Understanding Eating Disorders

ISSUES IN BIOMEDICAL ETHICS

General Editors
John Harris and Søren Holm

Consulting Editors
Raanan Gillon and Bonnie Steinbock

The late twentieth century witnessed dramatic technological developments in biomedical science and in the delivery of health care, and these developments have brought with them important social changes. All too often ethical analysis has lagged behind these changes. The purpose of this series is to provide lively, up-to-date, and authoritative studies for the increasingly large and diverse readership concerned with issues in biomedical ethics—not just health care trainees and professionals, but also philosophers, social scientists, lawyers, social workers, and legislators. The series will feature both single-author and multi-author books, short and accessible enough to be widely read, each of them focused on an issue of outstanding current importance and interest. Philosophers, doctors, and lawyers from a number of countries feature among the authors lined up for the series.

Understanding Eating Disorders

Conceptual and Ethical Issues in the Treatment of Anorexia and Bulimia Nervosa

SIMONA GIORDANO

CLARENDON PRESS · OXFORD

OXFORD

UNIVERSITY PRESS

Great Clarendon Street, Oxford OX2 6DP

Oxford University Press is a department of the University of Oxford.
It furthers the University's objective of excellence in research, scholarship,
and education by publishing worldwide in

Oxford New York

Auckland Cape Town Dar es Salaam Hong Kong Karachi
Kuala Lumpur Madrid Melbourne Mexico City Nairobi
New Delhi Shanghai Taipei Toronto

With offices in

Argentina Austria Brazil Chile Czech Republic France Greece
Guatemala Hungary Italy Japan Poland Portugal Singapore
South Korea Switzerland Thailand Turkey Ukraine Vietnam

Oxford is a registered trade mark of Oxford University Press
in the UK and in certain other countries

Published in the United States
by Oxford University Press Inc., New York

British Library Cataloguing in Publication Data

Data available

Library of Congress Cataloging in Publication Data

Data available

Typeset by SPI Publisher Services, Pondicherry, India
Printed in Great Britain
on acid-free paper by
Biddles Ltd, King's Lynn, Norfolk

ISBN 0-19-926974-2 978-0-19-926974-7

10 9 8 7 6 5 4 3 2

Acknowledgements

I wish to thank my father and my mother, who encouraged and supported my studies. Also Fabio Bacchino, Alan Cribb, John Harris, Søren Holm, Chiara Lalli, Eugenio Lecaldano, Harry Lesser, Paul McNeill, Raffaele Marchetti, Maurizio Mori, Paolo Rigliano, Walter Vandereycken, Hilary Walford, and the anonymous readers of Oxford University Press. A special thought goes to the patients of the psychiatric hospital 'Villa Rosa' of Viterbo (Italy), with whom I have worked from 1991 to 1999.

Parts of this work have been sponsored by the Consulta di Bioetica of Milan (Italy), the University 'La Sapienza' of Rome, the British Academy, and the European Union.

Contents

Non al denaro, non all'amore ne' al cielo . . .

Introduction

> [Eating disorders are] ... *really like a great, mythological artichoke ... a single flower, green and purple, where each leaf hides another, each layer covers another layer, jealously hidden. Whoever knows how to take off the outside leaves will discover unimaginable things, in a difficult voyage in time and space* ... [1]

Eating disorders are a complex condition: they have many sides and, like artichokes, are made up of layers. You have to have the patience to look beyond, to proceed step by step to find the core of a problem, to find 'the person within'.[2] Eating disorders are puzzling in many ways. They are puzzling because they are a *self-imposed* disease. People with eating disorders are normally young and bright. They do not complain about their eating habits and they either hide them or defend them, or both, sometimes in the face of advanced emaciation. However, as well as being *wanted*, eating disorders are clearly self-destructive and potentially lethal. The risks for health are great, and mortality (up to 20 per cent) is one of the highest among psychiatric disorders. Even when emaciation is not advanced, disordered eating threatens a person's life in ways that are not always apparent: the effects on the heart, for example, are particularly worrisome, especially as they may be undetectable. Moreover, abnormal eating contributes to the probability of the person spiralling down into a condition of unhappiness and loneliness, and one of the main causes of death in people with eating disorders is suicide.

Eating disorders have been the subject of extensive research in clinical psychology, sociology, and psychiatry. The disorder raises many different questions. This book will concentrate on the ethics of the care and treatment of the person with eating disorders. It will not deal with epistemological issues on the nature of mental illness. It will be clear throughout the book that this is irrelevant to the ethics of care and treatment of the eating-disordered person (in particular, see Chapters 2 and 3). Moreover, I will

---

[1] Carlo Levi, *Le mille patrie* (Rome: Donzelli, 2000).

[2] This expression was used by Hilde Bruch in the title of her *Eating Disorders: Obesity, Anorexia Nervosa and the Person Within* (London: Routledge and Kegan Paul, 1974).

not compare eating disorders to other forms of food refusal—medieval ascetic saints, for example, or hunger strikers. Other researchers have provided extensive studies on the matter, and it would be superfluous to repeat the results of these studies. Another aspect that will be marginal to this study is the impact of gender socialization in the development and treatment of eating disorders. We will discuss the family and society of the eating-disordered person, but there is much important work by feminist philosophers that will not be discussed in this book, as I do not wish to consider eating disorders from a feminist perspective or as a 'women's' issue and as thorough discussion of this topic would require a separate study and would direct us into areas of investigation that are not strictly pertinent to this book. The Bibliography at the end of the volume provides references for those who are interested in the subject.

Chapter 1 provides a description of the condition. It explores aetiology, incidence, and prevalence, and reports the risks for health that are caused by abnormal nutrition. I will focus on anorexia and bulimia nervosa, which are generally regarded as the main eating disorders, and mainly on anorexia nervosa. Diagnostic manuals identify borderline types and subtypes of eating disorders, which I will not analyse. I will focus only on the two major syndromes, and mainly on anorexia nervosa, because I am concerned with the phenomenon that seems to underlie all eating disorders that are psychological in nature,—namely, *the desire to be thin*. Rather than providing a clinical exploration of the various forms of eating disorders, I will try to answer a general question: why do people want to be thin? I will focus on attempts to control eating, rather than on the result of eating anomalies in terms of body weight or shape. In other words, I shall try to understand why people are preoccupied with body weight, and why they try to control their eating habits: whether they will become emaciated, keep normal weight, or become overweight is secondary. Whether people vomit as a way of purging themselves or only diet is also secondary. I will consider bulimia as one form in which the fight for thinness and lightness may take shape.

Anyone who is involved with a person with an eating disorder and who cares for her[3] will be troubled by an ethical dilemma: should one respect the person's self-destructive behaviour, should one try to persuade the person to modify it, or, if there seems to be no alternative, should one force the person not to perform self-destructive acts?

---

[3] For easiness, given that the majority of sufferers are women, I shall use the female pronouns she/her. However, it should be remembered that eating disorders also affect the male population. See H. G. Pope Jr, J. I. Hudson, D. Yurgelun-Todd, and M. S. Hudson, 'Prevalence of Anorexia Nervosa and Bulimia in Three Student Populations', *International Journal of Eating Disorder*, 3 (1984), 33–51; and the Eating Disorders Association reports at edauk.com, section 'Men's Issues'. See also Section 1.3 below.

These questions raise an issue of principle: is there an entitlement to intervene against people's wishes, in order to protect their welfare?

1. *Autonomy v. Paternalism*

Chapter 2 explores the value of autonomy as compared with the value of people's welfare and articulates a theory of ethically justifiable paternalism. It will be explained in what circumstances non-consensual interventions may be ethically acceptable.

I shall propose a theory of 'weak paternalism' according to which, at least prima facie, it may be legitimate to restrict freedom of action and choice only when the actions and choices that are impeded are non-autonomous in some important way (for example, when they are based on inaccurate information or on false beliefs). If a person is making autonomous actions and choices, these actions and choices, however harmful for the person herself, should be respected, at least prima facie. In principle, a person should be entitled to refuse other people's advice, and even to refuse life-saving treatment, provided that the choice is significantly autonomous.

I will apply this theory to the case of eating disorders, and I will analyse eating-disordered behaviour to determine whether it may be considered autonomous and whether, therefore, it should be respected (Chapter 12). It should be noticed that the theory articulated here is prima facie (other things being equal, this is what carers and health-care professionals should do). This theory applies prima facie to everyone, whatever their illness, and therefore is not specific to people with eating disorders. However, after we have analysed eating disorders, we shall notice that this theory loses a significant part of its normative strength. There are two reasons for this: first, it is extremely difficult (for a number of reasons that will be discussed in Chapter 12) to determine whether eating-disordered behaviour is significantly autonomous. Consequently, it is extremely difficult to answer the question as to whether that behaviour should be respected or not. Secondly, there are circumstances that are particular to anorexia nervosa in which, even if we could determine with certainty that some actions and choices are fully autonomous, it is not clear that these actions and choices should always be respected, or that the appeal to the principle of respect for autonomy would be enough to guarantee that the autonomous choice should be respected. I am here referring in particular to the choice of refusing life-saving treatment—and thus, to the choice of letting the patient die from starvation.

It has been suggested that in some cases refusal of life-saving treatment by anorexic patients may be autonomous. Based on the theory of weak paternalism, an autonomous refusal of life-saving treatment should be respected.

If we could determine that a patient with anorexia is autonomously refusing life-saving treatment, in theory we should respect that choice. However, the anorexic patient is normally a young woman, who is otherwise physically fit, and who could become healthy again, if she just accepted that she should eat. This simple awareness sets the whole situation in a peculiar light: the fact that the anorexic *may decide to eat* and *to go back to normal* (as many anorexics do) creates a situation in which it may be extremely difficult for carers and health-care professionals *to let the patient go*. The case of eating disorders thus imposes enormous psychological distress on the significant others (normally relatives and carers). The death of a young woman who *just refuses to eat* may be an intolerable event for the significant others, possibly more intolerable than other deaths. This is not only understandable but also ethically important.

Whereas prima facie the autonomous choice to refuse life-saving treatment should be respected, the peculiarities of anorexia lead us to widen the scope of the analysis also to include carers in the choice of how to deal with the patient. This is not to say that 'the relatives should decide'; rather, this is to say that *some weight* should be given to the particularities of the case and that it is possible that the normative strength of the principle of respect for autonomy, in some instances, is *weakened*.

An appeal to the principle of respect for patients' autonomy may be insufficient to allow the anorexic patient to starve herself to death. Not that this would necessarily be *wrong*. However, this would be, or could be, *psychologically unbearable*. It seems to me, and I will show this in Chapter 13, that, if we decided to respect the anorexic's choice to die, while we had the power to feed her and thus keep her alive, we would not do so only for the sake of respect for people's autonomy. It is more likely that we would also do so *because we are profoundly sorry for the person*, because we understand that all this is intolerable for her, *because we feel compassion for her*. I will argue that the principle of respect for autonomy loses part of its normative strength in the case of anorexia, and that the choice to respect the person's decision to die will be based on *our compassion*, or at least some sort of 'mixture' of respect for autonomy and compassion.

I should clarify one point. The autonomy of the psychiatric patient has historically been trumped, and this book shows that very often the reasons for which this has happened are untenable. This book will argue that people with a psychiatric diagnosis should be treated in the same way as people with other diseases. If, as I have just argued, in some cases there may be reason not to accept straightaway the anorexic's decision to die, even if that decision was autonomous, this is *not* because the patient has a mental illness, or because, since the patient has a mental illness, she should be treated differently.

2. *The Value of Autonomy in Psychiatric Health Care*

The value of autonomy is universally recognized in philosophy, ethics, law, medical ethics, and international protocols. The idea that autonomy is valuable and ought to be respected and protected is one of the pillars of democratic societies. The principle of respect for autonomy is to be found in the health-care law of most societies: people are normally entitled to consent to or refuse medical treatment for any reason, so far as they understand what they are refusing and the consequences of their refusal, even if they will die as a result of their choice. It is generally accepted that autonomy should be given priority over people's welfare.

However, many people believe that the principle of respect for autonomy should be suspended in psychiatry. People with mental illnesses are often thought to be deficient in autonomy in important ways. It is believed that mental illness compromises people's autonomy, at least in important areas of their life. Therefore, for example in the UK, a special statute regulates assessment and treatment of people with mental illness (the Mental Health Act 1983). The statute provides that people with mental illnesses or mental disorders who are hospitalized under the Mental Health Act 1983 shall not be required to give consent for treatment of their mental disorder. The rationale for this is that people with a mental illness are believed to lack autonomy when it comes to decisions relating to their mental health.

Because of the belief that mental illness 'may compromise people's autonomy', it is often accepted that people with mental conditions be treated paternalistically.

Empirical evidence seems to suggest that such a belief is false. Most people with mental disorders are able to make important decisions, including decisions about their health and mental health. And people with eating disorders are typically capable of running their life in any sense that may be considered relevant to autonomy: they are generally intelligent, skilled people, and often successful in school and professional life. So, in what sense may mental illness 'compromise' people's autonomy? What does this statement mean exactly?

Chapter 3 shows that the claim that mental illness compromises autonomy is meaningless. This statement is *tautological*.

This does not mean that people with mental illness *must necessarily be autonomous*, or that people with eating disorders *are and must be considered* autonomous. Indeed, it is questionable whether eating-disordered behaviour is autonomous. The point that I make in Chapter 3 is that, in most cases, it is mistaken to claim that *mental illness compromises people's autonomy*.

This has an important ethical implication: the fact that the person has been diagnosed as having a mental disorder does not provide us with a justification to act paternalistically. Clinical diagnosis has no ethical relevance. In other words, we cannot claim that we are justified in forcing people to accept treatment, or in restricting people's freedom of action and choice, on the basis of the fact that they have been diagnosed as having a mental illness.

People, whether they suffer from a mental or a physical illness, or from no illness at all, should be free to act and choose as they wish—so far as they do not harm others—if their actions and choices are autonomous to a relevant extent. Thus, if people with a mental illness prove capable of making decisions about their mental health, or about any other matter that is relevant to them, the protection of their own good is not a valid reason to deny them the exercise of autonomy.

People *with a mental illness* who are capable of making a decision (whether or not related to their illness) should be respected for the same reason that people *without a mental illness* who are capable of making a decision should be respected. And people *without a mental illness* who are going to harm themselves while acting non-autonomously (out of ignorance, or false beliefs, or because they are under the effect of some drug, for example) should be protected in the same way and for the same reasons that people *with a mental illness* who are going to harm themselves while acting non-autonomously should be protected.

This idea is very far from commonly accepted views, common practice, and legislation. The law entitles health-care professionals to section people with mental illnesses for assessment and treatment of their mental condition, and their competence to decide upon their mental health is not assessed. People with eating disorders are subjected to the same legislation. Chapter 11 analyses the law regulating assessment and treatment of people with mental disorders; it discusses issues of competence and consent. Chapter 11 focuses on cases specifically concerning people with eating disorders and discusses the resolutions taken in courts. Legal provisions are critically analysed.

The conclusion is that there is no ethical justification for the different treatment that the law reserves for people who have received a psychiatric diagnosis. Some may object that surely 'some' diagnoses justify different treatment. In this book I will argue that of course different diagnoses justify different treatment, in the sense that a diagnosis of cancer justifies chemotherapy whereas a diagnosis of diabetes justifies insulin. However, the *coercion* (*this* type of different treatment!) is not justified by the diagnosis. What may justify coercion is the fact that the patient is incapable of acting or choosing autonomously on a particular occasion. Lack of autonomy is sometimes (or maybe often) associated to a psychiatric diagnosis, but this is not always the case, because people with a psychiatric diagnosis may be autonomous to make numerous choices. In any case, it is not the type of diagnosis that justifies coercion: it is the lack of autonomy. By providing that people with a psychiatric diagnosis may be coerced in ways in which people without a psychiatric diagnosis cannot, legislation violates not only one of the requirements of ethics, *consistency*, but also a fundamental human right, that is, *equality*. It is universally understood that individuals should be treated as equal, unless an ethically valid reason justifies difference in treatment. The diagnosis of mental disorder—including eating disorders—is not an ethically valid reason to *enforce* treatment.

Although it is easy to agree in principle with the argument that we ought to respect people's autonomy, despite an ongoing mental disorder, it is hard to accept that we should respect the behaviour of people with eating disorders. There is something far too irrational in eating-disordered behaviour and it is hard to believe this is what a person genuinely wants: such an irrational behaviour cannot be autonomous. One tends to believe that there must be 'something wrong with the person': it is 'impossible' for someone to sacrifice her health and even her life for the sake of 'thinness'. She 'must be driven' by some irrational force: there must be some 'irrational fear', some 'obsession', or some 'perceptual disorder'. Or maybe some 'addiction' that 'compels' the person to act in that particular way. Or some endocrine disorder or some genetic factor that explains why the person behaves in this way.

The entire behaviour of the eating-disordered person is so puzzling that people need to make sense of it. The behaviour of the sufferer throws people around her into a state of utmost psychological and emotional confusion: sympathy and worry mixed with horror, on the one hand; on the other, frustration and anger. The person is perceived as stubborn and untrustworthy, as a manipulator who has no genuine illness and who imposes her suffering both on herself and on others for unknown reasons, maybe just for power—as a demonstration of her iron will.

For most of us eating-disordered behaviour seems completely impossible to understand. Carers and health-care professionals are thrown into the same whirlpool of emotional distress. Their best attempts to help clash with the person's unwillingness to cooperate. The person may seek help but then mislead everybody over and over again. Her attitude is likely to cause irritation or deep frustration. It is possible that at some point both those who care for her and professional health-carers will just be tempted to contrast the 'iron will' of the sufferer with authority: one had better save a life than give up to the caprices of a stubborn and unreasonable (most often) *girl*.

Such an attitude may be understandable, but is it right?

Inability to understand people's behaviour has a direct impact on ethics. Because of the apparent impenetrability of the condition, because of the contradictory feelings that it generates in carers and professionals, and because of the power game that is likely to be created between carers and the sufferer, it becomes extremely difficult to determine whether any coercive intervention is appropriate or justifiable. If we believe that this person 'in one way or another' has to be fed, for example, to what extent is our judgement determined by our irritation and frustration? Or, for example, if we suggest that such behaviour is too irrational and is not what the person really wants, or that the person behaves in this way because she is ill, therefore we need to protect her, to what extent are such judgements determined by our incompetence to understand what is going on with the person?

If we do not know why the person behaves in a certain way, it seems impossible to determine what we should do, or whether it would be right to act paternalistically. The ethics of care and treatment of the eating-disordered person therefore relies on better understanding of the disorder.

3. *Understanding Eating Disorders*

Eating disorders are commonly considered as complex, multidimensional diseases. They are thought to be affected mainly by genetic, neurophysio-logical, psychological (the personality of the subject), familial, and social factors (including cultural and moral elements). These factors are all thought to play a role in the genesis and maintenance of the disorders. They constitute a network of biological and psychological connections, and I will try to provide a comprehensive and accessible account of these. Moreover, I will add further aspects that I believe should also be taken into consideration, in addition to the genetic, psychological, sociological, and other aspects.

Chapter 4 analyses the genetics and neuro-physiology of eating disorders, Chapters 5–6 explore the personality of the subject, the rationale of her behaviour, and the values underpinning eating anomalies. These chapters focus in particular on the value of lightness. Chapters 7 and 9 explore the family of the eating-disordered person; Chapters 8 and 10 are a study of the society in which the disorder is found. Finally, Chapter 12 explores the system of beliefs informing eating-disordered behaviour, to assess whether eating-disordered behaviour is autonomous.

The main conclusion of this analysis is that eating disorders should be understood from a moral perspective. Eating disorders signify a person's belonging and adherence to a determined moral context. The disorder is the consistent expression of values that have ancient roots in Western culture and that have been incorporated into ordinary morality. Eating anomalies are not the *symptom of an underlying mental disorder*, as is often argued. They are the symptoms of ordinary morality, which is just being *taken seriously*—or more seriously than usual. The logic of anorexia and bulimia nervosa is not a *dysfunctional* logic: it is a *moral* logic. This is not to say that eating-disordered behaviour, since it is dictated by moral beliefs, is autonomous and should be respected. Nor is it to say that the person is fully conscious of the values that guide her behaviour. On the contrary, the person may be not completely aware of the meaning of her behaviour and may also not be fully autonomous, as we shall discuss in Chapter 12. However, eating-disordered behaviour may be understood if it is seen from the point of view of the moral values that may direct it. The analysis of morality *makes sense* of apparently irrational behaviour.

This result has important implications for the moral philosopher, and for anyone who looks at the eating-disordered person from the standpoint of ethics ('what is it good or right to do in these cases?'). No one will have a definite answer. Many ethically consistent arguments may be produced, but none will be fully satisfying. An honest look through eating anomalies in some way represents a challenge to the very moral concepts of 'goodness' and 'rightness'. If the logic that underlies eating disorders is a moral logic, then understanding and unmasking that logic has, as a consequence, the *loss of ethics*. Someone who follows this book on its journey towards the heart of eating disorders, with the aim of finding out what it is ethical to do in these cases, is left in the same position as the cook who takes off all the leaves of the artichoke in the search for the artichoke.

The question 'What is it ethical to do?' will appear to be, in an important way, the *wrong question*. The real issue is *why* people want what they want, why they want it so much, why they are ready to sacrifice their health and even their life in order to get it. From this point of view, ethics collapses into psychology. The ethicist who gets to this point has to accept that there may be no definite answer to the ethics of paternalism towards people with eating disorders and that in an important sense searching for 'what is the right or good thing to do' is just missing the point and reinforcing the logic that gives rise to eating anomalies.

It may be objected that sometimes carers and doctors still have to make decisions as to how to deal with an eating-disordered person. This becomes particularly evident when we are faced with the most difficult decision of whether or not we should save a person's life by forcibly feeding her. Ethics cannot be sidelined entirely.

Chapter 13 will discuss the case of coercive therapy for people with anorexia nervosa; it will explore the arguments for and against force-feeding. We shall see that the arguments both for and against force-feeding have some strength. Once more, a definite answer to questions about the ethics of care and treatment of the eating-disordered person cannot be provided. However, some general principles may be applied to individual cases. As

I have anticipated above, the principle that should guide carers is respect for the person's autonomy. However, the psychological distress of carers should also be given some weight in the decision as to how to deal with the dying anorexic. When the circumstances and peculiarities of the case are taken into consideration, we shall notice that the principle of respect for people's autonomy loses part of its normative strength. The decision eventually to accept the patient's choice to refuse food and to die as a consequence will be based not only on the principle of respect for autonomy but also, importantly, on compassion for the patient's intolerable life.

I draw conclusions in the final chapter. Wittgenstein said that anyone who understands his book the *Tractatus Logicus Philosophicus* must *throw it away*. 'He must, so to speak, throw away the ladder after he has climbed up it'.[4] In some way, something similar will happen to this book, once it has been read and understood. The perspective from which eating disorders are normally observed needs to be surpassed. If eating disorders have been understood, then one should no longer be interested in eating disorders, eating, fasting, autonomy, or competence. What one will want to discuss is not eating disorders but our ordinary moral values, our shared moral notions, such as moral perfection and moral integrity, and our moral categories. The perspective from which the investigation of this book started also needs to be surpassed. We started our investigation puzzled by ethical dilemmas, and we asked what we should do with eating-disordered people: should we respect their choices or protect their welfare? What is good or right to do? But the same ethical categories through which we looked at the disorder are to be questioned. It is our very concepts of 'good' and 'right' that are to be questioned. Their value needs to be discussed, and their possibly lethal consequences need to be openly addressed.

The analysis of eating disorders and of the ethics of treatment of eating-disordered people touches our very moral values and beliefs. The main argument of this book is that, if we really want to understand eating disorders, and to understand *what it is right to do* with eating-disordered people, we have to forget about how people eat and look at *what they believe*, and more generally at *what we all believe—at our morality*. This book shows extensively that eating-disordered behaviour is the consistent implementation of moral values that the person (the sufferer) *takes seriously*. This claim does not mean that people with eating disorders 'act morally' with their eating-disordered habits; or that eating anomalies are 'right' types of behaviour; or that a person who develops eating disorders will do something morally worthwhile. This claim means that eating-disordered behaviour

---

[4] Ludwig Wittgenstein, *Tractatus Logico-Philosophicus*, trans. D. F. Pears and B. F. McGuinness (London: Routledge and Kegan Paul, 1961), 6.54.

can be understood if one considers a determined moral background. Eating disorders are an expression of some moral beliefs. In this sense, it is morality that is at the heart of eating disorders, and is therefore morality that we need to understand and discuss: our very concepts of 'goodness' and 'rightness'— those concepts from which we started our investigation. At the end of our search, so to speak, the part of the artichoke we are left with will be the stem.

PART 1

Scientific Understanding of Eating Disorders

1

Eating Disorders:
Anorexia and Bulimia Nervosa

1. *Introduction*

Alison has anorexia, Lisa bulimia; here are their stories.

Alison lives with her parents in one of those big houses at the posh end of town. There's an old pony in the paddock, and a housekeeper in the kitchen. But Alison can't appreciate the luxury of her life. She's 28 now, but you'd never know it—she looks sixteen. She went to a London art school, and did very well. Now she works in a local graphic studio. Her work is good—when she's there. But increasingly, she's having days off.

Alison's been losing weight, quietly and insistently, for the past six years. Now she's down to about six and half stone—pretty thin for a woman of 5'6''. Her periods have stopped. She's cold all the time. Sometimes she wears a lot of loose, floppy layers, and fingerless gloves. But sometimes she slips on a glossy leotard, proud of her hard, lean body.

It's nobody's business if she's getting slim. She still feels a bit pudgy around the waist and thighs, but if she really works at it, one day she'll be really elegant. She's spending a lot of time at the gym, and goes to an aerobics class twice a week. She also has an aerobics tape at home, which she works out with every evening.

Alison has to have the same amount of food at each meal. Long ago she declined to eat with her parents, although sometimes, terrifyingly, her father will shout and rage at her to eat more. She must eat at exactly the same time too. She gets fearful and panicky if a meal is delayed for any reason.

It was when she was fifteen that Alison's younger brother, aged twelve, was killed in a car accident. Her mother was depressed for years—perhaps still is. Her father, a vigorous man who liked to stay in control, worked even harder at his high-level job, and said little. Her brother's name was seldom mentioned again. Noel was handsome, blond and funny, the darling of the family, and as her mother once said, 'suddenly the light was put out'. Now, Alison wonders if her parents' marriage was 'put out' too. Her mother spends a lot of time complaining about her father to Alison.

I wish to thank Mr Harry Lesser, who has read and commented on the entire manuscript and especially on the first 4 chapters. I also wish to thank Prof. Walter Vandereycken for helping me with the structure and bibliography of this chapter.

Alison can't bear to look into the future. She couldn't possibly leave her parents. Although men sometimes ask her out, she tries to avoid it. They might ask her to have a meal with them, and that, of course, would be impossible. She thinks that if only she can get down to a reasonable weight—just another few pounds—things might be all right. If only she can endure the terrible, gnawing hunger. Sometimes this seems to be eased by looking at all her cookery books, or even making a meal for her parents. But they don't seem to want her to cook for them any more.

What they do want, they've just said, is for her to go to the doctor's. She's been before, but he wanted to weigh her, and she wasn't having that! He might even want her to have tests, or go into hospital, and she's sure—well, almost sure—there's nothing whatsoever wrong with her. But in the quiet of her luxurious bedroom, she cries. There is something wrong, and she doesn't know what, or why, or how to put it right.

Lisa is bulimic. The fact rules her life. She is 23, and works in a garage office, dealing with orders for spare parts. She lives in terror lest her workmates (especially the men) think she is fat, or eats too much. She avoids talking much at anyone at work [...]

In her last year or so at school she lost weight dramatically, and her teachers began to notice that her work improved too [...] She was almost fifteen when she learned the trick of making herself sick. A year later, she plucked up the courage to buy some laxatives from Boots. Now she could stuff herself with all the food in the fridge—plus the chocolate, crisps and cakes which she brought home in carrier bags—and never put on weight. It was difficult, but her figure was all she had ever wanted.

Now she has a routine. She does without breakfast. She's starving hungry by lunch-time, and she goes out to buy herself several porkpies, and often a whole battenburg cake. She varies the shops so that the shop assistants don't become suspicious. Some-times she gets some Mars bars too, if she's got enough money. [To her shame, she sometimes steals them if she hasn't.] She locks herself in the office loo, and stuffs all this down, being careful not to rustle paper in case anyone else is around. Then she drinks a lot of water. Within minutes, she can go back into the cubicle and vomit the lot down the toilet. Then she washes her hot face, and goes back to work.

In the evening, Lisa's expected to eat a 'proper meal', as her mother puts it. Meat and two veg, and a pudding. Lisa is a good girl and does what she's told. But as soon as she can escape, she drifts upstairs to her bedroom and swallows between thirty and fifty laxative pills. Later in the night the cramps grip her and, while the household sleeps, she can get rid of all that food in the toilet. She often looks very tired. She never goes out in the evenings [...] She's wondering, now, about trying counselling [...] She's desper-ate. Perhaps killing herself would be better than revealing the disgusting world she carries inside her.[1]

These are two typical stories of anorexia and bulimia—stories in which the disorder is not directly lethal, but threatens the person's happiness, health, and life in a subtle and pervasive way. It is hard to understand why bright

---

[1] These two case studies are taken from Carole Waskett, *Counselling People in Eating Distress* (Rugby: British Association for Counselling, 1993), 13–14, 17–18.

and skilled people condemn themselves to the misery of obsession with food and why they sacrifice their life in the pursuit of thinness.

This chapter will start the analysis of anorexia and bulimia by looking at their clinical features. It will provide epidemiological data about incidence and prevalence and describe the physiological and psychological effects of abnormal nutrition.

Eating disorders include anorexia and bulimia nervosa.[2] Food orgies that are not followed by compensatory practices are sometimes considered as a separate clinical category, called 'binge eating'.[3] Obesity may also be regarded as the result of an eating disorder (excessive eating).[4] However, obesity is probably most often considered a 'medical' condition, rather than a 'mental' condition, and eating too much, contrary to what happens with other anomalies in eating, is not commonly regarded as psychopathological behaviour and is normally not included among psychiatric classifications of diseases.

This book will refer mainly to anorexia and bulimia nervosa, which are generally regarded in psychology and psychiatry as the main eating disorders.[5] However, it will hopefully say something about all phenomena of abnormal eating. It will be concerned mainly with the relentless preoccupation with body image and body weight that characterizes eating disorders in general. It will focus on attempts to control eating, rather than with the result of eating anomalies in terms of body weight or shape. In other words, we shall try to understand why people are preoccupied with body image and body weight and why they try to control their eating habits: whether they will become emaciated, keep normal body weight or become overweight as a result of this concern is secondary to our purposes. What will be said here will therefore help us to understand not only the extreme cases of anorexia and bulimia, but also the relationship that people in general have with food, and thus to understand all eating behaviours, whether 'normal' or 'abnormal'.

---

[2] H. Bruch, *Eating Disorders: Obesity, Anorexia Nervosa and the Person within* (London: Routledge and Kegan Paul, 1974). Italian version, *Patologia del comportamento alimentare* (Milan: Feltrinelli, 1977).

[3] U. D. McCann, E. M. Rossiter, R. J. King, and W. S. Agras, 'Non-Purging Bulimia: A Distinct Subtype of Bulimia Nervosa', *International Journal of Eating Disorders*, 10/6 (1999), 679–87.

[4] Hilde Bruch analysed obesity as an eating disorder in *Eating Disorders*.

[5] World Health Organization, *International Classification of Diseases, ICD-10 Disorders: Clinical Descriptions and Diagnostic Guidelines* (Geneva: WHO, 1992); see also American Psychiatric Association, *Diagnostic and Statistical Manual of Mental Disorders, DSM-IV-TR (Text Revision)* (4th edn., Washington: APA, 2000), 307.1.

2. *'Anorexia' and 'Bulimia': The Terminology*

The term 'anorexia nervosa' was coined by William Gull in 1873, and is currently the most commonly used in English. In 1874 Lasegue named it 'anorexie histérique', and then 'anorexie mentale'.[6] According to Mara Selvini Palazzoli, 'anoressia mentale' (mental anorexia) is preferable, as it avoids confusion with neurological and endocrine syndromes. However, most often the term 'anorexia nervosa' is used in international literature.

'Anorexia', in etymological terms, means 'lack of appetite'. However, the condition named anorexia is far from characterized by absence of appetite. On the contrary, the person feels hungry but tries to suppress the sensation. Moreover, food has an overwhelming importance in anorexics' life and thought, as it is in many other cases of low food intake. People in a condition of starvation think constantly of food.[7] Anorexics are no exception to this rule. Their lives are totally focused on food. For this reason Selvini Palazzoli points out that 'mental anorexia is not *primarily* a lack or a perversion of appetite, but an impulse to be thin, which is *wanted and completely accepted by the sufferer*'.[8] It has been argued that the most precise term is the German, *pubertätsmagersucht*, 'adolescent mania of thinness'.[9]

Etymologically, bulimia is the *contrary of anorexia*. Bulimia means 'ox hunger'. As so-called anorexia is not actually primarily characterized by a lack of appetite, so-called bulimia is not actually characterized by a huge hunger. Bulimia sufferers, in fact, do not 'eat a lot' because 'they are very hungry'. When they overeat, they cross the threshold of satiety.

Anorexia and bulimia, therefore, are not opposites, as the etymology of the words would suggest. Much has been written on the relationship, similarities, and differences between so-called anorexia and bulimia.[10] Although some

[6] Bruch, *Eating Disorders*, 213, Italian version, p. 281. A history of eating disorders may be found in Walter Vandereycken, 'History of Anorexia Nervosa and Bulimia Nervosa', in Christopher G. Fairburn and Kelly D. Brownell (eds.), *Eating Disorders and Obesity* (2nd edn., London: Guilford Press, 2002), ch. 27, pp. 151–4.

[7] H. Bruch, *The Golden Cage: The Enigma of Anorexia Nervosa* (London: Open Books, 1980), 90.

[8] M. Selvini Palazzoli, *L'anoressia mentale: Dalla terapia individuale alla terapia familiare* (9th edn., Milan: Feltrinelli, 1998), 46, my translation, emphasis added; see also Bruch, *The Golden Cage*, 4.

[9] Richard Gordon, *Anoressia e bulimia: Anatomia di un'epidemia sociale* (Milan: Raffaello Cortina, 1991), 75. The original English version of this book is *Anorexia and Bulimia: Anatomy of a Social Epidemic* (Oxford: Blackwell, 1990); see ch. 5.

[10] See e.g. R. A. Vigersky (ed.), *Anorexia Nervosa* (London: Raven Press, 1977); Arnold E. Andersen, *Practical Comprehensive Treatment of Anorexia Nervosa and Bulimia* (London: Edward Arnold, 1985); G. I. Szmukler, Chris Dare, and Janet Treasure (eds.), *Handbook of Eating Disorders: Theory, Treatment and Research* (Chichester: Wiley, 1995); S. Abraham, *Eating Disorders: The Facts* (Oxford: Oxford University Press, 1997).

clinicians consider the two syndromes as separate, and insist that there are important psychological differences between the typical 'anorexic' and the typical 'bulimic', the vast majority of experts consider the two syndromes interrelated. In most cases 'anorexics' also adopt 'bulimic' behaviours. 'Bulimia' seems to stem from preoccupation with thinness and appears to be one of the many manifestations of a relentless concern with food and body image.[11]

'Bulimics' do not often reach the state of emaciation of 'anorexics', and therefore bulimia can be regarded as less immediately life-threatening than anorexia. However, as we shall see later in this chapter, bulimic symptomatology may be life-threatening in ways that are not apparent. I will be concerned primarily not with 'the effects' of eating anomalies in terms of body weight, but rather with the *mania of thinness*, or with the *fear of* being fat or overweight. These may be considered as the problematic features that underlie both food restriction and the breakdown of dietary regime that characterizes bulimia.

3. *Eating Disorders: Epidemiology and Prevalence*

The official statistics report a prevalence of 0.5–1 per cent for anorexia and 1–3 per cent for bulimia.[12] However, we should note that epidemiological data on the incidence and prevalence of eating disorders are not always consistent. This is due to the methodological problems of screening a sufficiently large population for several years (the prevalence is the number of cases of eating disorders in the population; the incidence is the number of *new cases* of eating disorders per year in the population).[13] Another problem is that there are probably 'silent' sufferers who will never seek help, and who will never declare they have a problem with food. Obviously the population of silent sufferers will not appear in clinical estimates.

Eating disorders are found nearly exclusively in Western or Westernized countries,[14] although they have spread to other economically emancipated

---

[11] For a detailed account, see Andersen, *Practical Comprehensive Treatment of Anorexia Nervosa and Bulimia*; see also C. G. Fairburn and G. T. Wilson, *Binge Eating* (New York: Guilford Press, 1993).

[12] See American Psychiatric Association, *DSM-IV*. See also E. Faccio, *Il disturbo alimentare: Modelli, ricerche e terapie* (Rome: Carocci, 1999), 29, 32.

[13] Hans Wijbrand Hoek, 'Distribution of Eating Disorders', in Fairburn and Brownell (eds.), *Eating Disorders and Obesity*, ch. 41, pp. 233–7, at p. 233.

[14] Richard Gordon provides an analysis of eating disorders as an ethnic condition. Gordon, *Anorexia and Bulimia*, ch. 1; Pierre J. V. Beumont and Walter Vandereycken, 'Challenges and Risks for Health Care Professionals', in Walter Vandereycken and Pierre J. V. Beumont (eds.), *Treating Eating Disorders: Ethical, Legal and Personal Issues* (New York: New York University Press, 1998), p. 1.

countries.[15] Eating disorders are a relatively recent 'syndrome'. Only in the 1992 version of the *International Classification of Diseases*, the *ICD-10*, are eating disorders reported as an articulated and well-defined syndrome.[16] In the 1970s anorexia was 'a rarity'[17] and there seems to be evidence of a progressive increase in eating disorders between the 1970s and the 1990s.[18] Because of the alarming dimension of the problem, eating disorders are sometimes called 'a social epidemic'. It is unclear, however, whether this increase reflects a real increase in the incidence of the disorder or depends rather on variables that are unrelated to the number of sufferers, such as demographic changes, public awareness of the condition, specifications of diagnostic criteria, and other factors relating to clinical management.[19]

Anorexia and bulimia mainly affect young people. These are principally women between 16 and 19 years old, although some studies observe a rise in the age of the onset.[20] The disorder is often found in secondary schools, colleges, and campuses.[21] Also people in some professions seem to be particularly at risk, especially models and ballet dancers.[22]

Eating disorders also affect the male population, although with lower prevalence.[23] Males represent around 8 per cent of the anorexic sufferers, 15 per cent of the bulimic sufferers, and 20 per cent of binge-eating disorder sufferers.[24] The age of onset of anorexia in males is reported as ranging

[15] J. Wardle, R. Bindra, B. Fairclough, and A. Westcombe, 'Culture and Body Image: Body Perception and Weight Concern in Young Asian and Caucasian British Women', *Journal of Community and Applied Social Psychology*, 3 (1993), 73–181; Maher A. Nishizono, 'Eating Disorders in Japan: Finding the Right Context', *Psychiatry and Clinical Neurosciences*, 5/55 (1998), 320–3; D. Le Grange, C. F. Telch, and J. Tibbs, 'Eating Attitudes and Behaviors in 1435 South African Caucasian and Non-Caucasian College Students', *American Journal of Psychiatry*, 155/2 (1998), 250–4.

[16] *ICD-10*. In *ICD-9*, only 'Anorexia nervosa' is reported, at 307.1, together with 'Other and unspecified disorders of eating', at 307.5. In the previous version, anorexia nervosa was not reported. Only 'Feeding disturbances', at 306.5, were reported, under the category 'Physical disorders of presumably psychogenic origin' (305). See World Health Organization, *Manual for the Statistical Classification of Diseases, Injuries, and Causes of Death* (9th edn., Geneva: WHO, 1967).

[17] O. W. Hill, 'Epidemiological Aspects of Anorexia Nervosa', *Advances in Psycholomatic Medicine*, 9 (1977), 48–62, quoted in Gordon, *Anorexia and Bulimia*, 39.

[18] Faccio, *Il disturbo alimentare*, 28; Mara Selvini Palazzoli, S. Cirillo, M. Selvini, and A. M. Sorrentino, *Ragazze anoressiche e bulimiche: La terapia familiare* (Milan: Cortina 1998), ch. 2.

[19] See e.g. Faccio, *Il disturbo alimentare*, 28.

[20] Palazzoli et al., *Ragazze anovessiche e bulimiche*, 20.

[21] Faccio, *Il disturbo alimentare*, 30.

[22] Hoek, 'Distribution of Eating Disorders', 233.

[23] An account of the effects of eating disorders in males may be found in Arnold E. Andersen, 'Eating Disorders in Males', in Fairburn and Brownell (eds.), *Eating Disorders and Obesity*, ch. 33, pp. 188–92, at p.188.

[24] Manfred Fichter and Heidelinde Krenn, 'Eating Disorders in Males', in Janet Treasure, Ulrich Schmidt, and Eric van Furth (eds.), *Handbook of Eating Disorders* (2nd edn., Chichester: Wiley, 2003), ch. 23, pp. 369–83.

between 15.5 and 17.2, whereas bulimia normally manifests later.[25] According to other studies, the age of onset for eating disorders in males is 18–26, as compared to 15–18 for females.[26] In spite of these differences, epidemiological studies consistently report both a lower prevalence of eating disorders in males and a higher age of onset in males.

Studies report an increasing prevalence of 'bulimic anorexia' as compared to 'restrictive anorexia'. Bulimic anorexia is also consistently regarded as more difficult to treat.[27]

4. *The Family of the Eating-Disordered Person*

Eating disorders are found mainly in middle- and upper-class families in which both parents live at home (89.4 per cent) and in which the mother has an extra-domestic job. These families hold typical middle-class values (career, marriage, appearance).[28] Duker and Slade report:

One of the most consistent sociological findings has been that anorexic/bulimic illness occurs predominantly in relatively privileged sections of the community. Where upper- or middle-class status is not conferred explicitly by wealth or 'father's occupation', families have been found typically to be aspirant, either working to achieve higher social standing, or struggling to regain status that has been lost.[29]

The exact reliability of these findings cannot be determined. In fact, it is possible that these types of families are those who are most prone to seek help, and therefore it is possible that the disorder arises equally in other areas of population who either do not consider the person's behaviour to be a problem, or a psychological problem, or would not refer the eating-disordered person to a professional.

We shall discuss the family of the eating-disordered person at greater length in Chapters 7 and 9.

5. *The Society of the Eating-Disordered Person*

Eating disorders seem to be a socially and culturally bound syndrome. They are found in Western or Westernized countries. This has generated wide

---

[25] See e.g. Faccio, *Il disturbo alimentare*, 30, 32.

[26] Fichter and Krenn, *Eating Disorders in Males*, 369–83.

[27] Selvini Palazzoli et al., *Ragazze anovessiche e bulimiche*, ch. 2.

[28] Ibid. 22–3, 122.

[29] Marilyn Duker and Roger Slade, *Anorexia Nervosa and Bulimia: How to Help* (2nd edn., Buckingham; Open University Press, 2003), 124.

interest in eating disorders amongst sociologists. Some studies, among which we should include feminist studies, have related eating disorders to the changes in the role of the woman in modern Western and Westernized societies, whereas others have related the phenomenon to moral and cultural values that are accepted in these cultural settings. We shall say more about the society of the eating-disordered person in Chapters 8 and 10.[30]

6. *Diagnosis and Description*

There is a high level of agreement about the clinical features of anorexia and bulimia, since experiences reported by both sufferers and clinicians manifest notable similarities.

There are two widely accepted diagnostic manuals of mental disorders, the *International Classification of Diseases, ICD-10*, and the *Diagnostic and Statistical Manual of Mental Disorders, DSM-IV-TR (Text Revision)*.

According to both diagnostic manuals, the central feature of anorexia is *deliberate weight loss*, which is tenaciously pursued and/or sustained by reduction of food intake and strict selection of permitted food. Low weight is upheld by compensatory behaviour, practised in order to reduce the assimilation of calories. Compensatory behaviour includes vomiting (which is generally self-induced), abuse of laxatives, excessive exercise, and use of appetite suppressants and/or diuretics.[31]

Bulimia or 'bulimic' phases generally refers to bingeing, which is experienced as being 'out of one's own control', and which is followed by compensatory behaviour. The person feels compelled to overeat. Overeating normally occurs in secrecy. The person is overwhelmed by the thought of eating and tries to set up a situation (out of sight) in which she may perform her food orgy. She normally feels ashamed of this urge and will find it difficult to talk about it. The preferred food is usually simple carbohydrates, mainly in the form of sweets, but some studies report that the person may eat whatever is available, including food that has been thrown in the waste and even frozen food. She will then feel disgust over her orgy and will normally

[30] I should perhaps specify here that this book will not regard eating disorders as a 'feminist issue'. The impact of gender socialization in development and treatment of eating disorders has been discussed at length by feminist philosophers, who are referenced at the end of the volume. Although I will report the results of studies that have argued that there is a connection between the social changes in the role of the woman in Western society over the twentieth century and eating disorders, the observations that I will offer on the society in which the disorder is found are of a general nature.

[31] A brief account of the classification of eating disorders may be found in Paul E. Garfinkel, 'Classification and Diagnosis of Eating Disorders', in Fairburn and Brownell (eds.), *Eating Disorders and Obesity*, 2nd edn., ch. 28, pp. 155–61.

compensate the bingeing either by self-induced vomit and/or by other cathartic practices (restrictive diet in the next days, until the next breakthrough, exercise, diuretics, and laxatives). These practices are experienced as purification from the pollution of food.

Dread of fatness or a morbid fear of weight gain is a commonly reported feature of eating disorders.[32] In cases of open emaciation or rapid weight loss, denial of the state of emaciation is typical.[33] Sometimes, even though severely emaciated, people with eating disorders claim that they 'look fat' (or that they are still too fat). Sometimes it is believed that these claims show that the person has a disordered perception of body shape.

Boxes 1.1 and 1.2 report the clinical criteria of both the *ICD-10* and the *DSM-IV*. The *DSM-IV* distinguishes between the *Purging Type of Bulimia*, in which the person has regularly engaged in self-induced vomiting or the misuse of laxatives, diuretics, or enemas; and the *Non-Purging Type*, in which the person has used other inappropriate compensatory behaviours, such as fasting or excessive exercise, but has not regularly engaged in self-induced vomiting or the misuse of laxatives, diuretics, or enemas.

7. *Eating Disorders and Perception of Body Image*

The study of perceptual disorders is always a controversial one. Even in the case of paranoid schizophrenia, where the presence of disorders in perception is widely recognized and accepted, neither the nature nor the scope of perceptual disorders is defined.[34] However, many people assume that people with eating disorders have a distorted *perception* of their body (whereas the *DSM-IV* reports 'distorted experience' of body weight and shape, which does not necessarily mean that the person, put in front of the mirror, will actually see herself fatter than she is). Some people believe that the person with eating disorders diets because she has an altered visual perception of her body image.

People with eating disorders indeed often deny that they are too thin. They may claim they are fat and that they still have to lose weight, and they may refuse to eat even when they are severely emaciated. However, it is unclear

---

[32] See World Health Organization, *ICD-10*; see also American Psychiatric Association, *DSM-IV*; for a detailed account of current conceptions of anorexia and bulimia, see K. A. Halmi, 'Current Concepts and Definitions', in Szmukler, Dare, and Treasure (eds.), *Handbook of Eating Disorders*, 29–44; for a description of behaviour of anorexic people, see Bruch, *The Golden Cage*, 72–90.

[33] *ICD-10* reports a body-image distortion (see *ICD-10*, F 50), whereas *DSM-IV* reports an abnormal body-experience (see *DSM-IV*, 307.1).

[34] L. A. Sass, *Madness and Modernism* (London: Harvard University Press, 1992), ch. 2.

BOX 1.1. Eating Disorders Listed in *ICD-10*

F 50 EATING DISORDERS

[. . .]

F 50.0 Anorexia nervosa

A disorder characterized by deliberate weight loss, induced and sustained by the patient. It occurs most commonly in adolescent girls and young women, but adolescent boys and young men may also be affected, as may children approaching puberty and older women up to the menopause. The disorder is associated with a specific psychopathology whereby a dread of fatness and flabbiness of body contour persists as an intrusive overvalued idea, and the patients impose a low weight threshold on themselves. There is usually undernutrition of varying severity with secondary endocrine and metabolic changes and disturbances of bodily function. The symptoms include restricted dietary choice, excessive exercise, induced vomiting and purgation, and use of appetite suppressants and diuretics.

[. . .]

F 50.2 Bulimia nervosa

A syndrome characterized by repeated bouts of overeating and an excessive preoccupation with the control of body weight, leading to a pattern of overeating followed by vomiting or use of purgatives. This disorder shares many psychological features with anorexia nervosa, including an overconcern with body shape and weight. Repeated vomiting is likely to give rise to disturbances of body electrolytes and physical complications. There is often, but not always, a history of an earlier episode of anorexia nervosa, the interval ranging from a few months to several years.

Source: World Health Organization, *International Classification of Diseases, ICD-10* (10th edn., Geneva: WHO, 1992).

BOX 1.2. Eating Disorders Listed in *DSM-IV*

307.1 Anorexia nervosa. Diagnostic criteria

Early signs may include withdrawal from family and friends, increased sensitivity to criticism, sudden increased interest in physical activity, anxiety or depressive symptoms.

A. Refusal to maintain body weight at or above a minimally normal weight for age and height (e.g., weight loss leading to maintenance of body weight less than 85% of that expected; or failure to make expected weight gain during period of growth, leading to body weight less than 85% of that expected).

B. Intense fear of gaining weight or becoming fat, even though underweight.

C. Disturbance in the way in which one's body weight or shape is experienced, undue influence of body weight or shape on self-evaluation, or denial of the seriousness of the current low body weight.

D. In postmenarcheal females, amenorrhea, i.e., the absence of at least three consecutive menstrual cycles. (A woman is considered to have amenorrhea if her periods occur only following hormone, e.g., estrogen, administration.)

[. . .]

307.51 Bulimia nervosa. Diagnostic criteria

A. Recurrent episodes of binge eating. An episode of binge eating is characterized by both of the following:

- eating, in a discrete period of time (e.g., within any 2-hour period), an amount of food that is definitely larger than most people would eat during a similar period of time and under similar circumstances
- a sense of lack of control over eating during the episode (e.g., a feeling that one cannot stop eating or control what or how much one is eating)

B. Recurrent inappropriate compensatory behavior in order to prevent weight gain, such as self-induced vomiting; misuse of laxatives, diuretics, enemas, or other medications; fasting; or excessive exercise.

C. The binge eating and inappropriate compensatory behaviors both occur, on average, at least twice a week for 3 months.

D. Self-evaluation is unduly influenced by body shape and weight.

E. The disturbance does not occur exclusively during episodes of anorexia nervosa.

Source: American Psychiatric Association, *Diagnostic and Statistical Manual of Mental Disorders, DSM-IV-TR (Text Revision)* (4th edn., Washington: APA, 2000), 307.1.

whether these claims are linked to an actual distortion of perception of body image.[35] Results of clinical studies on perception of the body image are discordant.[36]

It has been found that distortions, though less remarkable, are also experienced by control groups.[37] Moreover, people with eating disorders seem to have an ambivalent perception of themselves. Distortions mainly concern the perception of the body as a whole, rather than individual parts.[38] In other words, people tend to err (by overestimation, obviously), nearly exclusively in the estimation of the size of the whole body, whereas the estimation of individual parts is generally much more realistic. This fact is rather curious. A person with colour-blindness (who evidently has a *perceptual* disorder) fails to distinguish colours whether she looks at a whole coloured object or a part of it. The perceptual disorder does not vary, whether a whole or a part of an object is being observed. How can we explain this perceptual disorder, which is peculiarly related to the overall estimation of the body but not to the estimation to the body parts? One option is to consider the problem as cognitive, rather than perceptual.

Moreover, it has been suggested that the notion of 'body image' is meaningless. The way we perceive our body does not simply depend on what we actually 'see' when we look at a mirror. We do not only see the inverted image of ourselves in the mirror. The perception we have of ourselves includes cognitive responses (what we think we look like), affective responses (what we feel we look like), and optative responses (what we want to look like). It has been argued that the notion of 'body experience', a multidimensional notion that includes all these responses, is preferable to 'body image'.[39]

Moreover, different techniques are currently used to assess the estimation of the body size. These techniques give discordant results.[40] It is thus difficult

---

[35] See T. F. Cash and E. A. Deagle, 'The Nature and Extent of Body-Image Disturbances in Anorexia Nervosa and Bulimia Nervosa: A Meta-Analysis', *International Journal of Eating Disorders*, 22/2 (1997), 107–25.

[36] See e.g. R. L. Horne, J. C. Vanvactor, and J. Emerson, 'Disturbed Body Image in Patients with Eating Disorders', *American Journal of Psychiatry*, 148/2 (1991), 211–15.

[37] G. Noordenbos, 'Differences between Treated and Untreated Patients with Anorexia Nervosa', *British Review of Bulimia and Anorexia Nervosa*, 3/2 (1989), 55–60.

[38] R. M. Gardner and E. D. Bokenkamp, 'The Role of Sensory and Non-Sensory Factors in Body Size Estimations of Eating Disorder Subjects', *Journal of Clinical Psychology*, 52/1 (1996), 3–15.

[39] Michel Probst, W. Vandereycken, Johan Vanderlinden, and Herman Van Coppenolle, 'The Significance of Body Size Estimation in Eating Disorders: Its Relationship with Clinical and Psychological Variables', *International Journal of Eating Disorders*, 24/2 (1998), 167–74; see also A. Meijboom, A. Jansen, M. Kampman, and E. Schouten, 'An Experimental Test of the Relationship between Self-Esteem and Concern about Body Shape and Weight in Restrained Eaters', *International Journal of Eating Disorders*, 25/2 (1999), 327–34.

[40] P. K. Bowden et al., 'Distorting Patient or Distorting Instrument? Body Shape Disturbance in Patients with Anorexia Nervosa and Bulimia', *British Journal of Psychiatry*, 155 (1989), 196–201.

to assess whether eating-disorder sufferers really have a perceptual dysfunction and what the extent of that dysfunction eventually is.

There seems to be insufficient proof to claim that people with eating disorders *do not actually see* that they have lost weight, or are losing weight, or that they are underweight. Their claims not to be thin enough (or similar) are certainly meaningful and need to be explored, but they do not seem to be primarily due to 'perceptual' dysfunctions.

The consequences of food restriction and compensatory behaviour may be severe and life-threatening, as the next section will show.

8. *The Effects of Abnormal Eating: Secondary Symptomatology*

The consequences of both weight reduction and compensation behaviour are called 'secondary symptomatology'. The secondary symptomatology includes a whole range of physiological effects of low or abnormal nutrition. It is called 'secondary' because it is not the primary disorder but the consequence of eating anomalies, and imbalances tend to go back to normal as weight is gained and normal eating patterns re-established.

Among the effects of low or abnormal nutrition we should include the following.

8.1. *Endocrine and metabolic changes*

Endocrine disorders[41] manifest in amenorrhoea in females and impotence and lack of sexual interest in males. The lack of estrogens linked to absence of menstrual periods causes bone thinning, even in the presence of hormone

---

[41] A. E. Taylor, Jane Hubbard, and Ellen J. Anderson, 'Impact of Binge Eating on Metabolic and Leptin Dynamics in Normal Young Women', *Journal of Clinical Endocrinology and Metabolism*, 84/2 (1999), 428–34. It should be noticed that the relation between body weight and leptin is currently controversial. It has been recently noticed that leptin is reduced in both underweight anorexics and normal weight bulimics, whereas it is increased in women who binge without engaging in compensatory behaviour. Some researchers suggest that factors other than body weight may affect leptin changes. See P. Monteleone, A. Di Lieto, A. Tortorella, N. Longobardi, and M. Maj, 'Circulating Leptin in Patients with Anorexia Nervosa, Bulimia Nervosa or Binge-Eating Disorder: Relationship to Body Weight, Eating Patterns, Psychopathology and Endocrine Changes', *Psychiatric Research*, 94/2 (2000), 121–9. A more technical account of endocrine abnormalities, electrolyte, and metabolic abnormalities, cardiac and cardiovascular disturbances, and gastrointestinal complications may be found in Katherine A. Halmi, 'Physiology of Anorexia Nervosa and Bulimia Nervosa', in Fairburn and Brownell (eds.), *Eating Disorders and Obesity*, 2nd edn., ch. 48, pp. 267–71; and Claire Pomeroy and James E. Mitchell, 'Medical Complications of Anorexia Nervosa and Bulimia Nervosa', in ibid., ch. 50, pp. 278–83. In particular, this chapter contains information on dermatological abnormalities, dental complications, and immunological disorders associated with eating disorders.

replacement.[42] This increases risks of fracture during exercise[43] and long-term danger of osteoporosis.[44]

A recent study reports that 'estrogen administration alone has not been shown to prevent progressive bone loss in current diagnosed anorexics and increases in weight alone appear to be insufficient in reversing bone mineral density losses [...] Even young women who recover before 15 years of age have been shown to have long-term decreased bone density in the lumbar spine and femoral neck.'[45]

Sometimes growth of skin hair (lanugo) also occurs.

8.2. *Heart disorders*

The effects of poor nutrition on the heart are particularly worrisome. The heart diminishes in size, like any other muscle in the body, and becomes weaker. Low heart rate (bradycardia) and low blood pressure (hypotension) are the normal outcomes of this process. The ability of the heart to increase oxygen delivery to the tissues while exercising is impaired, with potentially dangerous effects for the person who takes exercise (exercise is one of the methods for people with eating disorders to control body weight or to compensate calories intake). The mitral[46] valve may prolapse and potentially fatal arrhythmias may occur.[47]

8.3. *Electrolyte imbalances*

Vomiting may cause dehydration and usually produces electrolyte imbalance, which may cause cramps (especially because of the lack of adenosine

[42] D. W. Mickley, 'Medical Dangers of Anorexia Nervosa and Bulimia Nervosa', in R. Lemberg and L. Cohn (eds.), *Eating Disorders: A Reference Sourcebook* (Phoenix: Oryx Press, 1999), 47.

[43] L. Jack and M. D. Katz, 'Eating Disorders', in M. M. Shangold and G. Mirkin (eds.), *Women and Exercise: Physiology and Sports Medicine* (Philadelphia: Davis Company, 1994), 292–312.

[44] R. Shelley, *Anorexics on Anorexia* (London: Jessica Kingsley, 1992), 7; U. Cuntz, G. Frank, P. Lehnert, and M. Fichter, 'Interrelationships between the Size of the Pancreas and the Weight of Patients with Eating Disorders', *International Journal of Eating Disorders,* 27/3 (2000), 297–303; A. Marcos, 'Eating Disorders: A Situation of Malnutrition with Peculiar Changes in Immune System', *European Journal of Clinical Nutrition,* 54, supp. 1 (2000), 61–4.

[45] Patrick Lyn, 'Eating Disorders: A Review of the Literature with Emphasis on Medical Complications and Clinical Nutrition', *Alternative Medicine Review* (June 2002), 184–207.

[46] The mitral valve is the left atrio-ventricular valve. The prolaps consists in bulging or billowing of one or more parts of the mitral valve towards the left atrium. According to the degree and intensity of the prolaps, the blood may flow back to the left atrium. The prolaps of the mitral valve is not uncommon and in most cases does not prevent people from taking part in sport. However, it is important to determine the degree of the anomaly and the eventual cardiac anomaly associated with the anomaly of the mitral valve, as in the most serious cases the mitral valve prolaps may cause cardiac insufficiency.

[47] Mickley, 'Medical Dangers', 47; Jack and Katz, 'Eating Disorders', 299.

triphosphate (ATP), which is one of the carriers of energy in human cells[48]—and low potassium[49] level), epileptic attacks, and severe abnormalities in heart rhythms, even respiratory paralysis,[50] cardiac arrest, and death.[51] A major problem is that individuals with low-potassium levels are often asymptomatic, and it is therefore impossible to predict when a potentially life-threatening cardiac arrhythmia may occur.[52]

8.4. *Gastrointestinal complications*

Gastrointestinal complications in eating disorders may be life-threatening. These include swollen submandibular glands and parotid glands; esophagitis, esophageal spasm, and esophageal tearing and potentially fatal ruptures (this may occur from constant vomiting). Bulimics may suffer from undiagnosed esophageal disorders, which may contribute to involuntary vomiting. Bingeing may cause gastric dilatation.

'Acute pancreatitis can occur as a result of binge eating or in anorexics who are refed. Long-term laxative abuse can cause pancreatic damage and inhibit normal insulin release. Atrophy of the pancreas has been observed in anorexics and, although the size of the pancreas appears to revert to normal with recovery and increases in body weight, it is unknown whether pancreatic function returns to normal. Abnormal motility, reflected in delayed gastric emptying, increased transit time, constipation, loss of peristalsis, irritable bowel syndrome, steatorrhea, and melanosis coli (a dark brown discoloration of the colon secondary to laxative abuse) can have a variety of causes including binge eating, purging, food restriction, laxative abuse, electrolyte deficiency (potassium, magnesium) and dehydration'.[53]

Other complications connected with eating disorders are urinary problems,[54] kidney complications,[55] and olfactory impairment.[56] Abnormal eating is a serious threat to people's health. The mortality associated with eating disorders is '20 per cent at 20 years [. . .] by far the highest of any functional

---

[48] Adenosine triphosphate, or ATP, is one of the carriers of energy in human cells; ATP is often described as the 'coin' or the 'currency' of the cell.

[49] Jack and Katz, 'Eating Disorders', 300.

[50] Mickley, 'Medical Dangers', 47.

[51] Jack and Katz, 'Eating Disorders', 299.

[52] C. M. Shisslak and M. Crago, 'Eating Disorders among Athletes', in Lemberg and Cohn (eds.) *Eating Disorders*, 79–83, at 81.

[53] Lyn, 'Eating Disorders'.

[54] On this argument, see K. K. Hill, D. B. Hill, L. L. Humphries, M. J. Maloney, and C. J. McClain, 'A Role for *Helicobacter Pylori* in the Gastrointestinal Complaints of Eating Disorder Patients?' *International Journal of Eating Disorders*, 25/1 (1999), 109–12.

[55] R. Dresser, 'Feeding the Hungry Artists: Legal Issues in Treating Anorexia Nervosa', *Wisconsin Law Review*, 2 (1984), 297–374.

[56] I. C. Fedoroff, S. A. Stoner, A. E. Andersen, R. L. Doty, B. J. Rolls, 'Olfactory Dysfunction in Anorexia Nervosa', *International Journal of Eating Disorders*, 18 (1995), 71–7; quoted in Janet Polivy and C. Peter Herman, 'Causes of Eating Disorders', *Annual Review of Psychology*, 53 (2002), 187–213, at 203.

psychiatric illness, and high compared to most chronic medical illnesses'.[57] Other studies report 20 per cent for anorexia and bulimia nervosa (crude mortality) after a mean of 12.5 years of follow up,[58] and mortality rates (up to 20 per cent) are among the highest in psychiatry.[59]

Given the serious consequences on people's health and life, eating disorders give raise to important ethical issues of paternalism. The next chapter will explore these issues. It will discuss whether and in what circumstances paternalism may be justifiable. Before turning to the next chapter, I wish to introduce the reader to the ethical issues that surround the care and treatment of the eating-disordered person.

9. *Ethical issues*

It is hard to accept that a normally young, intelligent, skilled, and otherwise healthy person can destroy her life 'for the sake of thinness', and for no other reason, other than an apparently irrational desire to keep an abnormally low body weight—which can be unattractive as well as dangerous.

The ethical issues that surround eating disorders are extremely complex, given the complexity of the condition. Although this may appear somewhat paradoxical, the ethical issues are exacerbated by the fact that the person with the eating disorder is typically a very intelligent and otherwise 'normal' person. The person with an eating disorder is far removed from the common idea of the 'insane' and may be a skilled and competent person in virtually all areas of her life. Moreover, often she does not complain about her situation: she presents her choices as a private matter, a matter of personal preference, which she may even strenuously defend in the face of other people's criticisms and warnings. How can intelligent people behave in such a 'stubborn' and 'silly' way? Is it not appropriate for us just to stop them from performing clearly self-harming and 'unreasonable' behaviour? But, on the other hand,

---

[57] Rosalyn Griffiths and Janice Russell, 'Compulsory Treatment of Anorexia Nervosa Patients', in Vandereycken and Beumont (eds.), *Treating Eating Disorders*, 127.

[58] Stephen Zipfel, Bernd Lowe, and Wolfang Herzog, 'Medical Complications', in Treasure, Schmidt, and van Furth (eds.), *Handbook of Eating Disorders*, 2nd edn., ch. 10, pp. 169–90, at p. 195.

[59] Janet L. Treasure, 'Anorexia and Bulimia Nervosa', in G. Stein and G. Wilkinson (eds.), *Seminars in General Adult Psychiatry* (London: Royal College of Psychiatrists, 1998), pp. 858–902; S. Crow, B. Praus, and P. Thuras, 'Mortality from Eating Disorders: A 5-to-10 Year Record Linkage Study', *International Journal of Eating Disorders*, 26/1 (1999), 97–102; D. B. Herzog, D. N. Greenwood, D. J. Doer, A. T. Flores, E. R. Ekeblad, A. Richards, M. A. Blais, and M. B. Keller, 'Mortality in Eating Disorders: A Descriptive Study', *International Journal of Eating Disorders*, 28/1 (2000), 20–6; Søren Nielsen and Núria Bará Carril, 'Family Burden of Care and Social Consequences', in Treasure, Schmidt, and van Furth (eds.), *Handbook of Eating Disorders*, 2nd edn., ch. 11, pp. 191–206.

would this not be a violation of people's autonomy? If people are normally entitled to choose their lifestyle, however dangerous or irrational it may appear to others, why should not people be able to choose what and how they want to eat?

In part, these ethical issues reflect the profound psychological impact that eating disorders have on people who deal with the problem.

The behaviour of the person with an eating disorder generally produces a very articulate and complex response in people who deal with her.

Patients often evoke mistrust and even hostility in physicians who regard them as overprivileged manipulators and impostors because they have no genuine illness, deliberately harm themselves, and refuse to cooperate in treatment. The tactics that anorectic patients may display—from lying about food intake to manipulation of weight—are [...] regarded as [...] deceptions [...] Anorectic patients are often perceived as difficult: untrustworthy, obstinate, demanding, bothersome, manipulative, and likely to polarise family members and therapists [...] The cachectic condition evokes feelings of sympathy, worry and willingness to help. But soon the script of 'poor girl and caring rescuer' may change into that of 'naughty girl and angry doctor'.[60]

It is difficult to know what it is right or good or even appropriate to do in such a situation. The carer may swing between two extremes: there is the temptation, on the one hand, to act *with power*,[61] and, on the other hand, just *to give up*.

Eating disorders are a puzzling and frustrating condition to cope with. People who care for the eating-disordered person will be overwhelmed with anxiety and preoccupation. They are witnesses of a debilitating illness, which affects and destroys the entire life of the sufferer. The sufferer's shape changes, together with her habits, her way of thinking, and her lifestyle. She becomes increasingly withdrawn and more and more concentrated on her project of 'being thin'; everything is sacrificed to the ideal of 'thinness'. The psychological and physiological effects of starvation and/or abnormal eating become increasingly apparent, but, in front of the stubborn refusal on the part of the sufferer to offer any 'concession', concern and sympathy will become tension, a sense of impotence, and *anger*,[62] and a sense of being *wronged* by the sufferer's stubbornness. While, on the one hand, the person with an eating disorder appears as strong-willed, dominant, and intransigent, on the other hand, her suffering and difficulty to escape the trap of her condition are apparent. This contradiction is part of the condition itself: 'Sufferers seem to be choosing to restrict food intake. They seem to have

---

[60] Beumont and Vandereycken, 'Challenges and Risks for Health-Care Professionals', 4–5.
[61] Ibid. 5.
[62] Duker and Slade, *Anorexia Nervosa and Bulimia*, 11.

strong personal preferences and great determination to act on these, yet at the same time appear to be completely unable to alter course . . . even when they are so emaciated they are in danger of dying.'[63] The contradiction that the person herself experiences between *wanting* her condition and *being trapped* in it reflects on others, and produces in them a contradictory response, a mixture of irritation and preoccupation,[64] frustration, and an impulse to act with power, pity, and even admiration or jealousy, if not for thinness, at least for the sufferer's will power.

The strong and ambivalent psychological reactions that eating disorders elicit in others make it difficult for carers to have a clear picture of the ethical issues at stake and to know what is the right thing to do. On the one hand, it may be difficult to accept what seems to be unmotivated self-destruction (thinness is not generally perceived as a valid reason); but, on the other, why should one force the eating-disordered person to behave in a different way, when she herself wants to continue that behaviour and totally accepts the consequences of that behaviour for her health and life?[65]

The next chapter will articulate a general theory of paternalism. It will discuss whether paternalism towards people with eating disorders may ever be ethical. We shall first go through general issues of paternalism *v.* respect for autonomy, and we shall then see whether and, if so how, our theory of justifiable paternalism may be applied to the case of eating disorders—in other words, whether we may ever ethically intervene independently of or against the manifest wishes of a person with an eating disorder in order to protect her from harm resulting from her behaviour.

[63] Duker and Slade, *Anorexia Nervosa and Bulimia*, 17.
[64] Ibid. 13.
[65] Selvini Palazzoli, *L'amoressia mentale*, 46; see also Bruch, *The Golden Cage*, 4.

2

Paternalism v. Respect for Autonomy

1. *Introduction*

> I know that after tea she goes to the toilet and throws up. She walks up the stairs and puts the stereo on—she thinks the music will deceive us, downstairs. What should we do? Should we keep the door of the toilet locked?

> I know she gets up at night and eats and makes herself sick. Should I empty the fridge, so that she will not find anything to eat?

> I know that she goes running and to the gym far too much. She has been banned from one gym already. She drinks loads of diet coke and keeps going. Should I make sure she does not go to the gym or running on her own?

These fictional examples illustrate the ethical questions that inevitably arise for people dealing with someone in the grip of an eating disorder. Eating-disordered behaviour is often dangerous and self-harming, and it is likely to generate concern and anxiety in carers. The life of people with eating disorders is always focused on food and on how to avoid its assimilation, and therefore disordered eating is more than a disorder 'in eating', but involves a modification of the entire life of the sufferer. When dealing with someone with an eating disorder, carers end up wondering 'what is best' all the time: 'should we take her out of school?'; 'should we ban her from our sports centre?'; 'should I refuse to teach exercise to her?'; 'should I keep the cupboards of the kitchen empty?'; 'should I strive never to leave her alone, given that she may make herself sick?'; 'should I just force her to come out with us for dinner when we go?'; 'should I call her friends without telling her and ask them to pop around at night, so that she is not left alone?' In some cases eating disorders even involve and require a life-or-death choice.[1] What should we do when malnutrition threatens the person's life and she still refuses to eat? Should we forcibly feed and hydrate her? Carers and

---

[1] Pierre J. V. Beumont and Walter Vandereycken, 'Challenges and Risks for Health Care Professionals', in Walter Vandereycken and Pierre J. V. Beumont (eds.), *Treating Eating Disorders: Ethical, Legal and Personal Issues* (New York: New York University Press, 1998), 1.

BOX 2.1. Summary Box

Paternalism is literally 'the administration of the father'. There are different types of paternalism. Broadly, we distinguish between:

Strong paternalism. We are entitled to intervene against or independently of the person's wishes for her own good—for the protection of her own welfare—as defined by the person who intervenes.

Weak paternalism. A person may be entitled to prevent the *harmful conduct* of another person independently of or against the manifest wishes of that person only when this other person's actions and choices lack autonomy in some significant way, or when a temporary intervention is necessary to assess whether these actions and choices are autonomous. The autonomy of an action or choice is not to be assessed on the basis of its *content or outcome* but on the basis of the *process of deliberation* that leads up to that action or decision (formal or procedural conception of autonomy—these concepts are explained in the chapter).

Arguments supporting weak paternalism:

1. Strong paternalism does not account for the value of autonomy, as it is understood generally in liberal democratic societies.
2. Strong paternalism does not give sufficient importance to the process of deliberation leading up to a particular choice/action.

health-care professionals will be faced with 'ethical dilemmas' all the time. Sometimes the choices they will have to make will be about directly saving the sufferer's life; at other times these choices will be about preventing self-harm.

On which basis can we claim we have a right to prevent people from harming themselves, if this is what they want? Some people argue that those with eating disorders should be entitled to make their own decisions. For example, Rosalyn Griffiths and Janice Russell strongly discourage compulsory treatment for anorexia. They argue that, even if patients refuse treatment, their need for self-determination is fulfilled and they may eventually decide to be treated in the future.[2] However, most people

---

[2] Rosalyn Griffiths and Janice Russell, 'Compulsory Treatment of Anorexia Nervosa Patients', in Vandereycken and Beumont (eds.), *Treating Eating Disorders*, 129.

find it hard to accept what appears to be an 'unnecessary self-imposed disease'.[3]

Moreover, eating disorders arouse an ambivalent reaction in other people, carers, and family members. As Beumont and Vandereycken point out:

Patients often evoke mistrust and even hostility in physicians who regard them as overprivileged manipulators and imposters because they have no genuine illness, deliberately harm themselves, and refuse to cooperate in treatment. The tactics that anorectic patients may display—from lying about food intake to manipulation of weight—are [...] regarded as [...] deceptions [...] Anorectic patients are often perceived as difficult: untrustworthy, obstinate, demanding, bothersome, manipulative, and likely to polarise family members and therapists [...] The cachectic condition evokes feelings of sympathy, worry and willingness to help. But soon the script of 'poor girl and caring rescuer' may change into that of 'naughty girl and angry doctor'.[4]

For people faced with these types of reactions, it is difficult to know what is the right thing to do. Carers may be inclined just to 'let people be'; on the other hand, it is tempting[5] to force them 'to be reasonable'.

The question of whether we should intervene independently of or against the wishes of the eating-disordered person to protect her health and life is an example of a general issue of ethical theory—that is, the ethics of paternalism. The next section will address this general issue.

2. The Ethics of Paternalism

> E adesso imparo un sacco di cose
> In mezzo agli altri vestiti uguale
> Tranne qual e' il crimine giusto per non passare da criminale[6]

> And now I learn lots of things
> From people wearing the same uniform
> Except what's the right crime not to appear as a criminal

Is it ever ethical to intervene independently of or openly against someone else's wishes in order to protect her? This issue arises for health-care professionals in the management of any disease, and indeed it may arise for all of us in many situations of daily life. The fact that this is *an issue* depends on two

---

[3] H. G. Morgan, 'Fasting Girls and our Attitudes to them', *British Medical Journal*, 15 (1977), 1652–5, quoted in Stephen W. Touyz, 'Ethical Considerations in the Implementation of Behaviour Modification Programmes in Patients with Anorexia Nervosa: A Historical Perspective', in Vandereycken and Beumont (eds.), *Treating Eating Disorders*, 217.

[4] Beumont and Vandereycken, 'Challenges and Risks for Health Care Professionals', 4–5.

[5] Ibid. 5.

[6] Fabrizio De André, 'Nella mia ora di libertà', Storia di un umpiegato (1973; edizioni BMG Ricordi 2002©).

things. One is that we generally believe that people are entitled to make their own choices: people have different values and preferences, which ought to be respected. This is known in philosophy as the 'principle of respect for individual autonomy' (we shall see later what autonomy means and how it should be understood). The other is that we also acknowledge the value of other goods, such as life and health, or, in one word, people's welfare, and are reluctant to watch passively while people perform self-destructive behaviour, which may involve them harming or killing themselves; we seem to have a benevolent tendency to protect the loved person from (sometimes irreversible) harm. 'Welfare' refers to these goods, life, health, and well-being. 'Autonomy' refers to people's self-determination.

How we respond to the issue of paternalism depends to a significant extent on the value we attach to people's welfare as compared to the value we attach to their autonomy.

This chapter will answer the general question as to whether it may ever be ethical to intervene against or independently of someone else's wishes in order to protect her welfare. I shall argue that sometimes paternalism may be ethical, but only when certain conditions are met. I will explain what these conditions are. The theory of paternalism articulated here will take into account various philosophical and ethical notions. I will begin by clarifying the terms that are relevant to this discussion—namely, autonomy and paternalism. We shall see what autonomy means and how it should be understood. And we shall discuss the forms of paternalism that may be ethically justifiable. The theory of paternalism articulated here will be applied later to the care and treatment of the person with mental disorders and in particular of the person with eating disorders.

3. *Autonomy*

> Literally 'autonomy' means 'self-rule' (autos = self + nomos = rule of law). This term was originally applied to city-states of ancient Greece, and was meant to indicate independence of external political influences. Later on, its meaning was extended to the condition in which individuals' actions and choices are 'their own', and therefore are self-determined[7].

Individual autonomy is one of the pillars of liberal thought and democratic societies. The value of autonomy is universally recognized, secured by the constitutions of many states and subscribed to in virtually all declarations and conventions on human rights. Among these, we should quote the General Assembly of the United Nations, Universal Declaration of Human

---

[7] Gerald Dworkin, *The Theory and Practice of Autonomy* (Cambridge: Cambridge University Press, 1988), 12–13.

Rights, 10 December 1948; Council of Europe, Convention for the Protection of Human Rights and Fundamental Freedoms, Rome, 4 November 1950; Council of Europe, Convention for the Protection of Human Rights and Dignity of the Human Being with Regard to the Application of Biology and Medicine: Convention on Human Rights and Biomedicine, Oviedo, 4 April 1997. The value of autonomy is also often stressed in both moral/political philosophy and medical ethics and is protected by law in several contexts as well as in health care.

Isaiah Berlin expresses this value in a famous passage:

I wish my life and decisions to depend on myself, not on external forces of whatever kind. I wish to be the instrument of my own, not of other men's acts or will. I wish to be a subject, not an object; to be moved by reasons, by conscious purposes, which are my own, not by causes which affect me, as it were, from outside. I wish to be [. . .] a doer—deciding, not being decided for, self-directed and not acted upon by external nature or by other men as if I were a thing, or an animal, or a slave incapable of playing a human role, that is, of conceiving goals and policies of my own and realising them. [. . .] I wish, above all, to be conscious of myself as a thinking, willing, active being, bearing responsibility for my choices and able to explain them by reference to my own ideas and purposes.[8]

John Stuart Mill declared, with words that have become the anthem of liberal thought, that 'over himself, over his own body and mind, the individual is sovereign'.[9] Mill argued that:

The only purpose for which power can be rightfully exercised over any member of a civilised community, against his will, is to prevent harm to others. His own good, either physical or moral, is not a sufficient warrant. He cannot rightfully be compelled to do or forbear because it will be better for him to do so, because it will make him happier, because, in the opinion of others, to do so would be wise, or even right. These are good reasons for remonstrating with him, or persuading him, or entreating him, but not for compelling him, visiting him with any evil in case he do otherwise.[10]

Sometimes the state intervenes to restrict the autonomy of individuals, for example, with sanctions (the law on seat belts may be one example of the restriction of individual autonomy). However, in most liberal societies, these restrictions are kept to a minimum. People thus have freedom of religion, of speech, of choice in most matters of private life. They can choose to undertake risky jobs or risky sports. In health care, people have the right to consent to treatment or to refuse it, even if it is believed that this will harm them. The protection of the welfare of the individual is in general not considered a sufficient reason to exert power over the person and to force her to behave

---

[8] I. Berlin, 'Two Concepts of Liberty', in I. Berlin, *Four Essays on Liberty* (Oxford: Oxford University Press, 1969), 131.

[9] J. S. Mill, *On Liberty* (New York: Cambridge University Press, 1989), 13.

[10] Ibid.

differently. Liberal and democratic societies generally support and defend respect for people's autonomy in most areas of their life, so far as they do not directly threaten other people with their behaviour. Restrictions of people's autonomy for the sake of their own welfare are in general regarded as an abuse of power. This 'abuse of power' is sometimes called 'paternalism'. The equation between paternalism and abuse of power is, however, mistaken. There are in fact different forms of paternalism that need to be distinguished. Now we need to clarify what paternalism means.

4. *Paternalism*

Paternalism has acquired negative connotations. In health care 'paternalism' is equated to 'abuse of power' of the medical profession towards patients. Paternalism is seen as synonymous with disrespect for people's identity and diversity. However, paternalism should not be identified with abuse of power. There are different types of paternalism and some forms of paternalism are ethically justifiable.

'Paternalism' (from the Latin *pater* = father) means 'the principle and practice of paternal administration; government as by a father; the principle of acting in a way like that of a father towards his children' (*Oxford English Dictionary*). There is thus a positive meaning within the word. A person who behaves 'paternalistically' is a person who behaves like a father to his children. However, this type of 'administration' may take different forms. Paternalism is a wide-ranging term, and many characterizations of the notion have been attempted in both philosophy and medical ethics.[11] Before we discuss the different forms of paternalism, I will therefore clarify the way I use the term 'paternalism' here.

With the terms 'paternalism' and 'paternalistic interventions' I will refer to all non-consensual interventions aimed at the protection of the person towards whom these interventions are directed. By 'non-consensual interventions' I mean all acts that are independent of or contrary to the wishes of the person towards whom the interventions are directed. Paternalistic interventions always involve a restriction of a person's freedom of action or of choice. Moreover, they are always aimed by the paternalist at the protection of the person whose freedom of action or of choice is restricted.[12]

---

[11] For an account of paternalism, see e.g. T. Beauchamp, 'Paternalism', in W. T. Reich (ed.), *Encyclopedia of Bioethics* (rev. edn., New York: Simon and Schuster, Macmillan, 1995), iv. 1914–20; see also Allen E. Buchanan, 'Medical Paternalism', *Philosophy and Public Affairs*, 7 (Summer 1978), 372.

[12] As Mary Briody Mahowald points out, there is a link between paternalism and beneficence or non-maleficence. She also points out that there are other models of the doctor–patient

One of the reasons why it is difficult to characterize paternalism is that the term may refer to two different types of interventions. I will illustrate these two types of paternalism with two examples.

Lucy is in a crisis. She refuses to take psychotropic medication because she has a false belief that doctors want to poison her. If she does not take medication, she is likely to try to commit suicide—she tried before. Her refusal of medication is motivated only by her false belief. Doctors decide to force her to take medication.

Mrs P has a malignant breast lump. Good data suggest that with this kind of breast cancer, the five-year survival rate following a mastectomy is 90 per cent. The five-year survival rate following a lumpectomy is about 75 per cent. Without treatment, the five-year survival rate is less than 20 per cent. Mrs P's surgeon, Mr S, believes that a mastectomy followed by a breast implant is the treatment of choice. A previous patient of Mr S refused a mastectomy and decided to have a lumpectomy. She claimed that the implant might move to the side of the chest and that this would impinge on the quality of her life. She said that not only quantity of life, but also quality of life mattered to her. The patient died a few years later. Mr S now believes that he should not inform Mrs P that she has the option to have a lumpectomy. Since his previous patient died, Mr S has believed that his duty is to do what he thinks is best for the patient and to provide the patient with the most appropriate and efficient treatment. Therefore he offers only a mastectomy to Mrs P.[13]

Both examples illustrate cases of paternalism. In both cases, the doctor intervenes independently of or against the person's manifest wishes, in order to protect her welfare. However, the two cases present an important difference. In the first case the doctor decides to intervene against the person's wishes because the patient is unable to make a genuine choice about treatment (the patient lacks 'autonomy' or 'decision-making capacity'). In the second case the doctor decides to intervene independently of the patient's wishes—in fact, he withholds information that would be material to the choice—in order to avoid the patient making a 'mistake' (or what, in his opinion, would be a mistake).

Sometimes the difference between these two types of paternalism is bypassed in philosophy and medical ethics. This may depend on the fact that

---

relationship that could be employed as an alternative to the paternalistic one. One is the 'maternalistic' model, based on the mother's nurturant role. Another is 'parentalistic', which embodies both the principles of beneficence and non-maleficence and the principle of respect for autonomy. Those who have a parental role (not necessarily genetic parents) do for the other person what she cannot do for herself at a particular time (bathing or clothing, for example, at a young age or old age) and also encourage the other person's autonomy. She proposes the use of this model as an alternative to the paternalistic model. See Mary Briody Mahowald, *Women and Children in Health Care: An Unequal Majority* (New York: Oxford University Press, 1993), 28–35.

[13] The second case study is based on Tony Hope, Julian Savulescu, and Judith Hendrick, *Medical Ethics and Law, The Core Curriculum* (London: Churchill Livingstone, 2003), 53.

two notions are often confused. These are 'freedom of action' and 'autonomy'. To clarify the nature and ethics of paternalism, we should distinguish between interventions aimed at limiting the freedom of action and interventions aimed at limiting autonomy.

5. *Freedom of Action and Autonomy: Two Different Types of Paternalism*

All paternalistic interventions involve a restriction of freedom of action or of choice. The extent of such restriction may vary. There are different degrees of invasiveness. Restrictions may range from withholding information to physically restraining a person. Although all paternalistic interventions involve a restriction of freedom of action or choice, not all restrictions of freedom of action or choice are also a restriction of *autonomy*.

The distinction between interventions that are simply 'restrictive' and interventions that are 'autonomy-restrictive' is especially important in psychiatry. In this context, it is possible to argue that some restrictions are aimed at improving patient autonomy. For example, a psychiatrist may restrain a person with eating disorders from vomiting with the goal of strengthening her autonomy. The parents of a bulimic may decide to keep the cupboards empty in order to help the person manage without bingeing, thus reinforcing her will power.

Two versions of paternalism should therefore be distinguished: on the one hand, a form of paternalism that claims that it might be legitimate to restrict people's *autonomy* to protect their welfare; on the other hand, a form according to which we cannot restrict people's autonomy to protect their welfare. According to this second view, paternalistic interventions are justified only if the individual's autonomy is currently compromised. The former version of paternalism will be called 'strong paternalism'; the latter will be called 'weak paternalism'.[14]

> **BOX 2.2.** Paternalism
>
> A paternalistic act/intervention is any act/intervention that restricts a person's freedom of action/choice, and that is aimed at the protection of the welfare of the person whose freedom is restricted.

[14] J. Feinberg, 'Legal Paternalism', *Canadian Journal of Philosophy*, 1 (1971), 105–24.

6. *Strong and Weak Paternalism*

According to the 'strong' version of paternalism, a person's autonomy may be restricted for the protection of important goods, such as that person's life or health.[15] For example, Tom Beauchamp writes that paternalism maintains that restriction of *autonomy* is justified if it is likely that individuals will do serious harm to themselves, or if they deny themselves important benefits.[16] Similarly, Gerald Dworkin defines paternalism as the interference with the freedom of action of others justified by reasons concerning *exclusively* the individual's well-being, good, happiness, needs, interests, and values.[17] Finally, John Rawls characterizes paternalism as the interference that aims at avoiding the negative consequences of 'foolish' and 'imprudent' behaviour.[18]

According to the 'weak version' of paternalism, as it has been proposed by Joel Feinberg, a person may be entitled to prevent the *harmful* conduct of another person only when this other person is acting non-autonomously, or when a temporary intervention is necessary to assess whether she is acting autonomously or not.[19] The conduct to be prevented should be harmful, as paternalism has to be justified on the grounds that the person is to be protected.

Whether the 'strong' or the 'weak' version of paternalism is preferred depends on the view that one has about the importance and value of autonomy as compared to people's welfare.

BOX 2.3. Weak and Strong Paternalism

- Paternalism may involve the restriction of people's freedom of action/choice—but not of people's autonomy: *weak paternalism.*
- Paternalism may involve restriction of people's autonomy: *strong paternalism.*

---

[15] Ibid.

[16] Beauchamp, 'Paternalism', iv. 1914.

[17] G. Dworkin, 'Paternalism', *Monist*, 56 (1972), 64–84.

[18] J. Rawls, *A Theory of Justice* (Oxford: Oxford University Press, 1972), 249, emphasis added.

[19] Feinberg, 'Legal Paternalism'.

7. *Autonomy* v. *Life and Health*

The reason why we think paternalism is *an issue* is that we value autonomy. The questions about paternalism stem from the recognition of the value of autonomy, and also the answer we give depends on the value we attach to autonomy. Whether or not paternalism is justifiable and which forms of paternalism may be ethical depend on the value that we attach to autonomy generally,[20] and, in the case of eating disorders, to the autonomy of eating-disordered people.

Some people seem to believe that there are goods that are more valuable to the individual than the exercise of autonomy. In health care, the values that are most commonly considered of primary importance are life, health, and, in general terms, people's welfare. Those who consider these values as primary do not generally deny the importance of autonomy. They generally admit that the exercise of autonomy is also important, but consider autonomy as secondary to the primary goods and valuable in so far as it promotes the achievement of the goods that are regarded as primary. In psychiatric health care, for example, the exercise of autonomy (for example, through participation in therapeutic decisions) is deemed important, as it seems to promote the remission of psychiatric symptoms. Medical and psychiatric studies show that participating actively in the therapeutic process promotes the patient's recovery. Engaging in the informative process and choosing available options seems fundamental to the health and well-being of the patient, especially in cases of eating disorders.[21] Thus, the exercise of autonomy, as Buchanan and Brock have pointed out, may be considered 'instrumentally valuable in promoting a person's well-being'.[22]

However, claiming that autonomy has only secondary and subordinated importance, as compared to the patient's welfare, implies that autonomy is *rightly* restricted when this is necessary to protect these other goods. In other words, someone who gives a secondary and subordinated value to autonomy adopts a strong version of paternalism.

Whereas some people believe that welfare is primarily important and consider autonomy secondary to it or instrumentally valuable to it, other people believe that autonomy has a primary and intrinsic value. For them, autonomy is more important than welfare, and they believe people's autonomy should be respected, even if their choices may not be the best in terms of

---

[20] See Simona Giordano, 'Il principio di autonomia nel trattamento e nella cura dei malati di mente: Una prospettiva deontologica', *Bioetica, rivista interdisciplinare*, 3 (1999), 482–91.

[21] M. Selvini Palazzoli, S. Cirillo, M. Selvini, and A. M. Sorrentino, *Ragazze anoressiche e bulimiche: La terapia familiare* (Milan: Cortina, 1998), 96–7.

[22] Allen E. Buchanan and Dan W. Brock, *Deciding for Others: The Ethics of Surrogate Decision Making* (Cambridge: Cambridge University Press, 1989), 37.

protection or promotion of welfare, and even if they will mean that the person will die as a result of her choice. Moreover, autonomy is not valuable because and in so far as it produces or promotes other goods, but is valuable in itself. Although the exercise of autonomy may *also* be good because it promotes other goods (such as the patient's recovery, in the clinical context), its value does not depend on and is not secondary to these goods. For those who adopt this perspective, the fact that goods, such as life or health, may be compromised by the exercise of autonomy is not a sufficient reason to forbid people to act and choose according to their own lights. Believing that autonomy has a primary value, therefore, leads one to adopt a weak version of paternalism.

8. *Practical Similarities between Respect for Autonomy and Protection of Welfare*

It should be noticed that respect for autonomy and protection of welfare would in most cases produce similar practical outcomes. As R. M. Hare points out, in fact, patients are *on the whole* the best judges of their own interests.[23] Jonathan Glover also stresses that 'our preference for taking our own decisions is partly based on the greater likelihood of this bringing about outcomes we find satisfactory in other ways'.[24] Thus, normally, we know what is best for us and therefore in most cases the exercise of autonomy will promote our welfare.

In the case of eating disorders, the exercise of autonomy is thought to have an essential therapeutic potential. Beumont and Vandereycken have suggested that 'to speak of enforced treatment of anorexia nervosa is misleading. True therapy necessarily involves the patient's co-operation.'[25] If this is true, then respect for a person's decision is generally likely to produce the best outcome for her. It follows that those who attach a subordinated value to autonomy and those who attach a primary value to it would normally, in practice, both respect individual autonomy.[26]

Despite the fact that the practical outcomes will be the same on most occasions, the two theories described above are still the expression of two radically different perspectives on the value of autonomy as compared to the value of other goods, two different theories about what is most valuable in life, which may bring about very different courses of action.

---

[23] R. M. Hare, 'The Philosophical Basis of Psychiatric Ethics', in R. M. Hare, *Essays on Bioethics* (Oxford: Clarendon Press, 1993), 26.

[24] J. Glover, *Causing Death and Saving Lives* (9th edn., London: Penguin, 1988), 80.

[25] Beumont and Vandereycken, 'Challenges and Risks for Health Care Professionals', 10.

[26] Glover, *Causing Death and Saving Lives*, 78.

In one case, it will be argued that a person may legitimately be forced to accept an option (such as, to take an example, in the clinical field, a therapeutic option) for the protection of her own life or health. In the care of eating disorders, Birley, for example, argues that 'compulsory treatment is not a threat but a right'.[27] From this point of view, Dresser states that 'the refusing anorexia nervosa patient presents a case in which the discord between individual freedom and optimal health care is less extreme than in other instances of treatment refusal';[28] and Griffiths and Russell conclude: 'we hold no rescue fantasies, only the belief that our patients have a right to life and we have a responsibility to provide the best care possible.'[29]

In the other case, it will be argued that a person, whatever her disorder may be, cannot be forced to accept the option that best serves her own welfare, if this means violating her autonomy. Whether or not we are entitled to restrict her freedom (even the freedom to make self-harming choices, or to follow a 'dangerous' lifestyle) will depend on whether or not her actions and choices prove to be autonomous.

The choice between strong and weak paternalism is thus a matter of principle—that is, a choice relating to what we believe to be primarily important in life and worth protecting above all other things. Despite this, there are important considerations that support the perspective that gives priority to autonomy over welfare, and these are also relevant in relation to people with mental disorders.

9. *Welfare or Autonomy?*

Important arguments have been produced in support of the position that attaches value to the exercise of individual autonomy over the protection or promotion of welfare. The first concerns the value of autonomy.

9.1. *The value of autonomy*

The position according to which we may and should subordinate autonomy to other important goods, such as life or health, appears to contradict the value that is generally attached to autonomy. We have seen at the beginning of this chapter that the recognition of individual autonomy is one of the

---

[27] J. L. Birley, 'Psychiatrists as Citizens', *British Journal of Psychiatry*, 159 (1991), 1–6, quoted in Griffiths and Russell, 'Compulsory Treatment of Anorexia Nervosa Patients', 133.

[28] R. Dresser, 'Legal and Policy Considerations in Treatment of Anorexia Nervosa Patients', *International Journal of Eating Disorders*, 3 (1984), 43–51, quoted in Griffiths and Russell, 'Compulsory Treatment of Anorexia Nervosa Patients', 133.

[29] Ibid.

pillars of liberal thought and democratic societies. People generally regard themselves as 'agents', and are reluctant to accept that other people make decisions on their behalf, unless they delegate their choice to them.

With specific regard to health care, and in particular with regard to the patient's entitlement to accept or refuse medical treatment, John Harris has pointed out that deciding on the patient's behalf *for her own good* often means 'treating the agent as incompetent, [denying] the individual control over her own life and moral destiny and [treating] her as incompetent to run her own life as she chooses'.[30]

The subordination of people's autonomy to other goods, however motivated by the genuine intention to benefit them, and however important these goods may be, does not account for the value that people generally attach to their autonomy. There are, of course, occasions on which people prefer to delegate their decisions to others (for example, because they may believe others are better equipped than they are to make that particular decision). But the possibility of being able to delegate our decisions is part of our capacity to make decisions concerning our life and ourselves, and is therefore part of what exercising our autonomy means. Of course, it does not follow from the fact that we would sometimes ask other more competent people to make decisions on our behalf that these people are entitled to decide for us without our permission.

As Jonathan Glover writes:

For many of us would not be prepared to surrender our autonomy with respect to the major decisions of our life, even if by doing so our other satisfactions were greatly increased. There are some aspects of life where a person may be delighted to hand over decisions to someone else more likely to bring about the best results. When buying a secondhand car, I would happily delegate the decision to someone more knowledgeable. But there are many other decisions which people would be reluctant to delegate even if there were the same prospect of greater long-term satisfaction. Some of these decisions are relatively minor but concern ways of expressing individuality [. . .] Even in small things, people can mind more about expressing themselves than about the standard of the result. And, in the main decisions of life, this is even more so.[31]

Buchanan and Brock propose a similar argument:

Most persons commonly want to make significant decisions about their lives for themselves, and this desire is in part independent of whether they believe that they are always in a position to make the best choice. Even when we believe that others may be able to decide for us better than we ourselves can, we often prefer to decide for ourselves.[32]

---

[30] J. Harris, *The Value of Life* (London: Routledge, 1985), 194.

[31] Glover, *Causing Death and Saving Lives*, 80–1.

[32] Buchanan and Brock, *Deciding for Others*, 38.

If people sometimes prefer to direct their own lives, it is not because they believe that they are, or because they actually are, in the position to make the best decisions. The reason why people want to make their own decisions seems to amount to the very basic fact that they are 'these' particular individuals and that 'these decisions' are 'their' decisions. In health care, when people ask for information about their condition, available treatments, likely results, and so on, it is probably *not* because they believe that, once they are informed, they will be in the position to make the *best choices*, or that, if *they* choose, then the best outcomes are guaranteed. They might indeed not know what is *really best for them*, and they would not be 'irrational' for that. For example, if I had to choose to live either with my own severely damaged limb or with a well-functioning artificial limb, I might not know which would be best for me. Sometimes people do not know what is best for themselves, and sometimes they are even unable to imagine what their life would be like 'afterwards' (that is, after the choice is made). However, this does not make it less important to them to make their own decisions. On the contrary, it is especially in these cases, *when nobody knows* what the best outcome is, and when important goods are at stake, such as health or life, that individual autonomy and the burdensome responsibility that is involved in it become more valuable.

Another important argument that goes against the subordination of autonomy to other goods is that this theory implies underestimation of the reasons and values that lead a person to act in a particular way or to make a particular choice. By focusing on the outcome, this position does not give appropriate importance to the process through which the person articulates her behaviour or decision. Before considering this argument, something needs to be said on the way 'individual autonomy' should be understood.

9.1.1. *The substantive and formal conception of autonomy*

The previous section has shown that the position according to which individual autonomy should be subordinated to other goods does not account for the value that is generally attached to autonomy. However, 'individual autonomy' may be understood in different ways.

According to one position, whether or not individuals are acting autonomously depends on the type of choice they make. We may refer to this position as *the substantive conception of autonomy*. What matters most here is the *substance* or content of an action of choice. From this point of view, people act autonomously if the content or outcome of their decisions meets a stated standard of rationality. For example, a person would be acting autonomously if a rational agent would act similarly in similar circumstances (ideal rationality).[33] Or, a person would be acting autonomously if the

[33] Rawls, *A Theory of Justice*, 248–50.

majority of people would act similarly in similar circumstances (rationality as social acceptability).[34]

The substantive conception of autonomy seems to be rooted in Greek Stoicism and Cynicism, and finds its *acme* or peak in Kantian philosophy. In these philosophical theories, the notion of autonomy is co-extensive with the notion of rationality. Kant was noticeably clear in stating that human beings are autonomous because, and in so far as, they are rational, and they are rational (and therefore autonomous) in so far as their actions manifest a determined content (to the extent that they conform to the precepts of pure and practical reason).[35]

Thus, the substantive conception of autonomy links the concept of autonomy with that of rationality. Now, it is to be noticed that the notion of rationality, and in particular of practical rationality, often has substantive connotations. The 'rationality' of an action or choice is generally assessed on the basis of the goodness of the state of affairs that is promoted by that action or choice. Julian Savulescu, for example, writes that, in order for a choice or act to be considered rational, 'the state of affairs promoted by that choice or act must be worth promoting. That is, it must promote some objectively valuable state such as well being, achievement, knowledge, justice, and so on.'[36] Savulescu limits the substantive scope of this statement with Derek Parfit's Critical Present-Aim Theory, according to which we are not rationally required to choose always the state of affairs that is objectively the best: 'Some present rational concerns are good enough.'[37] In spite of such mitigation, and of relevant differences in theories of rationality, the notion of practical rationality is still generally linked to the evaluation of the *content and outcome* of actions and choices. Whether an action or a choice is to be considered rational depends on the evaluation of the state of affairs that is promoted. Accordingly, the rationality of agents is evaluated on the basis of the content of their actions and choices. This conception of rationality becomes co-extensive with the notion of autonomy, substantially meant.

Although a substantive conception of autonomy is central in some philosophical theories,[38] it manifests important problems, especially if applied to

---

[34] D. Scoccia, 'Paternalism and Respect for Autonomy', *Ethics*, 100/2 (1989–90), 318–34.

[35] I. Kant, *Critical Examination of Practical Reason*, in *Critique of Practical Reason and Other Works on the Theory of Ethics*, trans. and ed. T. K. Abbott (London: Longmans, Green and Co., 1948), 87–200.

[36] J. Savulescu, 'Desire-Based and Value-Based Normative Reasons', *Bioethics*, 13/5 (1999), 405–13.

[37] Ibid.

[38] In particular, this is true for the theory that Eugenio Lecaldano has called 'ideal contractarianism'. See E. Lecaldano, *Etica* (Turin: UTET, 1995), 93. Examples of this theory may be found in Rawls, *A Theory of Justice*, in particular p. 249; Dworkin, 'Paternalism', 83.

the physician–patient relationship. A substantive conception of autonomy, in fact, leads to the justification of an authoritarian attitude towards the patient and disregard for patient autonomy. If a patient makes decisions that do not manifest a particular content, these decisions will be considered not 'genuinely autonomous', and therefore respecting them is 'not *really* [respecting] what the individual wants'.[39]

For example, a doctor may believe that a patient is not autonomous, or is incompetent, simply because she refuses medical advice in circumstances in which he believes most people, or any 'rational' person, or a person of ordinary prudence would accept it. The doctor may conclude that the patient lacks autonomy simply in virtue of the fact that he believes the patient is being 'irrational', 'imprudent', or even 'unusual'. The doctor may thus conclude that, because the patient is lacking autonomy, forcing her to accept that advice is not a violation of her autonomy. How this approach may lead to disregard for individual autonomy is clear. We may have important reasons to sacrifice important goods, reasons that are personal and that concern our individual sphere, but that others would not share or even understand. This, of course, does not mean that we lack autonomy; it means rather that we are *these* particular individuals, and that our life is unique. Our choices, thus, may give other people reasons to talk to us, to question our decisions, and even to try to persuade us that we are making a mistake, but not to force us to do otherwise. Furthermore, it should be noticed that a substantive conception of autonomy may provide the medical profession with a powerful instrument not only of control over the individual patient, but also of social control, as, in its various forms, it implies (or reinforces) the idea that deviance from a presumed standard of rationality or normality is *symptomatic* of a *defect* in agency, or of a *disorder* in competence, or of *dysfunctional* decision-making capacity, or, in one word, of some sort of *mental* disorder.[40]

The alternative to the *substantive conception of autonomy* is a *formal or procedural conception of autonomy*. According to a formal conception of autonomy, autonomy is shown in the 'process of reasoning and deliberation' (see the next section) that leads to a decision. It is the *way* this process is articulated, rather than its content or outcome, that tells us whether a decision, or behaviour, should be considered as autonomous.

The *formal or procedural conception of autonomy*, which does not have substantive connotations and which therefore prevents abuse of authority in

---

[39] Harris, *The Value of Life*, 194.

[40] On the way psychiatric diagnosis may provide an instrument of social control, see T. Szasz, *The Myth of Mental Illness* (London: Paladin, 1984); G. Jervis, *Manuale critico di psichiatria* (5th edn., Milan: Feltrinelli, 1997); S. Bloch, 'Psychiatry, Abuses of', in *Encyclopedia of Bioethics*, iv. 2126–33.

the physician–patient relationship, is accepted and defended by a number of liberal philosophers, among whom we should mention Tristram H. Engelhardt.[41] It is also adopted by the US President's Commission for the study of Ethical Problems in Medicine and Biomedical and Behavioral Research,[42] and characterizes the legal approach to decision-making capacity that is adopted in the UK.

The Law Commission Report proposed a number of reforms relating to decision-making capacity. Among them, it was stated that a person should not be considered incapable 'merely because he makes a decision which would not be made by a person of ordinary prudence' (Draft Bill, 2(4)).[43] In common law, this conception is known as the 'functional approach',[44] as opposed to the 'outcome approach', which focuses on the content of the choice, and is the approach that the law has preferred.[45] The functional approach stresses the importance of factors like understanding[46] or the ability to balance costs and benefits of proposed alternatives, rather than the result of the choice.[47] Moreover, capacity for decision making is considered not as a general ability, but as relative to the specific decision and to the time it has to be made.[48] This means that people may be able to make a specific (competent) decision at one time, but not at another, or they may, at the same time, be able to make one decision but not another. Thus, decision-making capacity does not depend on the 'status'[49] of the subject, and is a decision-relative concept.[50] Furthermore, the law accepts that, even when life is at stake, people still have the right to make decisions that may appear

[41] Tristram H. Engelhardt, Jr., *Manuale di Bioetica* (Milan: Il Saggiatore, 1991; 2nd edn., 1999), 351; the English version of this book is *The Foundation of Bioethics* (2nd edn., Oxford: Oxford University Press, 1996).

[42] R. M. Wettstein, 'Competence', in *Encyclopedia of Bioethics*, i. 445–51.

[43] B. Hale, 'Mentally Incapacitated Adults and Decision Making: The English Perspective', *International Journal of Law and Psychiatry*, 20/1 (1997), 59–75.

[44] J. McHale and M. Fox, *Health Care Law* (London: Maxwell, 1997), 280–1.

[45] As also J. K. Mason and R. A. McCall Smith have recently reminded, the English Law Commission has 'preferred a "functional" approach to the question [of decision-making capacity] which focuses on the understanding and ability of the patient at the time of the relevant decision (paras. 3.1–3.23)' (See J. K. Mason and R. A. McCall Smith, *Law and Medical Ethics* (5th edn., London: Butterworths, 1999), 264 n. 5).

[46] See e.g. *State of Tennessee* v. *Northern* [1978] 563 SW 2d 197.

[47] The controversial character of the court decision in the case of *Re T (adult: refusal of medical treatment)* [1992] 4 All ER 649, (1992) 9 BMLR 46, CA, should be highlighted. See Mason and McCall Smith, *Law and Medical Ethics*, 263–4.

[48] *Gillick* v. *West Norfolk and Wisbech AHA* [1985] 3 All ER 402 at 409 e-h per Lord Fraser and at 422 g-j per Lord Scarman; see also *Estate of Park* [1959] P 112; *Re C (adult: refusal of medical treatment)* [1994] 1 All ER 819, (1993) 15 BMLR 77.

[49] For an account of the 'Status' approach, see McHale and Fox, *Health Care Law*, 280.

[50] On this point, see M. Brazier, *Medicine, Patients and the Law* (London: Penguin, 1992), chs. 2, 4 and 5; see also Harris, *The Value of Life*, ch. 10.

BOX 2.4. Substantive and Formal Conception of Autonomy

Substantive: Whether or not a person's action/choice is autonomous will be assessed on the basis of the outcome or of the content of the action/choice. The action/choice must be rational—that is, must promote some objectively valuable state.

Formal: Whether or not a person's action/choice is autonomous depends on the process of deliberation that leads up to that action or choice. The outcome or the content of the action/choice is irrelevant to autonomy.

---

unreasonable or irrational,[51] unwise[52] or wrong.[53] These legal notions will be presented in more detail in Chapter 11, when we discuss the issue of consent in psychiatry, and, in particular, legal issues surrounding anorexia nervosa. I will discuss the procedures that make an action or choice autonomous in more detail in the next section.

We should now consider the second important argument against the position that subordinates autonomy to other goods. We have anticipated above that this position, by focusing on the outcome, does not give appropriate importance to the 'process of reasoning and deliberation' through which the person articulates her behaviour or decision. We should now see what we mean by 'process of reasoning and deliberation' and what its ethical relevance is.

9.2. *The importance of the process of reasoning and deliberation*

Buchanan and Brock have argued that, when one has to decide whether to act paternalistically towards another person, it is not simply the *content* of the action or choice of that person that one needs to look at, but also the *way* in which she deliberates. One should 'focus primarily not on the content of the patient's decision, but on the process of reasoning that leads up to that decision'.[54] One always needs to consider the person's reasons and values and the way they are articulated. This 'way' of articulating behaviour is called by Buchanan and Brock the 'process of

---

[51] *Sidaway* v. *Board of Governors of the Bethlem Royal Hospital and the Maudsley Hospital* [1985] 1 All ER 643 at 509 B per Lord Templeman.
[52] *Lane* v. *Candura* [1978] 376 NE 2d 1232 Appeal Court of Massachusetts.
[53] *Hopp* v. *Lepp* [1979] 98 DLR 3d 464 at 470 per J. Prowse.
[54] Buchanan and Brock, *Deciding for Others*, 50.

reasoning and deliberation',[55] but, for brevity we may call it the 'process of deliberation'.[56]

In the psychiatric context, the decision-making process may be affected by abnormal experiences, such as, for example, hallucinations or delusions. If a patient refuses treatment because she fears she is being poisoned, arguably a delusion compromises the deliberation. The influence that abnormal experiences, such as hallucinations or delusions, may exert on the decision-making process can be considered similar to the influence of inappropriate information or false beliefs. For example, a decision cannot be considered as autonomous (or competent) unless based on appropriate and complete information (this is why we talk about *informed* consent, and not consent alone). Chapter 12 will further analyse the link between autonomous actions and choices and information and beliefs, with a focus on eating disorders. The fact that deliberation may be affected by inappropriate information or false beliefs has remarkable ethical importance, as it is not a violation of autonomy to protect a person from the harmful consequences of behaviour based on defective deliberation.

As John Stuart Mill, in his *On Liberty*, wrote: 'If either a public officer or any one else saw a person attempting to cross a bridge which had been ascertained to be unsafe, and there were no time to warn him of his danger, they might seize him and turn him back, without any real infringement of his liberty.'[57] In this case, not only the outcome, that is the fact that the person is going to harm himself, is ethically relevant, but also the fact that he is non-autonomously harming himself; the person may lack information, and therefore be unable to make a proper choice about his conduct. Since defects in information compromise the 'authenticity'[58] of the choice, non-consensual intervention is not a violation of the man's autonomy.[59]

The example offered by Mill is important, as it elucidates how lack of autonomy is sometimes related to lack of information. We may place ourselves in dangerous situations not because we wish to harm ourselves but simply because we do not know that the situation is dangerous. The example also illustrates that, if someone else has reason to believe that we are ignoring

---

[55] Ibid. 24.

[56] Buchanan and Brock also use the following terms to denote this process: 'process of decision-making' and 'process of the reasoning that leads up to that decision' (see Buchanan and Brock, *Deciding for Others*, 24–5, 50). It is important to notice that these terms do not have substantive connotations—that is, connotations relating to the content of the decision.

[57] Mill, *On Liberty*, 106–7.

[58] A. Mele, *Autonomous Agents: From Self Control to Autonomy* (Oxford: Oxford University Press, 1995), ch. 10.

[59] There is an intuitive link between defects in information and defects in autonomy. In fact, a decision based on a significant lack of information cannot be autonomous. In Chapter 12 it will be explained how the lack of information impinges upon autonomy in psychiatric healthcare and in eating disorders in particular.

the danger we are about to incur, he or she may paternalistically intervene to protect our life or welfare. I am not saying that everybody has a right to direct our lives because they believe we 'don't know' the relevant facts. All I am saying is that the example illustrates how having reason to believe that someone is going to harm herself based on a lack of information or false beliefs provides for an ethical justification to intervene paternalistically to save the person's life or to protect her welfare, provided that there is no time to warn that person.

It is important to anticipate here that the case of eating disorders is peculiar in the way the sufferer typically elaborates the information she has about food and about herself. Chapter 12 will analyse eating-disordered behaviour to assess whether eating anomalies are due to defects in information. We shall see that the model proposed by Mill does not entirely fit in the context of eating disorders. I shall point out important differences between the man who is going to harm himself on the bridge because he lacks relevant information and the self-destructive conduct of the eating-disordered person. I shall leave the discussion for now, as we need to know a lot more about eating disorders before we try to assess the autonomy of eating-disordered behaviour. Here I wish to provide a theoretical framework on the ethics of paternalistic interventions, which I will try to apply to the case of eating disorders. Mill's example of the bridge illustrates that being in possession of relevant information is essential to genuinely autonomous choices. It may happen that people make harmful choices while not realizing the dangers that they run, and this may entitle others to prevent the harm by intervening paternalistically.

In psychiatry, as well as in any other context, people may ignore important facts. People's behaviour and decisions, including medical and psychiatric decisions, may be based on inadequate or wrong information. Furthermore, it may happen that abnormal experiences may influence the patient—abnormal experiences such as delusions or hallucinations, for example.

In one sense, it is possible to predict that a person who has received a psychiatric diagnosis will make a certain type of choice. For example, suppose we have a patient who has delusions of persecution and who has a history of refusal of treatment based on her belief that doctors want to poison her. We may expect this patient to refuse medical treatment again, when she is in a crisis. In some cases and to some degree the psychiatric diagnosis may shift the balance of probabilities that actions and choices are based on a lack of information.[60]

However, in psychiatry as well as in any other context, there is no reason to assume that *all* types of behaviour and *all* decisions about medical or psychiatric treatment are 'defective' in these ways. With regard to health care,

---

[60] I wish to thank Mr Harry Lesser for pointing this out to me.

and therefore to medical decisions, or decisions on a patient's mental health, there may be many reasons why a person would rather not have medical or psychiatric treatment, or would prefer one type of treatment to another, which may have nothing to do with hallucinations, delusions, or other abnormal experiences that may impinge upon the deliberation process. This is true even if the person actually does suffer hallucinations or delusions. We cannot realistically assume that those who have received a psychiatric diagnosis have, by reason of their mental illness, diminished capacity to make any medical decisions or decisions on their mental health.

The analysis of the process of deliberation has thus a crucial ethical relevance, because violating a person's wishes to direct her life has a completely different weight, from an ethical point of view, from protecting a person who makes the harmful choice only in virtue of a delusion of which she may be unaware, or of incomplete or wrong information. Focusing on the result or outcome means that the reasons why a person makes a particular choice do not really count. However, most people would probably agree that it is one thing for me to refuse treatment because I am convinced that the doctor wants to poison me, and quite another thing for me to refuse treatment because, for example, having used that treatment on previous occasions, I consider the side effects outweigh the benefits and therefore wish to try something different. Since the process of deliberation has remarkable ethical importance, a theory that does not accord appropriate importance to the analysis of this process can hardly be prepared to address ethical issues and to propose a way to resolve them.

10. *The Value of Autonomy and Weak Paternalism*

Let me try to sum up my conclusions.

In the light of considerations made in the previous sections, relating to the implications of the position according to which autonomy is and should be subordinated to other goods and values, and of the value that is universally attached to individual autonomy, we need to conclude that, at least prima facie,[61] only a weak version of paternalism is acceptable, as this is the only form of paternalism that gives priority to the exercise of autonomy. We may articulate the weak version of paternalism as follows:

A person may be entitled to prevent the *harmful conduct* of another person independently of or against the manifest wishes of that person, only when

---

[61] Further considerations relating to the case of anorexia nervosa and competent refusal of artificial feeding will be found in Chapter 13.

this other person's actions and choices lack autonomy in some significant way, or when a temporary intervention is necessary to assess whether these actions and choices are autonomous (*weak paternalism*). The autonomy of an action or choice is to be assessed not on the basis of its content or outcome but on the basis of the process of deliberation that leads up to that action or decision (*formal or procedural conception of autonomy*).

This attitude guarantees respect both for a person's welfare and for the way in which she wishes to shape her life autonomously.

11. *Objections*

A number of objections may be raised against the theory of weak paternalism articulated in this chapter.

One objection may be that respecting individual autonomy may sometimes, especially the case involves people with psychiatric disorders and, in the specific, eating disorders, have very high costs for carers, and it should be considered whether autonomy has an absolute normative strength—that is, whether the autonomy of the individual should *always* and in all circumstances be respected. We shall address this issue in Chapter 13, when discussing the ethics of life-saving treatment for anorexia, but it may already be noticed that the theory of weak paternalism has been articulated as prima facie. In Chapter 13 we shall discuss the limits of the normative strength of the principle of respect for autonomy in some very particular circumstances that may occur in the care and treatment of the eating-disordered person.

Another objection may be that it may be difficult to determine (*a*) whether one's conduct is significantly autonomous or not, and (*b*) whether it is sufficiently harmful as to justify paternalism. It is, of course, true that there will be important theoretical and practical issues involved in the assessment of autonomy and of harm. For example, how much information should one possess to make an autonomous choice? How can we assess how this information is used in the deliberation process? Or, what type of behaviour counts as harmful? In the case of eating disorders, for example, is taking exercise sufficiently harmful to justify paternalism? Are compensatory practices such as vomiting sufficiently harmful to justify paternalism?

It is not possible to produce a general answer to these questions. These questions will have to be addressed on an individual basis and evaluated from time to time. In spite of these difficulties, the argument that we should respect people's autonomy and intervene to protect them only when their harmful actions and choices are non-autonomous remains, I believe, a valid argument. Respect for people's autonomy should be our aim, however difficult this may be in practice. The objections outlined above should be considered not as a proof that the theory articulated here is invalid, but as the expression of a more general difficulty that we all inevitably meet when trying to understand other people's experiences, and to relate to people whose actions and decisions are substantially different from the ones we would do or make if we were 'in their shoes', or we would expect from them. Any intellectually honest research on paternalism has to recognize that all acts of paternalism will probably always be controversial, and will usually conclude with *a moral doubt* (although often whether or not people have doubts about this will depend on the strength of their starting assumptions).

Remaining with a moral doubt, however, is not necessarily a bad or undesirable thing. When we are worried for somebody else's welfare, we are not bound to use force to protect that person. We may express our concern through a discussion of the matter and eventually persuasion, and, although these approaches take time, in the vast majority of cases they are likely to produce the same or better results than the exercise of force.

There is another important objection to the idea that we need to respect the autonomous choices of people with mental disorders. The objection is that 'pathological' behaviour is the result of an illness and not the result of an autonomous choice. The argument may take two directions.

One direction is to say that 'mental' illness affects the 'mind' and therefore jeopardizes the autonomy of the person. According to this type of argument, abnormal behaviour would just be a 'symptom' of a mental disorder. Although eating-disordered behaviour 'looks like' a deliberate choice, it is not, as it is the result of an underlying pathology that induces the person to behave in that particular way. Behaviour is 'pathological', and this means that it is directed by the illness and not by the person herself. In other words, that behaviour is *determined*, and not purposive or autonomous. People with mental illness, so the argument goes, behave in certain ways *because of their mental illness*. One cannot possibly claim that we should respect symptomatological behaviour. This behaviour is pathological in itself, is determined by the underlying mental disease, and there is consequently no autonomy in it to respect. Therefore, the very fact that the person has a mental illness means that we are entitled to prevent her from performing pathological behaviour and to protect her from the harmful consequences of the illness. This argument is very popular and seems to have some strength, at least at a first sight. The next chapter will answer the following questions:

- Is it true that people behave in some ways because 'they suffer from' a mental illness? Is it true that what we classify as symptomatological behaviour—for example, eating-disordered behaviour—is in fact the result of a mental illness?

- Is it consequently true that the fact that the person 'suffers from' a mental disorder entitles us to intervene against her manifest wishes to prevent self-harm?

The argument may take another direction as well. It is possible to say that abnormal behaviour is not autonomous in so far as it is caused by genetic or neurophysiological variations. Focusing on eating disorders, I will discuss their physiological basis in Chapter 4. The analysis of the genetics neuro-physiology of the disorders will clarify that we have no basis to believe that eating-disordered behaviour is only the result of genetic mutations or neuro-logical or physiological disorders (although clearly these may play a role in the articulation and maintenance of that behaviour).

12. *Conclusions*

This chapter has articulated a theory of paternalism. Emphasizing the value of autonomy and respecting the wish that each individual person has to direct her own life does not entail indifference towards people's destiny and is not in principle incompatible with paternalism. Claiming that autonomy is a pri-mary value and that it is 'more important' than welfare does not, of course, mean that welfare is not important. In psychiatry, in particular, adopting an attitude of respect for patient autonomy, wherever it is expressed and exer-cised, does not mean that we should passively stand before people's misery, and let them suffer and die, only because we are committed to the 'principle of respect for individual autonomy'. Stressing the primary value of auton-omy induces us, instead, to clarify the conditions, if any, of a morally justifiable form of paternalism.

As we have seen, in psychiatry as well as in other contexts, prima facie, the criterion that may possibly legitimize paternalism is the defect in the process of reasoning and deliberation that leads up to the harmful conduct. If the criterion that may legitimate paternalism is the defect in the deliberation, the fact that this defect is linked to psychological processes or to 'non-psychological' conditions (such as drunkenness, shock, or others) is surely clinically important, but has no ethical relevance. A person that is going to harm herself non-autonomously is can be protected, independently of whether her defect in autonomy depends on factors that are psychological in nature, or on conditions of a different type. Therefore, before intervening independently of or contrary to the wishes of the person with psychiatric disorders in order to protect her welfare, we should at least prima facie always analyse the reasons why that person behaves that way or makes that particular choice, and the way these reasons are articulated.

As anticipated in the previous section, the next two chapters will address the objection according to which we cannot possibly respect the autonomy of people with mental disorders because mental disorders impinge upon people's autonomy. Chapter 3 will answer the following questions:

- Is it true that people behave in some ways because 'they suffer from' a mental illness? Is it true that what we classify as symptomatological behaviour is in fact the result of a mental illness?
- Is it consequently true that the fact that the person 'suffers from' a mental disorder entitles us to intervene against her manifest wishes to prevent self-harm?

3

Is Pathological Behaviour Caused by Mental Illness?

1. *Introduction*

In Chapter 2 I have argued that there is a prima facie obligation to respect other people's actions and choices, provided that these actions and choices are autonomous. Paternalism, at least prima facie, may be justifiable only when self-harming behaviours are characterized by lack of autonomy (weak paternalism). Although many people agree with the idea that health-care professionals should respect or even encourage their patients' autonomy, many also believe that this model of patient–professional relationship cannot be applied to the management of mental disorders. The peculiar nature of psychopathology, so the argument goes, makes it impossible to respect patients' autonomy.

The argument may take different forms. One of the most common claims is that mental illness *jeopardizes people's autonomy*. This argument is very common in ordinary discourse, in discussions within psychiatry, and in law. According to this position, behaviour that we classify as 'symptomatic' or 'abnormal' is caused by the mental illness—therefore it is necessarily non-autonomous. A person is diagnosed as having a mental illness when she has abnormal experiences of different types and shows some types of anomalous behaviour. These experiences and behaviour result from an underlying mental disorder. Therefore, those experiences and behaviours are 'symptomatic' of the mental disorder. Mental illness is regarded as the cause, the reason, or the explanation of certain experiences, behaviour, and disturbances.

The argument is apparently straightforward and is accepted by many. It is very common to hear people saying, for example, that patients 'hear voices' *because* they suffer from paranoid schizophrenia; or that they lose interest in

An early version of this chapter has been published. See Simona Giordano, 'In Defence of Autonomy in Psychiatric Healthcare', *Tip Etigi, Turkish Journal of Medical Ethics*, 9/2 (2001), 59–66. I am very much indebted to Harry Lesser for discussing the paper and thinking through my ideas with me.

life *because* they suffer from depression; or that they gamble *because* they suffer from pathologic gambling; or that they fear open spaces because they are agoraphobic; or that they want to be thin *because* they suffer from anorexia; or that they binge and fast *because* they suffer from bulimia. These sorts of arguments are commonplace in ordinary discourse as well as in medical literature and in law.

The ethical implications of these sorts of statements are important. If mental illness causes people to have some experiences, and drives people to behave in a certain way, this means that people do not have much control over those experiences and behaviours. These will be considered 'pathological'. If pathological experiences and behaviours are the result of a mental illness, the sufferer has little control over them. It follows that the person's autonomy is diminished or compromised in important ways by the mental illness.

Where this is accepted, the diagnosis of mental illness or mental disorder will be considered as one of the criteria that justify coercive interventions. People who have a mental disorder will be regarded by definition as lacking autonomy in some important way. Since the psychiatric patient is regarded as non-autonomous at least in some way, the issue of respect for her autonomy in those ways simply will not arise. The diagnosis of mental illness will thus provide a justification for paternalism. For example, under the Mental Health Act 1983 (MHA) the statute that regulates assessment and treatment of mental disorders in England and Wales, the diagnosis of mental illness, severe mental impairment, psychopathic disorder, and mental impairment is the first criterion that justifies coercive detention and treatment (s. 2 and s. 3 of the Act).

But is it true that people with mental illness have abnormal experiences and behaviour *because of their mental illness*? Is it true that mental illness causes some forms of anomalous experiences and behaviour? Is it true that mental illness determines people's behaviour and jeopardizes their autonomy? Is mental illness the 'causal explanation' of some people's experiences and behaviour?

This chapter will challenge these types of claims. The claim that people's experiences and behaviours are due to their mental illness involves a logical fallacy, although one that may have a psychological *raison d'être*, as I now illustrate.

2. *'That man committed suicide because he was mentally ill'*

One of my colleagues, Mr Harry Lesser, tells this story. One day the news reported the suicide of a well-known British TV comedian. Harry Lesser was listening to the news with his young son. The son was very disturbed to hear about the man killing himself and asked why he did that. The father said that the TV personality had killed himself because he was mentally ill. Lesser told me that by saying that the man had killed himself because he was mentally ill, he did not mean to give an explanation of the suicide; rather, as he pointed out to me, that type of answer 'sets the action into a context' and 'makes it more tolerable' (his words). By saying that the man committed suicide because he was mentally ill, he wanted to make the suicide more tolerable to his son.

Probably, the suicide was rendered more tolerable to the general public as well in the same way. Similarly, saying to people that they have determined experiences because they are mentally ill makes these experiences more tolerable to them.

Moreover, this type of answer ('because he was mentally ill') also suggests that the man 'couldn't help it'. 'In the absence of a mental illness', one might expect people to realize that they have alternatives, and to try to control their desires and impulses. The emphasis on the 'mental illness' suggests that people cannot be held entirely responsible for their actions, that there is something overwhelming them, which compels them to act in a certain way—that their autonomy is diminished or jeopardized. It is, Lesser says, like the difference between saying that someone is a 'heavy drinker' and saying that someone is an 'alcoholic'. Saying that someone is a heavy drinker leaves space for control over drinking; saying that someone is an alcoholic is to suggest that he or she has lost significant control over him or herself. So, saying that things happen because of mental illness is to suggest that people have no control over certain experiences and behaviours.

But is it true that people have determined experiences *because they have a mental illness*? Is it true that the comedian committed suicide *because he was mentally ill*?

It seems to me, and in this chapter I will argue, that saying that things happen to people because they are mentally ill is just a ready-made answer. The problem with this statement is that it does not explain what it proposes to explain. It is *a way of putting it, a way of saying it*. As Lesser says, it is a way of putting things into context, and a way of making things more tolerable. Maybe it is also a way of making more tolerable *to us* the fact that we are unable to explain certain things. But it does not really say what it says. It does not really explain what happens. That *because* ('*because he was mentally ill*') does not provide an explanation of the action or of the experiences.

3. *'I had to wash my hair ten times today because voices commanded me to do so'*

Here is another story.

One day, while working in a psychiatric unit, I bumped into B. I had known B for a long time. B had paranoid schizophrenia and she had been living in the hospital for years. As always, she said hello to me and came towards me to kiss me. I asked how she was and what she had been up to today. She said: 'This afternoon I had to wash my hair ten times.' I asked why. She answered very simply: 'Because some voices ordered me to do so.'

For a long time I have been thinking about this brief conversation, about my question and her answer. She said: 'Because some voices ordered me to do so.' What did that word *because* mean? Was she really explaining her own behaviour? Did she really wash her hair because voices ordered her to do so—was that it?

After having thought about our conversation, I came to the conclusion that her answer was a *proper answer*, at least in an important way, and probably a better answer than one I could have had from a psychiatrist. She was not trying to provide any further explanation of her experiences and behaviour. She was not trying to explain why she heard voices, or why those voices were irresistible. She was just telling me why she washed her hair ten times—because voices gave the order. It is true, I was unsatisfied with that explanation—because I still did not know why she heard those voices, and why these voices were compelling to her. Of course, I could have asked her why she felt she could not resist that order, or what would have happened to her if she had refused to wash her hair, or whether she believed that the voices were right in asking her to wash her hair ten times, or whether she found it unreasonable to be asked to wash her hair ten times, or whether she found it unreasonable to obey the order, and so on. Indeed I could have asked her many things, but I did not.

I still wonder whether B thought the voices were right, or whether she could have refused to obey them. Although I still do not know many things about what happened to B that afternoon, I think her answer was appropriate in an important way. It was a proper answer *to my question*. In fact I did not ask her *why she heard voices*. I just asked *why she had to wash her hair ten times*. And the answer *to that question* was: because she heard voices that ordered her to do so.

Another thing that I could have done that afternoon (but I did not do) was to go to one of the psychiatrists in charge and ask why she was hearing voices—a question that is different from the original one 'why did you wash your hair ten times?' The reason why I did not ask 'why does she hear voices?'

is that I expected to receive the following answer: 'because she has paranoid schizophrenia', an answer that would have told me nothing more than I already knew about B. The truth, it seems to me, is that I do not know why B heard voices that afternoon, neither would a psychiatrist. I know why she washed her hair ten times—because she explained that to me: voices ordered her to do so.[1] But the other question—why does she hear voices—remains unanswered.

If I say that B has been washing her hair ten times because voices commanded her to do so, I think I am saying something meaningful. One may wonder why B is unable to resist these voices, but there is nothing tautological in the statement that B has been washing her hair because voices ordered her to do so. There is at most a missing premiss, and the whole argument would go as follows:

1. some voices commanded B to wash her hair 10 times;
2. B could not resist (for some unspecified reason);
3. therefore she washed her hair ten times.

This trilogy properly answers the question: 'Why has B washed her hair ten times this afternoon?'

If I ask, however: 'Why does B hear voices?', what answer can I have? Many would say: *because she suffers from schizophrenia.*

I will argue here that this sentence amounts to saying: B hears voices because she has hallucinations (= for example, hears voices). It sets B's experiences and behaviour into context; maybe it makes these experiences more tolerable to B; as Harry Lesser put it, it makes our incapacity to understand more tolerable to us; but, ultimately, it is logically fallacious—it is *empty*. The objection has been made to me that saying, for example, that voices are due to schizophrenia means ruling out other possible causes (such as brain tumours or the effects of drugs). Therefore, saying that the voices are due to schizophrenia is not an entirely empty statement. It is true that when one says, for example, that voices are due to schizophrenia one is implicitly saying that the person does not have a brain tumour or is not under the effect of drugs that produce hallucinations. However, from this it does not follow that the statement 'voices are due to schizophrenia' is logically correct. The statement may tell us a number of things about the person and her experiences, and also about how she may be treated, and therefore it may be a useful instrument in practice. However, this statement is still fallacious, from a logical point of view.

---

[1] I am not saying here that she could not resist the voices because the voices were irresistible. This would be another tautology. I do not know why she could not resist those voices—indeed, I did not ask.

4. *What do we Mean when we Say that a Person has a Mental Illness?*

When we say that a person has a mental illness, all we are saying is that that person manifests some types of experiences and behaviour. For example, B has received the diagnosis of 'schizophrenia' because she has manifested some of the many experiences and behaviour that Bleuler listed under 'paranoid schizophrenia' (for example, hallucinations and intrusive thoughts).[2] The psychiatric diagnosis summarizes in one word a large variety of disturbances (in perception, in language, in motion, and so on). Instead of saying: B has intrusive thoughts, auditory hallucinations, disorganized thought, and so on, we say: B has paranoid schizophrenia. All we mean is that B has intrusive thoughts, auditory hallucinations, disorganized thought, and so on.

The important thing to notice is that the psychiatric diagnosis summarizes these disturbances, but *does not explain them*. B has received the diagnosis of paranoid schizophrenia *because* she manifests a pattern of disturbances (for example, hallucinations). When I say that B is a paranoid schizophrenic, all I mean is that B has hallucinations, intrusive thoughts, ideas of reference, and possibly other symptoms. I do not know *why* she has these disturbances. I only know *that* she manifests these disturbances. I say that she is schizophrenic because I can see that she has these disturbances, *not* because I know the cause of her disturbances. I say that she is schizophrenic (= that she manifests hallucinations, intrusive thoughts, or ideas of reference), but I can give *no explanation* of why she is schizophrenic (= why she manifests hallucinations, intrusive thoughts, or ideas of reference).

The term 'schizophrenia' summarizes a number of disturbances, but does not say anything about the cause(s) of these disturbances. The diagnosis has descriptive value, not explicative value (diagnosis is not equivalent to scientific explanation).

The diagnosis certainly has an important predictive value.[3] If I am told that B has paranoid schizophrenia, I shall not be surprised when she tells me that 'voices' commanded her to wash her hair, and I will probably be able to predict, at least approximately, what is going to happen to her at some point. However good I may be in predicting her behaviour (what may be mistaken for the ability to explain it), I still do not know why she has these disorders.

---

[2] Schizophrenia is a clinical term that refers to a wide spectrum of disturbances. People manifesting such disturbances are called 'schizophrenic'. Eugen Bleuler used the term 'schizophrenia' for the first time. Bleuler called dementia praecox 'schizophrenia' 'because the "splitting" of the different psychic functions is one of the most important characteristics' of the disorder. In fact, in its etymological meaning, 'schizophrenia' means 'split-mind' (from the Greek $\sigma\chi\iota\zeta$ = *schizo* = split, and $\phi\rho\varepsilon\nu\iota\alpha$ = *phrenia* = mind). See E. Bleuler, *Dementia Praecox* (New York: International University Press, 1966), 8

[3] I owe this observation to Alan Cribb.

The philosopher Gilbert Ryle noticed that we often make a similar mistake (considering the description as an explanation) when we believe we can 'explain' people's behaviour by referring to their 'personality traits'. He wrote:

On hearing that a man is vain we expect him, in the first instance, to behave in certain ways, namely to talk a lot about himself, to cleave to the society of the eminent, to reject criticisms, to seek the footlights and to disengage himself from conversations about the merits of others. We expect him also to indulge in roseate daydreams about his own successes, to avoid recalling past failures and to plan for his own advancement. To be vain is to tend to act in these and innumerable other kindred ways. Certainly we also expect the vain man to feel certain pangs and flutters in certain situations; we expect him to have an acute sinking feeling, when an eminent person forgets his name, and to feel buoyant of heart and light of toe on hearing of the misfortunes of his rivals. But feelings of pique and buoyancy are not more directly indicative of vanity than are public acts of boasting or private acts of daydreaming. Indeed they are less directly indicative [. . .] When we explain why a man boasts by saying that it is because he is vain, we are forgetting that a disposition is not an event and so cannot be a cause [. . .] The vain man is a man who tends to register particular feelings of vanity; these cause or impel him to boast, or perhaps to will to boast, and to do all the other things which we say are done from vanity. It should be noticed that this argument takes it for granted that to explain an act as done from a certain motive, in this case from vanity, is to give a causal explanation. This means that it assumes that a mind, in this case the boaster's mind, is a field of special causes, that is why a vanity feeling has been called in to be the inner cause of the overt boasting [. . .] to explain an act as done from a certain motive is not analogous to saying that the glass broke because a stone hit it [. . .][4]

Ryle also pointed out:

There are at least two quite different senses in which an occurrence is said to be 'explained'; and there are correspondingly at least two quite different senses in which we ask 'why' it occurred and two quite different senses in which we say that it happened 'because' so and so was the case. The first sense is the causal sense. To ask why the glass broke is to ask what caused it to break, and we explain, in this sense, the fracture of the glass when we report that a stone hit it. The 'because' clause in the explanation reports an event, namely the event which stood to the fracture of the glass as cause to effect.[5]

Ryle proceeds to discuss in what other ways we may say that an occurrence is explained by this and that, and in what senses we may say that motives and inclinations explain our actions and behaviours. We do not need to get into

---

[4] Gilbert Ryle, *The Concept of Mind* (London: Penguin, 1978), 83–8. I owe this observation to Harry Lesser. We had interesting conversations and he made me think about these issues in a different way.

[5] Ibid. 86.

this discussion, because it is not entirely pertinent to our purposes. What is relevant here is to point out that when we ask: 'Why did someone act in a certain way?'[6] and we answer 'Because he was mentally ill', we may think we are providing a causal explanation, but we are not. As Ryle points out, saying that the man boasted because he is vain is not like saying that 'the glass broke because a stone hit it'. All we are saying is that 'we could have expected that to happen'. We have not established any causal explanation for the experiences and behaviours of that person; we have not given any 'reason for' those experiences and behaviours. Saying that 'B hears voices because she has schizophrenia' is like saying, as Ryle puts it, that 'the glass broke *because it was brittle*'—given that we know that the glass was brittle, we may expect that it will break easily. But what actually did break the glass was the stone, and the glass broke because the stone hit it. In the context of psychiatric illnesses, given that we know that a person is inclined to have certain sorts of experiences, we may expect him to behave in a certain way. But these statements ('the glass is brittle'—'the person has had a diagnosis of schizophrenia') are *descriptive* statements, with a predictive potential, and not *explicative* statements, in the same way as 'the glass is broken because a stone hit it' is explicative. In the case of mental illness, we are in a similar situation to the one in which we would be if we did not know that the glass was broken by a stone. We do not know what causes the experiences and behaviours that are listed under the psychiatric category. Psychiatry mostly offers descriptive statements (in contrast to physics and neurology as sciences,—if practised as such—that is, as efforts to obtain explanations of why).

To return to B, I think a logically correct way of constructing the situation is to say that B is (classified as, or described as) 'schizophrenic' *because* she manifests a pattern of disturbances (here the clause *because* is explicative—it explains why psychiatrists gave that particular diagnosis). She does not have these disturbances *because* she is schizophrenic. We do not know *why* she manifests these disturbances (unfortunately).

The way the situation of psychiatric patients is constructed in psychiatry is often logically fallacious, as the next section will show.

5. *The Fallacy of Psychiatric 'Explanations'*

Box 3.1 contains a schema of the fallacy that often occurs in psychiatry, when people seem to give 'explanations' of patients' experiences and behaviours.

---

[6] Ibid.

BOX 3.1. A Fallacy in Some Explanations of Schizophrenia

Paranoid schizophrenia

=

(a clinical term that) refers to/summarizes a number of disturbances (hallucinations, intrusive thoughts, etc.)

(*proper definition*)

Question 1 Why have you received the diagnosis of schizophrenia? (or: 'Why are you—called—schizophrenic'?)

Answer 1 Because you manifest the following disturbances: hallucinations, etc.

(*proper answer, logically correct*)

Question 2 Why do you manifest the following disturbances? (or: 'Why do you hear voices?')

Answer 2*a* We do not yet know.

(*proper and true answer*)

Answer 2*b* Because you suffer from schizophrenia.

(*tautological answer*)

=

You manifest the following disturbances, hallucinations, etc., because you manifest the following disturbances, hallucinations, etc. (schizophrenia in fact means that you manifest the following disturbances, hallucinations, etc.).

I shall focus on schizophrenia and other clinical categories. We shall see later in the chapter that the *same fallacy applies to eating disorders*. Answer 2*b* is a tautology.[7] This kind of logical error is recurrent in psychiatry. Here there seems to be the tendency to believe that, once we give a name to a phenomenon, then this name explains such a phenomenon.

For example, it is said that people fear open space *because they are agoraphobic*. However, being agoraphobic means *fearing open space*. Thus, that statement amounts to saying that people fear open spaces because they fear open spaces—given that being agoraphobic means fearing open spaces.

---

[7] I am not underestimating the importance of diagnostic categories. I am trying to point out logical errors that may lead to overcoming people's autonomy.

Similar arguments are very common. For example: 'I cannot control my gambling because I suffer from pathological gambling.' If suffering from pathological gambling means being unable to control gambling, then saying that I cannot control gambling because I suffer from pathological gambling is like saying that I cannot control gambling because I cannot control gambling.

These statements are tautological. These statements point out that 'we can't help it'. But the logic of the argument is fallacious. The fallacy in these statements consists in taking the description and using it as the explanation.

There are cases in which the fallacy is more difficult to detect. For example, many of us may have heard people saying: 'She quit her job and now she never goes out, she has lost interest in everything *because* she suffers from depression.' These arguments are very much used in ordinary discourse. They also *seem* meaningful. However, they are also *logically fallacious*. The term 'because' makes them tautological.

The logically correct way of constructing the situation here is: we say that people are depressed *because* they lose interest in things and have a feeling of unsustainable sadness. We have decided to call a certain pattern of experiences *depression* and when people manifest that pattern of experiences we say they are depressed. Given that we say that people are depressed because they lose interest in things and have feelings of unsustainable sadness, then saying that a person is sad and loses interest in things because she is depressed amounts to saying that that person is sad and loses interest in things because she is sad and loses interest in things.

Depression refers to a mental state—it is a state of being, not its cause. Saying that people have determined types of feelings and behave in a determined way *because they have depression* is logically fallacious. As we said above, these statements 'put the happenings into a context', as Lesser said, and give us a certain 'frame of mind' in dealing with a particular person. They raise a number of expectations in us and make it possible for us to predict a person's behaviour and also to *tolerate* it—and to tolerate our incapacity to understand and our impotence. These sorts of apparent explanations also make it easier for the sufferers to tolerate their own experiences and the scarce control they have over them. I am not saying that it is by all means 'impossible' to understand why people believe in these sorts of explanations—there is probably something positive about them. However, they are not real *explanations*—as they seem to be. They are *psychologically reassuring fallacies*.

The same argument can be applied to eating disorders. The argument is outlined in Box 3.2. However often this error occurs in psychiatry, and however 'positive' it may be for someone, it is still a logical error. Neither

BOX 3.2. A Fallacy in Some Explanations of Anorexia Nervosa

Anorexia nervosa

=

(a clinical term that) refers to/summarizes a number of disturbances (loss of weight over stated limits, amenorrhoea, etc.)

(*proper definition*)

Question 1 Why have you received the diagnosis of anorexia nervosa?
(or: 'Why are you—called—anorexic'?)
Answer 1   Because you manifest the following disturbances: loss of weight over stated limits, amenorrhoea.

(*proper answer, logically correct*)

Question 2 Why do you manifest the following disturbances?
(or: 'Why do you diet, do you have amenorrhoea . . . ?')
Answer 2a We are trying to understand it.

(*proper and true answer*)

Answer 2b Because you suffer from anorexia nervosa.

(*tautological answer*)

=

You manifest the following disturbances because you manifest the following disturbances (having anorexia nervosa, in fact, means that you are manifesting the following disturbances).

the number of times in which this sort of 'apparent explanation' is used, nor its positive potential, modifies its tautological nature.

Some people will object that anorexia and other neuroses differ from other psychiatric conditions, such as schizophrenia, in that schizophrenia is determined by biological causes whereas anorexia is 'mental'. Therefore the category of schizophrenia has an explicative potential that anorexia does not have.

Indeed, there is evidence that some of the disturbances that characterize schizophrenia (in particular, some psychotic disturbances, such as hallucinations) have organic bases. For example, hallucinations seem related to increased dopamine levels. Genetic factors may also be involved in schizophrenia.[8] Moreover, brain scans show differences between patients with

---

[8] Nicky Hayes, *Foundations of Psychology* (London: Thomson Learning, 2000), 246.

schizophrenia and control groups. Some researchers argue that the brain of the person may have been damaged either by a birth trauma or by an intra-uterine virus, and the illness, dormant for many years, may make its onset at a later age.[9] All these factors, together with family and social stressors, are thought to play a role in the arousal of schizophrenia.[10]

Of course my arguments do not intend to deny the scientific reliability of these and other studies on schizophrenia. I am not denying that there may be organic factors that contribute to explain the disturbances that characterize schizophrenia. And, of course, the importance of research in this field is great. I am only pointing out a theoretical problem. It seems that, although we may be able to explain why people have some disturbances, the sentence 'people have hallucinations, delusions, and so on *because* they suffer from schizophrenia' is not explicative and is not the equivalent of saying that people have hallucinations because of increased dopamine levels or a birth trauma. What people (or most people) mean when they say that someone has delusions, or hallucinations, or disorganized speech 'because he or she suffers from schizophrenia' is not that the person suffers from hallucinations prob-ably caused by increased dopamine levels, or that a birth trauma may have caused brain abnormalities, which in turn may be responsible for the dis-turbances the person manifests. It seems that what most people actually mean is no more than what they say: the person has delusions, hallucinations, and so on 'because they suffer from schizophrenia' (= the person has delu-sions, hallucinations, and so on). This is the argument that I am contesting. When these statements are accepted with these meanings, the description is taken for an explanation. These sorts of statements are similar to the claim that 'people fast and vomit because they suffer from eating disorders'. These sorts of statements are not explicative. They are logically mistaken, regard-less of whether we can also give a proper explanation of the phenomenon.

6. *Conclusions*

Acknowledging that in most instances the psychiatric diagnosis merely has a descriptive character is to admit that, in the vast majority of cases,[11] mental illness does not—and cannot—compromise people's autonomy. I have

---

[9] R. M. Murray, P. O. Jones, E. Callaghan, N. Takei, and P. Sham, 'Genes, Viruses and Neurodevelopmental Schizophrenia', *Journal of Psychiatric Research*, 26/4 (1992), 225–35.

[10] Hayes, *Foundations of Psychology*, 246.

[11] Exception made for mental illnesses such as dementia, Alzheimer's disease, Parkinson's disease, and maybe substance-use disorders, in which abnormal experiences and behaviour are in a proper sense caused by the illness, and in which the illness actually *explains* those experiences and behaviour.

argued that it is simply not true that 'mental illness' causes a pattern of experiences and behaviour.

Surely the diagnosis sometimes encapsulates the results of scientific data that explain some of the symptoms (for example, the term 'Alzheimer's disease' refers to the brain abnormalities that cause loss of memory and other disorders). In these cases, it makes sense to argue that the diagnosis refers to a disease that is responsible for (or that causes) some disturbances. However, this is often not the case for psychiatric diagnoses. In the majority of cases when it is said that a person has a mental illness, what is meant is that *she manifests some disturbances*. In most cases the psychiatric diagnosis is only a short cut to describe a pattern of disturbances: it has no explanatory value.

In all cases in which the diagnosis merely has a descriptive value (and this is the majority) it is simply not true that 'mental illness' jeopardizes people's autonomy. Mental illness is a 'description of events', and as such it does not and cannot 'jeopardize autonomy'.

The psychiatric diagnosis may, of course, refer to a constellation of characteristics that *typically* indicate that the person *may lack autonomy*. And, from this point of view, the diagnosis of mental illness may give us an extra reason to investigate the autonomy of the person's behaviour and choices. But this is very different from the claim that 'mental illness jeopardizes people's autonomy', and should not be confused with the idea that the fact that a person has a mental illness gives us some sort of entitlement to intervene paternalistically.

This may be seen as an overly logical way of looking at psychiatric diagnoses. However, this has crucial consequences for the ethics of care and treatment of the mentally ill: there is no reason to consider mental illness as 'something' capable of destroying people's autonomy and therefore the diagnosis of mental illness should not function as a justificatory criterion for non-consensual interventions. Diagnosis of mental illness should be regarded in the same way as other types of diagnoses. The mere fact that a person has an illness (whatever that is) does not justify coercion. The diagnosis of an illness justifies treatment, but not *coercive* treatment, and there is no reason why the psychiatric diagnosis should be treated in a different way. The psychiatric diagnosis, like any other diagnosis, does not justify paternalism. The fact that medical or psychiatric treatment is deemed clinically appropriate or even clinically 'necessary' does not make it right or ethical for health-care professionals to *enforce it*.

Paternalism towards people with mental disorders—including eating disorders—cannot be justified on the grounds that they have a diagnosis of mental illness. As we shall see in Chapter 11, in the UK there are Mental Statutes that apply to people with mental illness (Mental Health Act 1983 and Scotland Mental Health Act 1984). People with a diagnosis of mental illness may be 'sectioned' (forcibly hospitalized) and compulsorily treated because of their mental illness. We shall see how the arguments developed in this chapter will be relevant to the discussion of English law on the management of mental disorders. I will explain that the diagnosis of mental illness should not be utilized as one of the criteria that justify coercion towards people.

This, of course, does not mean that we should be indifferent to the destiny of sufferers. In the previous chapter I suggested that paternalism may be ethical when the person is going to harm herself while acting or choosing non-autonomously (weak paternalism). It is true of those with mental illness, as it is of all other people, that they may be acting non-autonomously. However, it is mistaken to think that mental illness causes people's experiences and behaviour and therefore that by definition people with mental illness lack autonomy. Statements such as 'this happens because he has a mental illness', as I have argued, do not mean what they say. They do not mean that mental illness in effect causes people's experiences and behaviours.

With regard to eating disorders, arguments that people diet and vomit 'because they have an eating disorder' are fallacious. Arguments that we are justified in intervening against the eating-disordered person because her behaviour is 'the result of a mental illness' are fallacious. Paternalism should not be based on such fallacious grounds. These arguments, however, have been and are currently used in English law (see Chapter 11).

Some people may believe that there must be 'an illness' somewhere in the person, which produces some sort of experiences or which compels the person to act in the 'symptomatological' way. These arguments appear no more scientific than the old belief that 'spirits' or the 'devil' lie inside mentally ill people, *possessing them*, and determining their behaviour.

A different and more scientific version of this argument is that abnormal experiences and behaviours are caused by some unidentified genetic and/or neurophysiological factor. From this point of view, the distorted experiences and behaviours of mentally ill people are thought to depend on defective physiological or biochemical mechanisms. The issue is to find where the fault lies and in what it consists. Much research is being carried out on the genetics and neurophysiology of mental disorders—including eating disorders. This type of research attracts much attention, in part because finding out 'the faulted part' would be the first step towards finding appropriate drug treatments for the disorders. The next chapter will review the most relevant research between 1980 and 2004 on the genetics and neurophysiology of eating disorders. Although this research is beginning to generate interesting results in many mental illnesses, there is as yet no convincing evidence that there is a biological abnormality in the brain of those with eating disorders that causes the abnormalities described as mental illness, as we shall now see.

4

Scientific Understanding of Eating Disorders

1. *Introduction*

It is often believed that people with mental disorders lack autonomy and that their 'pathological' behaviour is determined by the mental illness. Sometimes mental illness is taken to be a non-specified entity 'underlying' the behaviour of the person—lying under, somewhere. I have raised a number of objections to this idea in the previous chapter. A more sophisticated version of this argument is that 'pathological' behaviour is determined by genetic mutations or by some neurological, physiological, endocrine, or biochemical disorder. The mental illness here is the organic disorder. 'Pathological' behaviour, from this point of view, is not the result of a genuine choice of the sufferer: the sufferer has some sorts of experiences and behaviour because of some organic causes (which, sometimes, are yet to be discovered).

Since eating disorders have evident somatic manifestations, much research has been directed to the discovery of their organic basis.[1]

Many studies investigate the possibility of gene variations that may create a predisposition to eating disorders. The majority of scientists agree that there are gene variations for both anorexia and bulimia nervosa. However, it is unclear what these variations are and how they may interact with environmental stressors to determine the onset of the disorders. This chapter will review relevant literature in the field.

Part of this chapter relies on my previous work. The conclusions of my previous work are expanded in the light of the most recent literature on the field. See Simona Giordano, 'Addicted to Eating Disorders? Eating Disorders and Substance Use Disorders, Differences and Fallacies', *Italian Journal of Psychiatry*, 11/2–3 (2001), 73–7.

[1] See e.g. Sebastian P. Grossman, 'Contemporary Problems concerning our Understanding of Brain Mechanisms that Regulate Food Intake and Body Weight', in A. J. Stunkard and Elliot Stellar (eds.), *Eating Disorders* (New York: Raven Press, 1984), 5–15; J. Treasure and A. Holland, 'Genetic Factors in Eating Disorders', in G. I. Szmukler, Chris Dare, and Janet Treasure (eds.), *Handbook of Eating Disorders: Theory, Treatment and Research* (Chichester: John Wiley & Sons, 1995), 49–65.

Other studies focus on the hypothalamus, which regulates both appetite and other functions that are anomalous in eating-disordered people. The results of these investigations do not all lead to the same conclusions. There is clear evidence that physiological abnormalities are linked to eating disorders. However, variations are generally corrected as abnormal eating patterns are abandoned, and the relationship between these abnormalities and the onset of eating disorders is unclear. It is considered unlikely that these abnormalities are the primary cause of the disorder.

BOX 4.1. Scientific Terms used in this Chapter

Biochemistry: the science dealing with the chemical substances present in living organisms and with their relation to each other and to the life of the organism; biological or physiological chemistry.

Biology: the division of physical science that deals with organized living animals and plants, their morphology, physiology, origin, and distribution. There are multiple branches of biology: for example, genetics, neurology, psychology, molecular biology, etc.

Chemistry: the branch of physical science that deals with the elementary substances, or forms of matter, of which all bodies are composed, the laws that regulate the combination of these elements in the formation of compound bodies, and the various phenomena that accompany their exposure to diverse physical conditions.

Endocrine system: denoting a gland having an internal secretion that is poured into blood or lymph; a ductless gland, as the thyroid, pituitary, and adrenal glands.

Physiology: a branch of biology that studies the normal functions and phenomena of living things. It comprises the two divisions of *animal* and *vegetable (plant) physiology*; that part of the former that refers specially to the vital functions in man is called *human physiology*.

Neuroendocrinology: the study of the interactions between the nervous system and the endocrine system.

Neurophysiology: the physiology of the nervous system.

Source: based on *The Oxford English Dictionary*, available online at www.oed.com.

---

2. *Genetic and Eating Disorders*

The aetiology of eating disorders is generally considered to be heterogeneous.[2] Eating disorders are thought to result from a complex interplay between environmental and genetic risk factors. These types of diseases are known as *complex or multifactorial diseases*.[3]

As Winchester and Collier explain, in these diseases 'the genetic component may be oligogenic, involving a small number of gene variants, or polygenic, involving the simultaneous action and interaction of many gene variants. The genetic variants that contribute to complex diseases are common in the population.'[4] These variants (*susceptibility alleles*) are not necessarily deleterious and will not *certainly* cause the disease. They are 'neither necessary nor sufficient to cause disease'.[5] In the case of eating disorders, genetics is considered likely to contribute to the development of the disease. However, the proportion of the genetic contribution to eating disorders is unclear.

A number of studies have found a significantly increased prevalence of eating disorders in relatives of probands with anorexia nervosa. Both anorexia and bulimia nervosa are found to be 'statistically more common among family members'[6] than in the general population. Studies on twins have evidenced a concomitance of 50 per cent between monozygotic twins, as compared with 10 per cent between dizygotic twins.[7] The greater concordance rates among monozygotic twins as compared to the concordance rates among dizygotic twins are generally taken as evidence of a 'strong etiological role for genetic factors'.[8] However, it should be noticed that perhaps a methodologically more correct way of assessing the etiological role for

---

[2] A. Kipman, L. Bruins-Slot, C. Boni, N. Hanoun, J. Adès, P. Blot, M. Hamon, M. C. Mouren-Siméoni, and P. Gorwood, '5-HT2A Gene Promoter Polymorphism as a Modifying rather than a Vulnerability Factor in Anorexia Nervosa', *European Psychiatry*, 17 (2002), 227–9, at 229; D. E. Grice, K. A. Halmi, M. M. Fichter, M. Strober, D. B. Woodside, J. T. Treasure, A. S. Kaplan, P. J. Magistretti, D. Goldman, C. M. Bulik, W. H. Kaye, and W. H. Berrettini, 'Evidence for a Susceptibility Gene for Anorexia Nervosa on Chromosome 1', *American Journal of Human Genetics*, 70 (2002), 787–92.

[3] Elizabeth Winchester and David Collier, 'Genetic Aetiology of Eating Disorders and Obesity', in Janet Treasure, Ulrich Schmidt, and Eric van Furth (eds.), *Handbook of Eating Disorders* (2nd edn., Chichester: Wiley, 2003), ch. 3, pp. 35–64.

[4] Ibid. 35–6.

[5] Ibid. 36.

[6] Lyn Patrick, 'Eating Disorders: A Review of the Literature with Emphasis on Medical Complications and Clinical Nutrition', *Alternative Medicine Review* (June 2002), 184–207.

[7] E. Faccio, *Il disturbo alimentare: Modelli, ricerche e terapie* (Rome: Carocci, 1999), 92.

[8] Michael Strober and Cynthia M. Bulik, 'Genetic Epidemiology of Eating Disorders', in Christopher G. Fairburn and Kelly D. Brownell (eds.), *Eating Disorders and Obesity* (2nd edn., London: Guilford Press, 2002), ch. 42, pp. 238–43, at 239.

genetic factors would be the study of monozygotic twins brought up separately. To date, there are no adoption studies of eating disorders among separated monozygotic twins.[9]

The interpretation of the 'familiality' (incidence within a family) of eating disorders is not straightforward.[10] Some studies 'strongly suggest that the familiality observed in family studies is primarily due to genetic causes';[11] other studies suggest that this familiality is likely to result from both environmental and genetic influences.[12]

Whereas it is generally accepted that there is a prevalence of eating disorders among relatives, the modality of interaction between genetic and environmental factors, and the extent to which genetic factors are involved in liability to eating disorders, are unresolved issues.[13] This is due to methodological difficulties with case ascertainment and the low statistical power of available studies.[14] Some researchers argue that genetics is the most determining factor—or that there is a genetic predisposition to anorexia, which becomes manifest because of environmental stressors, such as inappropriate diet or emotional distress;[15] other researchers stress the importance of environmental stressors—and argue that environmental influences play a major role in determining the onset of eating disorders.[16]

In spite of these differences, the majority of scientists seem to agree that genetic predisposition plays an important role in the development of

---

[9] Ibid. 238.

[10] According to D. A. Campbell, D. Sundaramurthy, A. F. Markham, and L. F. Pieri, 'Fine Mapping of Human 5-HTR2 a Gene to Chromosome 3914 and Identification of Two Highly Polymorphic Linked Markers Suitable for Association Studies in Psychiatric Disorders', *Genetic Testing*, 1/4 (1997), 297–9, clinical results are conflicting.

[11] Grice et al., 'Evidence', 787.

[12] Kelly L. Klump, Stephen Wonderlich, Pascale Lehoux, Lisa R. Lilenfeld, and Cynthia M. Bulik, 'Does Environment Matter? A Review of Nonshared Environment and Eating Disorders', *International Journal of Eating Disorders*, 31 (2002), 118–35; L. R. Lilenfeld, W. H. Kaye, C. G. Greeno, K. R. Merikangas, K. Plotnikcov, C. Pollice, R. Rao, M. Strober, C. M. Bulik, and L. Nagy, 'A Controlled Family Study of Anorexia Nervosa and Bulimia Nervosa: Psychiatric Disorders in First-Degree Relatives and Effects of Proband Comorbidity', *Archives of General Psychiatry*, 55 / 7 (1998), 603–10; M. Strober, R. Freeman, C. Lampert, J. Diamond, and W. Kaye, 'Controlled Family Study of Anorexia and Bulimia Nervosa: Evidence of Shared Liability and Transmission of Partial Syndromes', *American Journal of Psychiatry*, 157 (2000), 393–401.

[13] Faccio, *Il disturbo alimentare*, 92; see also E. Waugh and C. M. Bulik, 'Offspring of Women with Eating Disorders', *International Journal of Eating Disorders*, 25/2 (1999), 123–33.

[14] Winchester and Collier, 'Genetic Aetiology of Eating Disorders and Obesity', 39.

[15] A. J. Holland, A. Hall, R. Murray, G. F. Russel, and A. H. Crisp, 'Anorexia Nervosa: A Study of 34 Pairs of Twins and One Set of Triplets', *British Journal of Psychiatry*, 145 (1984), 414–19.

[16] T. Wade, N. G. Martin, and M. Tiggeman, 'Genetic and Environmental Risk Factors for the Weight and Shape Concerns Characteristic of Bulimia Nervosa', *Psychological Medicine*, 28/4 (1998), 761–77.

eating disorders,[17] although it is unclear what this role is and how determining it is.

Studies of twins have also highlighted another important factor in the development of eating disorders. Some researchers have noticed that a number of aspects of eating disorders cannot be explained by genetics, and have found that non-shared environmental experiences are also significant in the genesis of the disorder. Non-shared environmental experiences are those unique to each individual, despite the fact that they live in the same family. Two siblings will share some familial and environmental experiences, but other experiences and influences will be non-shared—that is, unique to each individual person. Monozygotic and dizygotic twins studies have highlighted the importance of both genetic factors and non-shared environmental experiences in the development of eating disorders.[18]

The fact that genetics may have an important role in the way a person interprets environmental influences does not negate the impact of shared and non-shared environmental stressors; neither does genetics rule out the role of the individual in interpreting these stressors and in articulating her behaviour. Although it is important to understand the biological components of appetite regulation, in order to obtain better understanding and treatment for eating disorders one needs to be aware that the interplay between genetics, environmental influences, the individual's interpretation of these factors, and the individual's articulation of behaviour is very difficult, if not impossible, to capture.[19] One study concludes that 'in a complex behavioural syndrome such as eating disorders [. . .] there are so many possible influences that their particular combination in any given individual becomes almost unique, and thus impractical to generalise to others'.[20] This, of course, does not mean that we should give up hope of understanding eating disorders, but rather that the phenomenon of abnormal eating should be explored from different perspectives and that the study of eating disorder needs to take into consideration the contribution of different disciplines.

3. *The 'Addiction' Model*

According to some people, eating disorders are a type of addiction. People do not genuinely choose eating-disordered patterns, but are out of control and

---

[17] Patrick, 'Eating Disorders'.

[18] Klump, Wonderlich, Lehoux, Lilenfeld, and Bulik, 'Does Environment Matter', 120.

[19] Janet Polivy and C. Peter Herman, 'Causes of Eating Disorders', *Annual Review of Psychology*, 53 (2002), 187–213.

[20] Ibid.

addicted to them. The addiction model is particularly influential in some countries, especially in the United States.

If eating disorders could be conceptualized in terms of substance-use disorders, this would have important clinical implications. For example, it has been argued that the finding of a common neurophysiological basis for the two conditions would contribute to the specificity of the diagnosis of eating disorders and to the efficacy of treatment options.[21]

This would also have important ethical implications. In fact, the physiological and chemical processes involved in substance-use disorders *explain* (or contribute to the explanation of) some of the classical and most important symptoms of addiction.[22] People who suffer from addiction among other things experience a compulsion to take the psycho-active substance, have difficulty in controlling the substance-taking behaviour, develop a tolerance to that particular substance, and suffer from withdrawal syndrome, precisely *because of the addiction.*

If eating disorders could be conceptualized in terms of substance-use disorders, the same sort of *explanation*, or one very similar, would apply to disordered eating as is applied to substance-use disorders. It would then be clearer *why* people fast or binge, and *why* they experience a *compulsion* to do so. It is, therefore, important to our current purposes to assess whether, and if so to what extent, eating disorders may be considered as an addiction.

4. *Similarities between Eating Disorders and Substance-Use Disorders*

Empirical observation shows interesting behavioural and psychological similarities between people suffering from substance-use disorders and people suffering from eating disorders; co-morbidity of eating disorders and substance-use disorders is also reported.[23] The similarities manifested in people suffering from both substance-use disorders and eating disorders are shown in Box 4.2.

However, it has also been noticed that the chemical dependency is characterized by tolerance, physical dependence, and withdrawal reactions, which are absent in eating disorders.[24] These similarities apparently concern

[21] B. J. Blinder, M. C. Blinder, and V. A. Sanathara, 'Eating Disorders and Addiction', *Psychiatric Times,* 15/12 (1998), http://www.mhsource.com/edu/psytimes/p981230.html.

[22] J. M. Darley, S. Glucksberg, L. J. Kamin, and R. A. Kinchla, *Psychology* (Englewood Cliffs, NJ: Prentice Hall, 1984), 141–52, 498–503. C. Landau, 'Substance Abuse', in *Encyclopedia of Psychology* (New York: Wiley, 1994), 382–3.

[23] P. F. Sullivan, C. M. Bulik, J. L. Fear, and A. Pickering, 'Outcome of Anorexia Nervosa', *American Journal of Psychiatry*, 155/ 7 (1998), 939–46.

[24] G. Terence Wilson, 'Eating Disorders and Addictive Disorders', in Fairburn and Brownell (eds.), *Eating Disorders and Obesity*, ch. 35, pp. 199–203, at 199.

BOX 4.2. Similarities between Addiction and Eating Disorders

- a strong desire or sense of compulsion to take the substance (or food)
- difficulties in controlling substance-taking behaviour in terms of its onset, termination, or levels of use, or sensation of compulsion to take the substance (or to overeat)
- adverse medical/social consequences
- persisting with substance use (or disordered eating) despite clear evidence of overtly harmful consequences
- loss of control
- constant concern towards the desired object (or food)
- use of the substance (or food) to cope with stressful situations and negative feelings
- secrecy
- ambivalence towards treatment
- risk of relapsing

Source: Faccio, *Il disturbo alimentare*, 69, 44.

---

more 'bulimic' behaviour (bingeing), than 'anorexic' restrictive behaviour (fasting), for they concern the loss of control, and the experience of compulsion, rather than control of food intake.

In fact, according to some researchers, it is 'bulimia' (and not 'anorexia') that may be considered a form of addiction. For example, De Silva and Eysenk argue that, differently from restrictive anorexics, 'the overall personality profiles of the bulimic group tend to be similar to those of drug addicts'.[25] It has also been noticed that higher co-morbidity is present between 'bulimia' and substance-use disorders than between 'restrictive anorexia' and substance-use disorders. In other words, it seems that those who suffer from bulimic episodes are more prone to substance use and abuse.[26]

It has been found that particular kinds of food, which, apparently, are those typically preferred during food orgies, may generate addiction. This reinforces the hypothesis of a common neurophysiological basis between 'bulimia' and addiction.

---

[25] P. De Silva, and S. Eysenk, 'Personality and Addictiveness in Anorexic and Bulimic Patients', *Personality Individual Difference*, 8/5 (1987), 749–51.

[26] C. C. Holderness, J. Brooks-Gunn, and M. P. Warren, 'Comorbidity of Eating Disorders and Substance Abuse: Review of Literature', *International Journal of Eating Disorders*, 16/1 (1994), 1–34.

Research on the relationship between eating disorders and addiction is huge and often shows conflicting results. The next sections will try to clarify the issues at stake in the analysis of eating disorders in terms of substance abuse.

5. *Are Eating Disorders a Form of Addiction?*

We have seen above that there are behavioural and psychological similarities between eating-disorder sufferers and addiction sufferers. However, the question as to whether eating disorders are a form of addiction is not straightforward.

The question of whether people with eating disorders are 'addicted' is a complex one, for two reasons. The first is that it is often unclear what is meant by 'addiction'. The second is that it is unclear to what the person is addicted: to eating anomalies, to starvation, to bingeing, or to food?

Let us focus on the first point. What do we mean by addiction? There are two senses in which the term 'addiction' can be used.

In one sense 'addiction' may mean a strong desire to do something, which may have psychological and physiological roots. If used in this sense, addiction has a 'soft' meaning. In this sense we all experience 'addiction' to some things—for example, to things that we find pleasurable. Positive physiological and psychological feelings associated with a pattern of behaviour stimulate us to repeat it. Sex may be an example of such a type of 'addiction'. Physiological, emotional, and psychological well-being may induce us to want to repeat the pleasurable experience again. However, in this sense of the word, it is not merely the 'addiction' that leads us to behave in a certain way. The neurophysiological and psychological processes do not fully explain our behaviour and ultimately do not rule out wilful control over our actions. This is why, while it is recognized that, for example, sex may be an intensely pleasurable activity, it is widely accepted that rape is a criminal act. From this point of view, we may recognize that neurophysiological and psychological processes contribute to an explanation of why we behave in a certain way, but we also recognize that much more is involved in what we do—and how, when, in what circumstances, and with whom we do it. From this point of view, we know that a constellation of reasons and motives leads us to behave in a certain way; our behaviour may take different forms, have many different meanings and is to a significant extent under conscious control.

There is another sense of 'addiction'. By addiction we may also mean an irresistible urge to do something, which is rooted in neurophysiological and/or psychological processes. According to this 'hard' meaning of the word (which is probably the more appropriate), these neurophysiological and/or psychological processes explain why a person behaves in a particular way. In this sense, addiction is properly considered as 'a dependency'. The person's freedom of choice is curtailed. When we say that a person 'suffers from an addiction' in this sense we say that neurophysiological or psychological factors have annulled or severely compromised her capacity to exert control over her actions, and that her behaviour is therefore *determined* by the *addiction*, at least to a significant extent. The addiction is in this sense an 'external force' that is able to explain why the person behaves in a certain way (although there may be concomitant reasons that contribute to the explanation of her behaviour).

There is much research on eating disorders and addiction, but more often than not it is unclear whether 'addiction' is used in a soft or hard sense. It seems to me that researchers (and maybe most people) often tend to use the term in a strong sense. For example, when researchers try to assess whether starvation or bingeing are addictive, they try to verify whether neurophysiological processes are able to explain why people starve or binge and why they *cannot control* their behaviour. If these processes were found, this would mean that eating-disordered behaviour *is out of the person's control* and that the person's autonomy is curtailed in an important way.

The difference between 'soft' and 'hard' meaning of addiction is an important one.

If addiction is used in a 'soft' sense, then we are all addicted to some behaviour. A large part of our behaviour will be 'dictated' in this sense by the pleasure or by the positive feelings that that behaviour brings about. Some behaviours may be potentially very harmful (smoking, for example, or practising highly risky sports). If we use addiction in this sense, it is unclear why eating disorders should be considered a problem—eating-disordered behaviour is aligned to other behaviours that are not generally regarded as pathological (or psychopathological) and is thus 'normalized'. Abnormal eating would be just one of the many 'addictions' that we all have—some of these are harmful, some are not.

If addiction is used in a 'hard' sense, however, we have insufficient ground to claim that eating disorders are addictions. There is no scientific evidence to claim that eating-disordered behaviour is caused by an addiction in the strong sense of the word (see Sections 6, 7, and 8).

The second complication relating to the 'addiction' model of eating disorders is that the sufferer could be 'addicted' to a number of things: to starvation, to bingeing, to some types of food, to disordered eating. Some researchers insist on the addictive power of starvation, others on the addictive power of some foods. Whereas eating disorders are often compared to addiction because of the sufferer's experience of being 'out of control', it is unclear to what the person is supposed to be addicted.

6. *Starvation and Addiction*

Marilyn Duker and Roger Slade describe the physiological dependence on starvation in the following terms:

In physiological terms starvation, i.e. going without food for more than half a day, is perceived by the body's internal monitoring system as hunger stress. This results in the secretion of adrenalin which, as well as creating the keyed-up effect noticeable in the underfed person's wider open eyes, faster heart rate and deeper breathing, also mobilizes reserves of glycogen in muscle to provide more blood glucose. Where there is the continued presence of adrenalin in the bloodstream, it acts on the brain and causes it to secrete endokinins. These are chemicals closely related to morphine and have similar tranquillising and euphoric effects. At the same time, metabolites (such as ketones) which are produced by the breaking down or metabolism of fat also act on the brain and can create an odd and lightheaded experience.

The brain has receptors for morphine-like substances (endorphins) which are also produced by the body when it is stressed by vigorous exercise. (It is the presence of these receptors which makes human beings susceptible to pain relievers.) This is how an individual can come to derive a particular pleasure, or sense of well-being, from strenuous exercise. It is how, by further stimulating the body's production of endorphins, hyperactivity itself acts as its own spur in anyone who is excessively dedicated to running, dance, cycling, working in the gym, walking, going up and down stairs, or any other such persistent or repetitive movement. It is also how, with the 'floating', detached experience it induces, the sleeplessness that accompanies hunger and hyperactivity becomes woven into the process [...] It is thus that anorexic illness can be viewed as an addiction to food/body control. Sufferers occasionally refer to themselves as 'starvation junkies' or as needing their 'exercise fix'.[27]

Food restriction also has other important consequences at a cognitive level. Low weight causes intellectual changes. The thought becomes increasingly polarized between extremes, and cognitive complexity is consequently diminished.

However, as Duker and Slade also recognize, the physiological and cognitive changes related to diet and starvation do not seem to account for the whole of eating disorders. Although abnormal eating has psychological and physiological effects, at the basis of eating disorders there is also *a value choice*: the person *prefers* the pleasure and elation of fasting and exercise

---

[27] Marilyn Duker and Roger Slade, *Anorexia and Bulimia: How to Help* (2nd edn., Buckingham: Open University Press, 2003), 32.

instead of the pleasure and tranquillity of, for example, eating and sleeping. The person gives more value to *that particular type of pleasure* than to other types of pleasure, and openly *disvalues* other types of pleasures—the pleasure of eating, for example. Even if analysed from the point of view of the 'addiction model', eating disorders always involve value choices, and are therefore ultimately a moral issue.

Eating disorders show an ambivalent nature: they are at the same time determined and purposive behaviour. As Duker and Slade also point out: 'at any present moment, decisions to restrict or control food intake may be deliberate and reasoned, and yet [...] the dynamic relationship between the decisions that are made and the changes they bring about draws sufferers into a situation that runs away with them'.[28]

Other studies focus on the addictive nature of some food, which would contribute to explain some phenomena of abnormal eating, such as bingeing. According to some researchers, as we have seen above, it is 'bulimia' (and not 'anorexia') that may be a form of addiction. Also, co-morbidity between bulimia and substance abuse seems to be higher than co-morbidity between restrictive anorexia and substance abuse.[29] The question is whether some foods may generate addiction and may explain the urge to overeat, in a way that may be similar to the effect of psycho-active substances, which produce a biochemical reaction to continue the consumption of the substance.[30]

7. *Addiction to Sweet Foods: Reactive Hypoglycaemia*

Some researchers have found that sweet food (particularly simple carbohydrates) may generate addiction.[31] The fast assimilation of carbohydrates determines a sensitive increase of glycaemia. Glycaemia, in turn, acts on the secretion of insulin. The more intense is the secretion of insulin, the faster is the decrease of glycaemia percentage in the blood. The result of this circuit of feedback is the new sensation of hunger. This circuit is called 'reactive hypoglycaemia'.[32]

As carbohydrates, especially in the form of sweets, are often the favourite food during bingeing episodes, it may be hypothesized that bulimics have developed dependence to carbohydrates (Guido Razzoli points out that

---

[28] Marilyn Duker and Roger Slade, *Anorexia and Bulimia: How to Help* (2nd edn., Buckingham: Open University Press, 2003), 37.

[29] Holderness, Brooks-Gunn, and Warren, 'Comorbidity of Eating Disorders and Substance Abuse'.

[30] Wilson, 'Eating Disorders and Addictive Disorders', 200.

[31] T. Tuomisto et al., 'Psychological and Physiological Characteristics of Sweet Food Addiction', *International Journal of Eating Disorders*, 25/2 (1999), 169–75.

[32] Faccio, *Il disturbo alimentare*, 69.

sometimes the sufferer has no preference between sweet and salty carbohydrates).[33] Elena Faccio argues that reactive hypoglycaemia may *contribute* to explaining why 'bulimics' tend to prefer these foods and why it is so difficult to give up bingeing. However, reactive hypoglycaemia does not explain how bingeing practices start.[34]

In order to explain how they start, a different hypothesis must be formulated. It has been suggested that people with eating disorders may be biologically vulnerable at the level of the system of neurotransmitters. The next section will discuss research in the field.

8. *The Role of Central Nervous System Neurotransmitters*

Research reports evidence of a relationship between eating disorders and altered brain structures. Although morphological alterations are thought to be a consequence of abnormal eating, in individual cases the alteration continues to exist after abnormal eating has been corrected. It has thus been suggested that people with eating disorders may be vulnerable at the level of the neurotransmitters system.[35]

Reduction in plasma-dopamine, norepinephrine, and serotonin has indeed been found in people with eating disorders.[36] Elevation of plasma beta-endorphin unrelated to glucose ingestion has also been noticed. It has been suggested that this elevated level of beta-endorphin is due to psychological stress.

Most abnormalities seem to be linked to starvation or to practices of control of food intake and tend to come back to normal levels as weight is gained.[37] However, abnormalities in the level of serotonin may in some cases

---

[33] G. Razzoli, *La bulimia nervosa: Definizione, sintomatologia e treatmento* (Milan: Sonzogno, 1995), 62.

[34] Faccio, *Il disturbo alimentare*, 69.

[35] Martina de Zwaan, 'Basic Neuroscience and Scanning', in Treasure, Schmidt, and van Furth (eds.), *Handbook of Eating Disorders*, 2nd edn., ch. 5, pp. 89–101. It should be noticed that genetics influences all of one's biological functions, including those of the nervous system. Therefore it may be asked why I treat the nervous system as a separate issue. I am not treating the nervous system as a separate issue, but as an aspect of the disorder that needs to be explored. Scientific literature provides studies on the nervous system, and I report the results of these studies in the more general analysis of the organic bases of eating disorders. A recent articulated account of the neurotransmitter activity in anorexia and bulimia nervosa may be found in Walter H. Kaye, 'Central Nervous System Neurotransmitter Activity in Anorexia Nervosa and Bulimia Nervosa', in Fairburn and Brownell (eds.), *Eating Disorders and Obesity*, ch. 49, pp. 272–7.

[36] D. T. Fullerton, W. J. Swift, C. J. Getto, and I. H. Carlson, 'Plasma Immunoreactive Beta-Endorphin in Bulimics', *Psychological Medicine*, 16 (1986), 59–63.

[37] Allan S. Kaplan and Paul E. Garfinkel, 'The Neuroendocrinology of Anorexia Nervosa', in R. Collu, G. M. Brown, and Glen R. Van Loon (eds.), *Clinical Neuroendocrinology* (Oxford: Blackwell, 1988), 117.

persist after weight gain and it has therefore been hypothesized that a disorder in serotonin may create a vulnerability to anorexia and bulimia.[38]

It is also suggested that opioids may play a role in generating eating disorders. Opioids influence eating: they increase feeding, whereas opioid antagonists decrease feeding.[39] Reneric and Bouvard[40] have acknowledged a high rate of opioids in people with anorexia and other psychopathologies. Similarly, Marazzi and colleagues have noticed high level of opioids in both anorexics and bulimics. According to these authors, these opioids are released in the initial period of dieting and reinforce the starvation dependence.[41] Dopamine may also be involved in eating disorders, since it inhibits the initiation and the extent of feeding.[42]

However, the relationship between the change in the rate of opioids, dopamine,[43] and eating disorders is unclear. It seems that multiple neurotransmitters are involved in eating disorders, but the neurobiology of eating disorders is not yet fully understood. It is unclear whether the imbalance in the system of neurotransmitters is secondary to abnormal eating, or associated with eating disorder, or is the expression of a vulnerability to the disorder.

9. *Hypothalamic Abnormalities*

A significant proportion of research on eating disorders has been devoted to the investigation of neuroendocrinological implications of abnormal eating. In particular, research has focused on hypothalamic abnormalities.

[38] W. Kaye, K. Gendall, and M. Strober, 'Serotonin Neuronal Function and Selective Serotonin Reuptake Inhibitor Treatment in Anorexia and Bulimia Nervosa', *Biological Psychiatry*, 44/9 (1998), 825–38.

[39] Blinder, Blinder, and Sanathara, 'Eating Disorders and Addiction'.

[40] J. P. Reneric and M. P. Bouvard, 'Opioid Receptor in Antagonists in Psychiatry: Beyond Drug Addiction', *Drugs*, 10/5 (1998), 365–82.

[41] M. A. Marazzi et al., 'Endogenous Codeine and Morphine in Anorexia and Bulimia Nervosa', *Life Sciences*, 60/20 (1997), 1741–7; see also M. A. Marazzi et al., 'Male / Female Comparison of Morphine Effect on Food Intake: Relation to Anorexia Nervosa', *Pharmacology, Biochemistry and Behavior*, 53/2 (1998), 433–5.

[42] J. E. Morley, A. S. Levine, and D. D. Krahn, 'Neurotransmitter Regulation of Appetite and Eating', in B. J. Blinder, B. F. Chaitin, and R. S. Goldstein (eds.), *Eating Disorders: Medical and Psychological Bases of Diagnosis and Treatment* (New York: PMA, 1988), 11–19. Also serotonin seems to be involved. See D. C. Jimerson, M. D. Lesem, W. H. Kaye, and T. D. Brewton, 'Low Serotonin and Dopamine Metabolite Concentrations in Cerebrospinal Fluid from Bulimic Patients with Frequent Binge Episodes', *Archives of General Psychiatry*, 49/2 (1992), 132–8, quoted in Blinder, Blinder, and Sanathara, 'Eating disorders and addiction'.

[43] A connection between opioid receptors and the release of dopamine associated with feeding has been suggested by M. T. Taber, G. Zernig, and H. C. Fibiger, 'Opioid Receptor Modulation of Feeding-Evoked Dopamine Release in the Rat Nucleus Accumbens', *Brain Research*, 785/1 (1998), 24–30, quoted in Blinder, Blinder, and Samathara, 'Eating Disorders and Addiction'.

The functions of the hypothalamus include nutrition,[44] reproductive activity, temperature homeostasis, sleeping, and wakefulness. Since people with eating disorders unequivocally manifest disorders in all these areas—that is, in nutrition, in sleep and temperature control, libido and fertility[45]—the hypothesis is that hypothalamic dysfunctions may contribute to the onset of the condition.

The neuroendocrinological system and the biological processes regulating alimentary functioning in humans are not fully understood.[46] The functioning of the hypothalamus is also still unclear.[47] The hypothalamus is described as 'multiple intermingled groups of specialised neurones, each part of a complex neural system',[48] but the anatomy and functioning of this part of the brain is still not completely clear to scientists. As a consequence, the presence of an organic cause to eating disorders at the level of the hypothalamus can neither be proved nor disproved.[49]

Moreover, methodological problems in interpreting clinical data make it difficult to understand the relationship between eating disorders and neuroendocrinological functioning.[50]

In spite of these problems, as Roger Slade points out, 'the idea that there might be a purely physical explanation [to eating disorders] is one that is likely [. . .] to continue to attract attention'.[51] Research on eating disorders has focused on the three axes of the hypothalamus.

9.1. *Hypothalamo–pituitary–thyroid axis*

Among the health problems that are generally related to eating disorders are intolerance to cold, constipation, dry skin and hair, bradycardia, slowly relaxing reflexes, and low metabolism rate.[52] These problems suggest that there may be a dysfunction in the hypothalamo–pituitary–thyroid axis.

At the level of this axis, abnormalities have indeed been found in people with eating disorders.[53] Thyroid function is generally abnormal in both

[44] P. Dally, J. Gomez, and A. J. Isaacs, *Anorexia Nervosa* (London: Heinemann, 1979), 198. See also Polivy and Herman, 'Causes of Eating Disorders'.

[45] Dally, Gomez, and Isaacs, *Anorexia Nervosa*, 30–1.

[46] Ibid. 27.

[47] R. Slade, *The Anorexia Nervosa Reference Book: Direct and Clear Answers to Everyone's Questions* (New York: Harper & Rowe, 1984).

[48] Ibid. 34.

[49] Ibid. 35.

[50] P. De Giacomo, C. Renna, and A. Santoni Rugiu, *Anoressia e bulimia, inquadramento clinico e terapeutico con particolare riferimento alle terapie interattive brevi* (Padova: Piccin, 1992), quoted in Faccio, *Il disturbo alimentare*, 27.

[51] Slade, *The Anorexia Nervosa Reference Book*, 35.

[52] Dally, Gomez, and Isaacs, *Anorexia Nervosa*, 161.

[53] Ibid. 172.

anorexic and bulimic patients.[54] However, it seems that similar abnormalities characterize all states of undernourishment, therefore the interpretation of this data is extremely difficult.[55] In particular, the level of some hormones, such as prolactin, is within the normal range, whereas the distorted level of other hormones, such as the growth hormone, comes back to normal as weight is gained,[56] or as the person interrupts compensatory practices, such as self-induced vomiting, purgatives, and diuretics.[57]

9.2. Hypothalamo–pituitary–gonadal axis

The hypothalamo–pituitary–gonadal axis seems to be involved in eating disorders, in particular because of abnormalities in reproductive functioning that characterize the disorder (amenorrhoea in females and hypogonadism in males).

The decrease of gonadal steroids and the alteration of pituitary responsiveness seem to correspond to very low body weight, and, generally, abnormalities gradually cease as weight is gained.[58] In males, manifestations like low libido or difficulty with erection disappear with weight gain. In females, weight gain does not always lead to immediate onset of menstruation. It has been hypothesized that this is due to the peculiar sensitivity of the female reproductive function to psychological stress.[59] It seems that the menstruation cycle is affected not only by variations in body weight, but also by other factors, such as continuous and sustained physical exercise and other unspecified factors not yet understood.[60]

9.3. Hypothalamo–pituitary–adrenal axis

People with eating disorders also manifest abnormalities in the hypothalamo–pituitary–adrenal axis.[61] There is a decrease in peripheral metabolism of cortisol, and, in some people, abnormalities of hypothalamic control are

---

[54] Patrick, 'Eating Disorders'.

[55] Kaplan and Garfinkel, 'Neuroendocrinology', 105–22.

[56] Ibid. 109.

[57] For a study on the growth hormone cortisol and prolactin in the specific case of bulimia, see D. S. Goldbloom, P. E. Garfinkel, R. Katz, and G. M. Brown, 'The Hormonal Response to Intravenous 5-Hydroxytryptophan in Bulimia Nervosa', *Journal of Psychosomatic Research*, 40/3 (1996), 289–97.

[58] M. Pawlikowski and J. Zarzycki, 'Does the Impairment of the Hipothalamic–Pituitary–Gonadal Axis in Anorexia Nervosa Depend on Increased Sensitivity to Endogenous Melatonin?', *Medical Hypotheses*, 52/2 (1999), 111–13.

[59] Dally, Gomez, and Isaacs, *Anorexia Nervosa*, 200.

[60] Kaplan and Garfinkel, 'Neuroendocrinology', 107.

[61] Dally, Gomez, and Isaacs, *Anorexia Nervosa*, 200.

manifested.[62] Apparently, these abnormalities do not depend only on weight loss, for they are not found in people who have lost weight because of physical illnesses.[63] However, this imbalance appears reversible as weight is gained, therefore it seems unlikely that a dysfunction in the hypothalamo–pituitary–adrenal axis is the primary or original cause of eating disorders.[64]

10. *Conclusions*

Eating disorders have many physiological implications. However, the relationship between physiological abnormalities and the onset of the disorder is complex and difficult to interpret in any straightforward way. Many studies focus on the functioning of the hypothalamus. However, the anatomy and functioning of the hypothalamus are not completely clear and the importance of extra-hypothalamic controls of feeding is increasingly recognized.[65] As a consequence, it is impossible to assess the exact role of the hypothalamus in eating disorders, and the presence of an organic cause of eating disorders can neither be proved nor disproved.[66] It is generally noticed that endocrine and vegetative abnormalities of the hypothalamus tend to improve as body weight is gained. For this reason researchers generally do not regard such abnormalities as the primary disorder, but rather as an adaptation of the organism to the condition of malnutrition. This conclusion is supported by the study of other conditions of starvation, both voluntary and involuntary, such as war or imprisonment.[67]

Eating disorders are a complex set of conditions, which are likely to result from many different factors: sociological pressures, family influences, genetic predisposition, neurophysiological vulnerability, moral values, and personality variables—for example, perfectionism, need for control, low self-esteem—and from the way the individual articulates all these factors.

The study of the genetics, neurophysiology, and neuroendocrinology of eating disorders should therefore be considered within a wide-ranging

---

[62] Ibid. 188.

[63] Kaplan and Garfinkel, 'Neuroendocrinology', 109.

[64] Dally, Gomez, and Isaacs, *Anorexia Nervosa*, 200.

[65] Ibid. 198.

[66] Slade, *The Anorexia Nervosa Reference Book*, 35.

[67] Dally, Gomez, and Isaacs, *Anorexia Nervosa*, 198–200; see also K. A. Gendall, C. M. Bulik, and Joyce, 'Visceral Protein and Hematological Status of Women with Bulimia Nervosa', *Physiology and Behavior*, 66/1 (1999), 159–63; and A. Caillot Augusseau, M. H. Lafage Proust, P. Margaillan, N. Vergely, S. Faure, S. Paillet, F. Lang, C. Alexandre, and B. Estour, 'Weight Gain Reverses Bone Turnover and Restores Circadian Variation of Bone Resorption in Anorexic Patients', *Clinical Endocrinology*, 52/1 (2000), 113–21.

perspective, in which the role of the environment and the role of the individual are also considered.

At present, we cannot claim that we have definitely identified the cause or the causes of eating disorders, and probably there is no such a single determinant cause or set of causes. Since many different variables seem to be involved in the development of the disorder, the only plausible approach is a multidimensional and open one. In order to understand eating disorders, we need to analyse them from different angles, and to take into account all factors that may be relevant.

An implication of this approach is that we should avoid thinking of eating-disordered behaviour as either 'determined' or 'purposive'. Eating disorders should instead be regarded as the result of interplay of both determinant *and* chosen elements (the issue of whether these are chosen 'autonomously' will be explored in Chapter 12). This ambiguity well expresses the conflict that the sufferer experiences. Normally, the sufferer seems to want and to defend her abnormal eating habits, on the one hand, while, on the other, feels *compelled* to maintain those habits. The contradiction that is experienced by the person is probably the expression of a condition that is both the result of a choice and the result of factors that are beyond the individual's conscious control.

The idea that, in the study of mental phenomena, we should abandon the dichotomy 'determined' v. 'purposive' behaviour has been well articulated by Louis Sass in his book *Madness and Modernism*. In this book Sass mainly discusses paranoid schizophrenia, but his considerations are pertinent to our study.

Sass argues that the study of mental phenomena is characterized by a singular asymmetry. While 'normal' behaviour is generally understood in teleological terms (that is, behaviour directed towards some end), 'pathological' behaviour is generally understood in deterministic terms (that is, caused by something).[68] According to Sass, psychotic experiences, as any other mental experience, is not *only* causally determined, *but also* directed to a purpose, or to more purposes. He calls this characteristic 'directness of behaviour'.[69] Psychotic behaviour, according to Sass, is to a significant extent intentional. In this sense, schizophrenia cannot be considered simply as something that one *gets* or *has*, such as malaria, tuberculosis, or cancer,[70] but as something that, in a mysterious way and with a mysterious interaction with a number of other variables, the individual *contributes to produce.*

[68]   L. A. Sass, *Madness and Modernism* (London: Harvard University Press, 1992), 182.
[69]   Ibid. 68.
[70]   Ibid. 79.

Before Sass, other authors[71] stressed that 'mental illness' is not something 'that merely happens' to the individual: people are not passive recipients of mental illnesses, or mere victims of their disorder. They, instead, participate actively in the production and, to some extent, in the maintenance, of symptoms. What we conceptualize in terms of 'symptoms of mental illnesses' should not be considered as entirely determined. They are also, to a significant extent, purposive and meaningful. According to R. D. Laing, mental illness may be considered as a foreign language: the person is trying to say something, and what we need to do is try to understand what she is saying. Disordered behaviour and language thus require careful interpretation. Laing pointed out that, at first sight, schizophrenic behaviour and discourse seem completely meaningless, but usually, if adequately constructed, they appear coherent and meaningful. *Ill* behaviour is for Laing the expression of an existential condition. With their syndrome, patients want to say something about themselves, and express their wishes and needs. The symptoms are the only language they possess. The psychiatrist is therefore required to perform a patient work of interpretation, in order to understand what the person is trying to say or to achieve.[72]

Thomas Szasz also suggested that abnormal behaviour is a form of communication. For example, he used the term 'paranoid communication',[73] and other authors have argued that pathological behaviour has a 'means-to-ends' structure,[74] or that mental illness should be considered as a strategy that the person uses in the attempt to survive or to cope with demands that she perceives as contradictory.[75] The person tries in this way to reduce her existential suffering. Mental illness would, in this sense, have a 'positive' function, in that it would allow an individual to cope with an environment in which she would not be able to live otherwise, or to suffer as little as possible in it.

---

[71] See e.g. D. Cooper, *Psychiatry and Antipsychiatry* (London: Paladin, 1970); R. D. Laing, *Sanity, Madness and the Family: Families of Schizophrenics* (Harmondsworth: Penguin, 1990); R. Boyers, *Laing and Anti-Psychiatry* (Harmondsworth: Penguin, 1972); G. Jervis, *Manuale critico di psichiatria* (5th edn., Milan: Feltrinelli, 1997); G. De Leo, *Psicologia della Responsabilità* (Rome: Laterza, 1996); G. De Leo and P. Patrizi, *La spiegazione del crimine* (Bologna: Il Mulino, 1998); A. Esterson, *The Leaves of Spring: A Study in the Dialectics of Madness* (London: Penguin, 1972).

[72] R. D. Laing, *The Divided Self* (Harmondsworth: Penguin, 1990), in particular chs. 1, 2, 4.

[73] T. Szasz, *The Myth of Mental Illness* (London: Paladin, 1984), 26.

[74] K. W. M. Fulford, 'Mental Illness, Concept of', in *Encyclopedia of Applied Ethics* (London: Academy Press, 1998), iii. 230; M. Moore, 'Legal Conceptions of Mental Illness', in B. Brody and T. H. Engelhardt (eds.), *Mental Illness: Law and Public Policy* (Boston: Reidel, 1980), 60; C. Dunn, *Ethical Issues in Mental Illness* (Aldershot: Ashgate, 1998), 7.

[75] R. Baker, 'Conception of Mental Illness', in W. T. Reich (ed.), *Encyclopedia of Bioethics* (rev. edn., New York: Simon and Schuster, Macmillan, 1995), iii. 1731–41.

In the attempt to understand eating disorders, we should adopt a similar method. We should use different types of analysis, and different approaches, and explore the phenomenon from all possible angles. Up until now, I have mainly used a clinical approach: we have discussed what eating disorders are, their clinical features, their neurophysiological implications of abnormal nutrition, and their genetic components.

In the next chapter I shall adopt a different perspective. I shall look at eating disorders not as a medical or psychiatric condition, but as an expression of the person's needs and wishes, and therefore as meaningful and purposive behaviour. This approach is not new to the study of mental disorders. As we have just seen, there is a well-established phenomenological tradition that studies mental illnesses. With regard to eating disorders, many experts, coming from different schools of thought and using different approaches, have stressed the importance of understanding anorexic experience through the interpretation of the implicit *meanings and purposes* of symptoms. Abnormal eating is often considered as an expression of the person's difficulties,[76] and therefore both as meaningful behaviour and as a means to achieve some ends (or secondary gains). For example, with regard to obesity, Hilde Bruch argued that obesity is sometimes a defence from other psychiatric conditions. It may be used to compensate stress and frustration, or as a defence from anxiety and depression.[77] The hypothesis of the strategic or functional character of symptoms is widely considered plausible, and even survival has been mentioned as one of the 'objectives' of anorexia nervosa.[78]

The next chapter will try to make sense of the apparently irrational eating behaviour characterizing eating disorders. I will use a number of literary and artistic sources, which will help us to understand the meanings and purposes of eating-disordered behaviour. This analysis will be essential to our understanding of the condition, and therefore to our understanding of the ethics of care and treatment of the eating-disordered person.

---

[76] On this subject, see Faccio, *Il disturbo alimentare*, ch. 6; see also P. J. Hugo and J. H. Lacey, 'Disordered Eating: A Defense against Psychosis?', *International Journal of Eating Disorders*, 24/3 (1998), 329–33.

[77] H. Bruch, *Patologia del comportamento alimentare* (Milan: Feltrinelli, 1977), 164, 167. The original English version is *Eating Disorders: Obesity, Anorexia Nervosa and the Person within* (London: Routledge and Kegan Paul, 1974); see ch. 7.

[78] Ibid., chs. 5, 11.

PART 2

The Value of Lightness

5

Lightness and Eating Disorders

1. *Introduction*

Eating disorders are one of the most widespread and threatening conditions affecting young people in contemporary societies. More than 1,000,000 sufferers are registered in the UK and the mortality associated with the disorder (up to 20 per cent) is one of the highest in psychiatry (see Chapter 1). Eating disorders may be a long-lasting condition, with which the person 'will manage' to live sometimes for many years. The consequences of low or abnormal nutrition are severe and threaten people's lives in ways that are not always apparent (Chapter 1).

The person with eating disorders is trapped in a puzzling ambiguity: she both *chooses*[1] her condition, and *feels compelled* to maintain it. She is, at the same time, the *doer* and the victim of a condition that appears at the same time as the fruit of her great self-control and as a mysterious force that is completely out of her control. Being *in control* and *out of control* are the two extremes that, in a somewhat paradoxical and painful way, meet together in the eating-disordered person. The ambivalence that characterizes eating disorders also characterizes the response to eating disorders. Relatives and carers will respond to eating-disordered behaviour with frustration, a sense of defeat, anxiety, preoccupation and also anger, irritation and even admiration and envy, if not for thinness itself, for the sufferer's 'will power'.

A major problem in approaching eating disorders is that *we do not understand* the person's behaviour. Her behaviour appears totally unintelligible. We seem unable to comprehend it in any coherent manner. For this reason, it is also difficult for us to have a clear picture of what it is right to do when dealing with a person with eating disorders.

In an important way, the ethics of the treatment and care of the eating-disordered person relies on *understanding* the person's behaviour. It is only

Chapters 5 and 6 are partly based on Simona Giordano, 'Qu'un souffle de vent...', *Medical Humanities*, 28/1 (2002), 3–8.

[1] The extent of the autonomy of this choice is a separate issue, which will be analysed in Chapter 12.

when we understand a person's behaviour—why she does the things she does, or why she makes those choices—that we can say whether these are genuine or autonomous choices or not. Once we understand a person's behaviour we can figure out what we should do and how we should approach the problem with the person. We shall now look at the salient features of the disorder and try to understand the rationale that may explain them.

This analysis is not a clinical analysis. I shall not provide therapeutic advice. However, any effective intervention is arguably to be based on an understanding of the disorder. By shedding light on central features of the eating disorders, this analysis may also have a clinical significance.

I shall use literary and artistic sources to explore the most salient features of eating disorders. The imaginative sources will help to understand, *by way of analogy*, aspects of eating disorders that would otherwise appear unintelligible. I shall appeal to scientific sources to verify the plausibility of my hypotheses, and I shall therefore combine theoretical reflection with empirical observations. However, it should be recognized that my conclusions will be highly speculative. The only way to verify them is our 'inducement to say, "Yes, of course, it must be like that" '.[2] They do, however, throw a light upon salient traits of eating disorders, and therefore enrich the perspective from which a scientific analysis of the phenomenon should start.

2. *The Central Feature of Anorexia Nervosa: The Pursuit of Lightness*

According to the *International Classification of Diseases, ICD-10*, the central feature of anorexia nervosa is 'deliberate weight loss'.[3] The *Diagnostic and Statistical Manual of Mental Disorders, DSM-IV-TR (Text Revision)* also cites weight loss and fear of weight gain as central traits of anorexia nervosa. This means that anorexia nervosa is a *progressive pursuit of lightness* (weight loss, reduction of weigh). The person pursues lightness with different methods: mainly by control of food intake and by compensatory or cathartic practices—vomiting, exercise, and the use of diuretics and laxatives.[4]

The fact that the central feature of anorexia is deliberate weight loss is very important. It means that anorexia would not exist if it were not possible for people to value *lightness*. It is the value of lightness to some people that we need to understand, if we want to understand anorexia. This search for

---

[2] L. Wittgenstein, *Lectures and Conversations on Aesthetics, Psychology and Religious Belief*, ed. C. Barrett (Oxford: Blackwell, 1966), 52.

[3] World Health Organization, *International Classification of Diseases, ICD-10* (Geneva: WHO, 1992), F10–19.

[4] American Psychiatric Association, *Diagnostic and Statistical Manual of Mental Disorders, DSM-IV-TR (Text Revision)* (4th edn., Washington: APA, 2000), 307.1.

lightness, as we have seen in Chapter 1, has severe psychological and physio-logical side effects. Why do people risk and sacrifice so much for the sake of lightness? Why would some people die rather than put on weight? What is the value[5] that is associated with lightness? In order to answer these questions we need to look at the 'psychology' of people with eating disorders.

According to clinical studies, people with eating disorders typically fear invasions of personal space. It has been observed that they generally fear other people's interference and expectations, and experience them as viola-tions of their personal sphere. These people often avoid contacts because they experience relations with others as a possible threat to their privacy and to their control over their own life.

Fear of invasions, of intrusions, or of demands and expectations are experiences that sufferers commonly report. Some experts on eating dis-orders have related these experiences with emaciation. They have argued that people with anorexia use their own emaciation to defend themselves from the presumed intrusions of the external environment. People with eating disorders shut themselves up in their own thinness.

The question arises, however, as to why, in order to obtain such a protec-tion, people lose weight rather than adopting some other form of conduct. Why is being light, rather than say being angry or being joyful or being tearful or being heavy believed to offer protection from other demands and intrusions?

3. *The Pursuit of Lightness and Fear of Intrusions*

> I should rejoice to see you, and had earnestly asked you to my Home with your sweet friend, but for a Cowardice of Strangers I cannot resist.[6]

Clinical studies show that the fear of invasions of personal space is one of the main worries of people with eating disorders. From questionnaires given to her patients, as well as from other studies quoted in her book,[7] Morag MacSween concludes that people with anorexia do not like to be touched and always need space around them:

---

[5] I use the term 'value', rather than 'importance', because of the ethical connotations of lightness that will become clear in what follows.

[6] E. Dickinson, Letter No. 735, in T. H. Johnson (ed.), *The Letters of Emily Dickinson* (Cambridge, Mass.: Harvard University Press, 1958), 716.

[7] A. E. Anderson, 'Atypical Anorexia Nervosa', in R. A. Vigersky (ed.), *Anorexia Nervosa* (London: Raven Press, 1977), 14; L. K. G. Hsu, 'Outcome of Anorexia Nervosa', *Archives of General Psychiatry*, 37 (1980), 1044, quoted in M. MacSween, *Anorexic Bodies: A Feminist and Social Perspective* (London: Routledge, 1995), 218.

'I cannot cope with anybody coming close or touching me even if someone touches me on the shoulders or back.'[8]

'I like space around me.'[9]

According to Mara Selvini Palazzoli, people with eating disorders *oppose their emaciation* to these presumed invasions, and believe (or have the illusion) that thinness works as a defence against staring, criticisms, aggression, and sexual intrusions.[10] Anorexic emaciation would therefore be a way of declaring: 'I have sharp contours, I'm not soft, I don't merge with you.'[11] A person who had recovered said that anorexia satisfied her need to be 'closed up for a while, and very small, not receptive, not there for others'.[12]

We should notice here that not all people with eating disorders become extremely emaciated. However, what is important is *why people try* to be light, what they find desirable and appealing in lightness. Whether or not they actually become thin is secondary. We need to understand the *pursuit* of lightness, quite independently of whether a person, as a consequence of her efforts, becomes emaciated or whether, instead, she 'fails' in her attempts to become thin. This chapter, therefore, will not make a distinction between restrictive anorexia, non-restrictive anorexia, and bulimia nervosa. I am concerned with the *attempt to lose weight*, and therefore generally with *the value of lightness*. The 'physical' result, in terms of body shape, is, I believe, secondary. What matters here is why people pursue lightness and not why they are eventually unable to *succeed*. What is important, I believe, is to understand why people want to become light and would be prepared to sacrifice happiness, health, and even life for its sake. What is important is to understand *the value of lightness*.

According to clinical studies, people with eating disorders typically fear other people's intrusions and demands, and they use weight loss as a protection from presumed invasions of personal space.[13] However, we should ask

---

[8]   MacSween, *Anorexic Bodies*, 221–2.

[9]   Ibid.

[10]   M. Selvini Palazzoni, *L'anoressia mentale: Dalla terapia individuale alla terapia familiare* (Milan: Feltrinelli, 1998), 96. I also wonder whether the fear of demands and expectations has moral origins, to be found in the blame that is sometimes associated with the disappointment of others' expectations, and with the guilty feelings that people often experience when they are not willing to meet such demands.

[11]   MacSween, *Anorexic Bodies*, 65.

[12]   Ibid.

[13]   This analysis is an attempt at understanding experiences and behaviours that appear sometimes uncontrollable and incomprehensible to the person herself. For this reason, the hypotheses are necessarily speculative, at least to some extent. On this point see the opening paragraphs of this chapter. Similar objections have been raised against psychodynamic analyses. These objections concern, in particular, the scientific character of the psychodynamic approach, and the fact that its hypotheses and conclusions are impossible to verify, at least directly.

why these people lose weight, rather than adopting some other strategy of conduct. In other words: in what sense do thinness and lightness work as a defence against invasions of personal space? In order to answer this question, it is necessary to reflect upon the 'deliberate weight loss', or pursuit of lightness, that is the central feature of eating disorders.

4. *The Unbearable Lightness of Being: A Representation of Anorexia Nervosa*

At the heart of eating disorders there is a search for lightness. The pursuit of lightness is potentially endless: one can always make another effort to lose weight, until lightness becomes physically unbearable. The clinical picture of eating disorders—people who seek *an unbearable lightness* has curious cultural resonances. The Czech novelist Milan Kundera wrote a novel that became famous, *The Unbearable Lightness of Being*. This novel has nothing to do with eating disorders.

Published in 1982, the novel narrates the story of four Czech characters, Tomas, Sabina, Tereza, and Franz. Tomas is a successful surgeon. He is prosecuted by the Czech Communist Government: they want a statement from him declaring his faith in the Communist Government. If he does this, he will lose his credibility among his friends and colleagues. Thus he refuses. However, the Government does not give up, and he is asked to sign a letter avowing his love for the Soviet Union. Once more, he refuses. After this second refusal he decides to quit his job and takes a job as a window-washer. He hopes that the authorities will no longer be interested in the opinion of somebody at the bottom of society. However, he soon realizes that, now that he is declassed, not only are the police not interested in him, but neither is anyone else, including his friends. By the time the police knock on his door, Tomas's life is ruined, whatever he might have decided to do.

Franz is a university professor. Sabina, his partner, is a painter. She cannot decide whether she wants to stay with Franz or not. Her life is a life of betrayal and infidelity: infidelity to her lover, to her family, and to her country. Her absolute lack of sense of moral responsibility and commitment condemns her to a 'lightness of being'; she floats among situations that are all apparently interchangeable. Juxtaposed to Sabina is Tereza, Tomas's wife, who is all commitment and fidelity. While Sabina loses her identity transported by her lightness of being, Tereza loses her identity sinking under the unbearable weight of her moral sense.

An account of such a debate cannot be provided here. See G. Jervis (ed.), *Psicoanalisi e metodo scientifico* (Turin: Einaudi, 1967), pts. I, III.

Although this story has no direct link to eating disorders, the genesis of the *Unbearable Lightness of Being* may tell us something important about eating disorders. In *The Art of the Novel*, Milan Kundera says he thought about the 'unbearable lightness of being' for the title of his famous novel after reading about an idea of Gombrowicz's. This idea, which, according to Kundera, is as comic as it is ingenious, is that the weight of our being is inversely proportional to the growth of the population on the planet. Democritos represented 1/400,000,000 of humankind. Gombrowicz himself represented 1/2,000,000,000 of humankind. In this kind of arithmetic, says Kundera, each of us today weighs 1/6,000,000,000, and such lightness, which progressively reduces the weight of our being, starts becoming unbearable.[14]

From this perspective, because of the continuous growth of the population on the planet, we are condemned to a continuous (and potentially lethal) rush towards lightness. In fact, each of us would be confined to a smaller and smaller space, and condemned to a continuous loss of weight. Lightness may be physically unbearable, and may even kill us.

This picture is obviously a literary paradox, and these observations should not be understood as an explanation of anorexia nervosa. But they make it possible, by way of analogy, *to represent* the anorexic experience. Anorexic behaviour may well appear absolutely unintelligible, and the observations made by Kundera upon Gombrowicz's idea provide us with something of a representation of what those with anorexia nervosa experience. Anorexia is, in fact, a frantic rush towards lightness, a desperate escape from fatness and heaviness, a rush not only 'wanted', but also experienced as ineluctable; a process that, unless interrupted, is lethal. People with eating disorders seem trapped in a relentless (and apparently paradoxical) search for weight loss, without knowing exactly how this happened, or, above all, how they could interrupt it. This does not mean that people are blindly involved in this process. On the contrary, the rush towards lightness involves strong self-control. Weight loss is deliberate (see *ICD-10*), and this also gives us the hope that people with eating disorders may find in themselves the capacity to modify their situation. However, sufferers also experience this rush towards lightness as ineluctable. This contradiction is part of the complexity of the phenomenon, and contributes to making the anorexic condition so dramatic.

Of course, I am not claiming that people develop eating disorders because of the demographic growth on the planet. Otherwise, contrary to what happens, eating disorders would spread more in the most populated areas of the planet, rather than in the USA and in Europe. Moreover, all of us would have eating disorders, not only some of us. Neither am I arguing that

[14] M. Kundera, *L'arte del romanzo* (Milan: Adelphi, 1988), 47–8. There is an English translation of this book: *The Art of the Novel* (London: Faber, 1988).

there is a perfect symmetry between fear of expectations and pursuit of lightness. It is unlikely that all people who are particularly concerned with others' expectations develop anomalous eating habits. And, as we shall see in the next chapters, lightness is not only valuable because it may protect us from other people's intrusions. Lightness is also valuable for other reasons, and it is often presented as a positive quality to have, in contexts that are not related to this fear. The picture that we have drawn from Kundera's understanding of Gombrowicz's arithmetic should be seen only as a representation of the anorexic rush towards lightness, which people also experience as independent of their will. Likewise, the work of Modigliani[15] and Giacometti[16] provides an extraordinary representation of the filiform figure, which is both the result of Gombrowicz's arithmetic and the ultimate model to which anorexic bodies try to correspond.

From this perspective, Jean Paul Sartre's comments on Giacometti are illuminating:

In space, says Giacometti, there is too much. This too much is the pure and simple coexistence of parts in juxtaposition. Most sculptors let themselves be taken by this. Giacometti knows that space is a cancer on being, and eats everything; to sculpt, for him, is to take the fat off space; he compresses space, so as to drain off its exteriority. This attempt may well seem desperate; and Giacometti, I think, two or three times came very near to despair. Once he had a terror of emptiness; for months, he came and went with an abyss at his side; space had come to know through him its desolate sterility. Another time, it seemed to him that objects, dulled and dead, no longer touched the earth, he inhabited a floating universe, he knew in his flesh, and to the point of martyrdom, that there is neither high nor low in space, no real contact between things.[17]

As I have remarked earlier, these references should not be seen as an explanation of anorexic experience, but rather as a representation of it. By way of analogy, they make it possible to picture the difficult relationship that some people have with the idea of 'occupying space',[18] and provide a representation of the anorexic pursuit of lightness. It also becomes possible to understand the value that people with anorexia attach to lightness. In other words, as we shall now establish, it becomes possible to understand why

[15] Selvini Palazzoni, *moressia mentale*, 96. Easily accessible samples of Modigliani's works can be found at the following web pages: www.picturalissime.com/modigliani_femme_y.htm; www.a525g.com/art/modigliani.htm; www.picturalissime.com/art/modigliani/modigliani_lunia. htm; www.picturalissime.com/modigliani_hebute_c.htm; www.picturalissime.com/modigliani_fille_bleu.htm.

[16] Easily accessible samples of Giacometti's works can be found at the following web pages: www.nobl.k12.in.us/art/sculpt2unit1.htm, www.expressivetherapy.com/index_other.html.

[17] Cited in R. Hohl, *Alberto Giacometti: Sculpture, Painting, Drawing* (London: Thames and Hudson, 1972), 277.

[18] MacSween, *Anorexic Bodies*, ch. 7, sect. 5.

emaciation seems to offer protection from the expectations and intrusions of others, or why people lose weight to obtain such a protection, rather than adopting other types of behaviour.

5. *Lightness as a Defence from the Invasions of Personal Space*

Physically speaking, fat occupies space. Under Gombrowicz's logic, being fat means having a wider surface exposed to intrusions. On the contrary, being thin means having more space around, and being proportionally less exposed to intrusions. Intuitively, a bigger body is more likely than a slender body to come into contact with other bodies. As a slender body has more available space around it, the risk of its being touched by other bodies is lower. By reducing one's physical size, one reduces the threat of undesired physical contact. The fight against fat may in this perspective be interpreted as an attempt to become inviolable, and to reach physical detachment (see also Chapter 6).

Understanding eating disorders in this way also allows us to clarify another important aspect of anorexia: the link between thinness and lightness. In order for a body to defend itself from possible intrusions, and to free itself easily from eventual constrictions, it must be not only slim, but also light, because it is easier for a light body to float away. In fact, people with eating disorders seek not only thinness, but also lightness: they are not only slaves of the mirror; they also make indiscriminate use of the scales, often checking their weight several times a day. Lightness and emptiness are closely related. In order to be light, a body must be empty. Eating-disordered people are, in fact, persistently concerned with being 'full' and 'empty'. Eating means 'filling oneself up', or 'blowing oneself up', and, as a caloric content is introduced in the body, the main concern is how to eliminate it. A person who had anorexia said: 'Before I eat (or ate) I felt afraid that I had held out too long; while eating my main idea was how I could get rid of the food in one way or another—and this thought filled my head until I felt empty again.'[19]

By getting thin, therefore, people with eating disorders gradually become (or so they seem to believe) less exposed to possible invasions of personal space. The lighter they become, the more they feel ready to free themselves from the unpleasant interference of others. Paradoxically, therefore, the anorectic filiform figure, the fragile, a-carnal body, which looks vulnerable to anybody else's eyes, is experienced as invulnerable by the person herself.

---

[19] MacSween, *Anorexic Bodies*, 217–18; on the dichotomy between full/empty, see ibid., ch. 7.

Based on the psychological studies quoted in Section 3, the pursuit of lightness is thus a pursuit of inviolability.[20] Silently, with no apparent intervention on others or on the external environment, people with eating disorders expand that environment, thus expanding the space between themselves and other people. In the isolation of their thinness and lightness, people with eating disorders achieve an exceptional place, one that is out of reach. This achievement, as we shall see in the next chapter, has important links with morality. Isolation in fact allows detachment from the 'physical' world, and the achievement of a 'transcendent' dimension. Isolation, thus, not only responds to an overwhelming fear of intrusions, but also contributes towards satisfying an ethical ambition to spirituality. Moreover, because of the strenuous sacrifice involved, the defence of the personal sphere is also proof of will power, and this, as we shall see, is one of the keys for understanding the ethical connotations of eating disorders. In the next chapter I shall analyse all these different aspects of the pursuit of lightness. At the end of our discussion, these aspects will appear related and coherent.

6. *Is Lightness a Contemporary Obsession?*

> *La donna è mobile*
> *qual piuma al vento*
> *muta d'accento*
> *e di pensiero,*
>
> *Sempre un'amabile*
> *leggiadro viso*
> *in pianto e in riso*
>
> .   .   .
>
> *La donna è mobile*
> *qual piuma al vento*
> *muta d'accento*
> *e di pensier,*
> *e di pensier,*
> *e di pensier.*

The woman is mobile, such a feather in the wind, mute in the word and in thought. Always an amiable graceful face, in tears and laughter ... The woman is mobile, such a feather in the wind, mute in the word and in thought, and in thought, and in thought.[21]

---

[20] See also n. 13.   [21] Guiseppe Verdi, 'La donna è mobile', The Duke's aria in *Rigoletto*.

Whereas in the clinical field lightness is often regarded as a strategy to escape other people's expectations or as a defence from intrusions of personal space, in common discourse anorexia and eating disorders in general are often regarded as the effect of the pressure exerted by mass media to be thin. The common explanation for anorexia goes more or less like this: nowadays, if you want to be beautiful you have to be thin—so they say. Pressure to be thin is everywhere. You open any magazine, and you will find plenty of skinny models, dietary advice, slimming products, slimming therapies. You walk down the street, and are bombarded with beautiful women with not one extra pound of flesh ... You can't go shopping without feeling 'fat' even if you are slim: clothes are always advertised on skinny people; you will never be like that. If you are just a little bit round, you feel a failure! It is no surprise that people diet. Especially young girls. Adolescents are in a period of transition and are very sensitive to social symbols. They will want to be like their favourite singer or actress. This is where the diet comes in. Then, when they start losing weight, they are happy and prised by their peers, and they just will not stop—and day after day, the situation *slips out of their hands*. They become unable to control themselves. It becomes an illness.

These types of arguments are common explanations for anorexia nervosa. This is generally the way people seem to make sense out of the search for thinness. In these sorts of arguments, blame is not much on the person (who at worst is considered *vain*) but mainly on society, which spreads a dangerous model of beauty. The person is thus regarded as the *victim* of the social pressure to be thin.

Contemporary society is indeed replete with light and thin models of beauty. The presence of ultra-thin models has often been related to eating disorders, and magazines and the media have sometimes been blamed for causing or reinforcing eating disorders. The images that everyday are pictured in the magazines and the media are thought to provide an *anorexic* model of beauty. The fact that eating disorders are a relatively recent syndrome, and the fact that in the societies where the disorders appear thinness is regarded as a nearly essential element of female beauty, are seen as being related: it is believed that the aesthetic ideal exerts some influence on young people. Any normal-shape woman will feel inadequate and fat as compared to these models. The omnipresence of thin beauties may thus induce people to restrict food intake and 'spiral down' into the trap of eating disorders.

Whereas undoubtedly the pressure exerted by the fashion industry has an influence on eating disorders, the campaign against the use of thin models risks drawing attention away from the most important causes of eating disorders, which are moral in nature.

7. *Light Beauties*

Many people believe that anorexia is connected with the images that we see everyday in magazines, television programmes, newspapers, and advertisements. One of the *causes* of eating disorders is often claimed to be the 'thin' ideal of female beauty spread by the media. It is indeed hard to distinguish between some models and people with anorexia—the line between 'beauty' and 'illness' here is fine. The complaint is that there is nothing beautiful in skeleton-like bodies, but when young people are bombarded every day with these images they end up believing that those skinny bodies are really more beautiful than normal-shaped women. Consequently, people who are not skinny feel fat and ugly. The media are blamed for spreading an 'unnatural' model of beauty and consequently for inducing people to conform to shapes that bring them into the disease.

Some studies have considered the models of the 'Miss America' competition and of the magazine *Playboy* since the 1960s, and have indeed registered decreased weight and decreased curves through the 1960s and 1970s. During the 1970s the 'tubular' androgynous body was imperative. One of the most highly paid models was Jean Shrimpton, also called 'the shrimp'.[22] Another was Twiggy.[23] The fashion of the thin body persisted through the twentieth century. The ideal of thin beauty spread by the media and used by the fashion industry has raised concern in medical settings. In 2000, the British Medical Association published a report, *Eating Disorders, Body Image and the Media*. The images spread by the media were here connected with anorexia. The publication of the report stimulated a wide debate on the relation between eating disorders and the media. Interestingly, the director of a magazine pointed out that the reason why skinny models are pictured is that they are what the general public want to see. People, in fact, tend to buy the magazines where skeleton-like bodies are pictured more than other magazines. The blame, the director argued, should therefore not lie entirely on the media.[24]

The argument of the magazine's director is important, as it draws attention to the relationship between what we are offered and what we want to be offered: it is not simply that people like thinness because magazines are replete with thin models. It is (or, it is also) the reverse—magazines are full of thin models because this is what people like. The supply, in other terms,

---

[22] Richard Gordon, *Anoressia e bulimia: Anatomia di un'epidemia sociale* (Milan: Raffaello Cortina, 1991), 78. The original English version is *Anorexia and Bulimia, Anatomy of a Social Epidemic* (Oxford: Blackwell, 1990); see ch. 5. Some images of Jean Shrimpton can be found at: http://www.swinginchicks.com/jean_shrimpton.htm.

[23] Some images of Twiggy can be found at: http://www.swinginchicks.com/twiggy.htm.

[24] *Guardian*, 31 May 2000, www.guardian.co.uk/Archive/Article/0,4273,4023818,00.html.

satisfies the demand. The question, therefore, is: why do people like *these women*? Or: what is attractive about thinness?

Of course, eating disorders are connected with the idea that slender or thin bodies are (other things being equal) nicer than fatter bodies. And arguably the use of extra-thin models may be ethically controversial for a number of reasons. For example, it can be argued that to guarantee models fame and success only if they are skinny is a form of exploitation, which is comparable to paying extra money to workers in order for them to accept unhealthy work conditions. A number of objections and counter-objections can be made to the use of extremely thin models in the fashion industry, but I will not go into the merits of such arguments. I would instead like to stress that the connection between aesthetic ideals and eating disorders is a complex one. The claim that the aesthetic ideal of female beauty is the cause of eating disorders is too simplistic. Studies on the meaning of thinness reveal that the rationale for the value of thinness is linked to other values, which go beyond the aesthetic preference for slim bodies. Some studies, for example, show that, historically, thinness has been valued at times when women have been requested to demonstrate their intellectual skills. It has been registered that the more numerous are the women who aspire to 'male' positions, the more numerous are those who pursue a cylindrical or tubular (androgynous) body. The negative stereotype 'prosperous woman = stupid' (and maybe blonde) appears deeply internalized in Western societies, and maybe for this reason the pursuit of thinness coincides with the pursuit of careers and roles that are traditionally 'masculine'.[25] From this perspective, thinness is valued not *in itself* but for what it signifies.

Both the aesthetic ideal of female beauty and eating disorders are the expression of profound beliefs. As we are now going to see, these beliefs are moral in nature. These moral beliefs are rooted in our shared conception of what is good and right. Thinness does not have much to do with what we believe to be nice or beautiful—it is not simply a matter of what we find *pretty*. It is a matter of what we believe to be *good and right*.

It is difficult to see anything intrinsically or inherently beautiful in *thinness*, and, unless one can show that there is something intrinsically

---

[25] B. Silverstein, B. Peterson, and L. Perdue, 'Some Correlates of the Thin Standard of Bodily Attractiveness for Women', *International Journal of Eating Disorders*, 5 (1986), 895–905; B. Silverstein, B. Peterson, L. Vogel, and D. A. Fantini, 'Possible Causes of the Thin Standard of Bodily Attractiveness for Women', *International Journal of Eating Disorders*, 5 (1986), 905–16; B. Silverstein and L. Perdue, 'The Relationship between Role Concerns, Preferences for Slimness, and Symptoms of Eating Problems among College Women', *Sex Roles*, 18 (1988), 101–6; B. Silverstein et al., 'Binging, Purging, and Estimates of Parental Attitudes regarding Female Achievement', *Sex Roles*, 19 (1988), 723–33, quoted in Gordon, *Anoressia bulimia*, 92 (in English version, see ch. 5).

beautiful in thinness and what that is, it has to be accepted that there are *reasons why* we regard the thin body as beautiful, or more beautiful than the fat body.

Of course, the question of why we regard some things as beautiful is a complex one. It is a question about the foundations of our aesthetic judgement. I will not try to address this issue here. However, it seems that the fact that we attach aesthetical status to thinness and fatness has meanings that go beyond our 'shared tastes'. I may argue that I find a thin body more beautiful than a fat body 'because in the society where I live thinness and not fatness is considered beautiful'. This society has taught me to appreciate thinness and this is why I prefer thin bodies. However, this argument shifts the question to another level: why is thinness regarded as beautiful *in this particular society*? What are the sociocultural reasons that induce some people to appreciate lightness/thinness? Why do people *in this society* tend to spend money on magazines where skinny models are pictured?

One plausible answer is that a determined physical quality—in this case thinness—becomes beautiful (*admirable*) for what it symbolizes in that context. Thinness is admirable for the meanings that it carries, not because it is in itself a beautiful thing. Aesthetic judgements about people's shape are thus *value judgements*. The type of *value* that is at stake in the case of the beauty *of the human body* is *moral in nature*. Aesthetic judgements relating to people's shape are in fact judgements relating to people's worth. The fat body is not only *ugly*—and is not *ugly* 'by chance': the fat body symbolizes laziness, indulgence, lack of will power, lack of self-control, and self-disrespect. These are not neutral observations relating to the person's psychological characteristics: there is a sense of repugnance attached to them. Behind the adjectives 'ugly' and 'beautiful' there appear to be judgements relating to the value of the person. In this sense, the aesthetic judgement about people's shape is not only—as it seems obviously—a *value judgement*, but also a judgement relating to the *value of the person*.

In the following chapter we shall analyse the reasons why thinness and lightness are valued in Western societies, and we shall explore the moral reasons that lie under the aesthetic judgement about people's shape. We should now note that the ideal of thin female beauty is not a new one in the Western world.

8. *The Ancient Myth of Lightness*

Far from being a contemporary mania, fear of fat has obsessed Western women for a long time. In her book *Victorian Literature and the Anorexic Body*, Anna Krugovoy Silver argues that the ideal of slender female body was common in Britain in the nineteenth century. Concomitantly, fat was regarded as ugly and/or unfeminine.

Medical books of the 1800s indicate that women of that time dreaded fat. Beauty manuals and magazines of the time present fat as an element that spoils the beauty of forms and female's grace. Fat around the waist was considered as the most aberrant. Hence the use of tight lacing and corsets, which control and castigate female fat and which allow the woman to display a 'wasp-waist'.[26] Although it was known that tight laces and corsets might be detrimental to women's health, a slender waist was imperative and the practice of tightening females' stomachs was commonplace.

Krugovoy Silver reports countless examples of celebrations of female's slenderness in common discourse, medical books, magazines, and literature. Her work clearly demonstrates that slimness is not at all a *new* ideal of female beauty. More importantly, Krugovoy Silver's work shows that the ideal of female beauty is, and has been for a long time, unnatural to women. The androgynous body (big shoulders, narrow hips, no fat stores), which is argu-ably today's standard of female beauty, is in contrast with the physiology of women. But the 'wasp-waist' that was fashionable in the nineteenth century was also arguably in contrast with the physiology of women. Women had to *struggle* to conform to that ideal. There is also evidence that girls and women used methods to control their body weight, such as drinking vinegar and lemon juice, which were thought to help lose weight.[27] An interesting parallel should be drawn between these practices and those employed by people with eating disorders, who typically use laxatives and diuretics as an aid to diet, in order to lose weight or stay underweight. It is not how much fat a body should or should not have in order to be considered beautiful that is important: what is important in both cases is that the ideal of beauty is unnatural to women, and that women have to *castigate* themselves in order to conform to it.[28]

9. *Slimness and Lightness in Literature and the Arts*

The female ideal of light/thin beauty is also reproduced in literature. Victor-ian literature is full of light and thin heroines. Krugovoy Silver writes:

---

[26] Anna Krugovoy Silver, *Victorian Literature and the Anorexic Body* (Cambridge: Cam-bridge University Press, 2003), ch. 1.

[27] Ibid. 53.

[28] Mary Briody Mahowald makes similar observations. She also reports the example of footbinding in pre-Revolutionary China as another illustration of the castigation of women's bodies which has been identified with beauty and grace. See Mary Briody Mahowald, 'To Be or Not To Be a Woman: Anorexia Nervosa, Normative Gender Roles, and Feminism', *Journal of Medicine and Philosophy*, 17/2 (1992), 233–51.

The prototypical heroine of nineteenth-century fiction
[...] almost inevitably displays a tiny appetite: Dickens's Little Dorrit, Eliot's Dorothea Brook, and Brontë's Jane Eyre are only three of the most well-known heroines defined in part by their light, pale bodies. In *Ruth*, Elizabeth Gaskell establishes her fallen heroine's fundamental innocence and passionlessness with repeated allusions to her slimness, her 'little figure', and 'beautiful lithe figure'.[29]

An overview of Victorian literature—including Victorian children's literature—proves that since at least the nineteenth century a slender body was considered the ideal of female beauty. The beautiful woman is aerial, graceful, light, and transparent. The arts (the domain of Beauty) have often used such a model of female beauty. Music, literature, and the figurative arts have often presented light women as agreeable, and still do.

Anna Krugovoy Silver has asked why it is the *woman* who has been subjected to unnatural models of beauty, rather than the man. She argues that there are two reasons for this. One has to do with the dichotomous conception of mind and body, which is both a religious and a secular idea. In Western thought, since Greek times, the body has often been juxtaposed to the mind, or soul or spirit. In the mind/body split, the inferior part is clearly the body. The body is the corrupt side of the human being, the one that needs discipline and control, the one that may bring the human being into moral collapse. Krugovov Silver argues that thinness (and lightness) is the emblem of the subordination of the body to the spirit. Lightness corporealizes self-government and spirituality. We shall come back to this point in Chapter 6. In a context that denigrates the body, and fatness as an abundance of body or 'corpulence' (from the Latin *corpus* $=$ body$_+$ *ulentus* $=$ abounding in), body fat cannot be considered 'beautiful'—because it is *not acceptable*. Fatness is unacceptable as synonymous with corporeal vices.

The second reason relates to the common view of woman as a more instinctual and emotional creature than man. Women are commonly regarded as 'less rational' than men and therefore more in need of control and discipline.[30] Moreover, women have always had an 'ornamental role'. Being beautiful is one of the responsibilities of the woman to her man, to her family, and to society.[31] Since fat is not *aesthetically* and *ethically* acceptable, women more than men have a moral imperative to control their body weight.

Like the woman who achieves an exultant sense of control over her body by obsessively fasting and exercising, many nineteenth-century women pursued discipline over the body through their eating habits and through the use of the corset. In addition, the Victorian woman's attempt to indicate her sexual purity through a slim figure recalls the anorexic girl's refusal of her own physical needs and desires [...] through starvation [...] Ultimately, such a rejection of appetite can be interpreted as the

---

[29] Krugovoy Silver, *Victorian Literature*, 10.   [30] Ibid. 46.   [31] Ibid. 29.

transcendence of the true self, whether conceptualised as soul or mind, over the corrupt and temporal body.[32]

We shall not discuss the issues of gender and gender discrimination and the connection between refusal of food and sexual chastity further. Krugovoy Silver has provided a comprehensive account of these aspects of eating disorders. What is important in this context is that the aesthetic ideals of 'how a body should look' are normative ideals. Aesthetical judgements about the body have to do with what we think about the body and how we judge the body, and are ultimately moral judgements.

The next chapter will discuss other examples of lightness in literature, arts, and music, and will explain what lightness signifies and how it is related to morality.

[32] Krugovoy Silver, *Victorian Literature*, 48.

6

The Value of Lightness

1. *Introduction*

At the heart of eating disorders is a pursuit of lightness. The pursuit of lightness is not a *new obsession* but has, instead, very old roots. Since at least the nineteenth century, in Western societies, women have been concerned with body weight and shape, and have attempted to control body weight. Like contemporary people, they have also been ready to sacrifice their health in the *pursuit of lightness*.

In this chapter, I will argue that lightness (and fasting) is viewed in a positive way in our culture and is associated with the pursuit of worthwhile goals. Moreover, it is a valued means to other important moral ends, which are related to Christian morality, but which have been absorbed into the secular culture of Western countries.

2. *Lightness as a Positive State*

According to the definition of the *Oxford English Dictionary*, 'lightness is the quality or fact of being light', that is 'of little weight, not heavy'.[1] If it were not possible to value lightness, eating disorders would not exist. The central feature of anorexia is, in fact, the pursuit of *weight loss*, that is, lightness. People with eating disorders, however, are not the only ones who attach value to lightness. Lightness is in fact viewed in a positive way in Western societies. Thin models are probably admired because they incarnate the ideal of lightness—they represent what we value, lightness.

Lightness is often presented as a positive state or a positive quality to have in contexts that are apparently unrelated to the clinical sphere, such as music, literature, arts. Even in ordinary language lightness is often presented as a desirable state: lightness is associated with feelings of liberation, purity, and well-being ('I feel so light . . . ').

---

[1] Lightness, in English, also means 'brightness', 'illumination'. This may also illustrate a part of the meaning of anorexia nervosa. However, this meaning is absent in other languages and therefore I will not develop this point further.

3. *'Dans l'eau de la claire fontaine'*

George Brassens wrote a song, 'Dans l'eau de la claire fontaine' (1961),[2] a poetic celebration of lightness. The song tells the story of a minute woman who is bathing naked in the water of a fountain ('Dans l'eau de la claire fontaine elle se baignait toute nue'). A man passes by and, moved by the fragile beauty of this tiny creature, decides to look for grapevine leaves and flowers of lily and orange to cover her ('pour la vêtir, d'aller chercher des morceaux de feuilles de vigne, fleurs de lis ou fleurs d'oranger'). However, she is so petite that just one petal is enough to cover her breast, and just one leaf is enough to cover her hips ('mail la belle était si petite, qu'une seule feuille a suffi'). Once she is dressed, she extends her arms to him to thank him ('Elle me tendit ses bras, ses lèvres, Comme pour me remercier'), and in the ardour of the moment, she gets undressed again ('Je les pris avec tant de flevre qu'ell'fut toute dishabille').

We are left with the image of this nearly a-corporeal creature who is so light, graceful, and fragile 'that a breath of wind . . .'. Smallness and frailty here elicit a mixture of feelings—tenderness, sexual desire, a sense of protection—and there is certainly a sense of beauty surrounding this vulnerable girl.

This model of *light beauty* recalls the heroines discussed by Anna Krugovoy Silver in her book *Victorian Literature and the Anorexic Body*. The parallel between the Victorian heroines and the contemporary French song is an important one, as it testifies to the survival of the ideal of lightness. Not only do we still have a certain conception of female beauty (the ideal of the tiny and ethereal woman has been preserved through the nineteenth and twentieth centuries), but we still *value lightness*.

Consider two other literary examples. The first is from Leo Tolstoy, the second is from Emily Dickinson. In both cases lightness is presented as a positive state and is associated with the pursuit of worthwhile goals. In later sections I shall focus on Emily Dickinson; I will discuss her life and values, as this will help us to clarify the meaning and value of lightness in anorexia. Emily's life and her writing will demonstrate that lightness is not only associated with the pursuit of worthwhile goals, but has also been considered

---

[2] In the water of the bright fountain | She was bathing undressed | When a breath of wind from the south | Threw her clothes to the clouds. | Distressed, she asked me to help her | And to look for vine-leaves, fleurs-de-lis or of orange. | With petals of roses I made her a blouse | But she was so little that one single rose was enough. | With the vine-leaves I made her a skirt | But she was so little that one leaf sufficed. | She stretched forth her arms, her lips, to thank me . . . | I took her with such ardour | that she was again naked. | The candid lady enjoyed the play | And often she went back to the fountain | Wishing that a breath of wind, that a breath of wind . . . (George Brassens, 'Dans l'eau de la claire fontaine' (France: Éditions Musicales Mercury, 1961), my translation.

as a means to achieve important goals, especially those that are moral and spiritual in nature.

4. *The Value of Lightness*

> All the night and morning Levin had lived quite unconsciously, quite lifted out of the conditions of material existence. He had not eaten for a whole day, he had not slept for two nights, had spent several hours half-dressed and exposed to the frosty air, and felt not only fresher and better than ever, but completely independent of his body: he moved without any effort of his muscles, and felt capable of anything. He was sure he could fly... [3]

This passage is taken from *Anna Karenina* by the Russian writer Leo Tolstoy. In this novel Anna, married to the important businessman Karenin, falls in love with Vronskij. She leaves her husband and son to go abroad with Vronskij. When she comes back, however, she realizes how her choice has compromised and ruined her entire life, and kills herself. In antithesis to this love, the book narrates the love of Kitty for Levin. In the quoted passage, Levin is about to meet Kitty's family, after they have consented to her engagement.

This passage is important because it presents lightness in a positive way, and also because it associates lightness with a positive value, namely love. This passage depicts a man who had not eaten for a whole day, and who, on top of it, has not slept for two nights and is also half frozen. But his situation is presented as a highly *desirable state*. It seems we should admire and even envy this man, for his extraordinary experience. Lightness here is worthy of admiration and is associated with sense of elation, happiness, and love.

Lightness is also presented in a positive light in the following description of Emily Dickinson provided by Joseph Lyman, who courted Emily's sister.

A library dimly lighted [...] Enter a spirit clad in white, figure so draped as to be misty[,] face moist, translucent alabaster, forehead firmer as of a statuary marble. Eyes once bright hazel now melted & fused so as to be two dreamy, wondering wells of

---

[3] Leo N. Tolstoy, *Anna Karenina* (London: Penguin, 1977), ch. 15. It is sometimes argued that this sense of exhilaration and spiritual power is ultimately rooted in physiological processes. On this point, research is not in one direction. For example, Richard Gordon argues that fasting has a potentially addictive lure, and that is why health cultists usually prescribe time limits on fasting. See R. Gordon, *Anorexia and Bulimia: Anatomy of a Social Epidemic* (Oxford: Blackwell, 1990), 123–5. Other researchers are, however, more sceptical on this point. See R. Slade, *The Anorexia Nervosa Reference Book: Direct and Clear Answers to Everyone's Questions* (New York: Harper & Rowe, 1984), 34–5. Despite this controversy, what matters in this context is that mystical and ethical connotations are often attached to this experience of purity and spiritual enthralment (whether or not underpinned also by neurophysiological factors).

expression, eyes that see no forms but gla[n]ce swiftly [& at once] to the core of all thi[n]gs—hands small, firm, deft but utterly emancipated from all [fleshy] claspings of perishable things, very firm strong little hands absolutely under control of the brain, types of quite rugged health [,] mouth made for nothing & used for nothing but uttering choice speech, rare [words] thoughts, glittering, starry misty [words] figures, winged words.[4]

Emily is described as a mere 'spirit', 'draped' so as to be misty, whose hands are small and emancipated from all flesh. One gets the impression of a near-transparent waif who has moved from the earthly world of the flesh. Not only is she presented in a positive light, but Emily elicits fascination in Lyman, as she has apparently overcome the 'mortal' world and reached a nearly spiritual dimension. The description of Emily is full of admiration. She is ethereal and spiritual, a nearly a-carnal creature who is elevated from the material world in which mortal beings live: this makes her a *heroine*, a subject of admiration. Like the heroines of Victorian literature, and like the woman in 'Dans l'eau de la claire fontaine,' she is *transparent and light*. Emily is a heroine *because of* and is to be admired *for* the emancipation from fleshy and temporal things. The detachment from the temporal world renders her superior to the rest of us: she is emancipated from the physical world and in contact with the 'Great realities of Life.'[5]

As with Levin's fasting, Dickinson's lightness is both presented positively and associated with another great value. In Levin's case, it was love; in Dickinson's case, as we are about to see, it was the writing of poetry.

5. *The Life and Work of Emily Dickinson: Lightness and Spirituality*

Dickinson's life and work shed further light on the value of lightness in eating disorders. The value that Emily attached to writing and poetry was *moral* in nature. We shall see in what way moral values are connected with lightness. We shall also see that, for people with eating disorders, being light is a *moral imperative*. Being light is a moral imperative derived from a particular conception of moral integrity and moral goodness.

Emily Dickinson (1830–86) lived in Amherst, Massachusetts, under the influence of Puritanism. She lived a very private life. From her 30s onwards, Emily progressively withdrew from social life, and isolated herself in what

---

[4] R. B. Sewall (ed.), *The Lyman Letters: New Light on Emily Dickinson and her Family* (Amherst, Mass.: University of Massachusetts Press, 1965), 69.

[5] R. B. Sewall, *The Life of Emily Dickinson* (New York: Ferrar, Straus and Giroux, 1974), 222–3, emphases added.

has been called 'self-elected incarceration'.[6] She began avoiding social contacts. Meeting people, even her friends, disoriented and worried her. When her friends called at her house to visit her, she would often refuse to see them and stayed in her room upstairs. After they had left, she would write letters and cards of apology and self-accusation.

She spent most of her time alone, writing. 'For several years', she wrote, 'my Lexicon was my only companion.'[7] Intellectual activity had for Emily a special meaning. She believed that the written word, lasting over mortal bodies, makes the human being closer to eternity, as, for example, illustrated in the following lines, extracted from a letter that she wrote to the literary critic Thomas Wenthworth Higginson: 'A Letter always feels to me like immortality because it is the mind alone without corporeal friend.'[8] The following poem is another example of the near-divine connotations that she attached to the Word:

> A Word made Flesh is seldom
> And tremblingly partook
> Nor then perhaps reported
> But have I not mistook
> Each one of us has tasted
> With ecstasies of stealth
> The very food debated
> To our specific strength—
>
> A Word that breathes distinctly
> Has not the power to die
> Cohesive as the Spirit
> It may expire if He
> 'Made Flesh and dwelt among us'
> Could condescension be
> Like this consent of Language
> This loved Philology.[9]

According to Charles Anderson, this poem is to be connected with the New Testament and with the Christian concept of the Word. The Word is the metaphor for the Divine incarnate in Christ. Jesus Christ is 'the Word made Flesh'. The Word is 'the very food needed for nourishment of the spirit [...] The opening lines, by linking the "Word made flesh" with the Eucharistic term "partook", carry her poem from the advent, the first incarnation of the

[6] E. Dickinson, Letter No. 735, in T. H. Johnson (ed.), *The Letters of Emily Dickinson* (Cambridge, Mass.: Harvard University Press, 1958), p. xix.

[7] Charles R. Anderson, *Emily Dickinson's Poetry: Stairway of Surprise* (New York: Holt Rinehart and Winston, 1960), 43.

[8] E. Dickinson, Letter No. 330, in Johnson (ed.), *Letters*, 460.

[9] E. Dickinson, Poem No. 1651, in M. Guidacci (ed.), *Poesie e lettere* (Florence: Sansoni, 2000), 398.

spirit, to the ritual by which it is shared, the "fresh sojourning" of the Word among us'.[10]

Emily asserts the immortality of the Word and Spirit, which is juxtaposed against the mortality of flesh—a Word may expire if God were to make a Word flesh and dwell among us.

Anderson explains that 'the symbols of the Eucharist and the doctrine of the Word were simply metaphors to express her passionate conviction about the power of poetry'.[11] In her poem, therefore, we should read her commitment to Christianity, and the value that Emily attached to intellectual activity. For Emily, intellectual activity was clearly superior to physical or social activities, and the soul was clearly superior to the body.

In her letters, she writes:

'I do not care for the body, I love the timid soul, the blushing, shrinking soul; it hides, for it is afraid, and the bold obtrusive body . . . '[12]

Who cares for a body whose tenant is ill at ease? Give me the aching body, and the spirit glad and serene, for if the gem shines on, forget the mouldering casket.[13]

These lines may be taken as an example of the poet's 'religious inheritance in general, including its hierarchy of body and soul, or soul against body'.[14] Not that she blindly accepted religious teachings. On the contrary, she was very critical and even rebellious to religion. However, 'there is an extent to which the Christian metaphysical tradition inevitably informs her work, and indeed never ceases to do so'.[15]

Through isolation and dedication to intellectual activity, Emily aimed at detaching herself from 'material' existence. Overcoming the physical and social dimension of life was for her the expression of her spiritual nature and the proof of her moral character. Her biographers describe her as a person of remarkable moral integrity and devoted to the Puritan axioms 'of simplicity, austerity, hard work'.[16] Sewall writes! 'She abhorred sham and cheapness. As she saw more and more of society—in Boston [. . .] in Washington [. . .] she could not resist the feeling that it was [terribly] painfully hollow. It was to her so thin and unsatisfying in the face of the Great realities of Life.'[17] Anthony Johnson also reports Emily's adherence to

---

[10] Anderson, *Emily Dickinson's Poetry*, 43.

[11] Ibid. 44.

[12] E. Dickinson, Letter No. 39, , in Johnson (ed.), *Letters*, 103.

[13] E. Dickinson, Letter No. 54, in ibid. 140.

[14] Shira Woloski, 'Emily Dickinson: Being in the Body', in Wendy Martin (ed.), *The Cambridge Companion to Emily Dickinson* (Cambridge: Cambridge University Press, 2002), 129–41, at 132.

[15] Ibid.

[16] Sewall (ed.), *The Lyman Letters*, 22.

[17] Sewall, *The Life of Emily Dickinson*, 222–3.

Puritanism, and to one of its ground values, namely the scarce consideration for 'the flesh'.[18]

Here we touch on an important point, which is essential to understanding how lightness may be considered important as a means to moral goals. Emily's dedication to intellectual activity was related, first, to her conception of the body as a *bold obtrusive* 'accessory', as a *mouldering casket*; and, secondly, to her moral belief that detachment from carnal existence is proof of moral integrity—a belief that, as we shall see, is not only religious but also secular, and that has great contemporary significance.

It is not clear whether Emily Dickinson was anorexic herself, in the sense we would today describe anorexia. But she was a person who rejected bodily existence, and the values that directed her life tell us something important about anorexia. Both the life of Emily and anorexia express a desire for *elevation* that is connected to a need for moral integrity.

Lightness fits into this need for moral elevation: that is, not only do we view lightness positively, not only is it a frequent accompaniment of the pursuit of some worthwhile end, but it can be the *means to* worthwhile ends. In particular, lightness may be considered valuable as a means to spirituality and moral integrity. We are now going to see in what sense lightness is related to spirituality and moral integrity.

6. *Moral Integrity and Spirituality*

There is a long-established connection, in Western religious and moral thought, between spirituality and morality. Being spiritual usually means being morally good. Spirituality is generally identified with moral integrity. The moral person is the one who wins over the body and over the corporeal nature of things, and who is able to penetrate the realm of the spirit. The truth is all on the side of the spirit, whereas corruption and baseness are all on the side of the body. Animal instincts are identified with the physical side. The 'superior' *human* nature is identified with the *spirit*—or mind, soul, or reason. Moral degradation is all on the side of the animal—physical or instinctual—whereas it is believed that the *spiritual, mental, or rational* is something ontologically different from the instinctual, something that distinguishes human beings from 'brute' animals. Morality is all in the realm of spirituality. There is no space for morality in the realm of the instinctual. We are moral in so far as we are spiritual, mental, or rational. Morality is thus thought to belong to our spiritual, mental, or rational dimension.

[18] Anthony Johnson, 'Postfazione', in Guidacci (ed.), *Poesie e lettere*, 382.

As Anna Krugovoy Silver points out:

Historically, the body has been ... denigrated and reviled as inferior and needing to be disciplined, punished, and ultimately transcended. In one classic, foundational statement of such a body/mind split, Socrates argues, in Plato's 'Phaedo', that 'as long as we have a body and our soul is fused with such an evil we shall never adequately attain ... the truth. The body ... fills us with wants, desires, fears, all sorts of illusions and much nonsense, so that ... if we are ever to have pure knowledge, we must escape from the body and observe matters in themselves with the soul by itself.' Socrates' language associates the body with corruption, infection, 'contamination', and 'folly' that keeps a human being from the knowledge that can come only through the reasoning of the soul.[19]

Plato also writes: 'we shall be closest to knowledge if we refrain as much as possible from association with the body or join with it more than we must, if we are not infected with its nature but purify ourselves from it until the god himself frees us.'[20]

The idea that the developed human being is *composed* of mind (or soul or spirit) and body as two entities that are ontologically different, and the belief that morality is on the side of the mind (or soul or spirit), has entered Western philosophy and moral and religious thought in all eras.[21] It has been accepted within Christianity, in the patristic doctrines, in the Scholastic philosophy, in the different denominations of Christianity—such as Catholicism, Protestantism, Puritanism, and Calvinism—and likewise it has been accepted in Humanism and Renaissance, with their prosperity of Neoplatonic and neo-Aristotelean theories. Aristotle talked about the human being as a compound of form and matter. The material is the body, the animal part, and the form is the mind (the *nous*): 'the part of the soul by which it knows and understands.'[22] The *nous* expresses our very nature.[23] Having a mind is essential to being a human. There is no human being without *nous*. The Scholastic philosophy, which probably relied on Aristotle more than Plato,

---

[19] Anna Krugovoy Silver, *Victorian Literature and the Anorexic Body* (Cambridge: Cambridge University Press, 2003), 8.

[20] Plato, *Phaedo*, trans. by G. M. A. Grube, *Five Dialogues* (Indianapolis: Hackett Publishing, 1981), 93–155, at 103, quoted in Krugovoy Silver, *Victorian Literature*, 171.

[21] I am not excluding that the same dichotomy may also be found in Eastern traditions. However, I am not attempting to give an account of the different religious and metaphysical traditions present in the world. I am only trying to understand eating disorders and these particular aspects of Western culture may help us to understand eating-disordered behaviour, regardless of whether similar values may be found in different cultural contexts.

[22] Aristotle, *De Anima (On the Soul)* (Harmondsworth: Penguin, 1986), iii. 4, 429^{a}9–10; cf. iii. 3, 428^{a}5; iii. 9, 432^{b}26; iii. 12, 434^{b}3.

[23] Aristotle, *Metaphysics* (London: Penguin, 1998), i. 1, 980^{a}21; *De Anima* ii. 3, 414^{b}18; iii. 3, 429^{a}6–8.

indeed interpreted Aristotle's (and Plato's) work in the light of Christian values. This was due to a number of historical factors.[24]

Many modern philosophers have incorporated in their theories the metaphysics of body and mind (soul or spirit). Probably Descartes (with his partition of *res cogitans* and *res extensa*—literally the 'thinking thing' and the 'extended thing') and Kant (with his division of the *phenomenal*—or physical—dimension and the *noumenal*—or supernatural—dimension) provide some of the most remarkable systematization of the dichotomous conception of the human nature in philosophy.

This metaphysics has crucial consequences for ethics. Clearly, in the partition between physical and spiritual, the spiritual part is the one that is ontologically superior. Within this system of thought, goodness, integrity, and morality, are all on the side of the *spiritual*, while the natural, material, or physical is either synonymous with *corruption* or, at best, morally neutral. Moral judgement does not apply to our natural side: morality has to do with our *reason* and with the capacity of our reason to control our natural side (the reason, mind, spirit, soul, intellect, or will). In either case, the *natural side*

---

[24] An important factor was the spread of a *corpus* of doctrines written by philosophers and theologicians in the second or third century BC. This was known as *Corpus Hermeticus*, and was ascribed to Thoth, an ancient Egyptian God. It contained references to the Bible and a doctrine of salvation that appealed to the use of intellect to achieve communion with God. It also contained references to the Gospel by John, to the Son of God, and to other elements of 'later' Christian religion. The Christian Fathers believed it to be original. Because it presented a theological ideology that was similar and for some theologicians (such as Augustine) more satisfactory than the Bible, this induced them to read the whole Greek philosophy in the light of the doctrines contained in the *Corpus*, as if it were a 'later' development of an older religious tradition from which Christianity was born. The whole Greek, pagan, and Christian philosophy and theology were read as coherent in the light of the 'prophecies' of the *Corpus Hermeticus*. Agostin thought that the *Corpus Hermeticus* was a prophetic work and based most of his speculation on the belief that the *Corpus* was authentic and that therefore the whole Greek tradition could be interpreted in terms of the future Christian metaphysics. This is in part why in the Middle Ages we find a syncretism of Christianity Neoplatonism and pagan doctrines. And this is also why Aristotle was also read coherently with the metaphysics of Christianity and could be integrated in this metaphysics. Giovanni Reale and Dario Antiseri, *Il pensiero occidentale dale origini a oggi* (3rd edn., Rome: La Scuola, 1984), ii. 17–20. Another important factor that led to the interpretion of Aristotle in the light of the Christian metaphysics was that the first systematic source that presented Aristotle to medieval thinkers was Avicenna (born in 980 near Bukara, in Persia). Avicenna combined the philosophy of Aristotle with Neoplatonism and Islamic elements, and this is why many Christian thinkers welcomed Aristotle and based their religious and philosophical speculations on his philosophy. Reale and Antiseri, *Il pensiero*, 406. I will not go any further into the history of philosophy. It is important to make these few remarks because some may object that the Scholastic and large part of medieval philosophy is based on Aristotle, rather than Plato, and Aristotelean philosophy did not contain any split between mind and body. I have shown that the Aristotelean conception of the human being is hierarchic, in that the *nous* is considered as the more important part of the human being. Moreover, Aristotelean philosophy reached the medieval thinkers in a particular way, and was interpreted in the light of Christian values, among which there is the inferiority of the body and physical life, and the superiority of the intellect as an instrument of salvation.

has to be transcended. The significance of such ideas for Western culture is incalculable. It may help to explain the strenuous exercise of control that characterizes anorexia and bulimia nervosa. This idea in fact explains why many people value lightness. Within the systems of beliefs that are based on such a dichotomous conception, *being light* inevitably becomes *important, valuable*. Within these systems, lightness becomes a means to the achievement of *spirituality* (that is, moral integrity). Through this route, moral connotations are attached to lightness. *Being light* becomes a *moral issue*.

7. *Moral Integrity and Christian Asceticism: The Value of Lightness*

The idea that the human body is ontologically different and inferior to the spirit has had a tremendous impact in the Latin world, and Christianity has had an important influence in its spread. The partition of two different worlds, and the notion of the body as belonging to the least important of the two, is central to Christian theology. This type of dualistic metaphysics, as remarked above, has important consequences for ethics. Moral integrity consists of overcoming the physical side: human beings need to elevate and detach themselves from their physical nature and *ascend to God*. The moral systems based on such metaphysical dichotomous conception of the human being dictate that the body, with its wants, desires, and impulses, may corrupt the human being and must therefore be transcended. Christianity hallowed the idea that moral perfection has to be found in the detachment from the world and ascension to God. *Ascetic practices* were exercises aimed at promoting such an elevation.

Interestingly, the word *asceticism* comes from the Greek *askesis*, which means physical exercise or practice. *Askesis* was mainly used to refer to the physical training of athletes and had nothing to do with spiritual exercises and spiritual practices.[25] However, the early Christians translated *askesis* with *ad-scandere*, which includes in its meaning the notion of elevation/ascension, a notion that was absent in the original meaning. In this way *asceticism* started to be used to refer to *spiritual* practices,[26] which were aimed at attaining true perfection through detachment from the world and *elevation* to God.[27] Fasting has always been considered as one of the most

---

[25] W. Vandereycken and R. Van Deth, *From Fasting Saints to Anorexic Girls: The History of Self-Starvation* (London: Athlone Press, 1994), chs. 2, 11.

[26] *The Catholic Encyclopedia*, vol. i (copyright © 1907 by Robert Appleton Company; online edition copyright © 2003 by Kevin Knight available at http://www.newadvent.org/cathen/01767c.htm).

[27] Istituto della Enciclopedia Italiana, *Vocabolario della lingua italiana* (Rome: Treccani, 1986).

effective ascetic techniques.[28] St Jerome prescribed mortification of your body 'by abstinence and fasting'.[29] Fasting involves *weight loss*.[30] Thus, when ascetic practices spread as a means to moral integrity, moral connotations started being ascribed to *being light* (to *lightness*).

The reasons for this connection between *lightness* and *asceticism* (in the sense of ascension to God) are probably to be found in human psychology. The idea of lightness is related to images of lifting, floating, flying, rising, and ascending. Lightness is associated with the capacity to rise and fly, and in ordinary language 'lightness' is associated with feelings of liberation and detachment from the body (we have expressions like feeling 'light-headed', for example, or feeling light or 'high' when we are over excited).

As we have seen above, lightness means being 'of little weight, not heavy'. The most obvious way to become *light* is clearly *fasting*, and it is no surprise that fasting has always been considered functional to *asceticism* (elevation). It is not by chance that Levin, Tolstoy's character, *had not eaten for a whole day* when he had his experience of elevation. '*He* could *fly....*' says Tolstoy. Would he be ready to fly after a nice big Sunday lunch?

Here it is interesting to notice that the sensation of pleasure associated with lightness is partly *physiological*. Duker and Slade point out that starving for more than half a day is perceived by the body as hunger stress.[31] This results in the secretion of adrenalin. When there is a continued presence of adrenalin in the bloodstream, endokinins are released in the brain: these have tranquillizing and euphoric effects. Moreover, the metabolism of fat produces metabolites (such as ketones), which also act on the brain and may cause a light-headed experience.

The interesting thing in all this is the *interpretation* that people give of these sensations. In other words, the fact that fasting may give some form of pleasure is not the most relevant thing here. What is most important is that this sensation of pleasure, the physiological effects of food deprivation, is interpreted in a *positive way*. Whereas other forms of pleasure—such as drunkenness—are not related in any way to *moral* achievements, the sensation of pleasure due to food deprivation is interpreted in terms of *detachment from material existence*, as *spirituality*, as *transcendence of the body*, and therefore, ultimately as moral superiority. The most interesting thing about the pleasure related to starvation is not that there are physiological explanations that one may find for that pleasure, but that the sensations are considered within a moral set of values. The interesting thing, in other

---

[28] Vandereycken and Van Deth, *Fasting Saints*, chs. 2, 11.
[29] *The Catholic Encyclopedia*.
[30] With exceptions.
[31] Marilyn Duker and Roger Slade, *Anorexia and Bulimia: How to Help* (2nd edn., Buckingham: Open University Press, 2003), 32.

words, is not that people actually feel pleasure and that they do not *invent it*; the interesting thing is how they conceptualize their pleasure. As we have seen, the sensations derived from starvation are associated with moral and spiritual goals.

Lightness is thus considered valuable in a moral sense, as a means to spiritual and moral perfection. Food restriction, in turn, is considered valuable as a means to lightness. Therefore, both lightness and food restriction are regarded as morally valuable in that they are functional to asceticism—to spiritual elevation.

To summarize, the central feature of eating disorders is the deliberate pursuit of lightness, achieved as weight loss. If it were not possible to value lightness, eating disorders would not exist. This is not to say that no other value or no other factor may contribute to the onset and maintenance of eating disorders. People may value *thinness* for a number of reasons, some of which have been discussed in the previous chapter. However, as the main diagnostic manuals report, deliberate *weight loss* is central to eating disorders,[32] and, as weight loss is *deliberate*, there must be a value attached to it. We therefore need to understand what is good or valuable about *lightness*, if we want to understand eating disorders.

A positive value has often been attached and still is attached to lightness in the arts, music, and literature. Being light is associated with positive feelings and with beauty. In Brassens's 'Dans l'eau de la claire fontaine', lightness accompanies the nearly acorporeal beauty of the girl. As we have seen, society is replete with this ideal of 'light' beauty, and the anorexic figure may be seen as the extreme expression of this ideal. As the lives of Levin and Dickinson show, lightness can also accompany the pursuit of worthwhile ends. In Levin's case, love; in Dickinson's, the Word.

However, fasting and lightness are also seen as positive values in another way: they are instrumentally valuable as means to worthwhile ends. First, lightness is thought to be *morally* valuable, as an instrument to asceticism. Secondly, since lightness is morally valuable, food restriction is morally valuable, because it promotes lightness and therefore asceticism.

Here I have not sought to examine whether fasting and lightness are *intrinsically* valuable—that is, valuable in themselves. Nor have I sought to examine whether the end of asceticism and control over the body by the mind are really worthwhile ends. It is enough that these ends are thought by many in the Christian and other traditions to be valuable, and fasting and lightness are means to these ends. This is in fact sufficient to find a plausible answer to

[32] World Health Organization, *International Classification of Diseases, ICD-10* (10th edn., Geneva: WHO, 1992), F10–19; American Psychiatric Association, *Diagnostic and Statistical Manual of Mental Disorders, DSM-IV-TR (Text Revision)* (4th edn., Washington: APA, 2000), 307.1.

the question as to why being light is widely and in different ways deemed valuable.

There is also another sense in which food restriction is *morally valuable*. The next sections will focus on other related aspects that explain why some people value morally lightness and food restriction. I shall show the contemporary significance of moral values and I shall relate these values to eating disorders. We shall see that it is only in the light of a determined morality that eating-disordered behaviour may be understood.

8. *The Moral Value of Lightness*

Lightness is often presented as a desirable state or quality to have. In fashion, being light is associated with beauty. In ordinary language, lightness is related with feelings of liberation and well-being. Lightness is also related to asceticism. In a context that values lightness so much, it is obvious that diet is also valued. We have seen that there is a moral dimension in all this. Lightness is associated with the pursuit of worthwhile goals and with moral goals of spirituality and elevation to god.[33]

Control of food intake (diet, fasting, and maybe even 'healthy eating') involves morality in different ways. One way, as I have argued in the previous chapter, is that, by eating less, people *lose weight*, that is, they become *lighter*, and being light is associated with the pursuit of spirituality and moral perfection. But there is also another way in which control over food intake involves morality. Food restriction indicates self-government, discipline, and the submission of the 'corrupted' side of the human being. This is related to the mind/body split and to the notion of the body as ontologically different and 'qualitatively lower' than the spirit (or mind, reason, or soul). We have already discussed in the previous chapter the body/mind split. Here I make further observations on this point, and show the relevance of this metaphysics to eating disorders.

---

[33] It has to be noticed that lightness, in one sense, is also associated with immorality. A 'light' woman is one who does not take seriously the values of chastity and monogamy. This seems to be in direct opposition to the way the 'light' and 'ethereal' woman is often presented as an example of spirituality and morality. I owe this observation to Harry Lesser. Although 'lightness' may also have this pejorative meaning, it still remains true that lightness is associated with morality. In this case, someone is 'light' because she does not take on the 'burden' of moral values and is a 'slave' of the flesh. And it remains true that—despite other possible negative meanings of lightness—lightness is often presented as a positive quality to have and that the ideal of beauty, spirituality, and purity has often and for a long time been associated with lightness.

9. *Food Restriction and the Body/Mind Split*

In Western thought the mind has often been juxtaposed to the body.[34] The philosopher Gilbert Ryle has defined this idea as 'The Official Doctrine'. He has described this doctrine in the following terms:

There is a doctrine about the nature and place of minds which is so prevalent among theorists and even among laymen that it deserves to be described as the official theory. Most philosophers, psychologists and religious teachers subscribe, with minor reservations to its main articles and, although they admit certain theoretical difficulties in it, they tend to assume that these can be overcome without serious modifications being made to the architecture of the theory [. . .] The official doctrine, which hails chiefly from Descartes, is something like this. With the doubtful exceptions of idiots and infants in arms every human being has both a body and a mind [. . .] Human bodies are in space and are subject to the mechanical laws which govern all other bodies in space [. . .] But [. . .] the workings of one mind are not witnessable by other observers; its career is private [. . .] The events in the first history are events in the physical world, those in the second are events in the mental world [...] In consciousness, self-consciousness and introspection he [the man] is directly and authentically apprised of the present states and operations of his mind [. . .] It is customary to express this bifurcation of his two lives and his two worlds by saying that the things and events which belong to the physical world, including his own body, are external, while the workings of his own mind are internal. This antithesis of outer and inner is of course meant to be construed as a metaphor, since minds, not being in space, could not be described as being spatially inside themselves. But relapses from this good intention are common and theorists are found speculating how stimuli, the physical sources of which are yards or miles outside a person's skin, can generate mental responses inside his skull, or how decisions framed inside his cranium can set going movements of his extremities [. . .] Underlying this partly metaphorical representation of the bifurcation of a person's two lives there is a seemingly more profound and philosophical assumption. It is assumed that there are two different kinds of existence or status. What exists or happens may have the status of physical existence, or it may have the status of mental existence.[35]

Ryle called this theory 'the dogma of the Ghost in the Machine',[36] and argued that this dogma is a philosopher's myth. We do not need to go into the merit of a philosophical discussion of the dualistic conception of human nature. I would like to point out only one thing: those who are accustomed to contemporary bioethics or medical ethics will be familiar with similar assumptions. The most influential contemporary speculations on personhood

---

[34] Krugovoy Silver, *Victorian Literature*, 9.
[35] Gilbert Ryle, *The Concept of Mind* (London: Penguin, 1978), 13–14.
[36] Ibid. 15.

(Peter Singer,[37] John Harris,[38] Derek Parfit,[39] Tristram H. Engelhardt Jr.,[40] for example), rely on a similar conception of the human being, as a being that, in its 'complete' or 'higher' form, possesses 'mental' capacities—self-awareness, for example, capacity to consider itself as the same being over time, and so on. The existence of the 'mind' as something ulterior and separated from the 'body' is very little disputed. Only beings that are not 'persons' do not possess the 'mental' capacities.

Different terms are used to refer to the 'mental capacities' or 'mental entity': soul, spirit, reason, intellect, will. The terms 'soul' and 'spirit' normally have a religious afflatus, whereas in contemporary philosophy the terms 'reason' or 'rationality' are most often used. The 'reason' or 'rationality' is supposed to be the faculty that distinguishes humans from beasts. The locus of such mental entity is undetermined: maybe the reason or rationality is located in the brain, whereas the soul or spirit is maybe located in the heart or somewhere at the centre of the body. The functions may also be differentiated: maybe the soul and spirit direct our sentiments, whereas the mind or reason produce articulated thoughts. Usually, contemporary philosophers do not provide an elaborated gnoseology, or any theory about human faculties, as, for example, Locke, Berkeley, or Kant did. That we *have* 'a reason' seems something so self-evident that it does not require any justification. If we *have* a mind, then we *also have a body*—as something different from the mind. In the mind/body split, the inferior part is clearly the body. The body is the corrupted 'side' of the human being, the one that needs discipline and control, the one that may bring the human being into moral collapse.

The dichotomy of mind and body is characteristic of Western thought and the association between body and baseness recurs in all eras: in the Greek thought, in Christianity, in the patristic doctrines, in Scholastic philosophy, in the different confessions of Christianity, such as Catholicism, Protestantism, Puritanism, Calvinism; in Humanism and Renaissance, with their flourishing of Neoplatonic and neo-Aristotelean theories, in modern philosophy and in contemporary society as well.

Many thinkers objected against the conception of the human being as 'composed of' mind and body.[41] Ayer argued, for example, that 'mind' and

---

[37] See e.g. Peter Singer, *Rethinking Life and Death* (Oxford: Oxford University Press, 1995).

[38] John Harris, *The Value of life* (London: Routledge, 1992).

[39] Derek Parfit, 'Personal Identity', in J. Glover (ed.), *The Philosophy of Mind* (Oxford: Oxford University Press, 1976), 143–63.

[40] H. T. Engelhardt Jr., *The Foundation of Bioethics* (2nd edn., Oxford: Oxford University Press, 1996).

[41] E. Oslon, *The Human Animal: Personal Identity without Psychology* (Oxford: Oxford University Press, 1997), 65–6, 144–51.

'body' are logical constructions, inventions of philosophers and theologicians.[42] Other philosophers have shown that the splitting of the mind from the body meets with insurmountable logical difficulties. Peter Van Inwagen, for example, showed that any attempt to think sensibly about the concepts of 'mind' and 'body' as conceptually distinguishable functions inevitably falls in irresolvable logical problems.[43]

Furthermore, theorists of ethics and metaethics objected to the validity of this conception and its consequences for ethics. Just to quote some, sentimentalists, such as Shaftesbury and Hutcheson, emphasized the importance of emotions as a guide for morality. Pragmatists such as James and F. C. S. Schiller, at the end of the nineteenth century, emphasized the importance of emotions and psychology. Ludwig Feuerbach also thought that mind and body are just two aspects of one material organism. Emotivists, such as C. K. Ogden, I. A. Richards, B. Russel, and A. J. Ayer, despite their differences, all articulated metaethics doctrines based on the idea that the function of evaluative expressions is to manifest or to elicit emotions and behaviours.

Despite the fact that many philosophers and philosophical schools have contested the dualistic conception of human being and have not accepted that emotions and physical needs are base and corrupted sides of our nature, it is undeniable that the dualistic conception of the human being has been fundamental for Western thought and culture. The opposition of many philosophers in effect testifies the importance of such a conception.

Among the origins of the body/mind split is Orphism.[44] Orphism takes its name from Orpheus, a Greek (probably legendary) poet. The information that we have about Orpheus is poor and fragmentary, but Orphism had a very significant influence on the Greek thought and consequently on the Latin world. Orphism understands the human being as composed of soul and body. The soul is a *demon* (δαίμων), a divine principle that fell in the body because of an original fault. The soul is immortal and reincarnates in different bodies, until the rituals and practices of the 'Orphic life' put an end to the cycle of reincarnations (metempsychosis).

The impact on this schema of thought on Greek philosophy was great. For the first time the human being was presented as composed of two sides in contrast with each other. This conception had an irreversible effect on the original Greek naturalism: for the first time physical impulses were presented

---

[42] A. J. Ayer, *Language, Truth and Logic* (London: Penguin, 1990), 130. J. J. Thomson, 'People and their Bodies', in J. Dancy (ed.), *Reading Parfit* (Oxford: Blackwell, 1997), 202–9.

[43] Peter Van Inwagen, 'Philosophers and the Words "Human Body" ', in V. P. Inwagen (ed.), *Time and Cause: Essays Presented to Richard Taylor* (London: Dordrecht, 1980), 283–99.

[44] The following information is drawn from Reale and Antiseri, *Il pensiero*, vol. i.

as something worth repressing. Orphism had a major impact on the whole Greek culture, including philosophy and science.

For example, the mathematical studies of the School of Pythagoras were all informed by the conception of the soul as trapped or incarcerated in the body. Pythagoras and his scholars considered science as a means to purification. Science was the instrument of the liberation of the soul from the body. A similar idea is found in Empedocles. Empedocles was a *physicist*, a scholar of the *physis* (*nature*). He provided an explanation of how things come into being by analysing the elements of which they are composed—water, air, earth, and fire. But in his less known poem *Katharmoi* (Purifications) he developed the orphic teachings. Empedocles, similarly to Pythagoras, believed that the soul (*psyche*) was a demon expelled from the *Olimpus*, and destined to reincarnate itself in different bodies.

Plato also included in his philosophy the concepts of Orphism. In the *Gorgias*, he argued that 'the body is for us a grave'.[45] We *are* our soul, and until our soul is in the body, we are dead. It is by dying that the soul is set free and that we come to life. In his later thought, Plato softened this mysterifical conception, but always preserved the metaphysic distinction between *psyche* (entity similar to the intelligible) and body (sensitive entity). The theme of the soul recurs in virtually all writings by Plato: in the *Meno, Phaedo, Republic,* the *Phaedrus,* and the *Timaeus.*

The metaphysical distinction was clearly accepted in the Latin world. Christianity presented the body and physical life as secondary and non-important, and the scale of values was articulated accordingly: beatitude is for the weak and the poor, and for those who suffer. Suffering in the body and suffering in our 'physical' life are irrelevant provided that the soul is pure and not ill, and, if suffering helps purifying the soul, then that is a good thing. The real values are on the side of the spirit. Ultimately, the body does not ultimately matter.

This metaphysics, in different forms, provides one of the pillars of the Western thought. The conception spread throughout the world. In Puritan New England, Emily Dickinson was writing to her friends:

'I do not care for the body, I love the timid soul, the blushing, shrinking soul; it hides, for it is afraid, and the bold obtrusive body [. . .]'[46]

Who cares for a body whose tenant is ill at ease? Give me the aching body, and the spirit glad and serene, for if the gem shines on, forget the mouldering casket [. . .][47]

---

[45] Plato, *Gorgias,* quoted in Reale and Antiseri, *Il pensiero,* 112.
[46] E. Dickinson, Letter No. 39, in Johnson (ed.), *Letters,* 103.
[47] E. Dickinson, Letter No. 54, in ibid. 140.

As we shall see, this ideology is one of the determinants of eating disorders. Many authors agree that this ideology is not only religious but also secular.[48] Kant provided one of the clearest systematizations of such ideology in secular terms. He developed his moral system on the basis of this metaphysics.

10. *Kant and the* Mortification *of the* Flesh

According to Kant, there are two ontological dimensions: one is phenomenal and the other is noumenal. Animals belong to the phenomenal dimension, and human beings belong to it for what concerns their animal nature. However, there is also a noumenal, transcendent dimension (that we need to presuppose—despite the fact that we *cannot* know it; we can only *think of it*), and human beings also participate in this dimension, with their *reason*.

From his ontology and theory of human faculties, Kant drew his moral doctrine. For Kant, a person behaves morally if (and to the extent that) he or she submits the 'phenomenal' side (that is the physical side, with its impulses and desires) to the 'rational' or 'noumenal' side (the rational having transcendent origins). In order to be moral, human beings need to sacrifice their physical nature and to act according to the precepts of the pure (although practical) reason. Our reason, so far as it is *practical*, applies to the phenomenal world, but, so far as it is *pure*, belongs to the noumenal world.

Human beings act *morally* only when they *sacrifice* their desires and impulses, when they 'bend' them to their will. It is not sufficient for an action to conform to the law: this would be a *legal action*, not a moral one. If we, for example, obtain *pleasure* out of our action, our action is no longer moral, or is not moral to the extent that it gives us pleasure. In order for the will to be moral, it must be determined *immediately*—with no mediation of sentiment, whatever the sentiment may be.

Thus, we conform to morality only to the extent that we exert *power* over our desires, wants, and impulses. There must be *necessitation*. Without necessitation we are not *moral*. Unless we make a *sacrifice*, our actions do not count as morally valuable. Moral actions are not a source of pleasure: if they are, we are not acting morally, but are following our impulses and desires. Thus, it is in the strongest possible sense that morality requires us to submit our phenomenal side to our will and our reason.[49]

---

[48] Krugovoy Silver, *Victorian Literature*, 137.

[49] I. Kant, *Groundwork of the Metaphysic of Morals* (London: Hutchinson House, 1955), ch. 1; I. Kant, *Critical Examination of Practical Reason*, in *Critique of Practical Reason and Other Works on the Theory of Ethics*, ed. and trans. T. K. Abbott (London: Longmans, Green and Co., 1948), 87–200.

Kantian moral philosophy represents one of the clearest expressions of the idea that morality is achieved by the submission of the 'phenomenal' to the 'rational' or 'noumenal' (the rational having transcendent origins). Morality requires that we act according to the precepts of pure (although practical) reason—in other words, that we act on the basis of categorical imperatives, and that we exert power (necessitation) over our phenomenal side.[50] It also represents, I believe, one of the most coherent doctrines of morals. His moral theory is a consistent derivation of the 'body/mind' split.

This moral ideology may have an obvious impact on the way people perceive their physical impulses, including *hunger*.

11. *Moral Integrity and* Hunger

Within an ethic that demands the submission of the 'phenomenal' or 'physical' to the 'noumenal' or 'spiritual', it is obvious that control over one of the most pressing physiological impulses, hunger, is praised.

Fasting has been associated (and is still associated) with ideas of *control* over the chaotic passions of the body, and the person who is able to exert control over hunger, such a powerful physiological impulse, has often been presented as an example of moral integrity.[51] Moreover, fasting has been associated (and is still associated) with the idea of *purity*. Fasting is 'detox'; this, of course, means that eating is always, more or less, a form of pollution. Fasting 'cleanses' the organism. Being empty of food is being clean.

We may look at eating disorders in this light. Control of food intake is central to eating disorders, together with compensatory practices, such as self-induced vomiting, abuse of laxatives, and diuretics. Interestingly, these are also called 'cathartic' practices. These are practices through which the person purifies herself of food. Being empty from food is being 'clean'.[52]

The mortification of the body may be considered a way in which the person with eating disorders wishes to affirm her moral character: she is able to control the body, and to exert will power. It is the value placed on self-control and austerity, and the role of fasting in achieving these, that is the dominant background of the psychology of anorexics. People with eating disorders deliberately try to lose weight on the basis of moral reasons. I am not claiming that this process is fully conscious, and that anorexics want to

---

[50] Ibid.

[51] H. Bruch, *Eating Disorders: Obesity, Anorexia Nervosa and the Person Within* (London: Routledge & Kegan Paul, 1974), 25; M. Weber, *The Protestant Ethic and the Spirit of Capitalism* (London: George Allen & Unwin, 1976), 166; M. MacSween, *Anorexic Bodies: A Feminist and Social Perspective* (London: Routledge, 1995), 211.

[52] Ibid. 217–18; on the dichotomy between full/empty, see ibid., ch. 7.

become light because they think, at a conscious level, that this will make them morally good. What I am arguing is that the deliberate weight loss that is central to anorexia appears understandable if one considers this particular moral background. The pursuit of lightness—which may seem unintelligible and irrational—actually makes sense in the light of the moral values of self-control, austerity, discipline, and spirituality that are deeply rooted in Western culture, both sacred and secular, and have been incorporated in ordinary morality.[53] The level of awareness that anorexics may have of the importance of their moral background in the articulation of their behaviour is a different issue, and something that may be better established in clinical settings.[54]

12. *The Contemporary Significance of Ancient Moral Values*

The claim that eating disorders have to do with moral values in Christianity and other religions and even Orphism is open to an objection. The objection can be raised that the values that are supposed to underlie disordered eating are 'outdated', no longer relevant, and that old-fashioned moral values cannot be blamed for contemporary obsessions: the values professed by Plato and then hallowed by Christianity, and articulated in later centuries by Calvin, Luther, and others, might explain Emily Dickinson's withdrawal and the prevalence of light and spiritual heroines in Victorian literature, but are unlikely to direct the behaviour of today's young people.

We need to notice two things. The first is that these values clearly do have remarkable weight in Western culture. Their persistence through nearly 3,000 years shows that they are a crucial part of the Western conception of morality.[55] It is not unlikely that they persist in contemporary societies.

---

[53] These claims are partly logical, partly empirical, partly speculative—with all the limits for which I take responsibility. It seems to me that it is important to try to understand people's experiences and behaviour, especially when we are confronted with the choice of restricting their freedom for their own sake. As I said at the beginning of this book, eating disorders raise the issue of whether we should force people to behave differently from the way they would otherwise, for their own welfare. But, as Kundera pointed out in his *The Art of the Novel* (London: Faber, 1988), we seem to have a 'natural' tendency to judge before we understand, and it is to resist this 'natural' tendency that I have made an effort to understand the phenomenon of eating disorders. This way of understanding eating disorders—as a suffering that is related to people's moral values—may be incomplete and partly speculative, but is still valid, as it is a way of making sense of behaviours and experiences that otherwise would not make sense, and that would be (and have often been) judged as irrational or unintelligible.

[54] The objection can also be made that anorexics' thinking is impaired by food deprivation and therefore they cannot be acting rationally. While it is true that food deprivation may impair mental functioning, the issue still arises as to why people start fasting in the first instance and get to a stage of food deprivation that compromises thinking and reasoning.

[55] An anonymous reviewer from Oxford University Press has pointed out to me that religious ascetic practices are a part of other religions as well, such as Hindu, Islam, and others. I wish to

The second thing is that sociological studies highlight that the Christian/ Protestant ethic is still dominant in contemporary society.

Max Weber, in his *The Protestant Ethic and the Spirit of Capitalism*, argues that the entire Western modern culture 'was born [...] from the spirit of Christian asceticism', and provides a detailed analysis of how Christian/ Protestant values are translated and implemented in contemporary life.[56] Other more recent studies also show how this ethic has influenced the entire modern culture.[57] The middle-class family has internalized such an ethic and has elaborated a standard of 'good life' on the basis of its values. Self-discipline, work, activity, control, and achievement have been divested of their earliest religious meaning, but have been adopted as rules that should direct both individual behaviour and the functioning of the family and the society in the Western world.[58]

One of the fundamental pillars of this ethics is the idea that the physical and emotional sphere is inferior and should be submitted to the spiritual one. The 'mistrust of feeling and emotions [...] though it may be stripped of its original religious significance ... still persists quite strongly [...] giving way to feelings and emotions is a sign of personal weakness [...] it puts a brake on productivity, progress and success [...] emotions are an impediment to everything that is deemed essential to prove individual worthiness'.[59]

Kantian ethics, and especially its underlying metaphysics, is still meaningful. *Control* is proof of *moral rectitude*. Eating-disordered behaviour, which is all about controlling what happens in the body, is the expression, in extreme

thank this reviewer for the observation. I should point out that I am focusing on eating disorders, and eating disorders are mainly a Western phenomenon. I argue that eating disorders, apparently irrational and unintelligible behaviour, appear coherent and intelligible in the light of some values of a certain moral background, and even of certain metaphysics. This does not mean that similar metaphysics, or similar moral values, are absent in other cultural contexts. A question may be asked: if different societies have similar values, and I am arguing that eating disorders are related to those values, why are eating disorders found in some societies but not others? Does the fact that similar values are found in other societies in which eating disorders are absent invalidate the theory that eating disorders are related to certain metaphysics and ethics? It does not. The presence of eating disorders, a particular phenomenon that is occurring in our society, may become clearer in the light of certain metaphysics and ethics. This does not mean that this metaphysics and this ethics must necessarily cause something like eating disorders, or that other social, cultural, familial, and indeed genetic and biological factors do not play a role in the development of the disorder. Instead, it would be interesting to explore those other cultural contexts, to analyse the meaning and importance of their metaphysics and moral values, the similarities and differences between the metaphysics and morals of cultures in which eating disorders are not found and those of cultures in which eating disorders are found, but this goes beyond the scope of this book.

[56] Weber, *The Protestant Ethic*, 180.

[57] Slade, *The Anorexia Nervosa Reference Book*, 134–8. Brian S. Turner, *The Body and Society: Explorations in Social Theory* (Oxford: Blackwell, 1984), chs. 3, 7, 8.

[58] Ibid.

[59] Duker and Slade, *Anorexia and Bulimia: How to Help*, 121–2.

terms, of the belief that moral principles 'work in opposition to basic and unrestrained impulses'.[60] People with eating disorders are just people who (maybe also because they lack a 'firm sense of the self'[61]) have taken these values *seriously*.

Sociological and clinical studies show that, typically, people with eating disorders are particularly sensitive to the ethic of perfectionism, discipline, austerity, hard work, spirituality, guilt, and especially the belief that the submission of the 'physical' to the 'spiritual' is a manifestation of moral integrity.[62] Those who develop disordered eating are invariably 'rule-bound' people. Values such as hard work, self-control, responsibility, intellectual achievement, postponing gratification to work, and not accepting any form of pleasure unless it is earned are typically those around which the life of the person with eating disorders is organized.[63] Achievement is valuable only when one works hard for it: no pain, no gain!

Duker and Slade write:

There are three underlying characteristics that are particularly marked in any sufferer. These are an intense morality, an extreme sensitivity, particularly to the needs and feelings of others, and a profound sense of worthlessness [...] there is a large measure of agreement among authorities on anorexia nervosa that these are key characteristics [...] It is characteristic of those who become entrapped in the illness that they are completely rule-bound [...] They apply their moral rules to food, to eating, to exercising as to everything else in their life [...] sufferers typically adhere very strongly to a cluster of values that centre on hard work, self control, personal responsibility, high standards of achievement, deferred gratification, not receiving rewards that have not been earned, not receiving where this is not deserved [...] these values and aspirations can be applied to food and body regulation as effectively as they can be applied to work, educational achievements, career success, personal relationships and of course sports, where encouragement for these values to be extended to body regulation is explicit [...] Anorexics, bulimics, all those striving to get their body 'into shape' [...] are people who place very high value on control [...] it is the continuity between the sufferers' moral attitude and that of their social group or culture that again explains why the condition can be lethal.[64]

It is no surprise to find that people who take these values very seriously find strength in *lightness* and that, the more they become emaciated, frail, and vulnerable, the more powerful they feel. This is also why bulimia, food orgies, and lack of control over food and physical activities are reasons for *shame*

---

[60] Duker and Slade, *Anorexia and Bulimia: How to Help*, 130.   [61] Ibid.

[62] Vandereycken and Van Deth, *Fasting Saints*, chs. 2, 11. Marlin Lawrence, *The Anorexic Experience* (3rd edn., London: The Women's Press, 1995), 32–5; Bruch, *Eating Disorders*, 25.

[63] Duker and Slade, *Anorexia and Bulimia*, 110.

[64] Ibid. 108–10.

and guilt, whereas rigid restriction of food intake is a reason for *pride*, in people with eating disorders.

The body is a chaotic entity, whose needs and passions may fall out of control: many people, including anorexics, believe that there is something *moral* in the capacity to control this chaotic body, and something *immoral* in the incapacity to control it. When not openly considered immoral, the judgement may be more subtle and severe: incapacity to control or contain the body will cause hilarity and disgust. Lightness is the demonstration of successful abnegation, whereas heaviness is the expression of the most repugnant vices: indolence, weakness, and moral collapse.[65]

I am not saying, of course, that other variables do not play a role in the articulation of such a complex syndrome; neither am I saying that eating-disordered behaviour is 'determined' by morality, and that the person is just a victim of external influences and that she has no part in the articulation of her own behaviour. Quite the contrary; eating-disordered behaviour expresses the way in which the person articulates and implements moral values and ideals. The fight against fat that is at the heart of eating disorders appears unintelligible unless one also takes into account the fundamental part played by moral pressure.[66] The fight against fat is a fight for control, and therefore a moral crusade for moral affirmation, integrity, and perfection. Claims that eating-disordered behaviour is irrational, or symptomatic of an illness or a mental problem, are not, I believe, related to the fact that eating disorders are *difficult to understand*, but rather prove a general unwillingness to question ordinary morality, and to accept that there is something potentially very dangerous and even lethal in the concepts of 'right' and 'good'.

13. *Conclusions*

In this chapter I have asked what is good or valuable about lightness. If lightness were not considered valuable, eating disorders would not exist, given that they are a 'deliberate pursuit of lightness'.

---

[65] MacSween, *Anorexic Bodies*, 249–50.

[66] Duker and Slade, *Anorexia and Bulimia*, 130. The following objection may be raised: if it is true that these values still affect our life, and if it is true that eating disorders spring from these moral values, why is it that mainly women have eating disorders? However, the idea that eating disorders are a 'female' problem is misleading. It is true that, if one sticks to diagnostic criteria, the majority of those who are diagnosed as having anorexia and bulimia are women. However, dynamics that are very similar to those that shape eating-disordered behaviour inform male behaviour in a number of areas, ranging from sports to work activities. It will not be uncommon to find similar patterns of behaviour as those adopted by the person with eating disorders in the body-builder, in other sportsmen, and in all those, men and women, who have accepted the idea that achieving is proof of adequacy (see Duker and Slade, *Anorexia Nervosa and Bulimia*, 132). It is, however, true that the search for lightness is mainly a women's issue. I cannot offer a conclusive explanation for this. The issue will be addressed in Ch. 8, Sect. 2.

A positive value has often been attached and still is attached to lightness in the arts, music, and literature. Being light is associated with positive feelings and with beauty. However, fasting and lightness are also seen as *instrumentally* valuable, as a means to worthwhile ends. In particular, we have seen that lightness is thought to be *morally* valuable, as an instrument to asceticism. Since lightness is morally valuable, food restriction is morally valuable, because it promotes lightness and therefore asceticism.

This chapter has also shown another aspect of lightness. One of the fundamental notions of Western thought and culture is the idea that body and mind are two different parts of the human being. The mind (or soul, spirit, or reason) is ontologically superior to the body, and morality and goodness are all on its side. This idea, which is both sacred and secular, has deeply influenced the entire modern culture. I have traced its origins in Orphism and have briefly looked at how it spread in the Latin world and in Western philosophy.

One of the consequences of this metaphysics for ethics is that moral perfection is identified with the transcendence of the physical side by the spiritual (or mental) one. Food restriction becomes valuable in this logic as it symbolizes the submission of the body, and for this reason becomes one of the most significant ascetic techniques. Food restriction corporealizes self-government, self-discipline, will power, and control, all of which are prised within such an ideology.

I believe that this provides one of the explanations for the pursuit of lightness that is at the heart of eating disorders. I have argued that there must be something valuable in lightness, if people are ready to sacrifice their health and life for its sake. In the light of what we have said so far, *lightness* is valuable as it indicates the *submission* of the body, and therefore the conformity to the law of the reason and of morality. The value attached to lightness may be understood if one takes into account the notion of the body as corrupted or corruptible. On this perspective, being light and thin is not merely *beautiful*, but *valuable*. Lightness and thinness indicate the transcendence of the body. Lightness and slenderness are the emblem of the person's self-control and discipline. Concomitant denigration of fat reflects the low conception of the body, which is invariably found in all eras in Western culture. From this point of view, lightness and thinness are much more than *aesthetic* ideals: they are normative, moral ideals that reflect the body/mind juxtaposition and the idea that the body is inferior to the spirit or mind.

This may have important clinical and social implications in terms of how eating disorders are understood and approached, and may also have important implications for the moral philosopher. Eating anomalies should be seen as the coherent implementation of moral imperatives that are just being taken seriously. These moral imperatives are part of ordinary morality;

they express moral codes that are routinely applied to all areas of daily life. What one should discuss, therefore, is not *eating*, but *morality*. The focus should shift from the person with eating disorders, from her eating habits to shared moral assumptions about being 'good' and 'right' and their repercussions. It is not 'abnormal eating' that has to be corrected. It is rather ordinary morality that has to be surpassed. It should be recognized that an analysis of our moral beliefs involves many conceptual difficulties. Resistance to critical analysis of moral values may also be understandable, given the obvious function that morality has in the preservation of the human species.[67] Eating disorders thus represent a big challenge: if we really want to understand eating disorders, it is necessary to change the perspective from which we look at things that happen and surmount the way we think ordinarily.

[67] Since morality obviously has an important function in the preservation of the human species. See e.g. K. Lorenz, *On Aggression* (London: Methuen, 1967), 94.

PART 3

Families, Society, and Eating Disorders

7

The Role of Expectations in the
Genesis of Eating Disorders

1. Introduction

Eating disorders manifest recurrent features. The diagnostic picture is repetitive—that is, it is very similar in all cases. This is not often the case in psychiatry. Normally psychiatric categories group together very different patterns of behaviour, and sufferers vary very much in experiences and behaviour. For example, people with different disturbances may all be labelled as having 'schizophrenia' or 'having psychotic experiences'. For this reason it is possible that different psychiatrists will give a different diagnosis to the same patient. The clinical picture of eating disorders is instead very consistent. People with eating disorders have very similar behaviour and experiences. Eating disorders are therefore a well-defined syndrome. This is one of the peculiarities of the condition. But there are other peculiarities as well.

Eating disorders mainly affect *women*; they are mainly found in some of the societies (Western or Westernized),[1] where food is widely available; and, apparently, in most cases they arise in families that share distinctive traits and values.[2] Because of these characteristics, feminist,[3] sociological,[4] and systemic studies have analysed the contexts (society and family) where the

---

[1] Pierre J. V. Beumont and Walter Vandereycken, 'Challenges and Risks for Health Care Professionals', in Walter Vandereycken and Pierre J. V. Beumont (eds.), *Treating Eating Disorders: Ethical, Legal and Personal Issues* (New York: New York University Press, 1998), 1.

[2] M. Selvini Palazzoli, S. Cirillo, M. Selvini, and A. M. Sorrentino, *Ragazze anoressiche e bulimiche: La terapia familiare* (Milan: Cortina, 1998), 22–3, and 122.

[3] See e.g. S. Orbach, *Fat is a Feminist Issue* (New York: Hamlyn, 1978); B. Ehrenreich, *For her own Good: 150 Years of the Experts' Advice to Women* (London: Pluto Press, 1979); H. Malson, *The Thin Woman: Feminism, Post-Structuralism and the Social Psychology of Anorexia* (New York: Routledge, 1998); P. Fallon, *Feminist Perspective on Eating Disorders* (New York: Guilford Press, 1994).

[4] See e.g. Brian S. Turner, *The Body and Society: Explorations in Social Theory* (Oxford: Blackwell, 1984); S. Bordo, 'Anorexia Nervosa: Psychopathology as the Crystallization of Culture', *Philosophical Forum*, 17 (1985–6), 73–104; Jules R. Bemporad, 'Cultural and Historical Aspects of Eating Disorders', *Theoretical Medicine*, 18/4 (1997), 401–20.

disorder is most commonly manifested. The systemic approach considers the person with a mental condition as a part of a 'system' and analyses her behaviour in relation to the environment where she lives. All these studies suggest that eating disorders can be understood if viewed in the light of the environment in which the sufferer lives. Mara Selvini Palazzoli, for example, is one of the principal theorists of family therapy for eating disorders. She writes that she and her team started analysing the family because they wanted 'to see whether families with an anorexic patient presented common modalities of functioning, that could be considered typical of that kind of family'.[5]

Apart from showing the common modalities of functioning of eating-disordered families and societies, these studies often present these modalities as an *explanation* of eating disorders. These studies not only report at a *descriptive level* that these families and societies present common traits, and describe what these traits are; they go further, and normally present these traits as an *explanation* of the disorder. According to these studies, the reason why people develop eating anomalies is to be found (among other things) in the dynamics within the society and the family.

In this and in the next chapter, I will provide an account of the family and sociological studies of eating disorders. In Chapters 9 and 10 I will make a critical analysis of these studies. I will show that the explanations provided by these studies leave important questions unanswered. I will argue that the argument that eating disorders are the expression of family crises or of social crises is based on assumptions that are far from self-evident.

This critical analysis will confirm that eating disorders are a *moral issue*. They are the coherent implementation of moral values. In Chapter 10 I will also address the methodological problems involved in the explanation of eating disorders provided by systemic and sociological studies.

I will consider the family first. Family dynamics have always been considered as one of the principal factors in the development of eating disorders. Since the earliest studies of eating disorders, psychodynamic descriptions have stressed the importance of the family in the arousal of the disorder.[6]

One of the first systematic studies of the eating-disordered family was provided by Salvador Minuchin. According to Minuchin, there is a particular family context in which eating disorders appear. He called this a 'psychosomatic family'. These families, according to Minuchin, are clearly dysfunctional. Specific processes are typical of these families: rigidity, enmeshment, overinvolvement, and conflict avoidance. Although not being

[5] Selvini Palazzoli et al., *Ragazze anoressiche e bulimiche*, 22–3, 122.

[6] Mervat Nasser and Melanie Katzman, 'Sociocultural Theories of Eating Disorders: An Evaluation in Thought', in Janet Treasure, Ulrich Schmidt, and Eric van Furth (eds.), *Handbook of Eating Disorders* (2nd edn., Chichester: Wiley, 2003), ch. 8, pp. 139–50, at p. 139.

the sole cause for the disorder, such dynamics are an essential element in the development of eating disorders.[7]

Studies in 2003–4 have found that the families with an eating-disordered member are not such a homogeneous group as Minuchin originally thought. Moreover, it is agreed by the vast majority of experts that eating disorders are multifactorial: many different elements are today believed to lead to the disorder, not only the family. However, the relevance of family influences on the future eating-disordered person remains very little disputed. For example, research consistently reports that the eating-disordered person has typically suffered abnormal attachment patterns[8] and that the family is decisive in both the aetiology and the treatment of the disorder.[9]

2. *The Family of the Eating-Disordered Person*

Studies of the family of the eating-disordered person overall provide very consistent results.

> *Anorexic/bulimic illness occurs predominantly in relatively privileged sections of the community. Where upper- or middle-class status is not conferred explicitly by wealth or 'father's occupation', families have been found typically to be aspirant, either working to achieve higher social standing, or struggling to regain status that has been lost.*[10]

Families with an eating-disordered member are mainly middle-class families. In the vast majority of cases (89.4 per cent), parents live together, and the mother (81 per cent) has an extra-domestic job.[11] The values of these families are typical middle class (career, marriage, appearance). According to Duker and Slade, the Protestant values of work ethic are particularly congenial to these families.[12]

Richard Gordon has noticed that in these families moral connotations are attached to matters such as obesity, diet, and health. The majority of these families adopt a puritan ideal of self-control, and therefore consider fatness as a sign of indolence and self-indulgence. Ultimately fat symbolizes the

---

[7] S. Minuchin, *Families and Family Theory* (London: Routledge, 1991). For a discussion of Minuchin's theory, see Ivan Eisler, Daniel Le Grange, and Eia Asen, 'Family Interventions', in ibid., ch. 18, pp. 291–310, at p. 292.

[8] Anne Ward and Simon Gowers, 'Attachment and Childhood Development', in ibid., ch. 6, pp. 103–20, at p. 115.

[9] Eisler, Grange, Asen, 'Family Interventions', 291.

[10] Marilyn Duker and Roger Slade, *Anorexia and Bulimia: How to Help* (2nd edn., Buckingham: Open University Press, 2003), 124.

[11] Selvini Palazzoli et al., *Ragazze anoressiche bulimiche*, 22–3, 122. The study does not specify whether all fathers also have an extra-domestic job.

[12] Duker and Slade, *Anorexia and Bulimia*, 124.

'sins of the flesh', which include sexual sins. These families are highly 'sex-ophobic', and sex is never approached in any relaxed way. Pleasure is a luxury and must be subordinated to work and activity. In these contexts, Gordon points out, being busy is regarded as good: even feeling tired and exhausted is a sign of hard work.[13]

It is not possible to determine the exact reliability of these findings. In fact, it is possible that these types of families are those who are most prone to seek help, and therefore it is possible that the disorder arises equally in other parts of population who either do not conceptualize the person's behaviour as a problem, or as a psychological problem, or would not refer the eating-disordered person to a professional (see Chapter 1).

Families with an eating-disordered member are normally described as highly problematic.

Colleagues commonly comment that we 'must be tired of working with those people' or 'how do you stand it?' This attitude reflects a general belief that eating-disordered families are manipulative and resistant to change. In some instances our colleagues see the individual with the eating disorder as a victim of her disturbed family or at the opposite extreme as a scheming manipulator who is purposefully destroying her long suffering family in her search for attention. These views are usually derived from simplistic interpretations of the theories of specific schools of family therapy, such as the Structural [...] or Milan Strategic [...] school.[14]

Truly affective bonds are seldom found in these families. They appear overall as extremely rigid in their beliefs and behaviours.[15]

Mara Selvini Palazzoli, who has studied and worked with these families extensively, notices that in these families each member claims that he or she is doing a lot and is sacrificing him or herself for the others. In this way, nobody is really willing to take responsibility if anything goes wrong: everyone has done everything already. For example, the mothers generally profess their guilt for their daughter's illness in a rather theatrical way. However, they also typically argue that their fault is justified by an excess of zeal and dedication to the family. In this way they reconstruct and summarize their fault in a way that absolves them from any responsibility. If they have made any mistake, that was for an excess of *goodness*. Mara Selvini Palazzoli argues that normally fathers appear more balanced than the mothers, but their

---

[13] Richard Gordon, *Anoressia e bulimia: Anatomia di un'epidemia sociale* (Milan: Raffaello Cortina, 1991), 96. The English original text is *Anorexia and Bulimia: Anatomy of a Social Epidemic* (Oxford: Blackwell, 1990). See ch. 6.

[14] Jan B. Lackstrom and D. Blake Woodside, 'Families, Therapists and Family Therapy in Eating Disorders', in Vandereycken and Beumont (eds.), *Treating Eating Disorders*, 106–26, at 107.

[15] Ibid. 108.

attitude reveals a lack of interest and an unwillingness really to understand the sufferer's problems and to share responsibility for the family dynamics.[16]

3. *The Father of the Anorexic Person*

As we have seen above, most families that seek help for eating disorders share common features and values. In most cases, there is no history of separation or divorce. This is an interesting fact: in an era in which marital instability and separations are relatively common, these families appear as rigidly inseparable. The partners are unable, or unwilling, to make their marital crises explicit, and to articulate them in an open way.[17] Any crisis has to be suppressed. It cannot be addressed clearly.

The father of the eating-disordered member is often closed to dialogue with his wife. In this way, he refuses to spell out the problems of the family and consequently to cooperate in the finding of solutions to these problems.

Two modalities of behaviour are normally found in these fathers. One is submission. Some react to their wives' complaints with silence. When fathers choose this attitude, the children will either blame them for their 'cowardice' or pity them for their 'weakness'. Other fathers, instead, react by shouting. Although the method is different, in both cases the result is the same: they all silence the problematic issues and thus reject dialogue.

Typically the fathers of the eating-disordered person are highly dedicated to work. They are competitive and individualist hard workers who aim at professional success: they have to *do*, rather than to *speak*. These fathers are normally detached from their children, both emotionally and physically. They do not participate in the rearing of the children in the first years of their life. The children's upbringing is completely delegated to the mother. It is only during their adolescence that some meaningful interaction begins. Sometimes these fathers are violent, and it is not uncommon to find that they have sometimes physically abused their wife or children.

Their expectations of their daughters are likely to be ambivalent: on the one hand, they expect their daughters to adopt a conventional role. However, on the other hand, they want to be 'proud' of their daughters: they want competence and success.

Selvini Palazzoli and Colleagues argue that these fathers present the narcissistic traits that are common of their generation. There are, according to these authors, historical and cultural reasons for this. Normally these fathers

---

[16] For an account of the systemic model, see Elena Faccio, *Il disturbo alimentare: Modelli, ricerche e terapie* (Rome: Carocci, 1999), 78–9.

[17] Ibid. 152.

were born around the Second World War, and they have internalized a strongly male chauvinistic culture: the man has to be hard and must not show his feelings. His suffering has to be jealously hidden. No sign of frailty or weakness should be manifested. These men are described as emotionally deficient. Despite their efforts to appear strong and independent, the pillar of the family, emotionally they are highly dependent on their wives.

4. *The Mother of the Eating-Disordered Person*

The mothers of the eating-disordered person also have common traits.[18] As in the case of the fathers, to understand the personality of the mother, Palazzoli and Colleagues argue that it is essential to consider their cultural context. Within this context the woman is normally submissive to the needs of both the family and the husband. This submission is not simply financial. Even when the mother is financially independent, the emotional burden she bears is much higher than that of the husband. These mothers think they are the ones who have to fulfil the emotional needs of the children.

A related typical feature is their *sacrificial tendency*. These mothers want to do everything: they take over other people's tasks, they rarely ask for help even in emergencies, and they want to run the house unaided even if they have an extra-domestic job. They will behave like full-time housewives even if they are not. However, they are driven by a sense of duty, and this makes them blind both to their own affective and emotional needs, and those of others. Since they find it hard to reflect about themselves, they also find it difficult to reflect about others and understand them. This lack of introspection makes it impossible for them to concretize any meaningful communication.

One of the feelings that are invariably found and constantly hidden in these mothers is anger. They are angry about their sacrificial role. However, because they also want to keep that role, they will not express their anger openly. This, of course, does not mean that they will not express it at all. They will express it, but in more subtle ways. So their families become theatres of continuous arguments about the most futile issues, which is the symptom of an underlying aggression that is consistently silenced and hidden.[19]

Another feature of these mothers that has been held responsible for the arousal of the disorder in their daughters is the inability to respond to their call for food in early childhood. This hypothesis was first elaborated by

---

[18] For an account of the systemic model, see Elena Faccio, *Il disturbo alimentare: Modelli, ricerche e terapie* (Rome: Carocci, 1999), 159–67.

[19] Ibid. 61–2.

Hilde Bruch.[20] She argued that the mothers of anorexic patients had not been sensitive to their children's requests for food, which had impinged upon the child's capacity to have a correct perception of hunger and satiety. These mothers have generally been either repressive or too permissive; they would feed their babies, not according to the requests and signals sent by the babies themselves, but, instead, to predetermined timescales. The baby is thus prevented from learning how to recognize her physical sensations and needs. The baby who has not gone through this learning process is likely to become someone who will live according to the thoughts, feelings, and needs of others. She will always lack a firm sense of the self and will assume that her needs either do not count or cannot have any determinant influence on the external environment. Chapter 12 will further discuss the process through which we learn how to distinguish hunger and satiety and how the perception of hunger and satiety appears unrealistic in people with eating disorders.

The blindness of these mothers to their daughters' needs, so it seems, begins early in the baby's life. This, so it is argued, will have a decisive impact on the sense of inadequacy and lack of control that characterizes the psychological life of eating-disordered people.

The transmission of values from mother to daughter is also thought to account for the arousal of eating disorders. It has been argued that it is likely that the mothers have in some way encouraged their daughters to adopt a traditional nurturant female role (the one they have probably had—the one that is familiar to them). However, it is also likely that they have shown their daughters that, in order to survive, a woman needs to be independent—more independent than they have been. The message is contradictory: on the one hand, the future anorexic is taught to achieve high standards of performance at school and work, as she has to be independent and to rely on herself (men cannot be trusted—a daughter should not repeat her mother's mistakes). On the other hand, though, the daughter is also expected to be caring and sensitive towards the family, and to give priority to the needs and desires of others.

Brian Turner also points out that 'the anorexic family' is characterized by contradictory requests of their daughters. On the one hand, these families value competitive success, for example, in school and professional life; on the other hand, they also encourage submission rather than the autonomy and independence that are necessary to obtain the valued success.[21] This is reported as being the background of anorexia and bulimia nervosa sufferers.[22]

---

[20] Hilde Bruch, *Eating Disorders: Obesity, Anorexia Nervosa and the Person within* (London: Routledge and Kegan Paul, 1974), ch. 4.

[21] Turner, *The Body and Society*, 192.

[22] Duker and Slade, *Anorexia and Bulimia*, 127.

5. *The Family Expectations of the Future Eating-Disordered Person*

In this scenario of incommunicability, the person is submitted to a number of pressures and is required to meet determined standards, without any encouragement to introspection and consequently without a real understanding of her inclinations and needs. The affective needs of the future anorexic are overlooked.

I report here some descriptions of these families provided by clinical studies:

To the superficial observer, this may look like quite an ideal family. Generally, parents are completely dedicated to their work or to the house, they have a high sense of duty and of social and conventional norms [. . .] there was, in all cases, a permanent state of underlying tension . . . a marked inclination to endless and unnerving arguments about the most futile issues, which is symptomatic of a hidden aggressiveness which needs an outburst [. . .] the dominant figure, in the family of the anorexic, is the mother: the father is often emotionally absent [. . .] secretly or openly underestimated by his wife. Even in cases in which the father, thanks to his intolerant and dictatorial behaviour, seems to be the dominant figure, the mother wins [. . .] *stubbornly playing the part of the victim* [. . .] *The daughter easily becomes the victim of the mother* [. . .] the daughter is the ideal baby of an invasive, *intolerant and hypercritical mother* [. . .][23]

The mother, as we have also seen above, is normally very demanding of herself, but equally demanding of her daughter. She is often moved by a sense of duty in fulfilling her role, and is therefore blind to her own emotional needs. Being unused to introspection, she is also emotionally distant from the daughter. These mothers are described as

perfectionist mothers, who hold on to their belief that they have done everything they could for their family, in an attempt to preserve their self-esteem.[24]

Cases reported by psychotherapists unfailingly reveal the difficult role of the child, who is the *victim* of highly demanding parents. Notably, she is the *real victim*, as opposed to some other family member (for example, the mother), who just *plays the part of the victim*.

Hilde Bruch also provides important information on the family of the eating-disordered person, and on the relationship between the mother and the sufferer. In her major work, *Eating Disorders: Obesity, Anorexia Nervosa, and the Person within*, she reports a number of cases that all share similar characteristics. The common point seems to be that parents have high and inappropriate expectations of their children.

---

[23] Selvini Palazzoli et al., *Ragazze anoressiche e bulimiche*, 61–2; my emphasis and translation.
[24] Ibid. 132.

She needed her high class standing, not only for her own peace of mind, but also as an obligation she owed her parents, who, she feared, *would be disappointed if she were not quite so popular and superior* [...][25]

Her parents still did not believe that there could possibly be any psychological problems because Christine had been normal and happy to an unusual degree. She was the oldest of 4 children, had been very helpful with the younger ones, and had been the object of much praise and admiration. She had been a straight A student, had participated in sports and social activities, and had been popular. It was a shock to see that she hadn't done so well at the college entrance examinations, *as everybody had expected* [...] it was gradually recognized that her life had not been as idyllic as her parents had described. She had been born during the war when her father was overseas. An often-repeated anecdote was about how surprised her father had been when meeting his little 4-year old daughter. Pictures sent to him overseas had depicted her as a blonde curly-haired child; when her father met her she was a brunette with straight hair. To Christine this story was the symbol of *her having been a disappointment to her father* [...] She described in many details the agony of living a life of perfection, never being able to do what she wanted to do or felt like doing, always under the compulsion to do *what she felt was expected of her* [...][26]

6. Conclusions: The Effects of these Expectations on the Future Eating-Disordered Person and the Struggle for Control

Clinical and sociological studies consistently report that a person who is going to develop eating disorders is typically overwhelmed by familial pressures. As we shall see in Chapter 8, she is also overwhelmed by societal pressures. According to these studies, eating disorders may be regarded as a response to the high and contradictory expectations that are directed towards the person, either within the family or in the social environment, or in both. The person, according to this explanation, develops the syndrome in contrast to these expectations. Disordered eating, in other words, would be a defence against the inappropriate demands directed towards that person. The sufferer develops the syndrome specifically to confront these expectations, and thus to gain power and control over the surrounding environment as well as over her life. Chapter 9 will discuss this argument. Now we should look at what happens *outside* the family of the eating-disordered person, in the social environment. In the social environment, the person with eating disorders also faces a number of high and contradictory expectations.

[25] Bruch, *Eating Disorders*, 262, emphasis added.
[26] Ibid. 264, emphasis added.

8

The Society of the Person with Eating Disorders

1. *Introduction*

Eating disorders have always been thought to be related to social factors. They are found almost exclusively in Western countries[1] or Westernized societies. Medical literature does not report cases of eating disorders in developing countries. The almost exclusive presence of eating disorders in some areas of the world seems to be related to cultural rather than geographical factors. For example, eating disorders are registered in South Africa and in Santiago (Chile).[2] They are spreading in areas that are becoming more Westernized, such as Japan, or in areas that are becoming economically emancipated, such as China after Mao.[3] For these reasons, it is agreed that eating disorders are a culturally bound syndrome.

Moreover, eating disorders are a relatively recent syndrome (only in the most recent version of the *International Classification of Diseases*, the *ICD-10*, are eating disorders reported as an articulated and well-defined syndrome.[4] Anorexia made its appearance at a time when hysteria was declining. It was therefore thought that anorexia represented the way in which women responded to new social pressures. The idea was that, whereas hysteria was a response to sexual repression, anorexia was the expression of the social pressure to be thin.

As it is well known, eating disorders mainly affect women. Feminist studies therefore regard eating disorders as a gender problem. Anorexia is seen as representing 'a rebellion against the adult female form and all that is implied with being a woman in today's society—an effort to obtain an androgynous

---

[1] Richard Gordon, *Anorexia and Bulimia: Anatomy of a Social Epidemic* (Oxford: Blackwell, 1990), ch. 1.

[2] Ibid., ch. 3.2.

[3] Mara Selvini Palazzoli, S. Cirillo, M. Selvini, and A. M. Sorrentino, *Ragazze anoressiche e bulimiche: La terapia familiare* (Milan: Cortina, 1998), 201.

[4] World Health Organization, *International Classification of Diseases, ICD-10* (10th edn., Geneva: WHO, 1992).

physique at a time when men are still viewed as more powerful, as a mean of demonstrating mastery and control'.[5]

So why do eating disorders mainly affect women?

2. *Why Women?*

The argument of this book is that eating disorders are in an important sense a moral issue. In Chapters 5 and 6 I have argued that lightness is valuable as a means to moral perfection and moral integrity. Unless one takes into account a specific moral framework, eating-disordered behaviour appears impossible to understand. If this is true, why do mainly women adopt that behaviour? Is it because women are more sensitive than men to morality?

First, it is not true that eating disorders affect only women. Men are also affected, albeit in smaller numbers (see Chapter 1). Secondly, the ideal of 'self-sufficiency' and the capacity to 'master' our own emotions and reactions seems to apply strongly to men as well as to women. Many men adopt patterns of behaviour that are in many ways similar to eating disorders: many of them are as body conscious as eating-disordered people. For example they spend much time in the gym attempting to 'sculpt' their body and to 'control' what happens to it. This attempt to master the body may be seen as an expression of men's sensitivity to certain moral values of 'control' and 'transcendence' from the body. Self-esteem seems to be, for men as well as for women, related to the capacity to overcome the impulses of the body, and a certain type of 'figure' is the expression of an achievement that is ultimately moral in nature. Men, as well as women, should be able to show strength and will power, and to overcome the 'natural' tendency to laziness. These ideals are translated into the fight for control of the body by men as well as by women. The same moral ideals that seem to lead to eating-disordered behaviour in women may also direct men's lives in many ways.

However, although men appear to be sensitive to the same moral values that lead to disordered eating, the *search for lightness* seems to be a mainly 'female' prerogative. It is mainly women who seek lightness. This is probably one of the most puzzling aspects of eating disorders. Lightness is an ideal for both men and women, for what it signifies. We have seen in Chapter 6 that lightness is presented as a positive state for Lenin in the passage quoted from Tolstoy's *Anna Karenina*. The values symbolized by lightness are part of ordinary shared morality in Western societies. But if lightness is valuable for both men and women, why is it mainly women who struggle to become light?

[5] Mervat Nasser and Melanie Katzman, 'Sociocultural Theories of Eating Disorders: An Evaluation in Thought', in Janet Treasure, Ulrich Schmidt, and Eric van Furth (eds.), *Handbook of Eating Disorders* (2nd edn., Chichester: Wiley, 2003), ch. 8, pp. 139–50, at p. 141.

Anna Krugovoy Silver has tried to provide an answer to this question. She has argued that traditionally women have been seen as emotional beings, or more emotional than men, and therefore more in need of control and discipline. A woman's body has historically been connected with corruption and irrationality more than a man's. Women have, therefore, been subjected to higher pressure to conform to that ideal of 'transcendence of the body'.

From this point of view, whereas the ideal of lightness stands for both men and women, and both men and women are supposed to do something to conform to that ideal, women have had to do much more than men. It may be sufficient for a man 'not to let himself go' to exert some form of control over his body, but for a woman to feel that she is conforming to the ideal she has to deny her body as much as possible. And maybe this is also why *aesthetically* the pressure to be light has generally been higher on women than on men.

However, it is not fully clear why under the influence of similar pressures women become light whereas generally men do not. Further empirical studies are necessary better to understand men's motivations and the influence of social and cultural ideals on their behaviour. The response of men to the dominant moral framework in society is an important but under-explored field of study.

3. *Factors that are Thought to be Related to the Spread of Eating Disorders*

The fact that eating disorders have appeared in some societies in recent times, and that they mainly affect women have been thought by many to be connected. It is widely believed that the rise and spread of eating disorders are related to social changes that have taken places in these areas. The following social factors have been identified as significant to the rise and spread of eating disorders.

1. Centrality of the children in the family: whereas in the past children had a peripheral place within the family, during the twentieth century children become central to the family. The duties towards children are currently considered very important and being a good/bad parent is a socially discriminatory factor.
2. Longer dependency: the period of dependency of children upon their parent is extended.
3. Greater responsibility for the parents. 1 and 2 imply that parents have more responsibilities and for a longer period of time.
4. Change of the social/familial role of the woman.

5. Abundance of food.
6. The social imperative of thinness.[6]
7. The modification of eating habits (culinary multiculturalism, presence of fast foods; missing lunch; eating alone).
8. Sedentary life and increasing obesity rates (in 2003 30% of US population was classified as being obese).[7]

4. *The Role of Women in Modern Western Societies*

All these factors account for highly contradictory pressures. In particular, according to some authors, to understand eating disorders, one has to consider the experience of women through centuries. Anguish and a sense of inadequacy are two constant existential dimensions for women. But while they have been recurrent for centuries in the Western world, the way women defend themselves from these feelings is culturally and historically determined. The Western woman believes that 'thin is beautiful' and therefore can *concretize* her anguish in the adipose tissue of the thighs and buttocks. In the traditional Arabian countries, where 'fat is beautiful', a similar defence mechanism cannot be articulated.[8]

One of Europe's most influential studies of the sociocultural components of anorexia reports:

Undoubtedly innumerable cultural and social factors affect contemporary young women. Conflicting situations are multiplied, which predispose them to neurotic and psychotic reactions [...] We may list the following as the most important: the participation of the woman in [...] education [...] and [...] a career (as opposed to the previous, atavic tradition of feminine ignorance, submission, passive acquiescence to sexual and maternal tasks as the only possible valorisation), united with the undiminished, on the contrary, increased, female narcissism, stimulated by fashion, mass media [...] increased wealth. Basically, nowadays the woman is asked to be beautiful, elegant and well-kept, and to spend time on her looks; this, however, should not prevent her from competing intellectually with men and other women, from having a career, and also from falling romantically in love with a man, from being tender and sweet to him, from marrying him and from representing the ideal type of lover-wife and oblational mother, ready to give up her degrees [...] to deal with nappies and domestic stuff. It seems evident that the conflict between the many demands [...] represents a difficult challenge for adolescents, especially the most sensitive [...] To these predisposing pathogenic factors we may add some that are more specific: the fashion of being thin and sophisticated, the widespread propaganda

---

[6] Selvini Palazzoli et al., *Ragazze anoressiche e bulimiche*, 201; Gordon, *Anorexia and Bulimia*, ch. 3.2

[7] Nasser and Katzman, 'Sociocultural Theories', 145.

[8] Selvini Palazzoli et al., *Ragazze anoressiche e bulimiche*, 91.

for diets and slimming drugs, the continuous chatting, within the family and the peer group, about calories and weight, and, especially, the social ridicule that is reserved for Ruberesque women. Our cultural environment today does not accept the fat girl [...] Young women [...] become anorexic: this is the attempt of a fragile Self to refuse a passive role. The more the stimulus is ambiguous, the more the role is ambiguous, the more the situation is ambiguous, the more these women claim what they want in an extremely precise manner: being very, very thin as a denial of what they feel in themselves in conflict with the active and efficient role that social expectation seems to require of them.[9]

Although these comments were made in the 1960s, they are still quoted and are still relevant in the twenty-first century. Most authors relate the spread of eating disorders to social changes and to the way these have affected women. In particular, the changes in the role and expectations of women identify one of the possible explanations of eating disorders.

Hilde Bruch, for example, argues that one of the causes of the spread and prevalence of anorexia is the change in the status and expectations of women. This can cause serious problems of identity and of a sense of uncertainty.[10]

Richard Gordon also points out the significance of radical changes in the social expectations of women especially since the 1970s. He emphasizes that the demands to be successful, competitive, and independent express a system of values that is strongly in conflict with the traditional definition of the role of women in the West. Many women in Western societies suffer a sense of fragmentation, confusion, and insecurity and find it difficult to develop a functional identity. Gordon hypothesizes that the psychological problems of people with eating disorders are related to matters such as self-esteem, autonomy, and success. He argues that these problems reflect the much more pervasive conflicts about the role of women in wider cultural contexts. The sufferer unconsciously expresses a widespread cultural crisis.[11]

Like Mara Selvini Palazzoli, Gordon also points out the contradictory expectations of women in modern Western societies. He argues that the definition of the social role of women, and consequently of their psychological identity, is still unclear. The pressure on women is twofold: as well as the drive towards success and independence, there is still a pressure to comply with a traditional femininity, of beauty, compliance, and passivity. Research shows that only women who accept the 'ideology of the superwoman' manifest symptoms of eating disorders. Those who reject this stereotype are free

[9] M. Selvini Palazzoli, *L'anoressia mentale: Dalla terapia individuale alla terapia familiare* (9th edn., Milan: Feltrinelli, 1998), 75.

[10] Hilde Bruch, 'Four Decades of Eating Disorders', in D. M. Gardner and P. E. Garfinkle (eds.), *Handbook for the Psychotherapy of Anorexia Nervosa and Bulimia* (New York: Guilford Press, 1985), 9.

[11] Gordon, *Anorexia and Bulimia*, ch. 4.

from the disorders.[12] Gordon also reports research on the link between intellectual capacity and physical shape. Studies conducted by Silverstein and colleagues at New York University[13] show that, historically, the ideal of thinness has been predominant when women have had to demonstrate their intellectual capacities, whereas the stereotype of rounded shapes in women is associated with scarce intelligence and skills.[14]

Analogous considerations are found in the study of Morag MacSween. She points out that the social values of independence, competency, and intellectual productivity conflict with the values of passivity, dependency, and weakness, as well as with the decorative role of the woman. Whereas many women are able to combine the two conflicting demands, the person who develops eating disorders is unable to do so. She has internalized the imperative of being receptive to others' desires and needs, and, paradoxically, because of her 'feminine receptivity', she feels obliged to take over 'masculine' tasks. Paradoxically, because she accepts *one role* (the acquiescence to others' demands), she also feels obliged to accept the other (the demand to be successful and independent), and she is thus torn apart in two opposite directions.[15] MacSween also argues that eating disorders should be considered as generated by women's experience in the world. She argues that the social pressure to succeed in school and professional life, combined with the pressure to care for others, are crucial to the crisis that gives rise to eating disorders. This means, according to MacSween, that the confusion and the crisis of the anorexic are not due to her own disturbances and defects: it is rather the social world that is lacerated by conflicting expectations about the behaviour of adult women.[16] Chapter 10 will discuss these arguments and point out the logical problems involved in these types of claims.

---

[12] Ibid.

[13] B. Silverstein, B. Peterson, and L. Perdue, 'Some Correlates of the Thin Standard of Bodily Attractiveness for Women', *International Journal of Eating Disorders*, 5 (1986), 895–905; B. Silverstein, L. Perdue, L. Vogel, and D. A. Fantini, 'Possible Causes of the Thin Standard of Bodily Attractiveness for Women', *International Journal of Eating Disorders*, 5 (1986), 905–16; B. Silverstein and L. Perdue, 'The Relationship between Role Concerns, Preferences for Slimness, and Symptoms of Eating Problems among College Women', *Sex Roles*, 18 (1988), 101–6; B. Silverstein et al., 'Binging, Purging, and Estimates of Parental Attitudes regarding Female Achievement', *Sex Roles*, 19 (1988), 723–33, quoted in Richard Gordon, *Anoressia e bulimia: Anatomia di un'epidemia sociale* (Milan: Raffaello Cortina, 1991), 92; English version, ch. 5.

[14] Ibid. 93. English version, ch. 5.

[15] M. MacSween, *Corpi anoressici* (Milan: Feltrinelli, 1999), 39. The English original version is *Anorexic Bodies: A Feminist and Social Perspective* (London: Routledge, 1995); see ch. 2.4. See also Mary Briody Mahowald, 'To Be or Not To Be a Woman: Anorexia Nervosa, Normative Gender Roles, and Feminism', *Journal of Medicine and Philosophy*, 17 (1992), 233–51.

[16] MacSween, *Corpi anoressici*, 71. English version, ch. 3.3.

5. *Contradictory Aesthetic Expectations of Women*

Feminist studies have identified another set of contradictory expectations of women. These are aesthetic expectations. These expectations are contradictory in the sense that they are *unnatural* to women. They are in contrast with women's physiology.

Studies of women magazines, such as *Vogue* and the *Ladies Home Journal*, confirmed the tendency to privilege thinness in eras of increased education for women. Some studies analysed photos of models wearing bathing costumes or lingerie. The samples went back to the beginning of the twentieth century. The difference between torso and waist was minimal in the 1920s and in the late the 1960s and during the 1970s. During these times, the 'beautiful' woman was 'cylindrical' (no curves). Interestingly, at times when women are asked to undertake tasks that were traditionally assigned to men, they are also required to deny their femininity *aesthetically*.[17] They have to be and to look androgynous.

The aesthetic expectations that are today directed towards women also seem to reflect this androgynous ideal of woman. Lean—or openly emaciated—bodies with 'wide shoulders/narrow hips' seem to be preferred to the traditional model 'round breasts/round hips'. The 'wide shoulders/narrow hips' model of female beauty is clearly masculine, and therefore inadequate to the physiology of the woman. Also, given that the total percentage of essential fat in women, including the sex-specific fat, is four times higher than in men,[18] it is unrealistic to expect the vast majority of women to achieve the 'manlike' or openly emaciated look of mainstream women models.[19]

Although these aesthetical expectations are evidently unrealistic, it is argued that they are so firmly established that the value of the individual (especially of the young woman) is measured in terms of the way she looks; consequently, self-esteem is directly affected by the physical aspect (this has been called 'lookism')[20]. It should also be noted that each individual corresponds to a different somatotype. Since most of us will never reach the proportions of models, even if diet and training became our main activity, it is certainly possible that the omnipresence of ectomorphs in magazines and the media may induce people who correspond to different somatotypes to feel hopelessly inadequate ('big', 'ugly').

[17] Gordon, *Anoressia e bulimia*, ch. 5.5.

[18] Essential fat is the fat stored in the bone marrow, in the heart, lungs, liver, spleen, kidneys, intestines, muscles and lipid-rich tissues of the nervous system. Essential fat includes sex-specific fat, in females. This is thought to include deposits in the pelvic, buttock, and thigh regions.

[19] *Guardian*, 31 May 2000, www.guardian.co.uk/Archive/Article/ 0,4273,4023818,00.html.

[20] Selvini Palazzoli et al., *Ragazze anoressiche e bulimiche*, 215; S. Orbach, *Hunger Strike: The Anorectic's Struggle as a Metaphor for our Age* (London: Faber and Faber, 1986), 35–48.

Clinical and sociological studies fairly unanimously present eating disorders as a way to cope with the types of pressures that seem to overwhelm a person in both her family and her social life. Through the symptoms, the person tries to defend herself from these expectations and to achieve better control over others and over the social environment by whose requests she feels overwhelmed and in which she feels deeply inadequate.[21] The next section focuses on the potential of eating disorders to be a means of gaining power and control over the family and the social environment. In Chapter 10 I will offer a critical analysis of these arguments.

6. *Eating Disorders as a Response to Familial and Societal Expectations*

In an environment that pulls her in different directions, the person who develops eating disorders needs to find a way to gain control over her life. Many authors agree that the need for autonomy and control is central to the development of eating anomalies. MacSween, for example, gave a series of questionnaires to her patients. She asked them why they thought they had become anorexic. The most common answer was that they felt powerless in their environment and they needed to exert control over at least one portion of their life. Her patients normally claimed that they felt powerless because of their parents' power and expectations of them, but also because of the expectations of their friends or their school, or of their own expectations of themselves. Through diet these patients felt they were realizing some sort of control over their life and over others. Diet, MacSween points out, allows control and manipulation of the body—of one important section of a person's life.[22]

Once diet is chosen as a means to exert power and control, a complex series of rituals is articulated around food. These rituals concern both what and how to eat, and more generally the body. Only 'safe' food has to enter the body. Hence the distinction between 'safe' and 'dangerous' food. Everything needs to be controlled and scheduled: what to eat, how, when, and where. The chaos of appetite is regulated within a rigid scheme that relieves the sense of threat associated with eating. By controlling one of the most compelling impulses of the body, the person achieves a high sense of order and discipline.[23]

---

[21] Selvini Palazzoli, *L'anoressia mentale*, ch. 6.
[22] MacSween, *Corpi anoressici*, 201.
[23] Ibid. 203–4.

The arguments may be summarized as follows. The person who develops eating anomalies, being burdened by a number of high and contradictory expectations, feels inadequate, vulnerable, and fragile. Whatever she chooses, she is destined to fail: whatever she chooses, she will disappoint somebody or will fail in the achievement of significant social requests. Therefore she identifies an area of her life that is *her own*, to which others do not have access, and over which she will exert total control. The perception of her own impotence is the route that leads a person to develop a rigid and implacable control over food and the body. For her, control over the self is possible only in the realm of the body: everything else is in one way or another controlled by others—or so she feels. People with eating disorders, who feel powerless in the interaction with others, choose, as the only possible option that is open to them, to exert control over their body. Self-control satisfies their need for power, which remains unsatisfied in the relationship with others and the surrounding environment. People with eating disorders, because of the contradictory demands that are directed towards them, regularly have the sensation of being dominated by an external force. Therefore, the person *creates* a self-sufficient body, which refuses everything that comes from the external environment, and which is absolutely under control (or, at least, this is the ideal). This is why the body needs to be empty: emptiness concretizes freedom from intrusions and demands (see Chapter 5).

Some studies have also argued that historically, during periods of cultural transition, the body has been identified as the *locus of power*. Morbid forms of control over the body occur in periods of drastic social change. The notion of 'social predicament' has been coined. Social predicaments are 'painful social situations or circumstance, complex, unstable, morally charged and varying in their import in time and place'.[24] Social predicaments should uncode the metaphors implied in eating disorders.

Many clinical studies thus agree that eating disorders are a strategy to obtain power and control over the self, over others, and over the surrounding environment in general. Control over herself and control over others are synthesized in the control over eating and over the body. Through control over herself, the person obtains control over others: she gives shape to a sphere over which others have no power. Control over herself, thus, means control over others. The battle for control is rooted in the sense of impotence derived by the many contradictory expectations of the sufferer, and is a response to those expectations.

Virtually everybody agrees that eating disorders are a defence against the contradictory expectations of the sufferer. W. Vandereycken and R. Van Deth argue that eating disorders may be regarded as an attempt to impose a

---

[24] Nasser and Katzman, 'Sociocultural Theories', 139–50.

negotiation, or, at least, to call for attention.[25] Elena Faccio makes a similar observation.[26] Hilde Bruch also points out that, by controlling her eating, the person feels that she is gaining power over others. Bruch provides a detailed description of the positive reinforcements that give the person the strength to perpetuate her unpleasant situation.[27] Rosemary Shelley stresses that eating disorders may be a way to shift the attention of the family from other kinds of problems.[28] Again, the person utilizes abnormal eating rituals to control the external environment—in this case, to enforce a change, shifting the attention of her relatives. Similarly, Mara Selvini Palazzoli contends that, when the person performs her abnormal eating patterns, she has the 'certainty of having acquired power *over* others' (albeit an erroneous certainty).[29] More recently, Selvini Palazzoli and collaborators have used the following terms to describe this experience of power: 'To the inebriating experience of exerting control over hunger and over the body is added the similarly valuable experience of exerting control over the family and over the social environment, which are submitted to [the sufferer's] will.'[30]

The authors report the case of a chronic anorexic: while she tried to achieve control over her parents through her alimentary rituals, they, in turn, tried to persuade her to eat according to their own preferences. There was a 'fight for power' between the parties, and the weapon was 'food'. According to Mac-Sween, people with eating disorders are trying to maintain control over their life, but, as is clarified by Lawrence, in order to maintain control over our life, it is sometimes necessary to exert power over others.[31] Brian Turner's hypothesis is similar. He interprets eating-disordered behaviour as an attempt to obtain power over the body and, therefore, *over one's life as a whole*.[32]

7. *Conclusions*

The studies reported in this chapter and in the previous chapter provide precious sources of information on eating disorders. However, neither the

---

[25] Walter Vandereycken and Ron Van Deth, *From Fasting Saints to Anorexic Girls: The History of Self-Starvation* (London: Athlone Press, 1994), 91.

[26] Elena Faccio, *Il disturbo alimentare: Modelli, ricerche e terapie* (Rome: Carocci, 1999), ch. 1.

[27] Hilde Bruch, *The Golden Cage: The Enigma of Anorexia Nervosa* (London: Open Books, 1980), 5, 72–90.

[28] Rosemary Shelley, *Anorexics on Anorexia* (London: Jessica Kingsley, 1992), 5.

[29] Selvini Palazzoli, *L'anoressia mentale*, 16, my translation.

[30] Selvini Palazzoli et al., *Ragazze anoressiche e bulimiche*, 54.

[31] Marlin Lawrence, 'Anorexia Nervosa: The Control Paradox', *Women's Studies International Quarterly*, 2 (1979), 93.

[32] Brian S. Turner, *The Body and Society: Explorations in Social Theory* (Oxford: Blackwell, 1984), chs. 4, 8, pp. 195–6.

types of interactions that take place within a given context, nor the kind and number of expectations directed towards a person, are able to explain *why* it happens that people suffer, and why eating disorders may somehow give them power or control over others.

All the studies reported above, in fact, assume two things: first, that it is normal and obvious that, if significant others have inappropriate expectations of us, we shall suffer; and, secondly, that controlling eating, rather than adopting other types of behaviour, is a means to power.

None of these claims is self-evident. It is not self-evident that people are 'made to suffer' by the inappropriate expectations directed towards them; and it is by no means self-evident that people should seek power through control over their body and through *suffering*.

The next chapter will thus pose and answer two questions:

1. Why does it happen that people are 'made to suffer' by the inappropriate expectations directed towards them?
2. Why are eating disorders experienced as a means of obtaining some form of control over the surrounding environment? Why do people with eating disorders feel that suffering, instead of, for example, singing or laughing will empower them?

Once these questions are answered, it will become evident that eating disorders are not a problem of *expectations*, as clinical and sociological studies agree; they are a problem of *morality*. They do not depend on the fact that the person has been or is burdened with high and contradictory expectations that she is unable to meet. Eating disorders depend on a moral logic that is shared by the sufferer herself. What need to be unmasked, therefore, are not familial or societal expectations, but the way people *think* morally of themselves and others. This way of thinking may be called 'a moral logic'.

9

Victims or Persecutors? The Moral Logic at the Heart of Eating Disorders

Quelles voix! quels cris! Quels gémissements!
Qui a renfermé dans ces cachots tous ces cadavres plaintifs?
Quels crimes ont commis tous ces malheureux?
Les uns se frappent la poitrine avec des cailloux; d'autres se déchirent le corps avec des ongles de fer; tous ont les regrets, la douleur et la mort dans les yeux.
Qui les condamne à ces tourments? [...] Quel est donc ce Dieu? [...] Un Dieu [...] trouverait-il du plaisir à se baigner dans les larmes?

What voices! What screams! What groans!
Who has locked in these dungeons all these groaning corpses?
Which crimes have all these unfortunate people committed?
Some of them hit their chest with stones; others tear their bodies with nails of iron; all have regrets, pain and death in the eyes.
Who is condemning them to these torments? [...] Who is this God then? [...] Would a God [...] find pleasure in bathing in tears?[1]

E guardano in alto, trafitti dal sole
Gli spasimi di un redentore.
Confusi alla folla ti seguono muti
Sgomenti al pensiero che tu li saluti
A redimere il mondo, gli serve pensare,
Il tuo sangue può certo bastare.
La semineranno per mari e per terra,
Per boschi e città la tua Buona Novella...

And they look up, wounded by the sun,
at the spasms of a redeemer.
Confused in the crowd, they silently follow you

An earlier version of this paper has been published as Simona Giordano, 'Persecutors or Victims? The Moral Logic at the Heart of Eating Disorders', *Health Care Analysis*, 11/3 (2003), 219–28. I wish to thank Prof. Søren Holm and Prof. John Harris, who have read and commented on early versions of this paper. My gratitude also goes to Dr Raphaelle Bermond for the translation of Diderot from French into English, and Mr Steve Lambert for having proof-read the text.

[1] D. Diderot, *Pensées philosophiques* (Paris: Garnier-Flammarion, 1746), 35.

surprised to see that you greet them.
They need to think that your blood
is certainly enough to redeem the world.
They will spread by sea and by land
Through the woods and through the cities
Your Good News...[2]

1. *Introduction*

Clinical and sociological studies have looked for an explanation of eating disorders in the relational systems—family and society[3]—in which they mainly arise. It is now widely agreed that eating disorders are not only the result of a dysfunction within the person, or the symptoms of a totally internal or intra-psychical (dysfunctional) mechanism, but are significantly linked to the relationships that take place within these systems.[4] As we have seen in Chapters 7 and 8, the person who develops eating disorders is typically overwhelmed by family and social pressures,[5] and develops the syndrome especially to confront these expectations, and thus to gain power and control over her surrounding environment as well as over her life.[6] This sort of explanation leaves important questions unanswered.

2. *Why are People Made to Suffer by Others' Inappropriate Expectations?*

It may seem obvious that people are sometimes made to suffer an excess of inappropriate[7] expectations (as we have seen in Chapter 7, clinicians refer to the person with eating disorders as a *victim*, or as the *real victim*, as opposed

---

[2] F. De André, *Via della Croce* (Milan: Edizioni Musicali BGM Ricordi, 1971). My translation from Italian into English.

[3] 'Relational system' refers to the context (family/society) in which the disorder is mainly found. According to the 'systemic approach', the psychic suffering results from an adaptation to an illogical and dysfunctional system. J. Haley, 'The Family of the Schizophrenic: A Model System', *Journal of Neurologic and Mental Disorders*, 129 (1959), 357–74.

[4] M. Selvini Palazzoli, *L'anoressia mentale: Dalla terapia individuale alla terapia familiare* (Milan: Feltrinelli, 1981), 224.

[5] Ibid.

[6] Walter Vandereycken and Ron Van Deth, *From Fasting Saints to Anorexic Girls: The History of Self-Starvation* (London: Athlone Press, 1994).

[7] 'Inappropriate' here means unreasonable, or unreasonably high when considering the person towards whom they are directed. For example, it may be realistic or appropriate to expect *some people* to excel at school and to study four hours every afternoon. It may be unrealistic or inappropriate to expect the same thing of *other people*.

to some other member of the relational system, who just *plays the part of the victim*). However, contrary to what one might think, it is not at all self-evident that the inappropriate expectations that others have of us should cause us suffering.

If we ask why a person is made to suffer by others' inappropriate expectations of her, clearly we cannot answer 'because others have inappropriate expectations of her'. Any similar answer ('because their expectations are inappropriate'; 'because she suffers when others have inappropriate expectations') would be tautological. There are deeper reasons that explain why we may suffer when others have inappropriate expectations of us, beyond the mere fact that others have inappropriate expectations. These reasons, as we are now going to see, are *moral* in nature.

There are two senses in which we may 'suffer' in these cases: one is that we may 'feel bad' about being unable to fulfil these expectations; the other is that we see in these expectations a lack of understanding of us ('if they really understood and accepted me, they would not expect this of me'). In both cases, we seem to think that a *moral wrong* is involved in the disappointment. If we perceive ourselves as the ones who disappoint, we feel *guilty*. If we perceive ourselves as the ones who are being disappointed ('they should not expect that of us'), then they are the ones who *should feel guilty*.

The person who 'feels bad' because 'she is disappointing' someone has thus accepted and absorbed a way of thinking according to which disappointing is something one should feel bad about. But, according to the same logic, those who raise expectations that are too high also disappoint that person, by making demands that reveal a failure to understand and accept the person's inclinations and needs. This way of thinking may be called *moral logic*.

Within the systems in which interactions are articulated around the dynamics of 'expectations-disappointments', such as the eating-disordered systems, it is inappropriate to talk about *persecutors*, on the one hand, and *victims*, on the other, as if they were two groups that confront each other. If the victim is the person of whom 'such and such is expected', and the persecutor is the person 'who expects such and such', then both are both. The victim, by the time she thinks of herself as a victim, automatically becomes a persecutor: she has absorbed the belief that disappointing others is *wrong*, therefore she thinks she may *rightly expect* others to modify their *wrong* expectations of her, and will blame them if they do not. The *persecutors* automatically become *victims*: they are expected to show understanding, to modify their expectations, and will be blamed if they do not. In these systems, therefore, the relationship between victim and persecutors is circular.

The Gestalt picture featured exemplifies well the relationship between the victim and the persecutors in eating-disordered systems. This relationship is not like the one between the two profiles that confront each other, but is like the one between the profiles and the vase: each of the two *is* the other and would not be as it is, if it were not the other at the same time. We can see the thing in two different ways, but the one and the other are the same thing, just seen in two different ways.

Persecutors or victims?

It thus seems that the eating-disordered person is made to suffer not by the expectations, but *by the feeling of being wronged*. Therefore she suffers because she accepts a determined set of moral beliefs and interacts with others accordingly.

This has important ethical and clinical implications. In fact, this means that reactions—such as suffering—and the behaviour that inevitably seems to follow that suffering are not things that *obviously happen* given the circumstances, but are the result of dynamics that people, at some level, direct and control. This also means, as we have seen in previous chapters, that any meaningful intervention involves exploring the morality at the heart of eating disorders, and questioning widely shared moral beliefs.

Now we should turn to the second issue: why people feel that eating disorders will give them power over the surrounding environment.

3. *What Makes People Treat Eating Behaviours as an Instrument of Power?*

According to clinical studies, the suffering involved in eating disorders is meant to *empower* the sufferer and to give her control over others and the surrounding environment. The misery, thus, instead of making the sufferer 'more vulnerable', is experienced as a means of empowerment. The more abnormal eating weakens the person with eating disorders, the more she experiences herself as invulnerable.[8]

However, it is not clear why a person may feel empowered by the suffering she inflicts on herself. Why do people who want to gain power impose

[8] Simona Giordano, 'Qu'un souffle de vent', *Medical Humanities*, 28 (2002), 3–8.

suffering on themselves? Why do they not make themselves happy instead? Or make themselves more beautiful, or blonde, or tanned? Why do they not sing and dance instead of suffering? *Why suffer?*

The answer is in *the question*. They make themselves miserable because suffering is in fact an instrument of power. Hunger strikers, to take an obvious example, use suffering in the same way.[9] More generally, it is not unusual to see people displaying their misery to various degrees and in various sorts of circumstances to achieve the same goal—that is, better control over others.[10]

We are also all familiar with the old and macabre tale of a God who kills 'His one and only Son that everyone who believes in him should not perish' (John 3: 16), another example of the power of suffering. In order to enforce a change in the destiny of humankind, to redeem and to save it, God utilizes *tears and suffering*. And all of us, at some time and to varying degrees, display misery in order to obtain something.

A moral belief is the basis of this potential of suffering—namely, that suffering is something we should be sorry for and do something about.[11] While it is believed that we should feel sorry for each other's misery and do something about it, displaying our suffering and making others feel sorry (or guilty, if they are somewhat responsible for it) represent an important instrument of power and control over them. In fact, as Szasz pointed out, guilty feelings are important mental constraints;[12] therefore, blame and inducement to feel guilty are powerful instruments of control. When we feel guilty, we are more likely to delegate a part of our control over ourselves and over things that are in our power. Feeling guilty makes us more open to question our conduct and to negotiate. For this reason, redemptive value is generally attached to the feeling of guilt.

These considerations help us understand why a person with eating disorders may feel that inflicting torments on herself, sometimes up to the point of dying, might *empower* her. Eating disorders are an *exhibition* of sacrifice and suffering. In their dichotomy of hiding and displaying, they are unfailingly addressed to others, and may have a resonance in the surrounding

[9] On similarities and differences between hunger strikes and eating disorders, see e.g. Rebecca Dresser, 'Feeding the Hungry Artists: Legal Issues in Treating Anorexia Nervosa', *Wisconsin Law Review*, 2 (1984), 297–374; Richard Gordon, *Anorexia and Bulimia: Anatomy of a Social Epidemic* (Oxford: Blackwell, 1990), ch. 8; Elena Faccio, *Il disturbo alimentare: Modelli, ricerche e terapie* (Rome: Carocci, 1999), ch. 1.

[10] One may certainly ask why they induce suffering through abnormal eating patterns rather than adopting some other modality of behaviour—that is, why do they develop 'eating disorders' rather than, say, 'breathing' disorders or some other type of disorder. The answer cannot be provided here, but considerations on the value of suffering resulting from food control may be found in Giordano, 'Qu'un souffle de vent'.

[11] Thomas Szasz, *The Myth of Mental Illness* (London: Paladin, 1984), 20.

[12] Ibid.

environment because they are a *displayed misery*. Eating disorders are the consistent claim of a person's presumed right (which she believes herself to have) to be listened to and understood, and to the modification of others' attitudes towards her (which she conceptualizes as *morally wrong*). They are in effect a strategy of power because they are implemented in contexts in which it is believed that we should feel sorry for other people's suffering and do something about it,[13] and in which a moral logic is articulated around this belief. In these contexts, it is not unreasonable of the eating-disordered person to expect her disorder to enhance her power over the surrounding environment, and that others will be more open to negotiation, will be more willing to delegate their power, and will eventually surrender to her displayed misery.

4. *Conclusions*

According to clinical studies, one of the factors that explain the onset of the disorder is the excess of expectations that both family and society direct towards the person who is developing the syndrome. The eating-disordered person, it is often argued, lives in a highly dysfunctional family and a burdensome society. She is a 'vulnerable member' of the system. She is made to suffer from high and contradictory demands, and develops the syndrome to contradict them.

As we have seen, however, it is not as obvious as it may seem that people 'are made to suffer' by others' expectations of them. If the arguments elaborated here are persuasive, the conclusion is that people are not made to suffer by dysfunctional systems. They are instead made to suffer by their own adherence to a moral logic within which disappointment is experienced as morally wrong.

We have also seen that, according to clinical studies, people develop eating anomalies to fight against this excess of expectations, and therefore to obtain the needed power and control over the surrounding environment. I have asked why eating anomalies may be considered an instrument of power. We have seen that this is also linked to the belief that 'causing suffering is wrong'. Where this belief is accepted, sacrifice and suffering become powerful instruments of control, and displaying misery becomes an appropriate and consistent instrument of power.

Eating disorders are thus the expression of the way in which people *think of*, and *judge*, interpersonal relationships occurring within their relational systems. Eating disorders are impossible to understand and to resolve unless the moral logic that underlies these systems is also understood. It seems to follow that any meaningful intervention should involve a direct analysis of

---

[13] Thomas Szasz, *The Myth of Mental Illness* (London: Paladin, 1984), 20.

the moral beliefs and of the moral logic that is at the heart of eating-disordered behaviour. Any other intervention (such as campaigns against thin models pictured in magazines and the media) taken alone, will probably provide little help. It should be noticed that an analysis of this underlying morality involves many conceptual difficulties. Resistance to critical analysis of this moral logic may also be understandable.[14]

A critical analysis of morality underlying eating disorders, however difficult it may be, will bring great benefit to the sufferers. Thanks to such an analysis, they may be made aware that their suffering is based neither on 'the misfortune of an illness' nor on what other people or society 'expect of them', but rather on what *they* believe or are prepared to believe, and on how *they* *choose* to act on the basis of the beliefs they accept.

---

[14] Morality obviously has an important function in the preservation of the human species. See e.g. Konrad Lorenz, *On Aggression* (London: Methuen, 1967), 94.

10

A Critique of the Systemic and Sociological Approaches to Eating Disorders

1. *Introduction*

As we have seen in the previous chapters, many experts have asked whether there are identifiable familial or social factors that could lead to eating disorders. In particular, sociological,[1] feminist,[2] and systemic analyses have tried to assess whether there are variables that are typical of the families and societies in which eating disorders are found and that may explain the arousal of the disorder.

Systemic analyses have had particular fortune in the field of eating disorders. They have led to the articulation of family therapies. The systemic approach to eating disorders derives from Haley's studies of the families of people with schizophrenia. In his 'The Family of the Schizophrenic: A Model System', Haley proposed a theoretical model to describe the family with a schizophrenic member in terms of interactional system.[3]

The systemic model articulates an original methodology that takes into account a cybernetic general theory of systems and a pragmatic study of human communication. The fundamental assumption of any systemic approach to mental diseases is that any mental disorder is the result of an adaptation to an illogic and deviant relational system. Any mental disorder is thus a transactional problem. This model represents a radical departure from the classic psychoanalytic model and from the psychodynamic model derived

---

[1] See e.g. Brian S. Turner, *The Body and Society: Explorations in Social Theory* (Oxford: Blackwell, 1984); S. Bordo, 'Anorexia Nervosa: Psychopathology as the Crystallization of Culture', *Philosophical Forum,* 17 (1985–6), 73–104; Jules R. Bemporad, 'Cultural and Historical Aspects of Eating Disorders', *Theoretical Medicine,* 18/4 (1997), 401–20.

[2] See e.g. S. Orbach, *Fat is a Feminist Issue* (New York: Hamlyn, 1978); B. Ehrenreich, *For her Own Good: 150 Years of the Experts' Advice to Women* (London: Pluto Press, 1979); H. Malson, *The Thin Woman: Feminism, Post-Structuralism and the Social Psychology of Anorexia* (New York: Routledge, 1998); P. Fallon, *Feminist Perspective on Eating Disorders* (New York: Guilford Press, 1994).

[3] J. Haley, 'The Family of the Schizophrenic: A Model System', *Journal of Neurologic and Mental Disorders,* 129 (1959), 357–74.

from it. Whilst the psychodynamic approach focuses on the individual, on her mental experiences, and on her past experiences, the systemic approach widens its field of observation to the significant others. The subjects of the analysis may be two (for example, the mother and her daughter), three (the sufferer and her parents), more than three (the whole family), indeterminate (the sufferer and her social context), or intergenerational (it may include the parents of the sufferer's parents).

This approach has been further articulated and applied to eating disorders, and, as mentioned above, it has led to the development of family therapy. Although many different therapies are available for treating eating disorders (for example, psychoanalytic therapy, cognitive behavioural psychotherapy, hypnobehavioural psychotherapy, interpersonal psychotherapy), there seems to be 'evidence that the best method of treatment is to work with the family'.[4] There are today two major schools of family therapy, based on the systemic approach: the 'Structural', elaborated by Salvador Minuchin,[5] and the 'Milan Strategic', elaborated by Mara Selvini Palazzoli.[6]

One of the most influential authors to apply the theory of systems to the study of families with an anorexic member is Mara Selvini Palazzoli. Selvini Palazzoli and her team write that their aim was 'to see whether families with an anorexic patient presented common modalities of functioning, which could be considered typical of that type of family'.[7] From her study, it seems that the way family members interact with the future anorexic is crucial to the genesis of eating disorders. Minuchin, as we have seen in Chapter 7, called the eating-disordered family a 'psychosomatic family'. He argued that these families are clearly dysfunctional, and are characterized by specific and identifiable processes (conflict avoidance, for example, and others – see Chapter 7). He also argued that such dynamics are an essential element in the development of eating disorders.[8] Other authors also point out the importance of the way family members interact with the (future) anorexic. It has, for example, been argued that the modalities of interactions that

[4] Günter Rathner, 'A Plea against Compulsory Treatment of Anorexia Nervosa Patients', in Walter Vandereycken and Pierre J. V. Beumont (eds.), *Treating Eating Disorders: Ethical, Legal and Personal Issues* (New York: New York University Press, 1998), 198.

[5] S. Minuchin, *Families and Family Theory* (London: Routledge, 1981).

[6] M. Selvini Palazzoli, *L'anoressia mentale', Dalla terapia individuale alla terapia familiare* (9th edn., Milan: Feltrinelli, 1998), 224.

[7] Ibid. 224, my translation.

[8] Minuchin, *Families and Family Theory*. For a discussion of Minuchin's theory, see Ivan Eisler, Daniel Le Grange, and Eia Asen, 'Family Interventions', in Janet Treasure, Ulrich Schmidt, and Eric van Furth (eds.), *Handbook of Eating Disorders* (2nd edn., Chichester: Wiley, 2003), ch. 18, pp. 291–310, at p. 292.

are found in eating-disordered families are so clear and typical that these families may be defined as 'generative of eating disorders'.[9]

Although not everybody agrees that the family dynamics are so homogeneous and well identifiable,[10] it is generally accepted that eating disorders are not only the result of a dysfunction *within* the person, but are significantly linked to the relationships that take place within the contexts in which the sufferer lives.[11]

Eating-disordered behaviour would be the expression of the problems of the family (Chapter 7) and not the expression of the problems of the person herself. Similarly, sociological studies have argued that anorexia is the expression of *social crises* concerning the role of the woman—again, not a problem of the person, but the expression of the problems of the system (Chapter 8).

These types of arguments may appear straightforward, but the claim is sometimes a very strong one: from the point of view of the systemic approach, the symptoms are 'the *effect* of a complex labyrinth of family relationships'.[12]

I will not attempt a clinical evaluation of these studies. Sociological and systemic analyses of eating disorders provide information that is essential to the understanding of the phenomenon. They offer detailed descriptions of the contexts where the disorders most typically arise, and therefore are certainly of great interest to all those concerned with eating disorders. However, they meet with some methodological difficulties. There are three major problems with these types of analysis.

The first is that they risk falling into the same 'moral logic' that is at the heart of eating disorders (Section 2).

The second problem concerns the interpretation of empirical data in terms of *causes* of eating disorders, or in terms of factors that *explain* why people develop eating disorders (Section 3). The problem of the interpretation of empirical data as causal explanations is a complex one. It is generally accepted that eating disorders have 'multifactorial' causes. This means that many different factors are thought to play a role in the arousal and maintenance of the disorders. Most practitioners would probably not be primarily interested in determining the 'only or main cause' of eating disorders. They

[9] Valeria Ugazio, 'La semantica de potere: Anoressia, bulimia e altri affanni alimentari', in Ugazio, *Storie permesse storie proibite: Polarità semantiche familiari e psicopatologiche* (Turin: Bollati Boringhieri, 1988).

[10] Anne Ward and Simon Gowers, 'Attachment and Childhood Development', in Treasure, Schmidt and van Furth (eds.), *Handbook of Eating Disorders*, 2nd edn., ch. 6, pp. 103–20, at p. 115.

[11] Selvini Palazzoli, *L'anoressia mentale*, 224.

[12] Mara Selvini Palazzoli, S. Cirillo, M. Selvini, and A. M. Sorrentino, *Ragazze anoressiche e bulimiche: La terapia familiare* (Milan: Cortina, 1998), 51, emphasis added.

would probably be primarily concerned with how to treat the condition and the prognosis, independently of 'the cause(s)'. Most practitioners probably do not believe that there is only one or one major cause of eating disorders, but many different factors that contribute to the arousal of the condition. Despite the fact that most practitioners would probably not commit themselves to any specific causal explanation of eating disorders, or would at most claim that there are many possible causes of eating disorders, there are theoretical issues that need to be clarified in relation to both clinical practice and scientific explanations of eating disorders. Some authors have presented social and family dynamics as causal explanations of eating disorders, and I will highlight the theoretical difficulties involved in these ways of presenting the problem.

The third problem is that these studies sometimes seem to suggest that external forces beyond the individual's control determine that she will develop eating disorders, or suffer psychological problems. Moreover, her suffering is also presented as something beyond her control (determinism) (see Section 4).

I will discuss these three problems in the next section.

2. *The Need for Neutrality in the Analysis of Mental Phenomena*

The first problem is that sociological and systemic analyses in some instances reinforce the moral logic that supports eating disorders. It is generally accepted that a clinical analysis of mental conditions should be 'neutral'. The patient should never feel 'judged', and should feel free to express emotional and psychological content without having the impression of being 'censured'. Moral neutrality is one of the pillars of psychological analyses. It has been argued that 'the shift from a blaming stance to a more neutral position helps everyone'.[13]

Indeed, whereas the concept itself of *mental illness* has been discussed for a long time, and often criticized, even those who do not agree with the conceptualization of human behaviour in terms of 'mental illness' recognize that psychiatric categories have at least one potentially positive side: they have a 'neutralizing' power.[14] If the 'odd' behaviour of the person is 'the symptom' of a mental illness, then the person is not 'guilty' or 'responsible' for it.[15] Or, at least, her responsibility/guilt is diminished.

---

[13] Jan B. Lackstrom and D. Blake Woodside, 'Families, Therapists and Family Therapy in Eating Disorders', in Beumont and Vandereycken (eds.), *Treating Eating Disorders*, 107.

[14] See e.g. G. Jervis, *Manuale critico di psichiatria* (5th edn., Milan: Feltrinelli, 1997), ch. 3; C. Dunn, *Ethical Issues in Mental Illness* (Aldershot: Ashgate, 1998), 23–4.

[15] T. Szasz, *The Myth of Mental Illness* (London: Paladin, 1984), 27.

Despite the fact that neutrality seems indispensable to a correct interpretation of human behaviour and experiences, a strong tendency may be registered to attach moral value to facts that are a part of our psychological life. This tendency is often manifest in everyday life, and is also sometimes detectable in the analysis of eating disorders. I quote only one illustrative example.

While discussing the way the members of the family interact with the person with eating disorders, Valeria Ugazio writes that 'their apparently *good intentions* often reveal a *false and manipulative* tone'.[16] She notices that peculiar recurrent dichotomies characterize the families of the eating-disordered person. One of these, she argues, is the dichotomy 'cooperation/abuse'. The antonym of 'cooperation', for one who wishes to be neutral, is 'competition' and not 'abuse'. The word 'abuse' has an immediate moral connotation. The same may be said about the adjectives 'false' and 'manipulative'.

It is not uncommon to find that the person with eating disorders is presented as a 'victim' of familial (or social) factors, or, at the other extreme, that she is the manipulator who is trying to submit everybody to her iron will. Some psychiatrists report: 'In some instances our colleagues see the individual with the eating disorder as a *victim* of her disturbed family or at the opposite extreme as a *scheming manipulator* who is purposefully destroying her long suffering family in her search for attention.'[17]

As Chapters 7 and 8 have shown, clinical and sociological literature is replete with attempts to explain eating disorders in terms of family and social dynamics. The eating-disordered person is presented in turn as the victim of her parents' unresolved problems, of generational splits, of social crises, of inappropriate or contradictory expectations, and so on. Clinical and sociological literature is full of similar claims. Finding an explanation for eating disorders seems to amount to finding someone or something that is responsible for the arousal of the condition, and the scapegoat may be, in turn, the society, the family, the genetic material, the hormones, the hypothalamus, and so on.

But when the scapegoat is the family or the society, the line between empirical observation and moral judgement is a fine one. To take just one example, saying that the father's emotional absence contributes to the development of eating disorders is very near to saying that the father is partly responsible (or 'guilty') for the person's suffering. Responsibility here is understood as 'guilt', given the ordinary assumption that 'causing suffering is wrong'. Again, we are moving within the moral categories that give shape

---

[16] Ugazio, 'La semantica', my translation and emphasis.

[17] Lackstrom and Woodside, 'Families, Therapists and Family Therapy in Eating Disorders', 106, emphasis added.

to eating disorders. Chapter 9 has shown that the belief that 'causing suffering is wrong' is one of the pillars of eating disorders.

Thus, on the one hand, we conceptualize abnormal eating as an illness. Normally sufferers are not openly accused of 'having developed eating disorders'—they are usually protected from moral judgement. However, on the other hand, people with eating disorders are also often, more or less explicitly, presented as the 'victims' of peculiar familial or social interactions. Thus they are not presented as *guilty*, but still as the object of other people's *faults*. Obviously, where there is a 'victim', there is a 'persecutor', and, as persecuting is a moral wrong, the morality that was turned out of the window (by the clinical diagnosis) then comes in again by the door. If the psychiatric diagnosis has the positive 'neutralizing' effect, this is limited to the 'ill person'. She is not deemed guilty, but others are. The moral logic that is at the heart of eating disorders is in this way reinforced. It is implicitly 'approved' by the analyst, who adopts it in his or her analysis.

3. *'Whatever has a Beginning has also a Cause of Existence':* *The Logical Fallacy Involved in the Search for the Causes* *of Eating Disorders*

The second problem concerns the interpretation of empirical data in terms of causes of the condition. Sociological and systemic empirical observations of the contexts in which eating disorders most typically arise certainly offer a valuable contribution to the understanding of the condition, as they provide detailed descriptions of the contexts where eating-disordered people live. They provide elements on which we can and should reflect, and therefore the following observations should not be understood as a critique of the value of these disciplines. However, these analyses often meet with methodological problems. One of these problems is the interpretation of typical features of families and societies in which the disorder is manifested in terms of *causes* of the disorder.[18]

Empirical observation shows that there are features that are typical of these families and societies. Such features are often presented as characteristics that are *able to explain* the condition.[19] However, the shift from an empirical, descriptive level (one that says that there are recurrent traits in these families and societies) to an explicative level (one that says that these traits are the cause of eating disorders) needs to be justified. This shift, unless

---

[18] D. Hume, *Treatise of Human Nature* (Oxford: Oxford University Press, 1967), 74.

[19] See e.g. Hilde Bruch, *Eating Disorders: Obesity, Anorexia Nervosa and the Person within* (London: Routledge and Kegan Paul, 1974), ch. 5.

properly justified, risks being logically fallacious. We should explain why sociological and systemic approaches risk incurring such a logical error.

These studies take their point of departure, as do many studies of eating disorders, from the question: *why do people develop eating disorders?* In other words, in virtually all studies of eating disorders a search for the *causes* of the problem is implied.

The belief that eating disorders must have a cause responds to an *intuitive certainty*. As was pointed out, a long time ago, by David Hume, we have the *intuitive certainty* that everything must have a cause: 'Whatever has a beginning has also a cause of existence.'[20] The fact that eating disorders are generally considered as an illness reinforces the idea that they must depend on some cause, which may still be unknown. In fact, it is commonly assumed that all illnesses have a cause, which may be either organic or psychological.

However, as Hume pointed out, it is one thing to verify, by empirical observation, that two or more phenomena are connected, and quite another thing to say that this connection is a *causal* connection; that is, that some of these phenomena are the *cause* of some others. In his *Treatise of Human Nature*, Hume pointed out that *causal* connections are not something that we *see* or *experience*. Instead, they result from a particular *reasoning* or, better, *inference*. When phenomena are connected by contiguity and priority of time, we *conclude* (or *infer*) that they are causally related.[21] This, however, does not mean that they are *actually* causally related. In other words, we may have the *strong impression* that phenomenon 1 (contiguous and prior in time to 2) is the cause of phenomenon 2 (contiguous and second in time to 1). And, every time we see phenomenon 1, we may have a *strong expectation* to see phenomenon 2. This says something about the *way our mind works*, about our psychology, but says much less about how things in fact are. This kind of fallacy is still debated in philosophy.[22]

The fallacy discussed by Hume highlights an important methodological limit of sociological and systemic analyses. The variables that are identified in the systems give us elements to aid our understanding of what the person feels and experiences, but do not explain *what the person does and why she chooses that particular type of behaviour*.

I have the impression that there is something more in this search for 'external' causes for eating disorders. Not only is this search moved by our intuitive (and problematic) certainty that everything must have a cause, as pointed out by Hume. I think that this search for the causes of eating disorder is also symptomatic of our general difficulty in facing the real nature of eating

---

[20] Hume, *Treatise of Human Nature*, 79.
[21] Ibid. 69–94.
[22] M. Tooley, *Time, Tense and Causation* (Oxford: Clarendon Press, 1997).

disorders. The following observations are, I believe, remarkable and very pertinent:

'Because it is disturbing to realize and acknowledge the extent to which the *extreme actions* of anorexic/bulimic sufferers *grow out of ordinary values and everyday notions of moral goodness*, many parents find more comfort in believing their offspring is suffering from an as yet unspecified brain disorder or endocrine disturbance or that it is a genetic illness [. . .] The predominance of physiological research into the problem has gained much of its plausibility from the *general unwillingness to accept the idea that moral goodness can have undesirable* [. . .] *consequences* [. . .] *There is a cruel irony in the persisting notion that anorexia nervosa is a mysterious illness.*'[23]

4. *Eating Disorders: The Role of the Person*

Another important conceptual problem involved in the sociological and systemic analyses of eating disorders concerns the role that the individual is thought to have in the articulation of her behaviour. These analyses are either inherently deterministic, or do not elaborate in any clear way the relationship between external influences and the person's self-determination. The following passage may be quoted as an example of how behaviour is sometimes presented as the result, perhaps inevitable, of variables that operate beyond the individual, and that are out of the individual's capacity to control them. This is a description of the family of a person with eating disorders.

Each family, considered as a transactional system, tends to repeat these modalities with high frequency, and, consequently, generates redundancies. These redundancies allow the observer *to deduce* the rules, often secret and generally implied, that *govern* the functioning of a given family at a given time, and that are necessary to keep the family stable.

If we define the family as a *self-correcting system* based on some rules [. . .], then *its members become as many elements of a circuit, in which no element is able to control the others.* In other words [. . .] *the behaviour of one member of the family* [. . .] is the *effect* of modalities of interaction characterizing the whole family. The study of these kinds of family transactions is therefore the study of *fixed behavioural responses* and of their repercussions.[24]

In this passage, the family is considered as a circuit, and its members' behaviour is regarded as the effect of the set of rules that govern the system. The individual is presented as a puppet in the hands of the system, and is thought to be somewhat compelled to act in a certain way, depending on the interactions that take place in the system.

[23] Marilyn Duker and Roger Slade, *Anorexia and Bulimia: How to Help* (2nd edn., Buckingham: Open University Press, 2003), 154, emphasis added.

[24] Selvini Palazzoli, *L'anoressia mentale*, 253, my emphases and translation.

From this point of view, the psychological state of a person is to a great extent determined by variables that operate in the surrounding environment and that are beyond her capacity of control. If this is accepted, it seems to follow that her recovery or improvement relies, to a significant extent, on the possibility of modifying these external causes. If abnormal eating is the consequence of family and social problems, dynamics, or pressure, then it seems that whether or not the individual may be better off depends on whether or not family and social factors can be changed. If the family or the society cannot be changed, then it seems to follow that the individual is condemned to suffer—a conclusion that is difficult to accept.

Morag MacSween has also noticed that sometimes clinical and sociological studies of eating disorders present the relation between social forces and sufferer as deterministic.[25] I will not attempt a clinical evaluation of these studies, nor shall I deny the importance of the family and social environment in the development of eating disorders. I will instead stress that the individual *always* has a decisive role in the articulation of her own behaviour, whatever the familial and societal influences may be, and it is on this role that we should focus, so as to give sufferers the confidence that they do have the power to make themselves happier.

5. *The Role of the Individual in the Articulation of External Influences*

Consider the following example.

Suppose that media and magazines start advertising a 'New Fitness Programme'. The programme includes diet and training and guarantees lasting results. However, both training and diet are extremely strict and demanding. Suppose that I decide to try the programme, enrol, and start. After two or three days I feel exhausted and doubt I am able to proceed with it. Suppose that you also tried the programme, and experienced the same exhaustion. After a couple of days you decided to reduce the intensity of the programme, and after ten days you gave up. You found that the programme was unbearable, and you were not convinced that it was really healthy. Indeed, you did not feel well from the moment you started, and saw no reason to complete it.

Now suppose that, rather than reducing it or quitting it because I feel exhausted, I start thinking that I feel exhausted because I am unfit. 'If I feel exhausted after two days—I think—that must mean that I need the train-

---

[25] Morag MacSween, *Corpi anoressici* (Milan: Feltrinelli, 1999), 41. The English original version is *Anorexic Bodies: A Feminist and Social Perspective* (London: Routledge, London, 1995); see ch. 2.

ing: then I will complete the programme!!' Therefore, I carry on, and, after a few weeks I start feeling unwell (I feel muscular weakness, suffer cramps, my period is unusually irregular, and I catch a cold for the first time after a long time[26]).

One might well blame the fitness programme for my ill health. No doubt, the programme was badly designed. And, of course, there was strong (perhaps unethical) advertising. Of course if I had not seen an advertisement, the idea of enrolling the 'New Fitness Programme' would have not crossed my mind. However, perhaps what led me to stick to it was not the advertisement: if I had trusted my own sensation of tiredness, I would have stopped training, or at least reduced its intensity, as you had done. The difference between you and me does not lie in the amount of pressure we have received, but in the fact that you have trusted your physical sensations whereas I did not. I *interpreted* my tiredness as a sign of my 'weakness' and of my 'poor fitness level'. From this point of view the problem is not the amount of pressure I received, but my insecurity about the perception that I have of my own physical sensations. The problem is, therefore, that I do not have a realistic perception of my possibilities and limits, and the real issue is why I give that particular interpretation of my physical sensations. Unless I articulate properly the way I tend to interpret my physical sensations, banning fitness/dieting advertisements will not guarantee that I shall not have some similar experience in the future (Chapter 12 will focus on the way people with eating disorders perceive their body and their physiological sensations, and interpret information).

This example is meant to show that the way I respond to pressure that both family and society operate on me depends largely on the way *I perceive* the surrounding environment and *myself*. Of course, as we all know, we cannot just 'choose' the way we respond to familial/social pressure, in the same way we seem to choose, for example, how to decorate our house. However, the way we respond is *subjective* and *meaningful*, as subjective and meaningful as our aesthetic choices are.

The way each individual experiences the pressures that operate on her, and the information she receives, is somewhat original and subjective, and meaningful of her own perception of the surrounding environment *and of herself*. The fact that I respond in one way rather than another is not just something that *happens to me*—in the same way as I happen to catch flu. Although, at some level, it *also* happens to me, it never *only* happens to me, and,

---

[26] Negative effects on the immune system and on the menstrual cycle, muscular weakness, and cramps—linked to muscular weakness, to low calcium levels, and, in some cases, to electrolyte imbalance—are some of the effects of over-exercise. See Julia Dalgleish and Stuart Dollery, *The Health and Fitness Handbooks* (Harlow: Longman, 2001), 7–10.

moreover, it always *means* something. It means that I perceive the surrounding environment and myself *in a particular way*. The fact that I suffer from pressures on me not only means that these pressures are inadequate (inappropriate for me, being this particular person) or wrong. It also means that I have given myself a *particular place in that context*, and that *from that perspective I view that context and myself*. This is not meant to minimize the importance of what happens around us. It is instead meant to indicate that people react in some ways to what happens around them *because they are these particular individuals*.

Coming back to the example of the 'New Fitness Programme', if I start considering the programme from a different point of view, then of course this does not mean that the programme is 'good' or 'right'. However, this means that I perceive the programme *and myself* in a different way, and therefore, although still 'bad' or 'wrong', the programme becomes innocuous to me. From this point of view, sociological and systemic analyses are mistaken in the way they sometimes present the individual's behaviour as the result of family interactions, and of social variables that are beyond the control of the person herself. The person may in fact always try to reach a better understanding of the place she gives herself in the contexts in which she lives, of the way she filters and articulates information and demands coming from the surrounding environment, and of the personal reasons that induce her to respond in that particular and subjective way to them. The articulation of this very personal and individual process is in itself a modification of the way familial and social pressures operate on the individual person, as it is in itself a change of perspective and therefore a small revolution within the system.

6. *Conclusions*

In this chapter, we have looked at some sociological and systemic approaches to eating disorders. These studies provide important information about eating disorders, as they observe and describe the contexts (families and societies) where the disorder is most commonly manifested.

However, these approaches have important conceptual difficulties. First, they risk reinforcing the moral logic that underlies eating disorders. Secondly, there are methodological problems relating to the interpretation of empirical data as causes of eating disorders, or as factors that can explain why people develop eating disorders. Finally, they underestimate the role of the individual in the articulation of her reaction to familial and societal influences.

Eating disorders are sometimes viewed as the effect of peculiar familial/social interactions. But, if an individual's suffering and consequent behaviour are the effect of factors that are beyond her control, it seems that she should be waiting for these factors to change, in order to be better. I have argued that, instead, the person always experiences information, demands, and expectations coming from the surrounding environment in an original and meaningful way, a way that she can always try to understand better and that is not ultimately beyond her own control. The very rearticulation of the way we perceive the surrounding environment and ourselves represents a *revolution* of the system and therefore a modification of the influence that these dynamics have on us.

This does not mean that there are no inappropriate pressures on individuals within families and societies. However, we should trust that eating-disordered behaviour, like any other human experience, is not merely the 'effect' of other people's behaviour and expectations. People with eating disorders are not simply the victims or the abnormal product of dysfunctional families and societies.

PART 4

Law, Ethics, and Ending Lives

11

Eating or Treating? Legal and Ethical Issues Surrounding Eating Disorders

1. *Introduction*

An anonymous story:

Hi, I am 16 yrs old and battling anorexia. I was a skinny child, not thin, but skinny. From the stages of being a kid and becoming a teenager I had never exercised, ate whatever I wanted and somehow by the age of 14 I thought I was fat. I lost my dad when I was 3 and lived with my grandma because my mom was a drug abuser. My grandmother died when I was 9 so I had some tied up feeling going through me.

I kept it to myself, never sharing anything with anybody. Every time I looked in the mirror I couldn't stand my appearance. I was fat, I wasn't really fat but could stand to lose bout 5 lbs. I started a new school in 7th grade and had a great 8th grade year. I guess my anorexia started in the summer before my 9th grade year when a friend told me this guy said I was getting fat. I couldn't stand the fact that people thought I was fat. I hated myself.

So I started eating no junk food, doing 200 sit-ups a night and in a month I lost 7lbs. This wasn't enough for me I wanted to lose more on my 5′7 135 body frame. So I started eating almost nothing but 5 crackers a day and some fruit and only water. I decided to run cross country as a sophomore and was running 4 miles a day plus 500 sit-ups every night in that whole month I lost 25 lbs. and still thought I was fat I loved the compliment 'oh you're so skinny you look so good...' but I still wasn't happy. I remember looking at the scale, 110pds and I wanted 100 lbs. so I determined to get there.

I eventually started eating absolutely nothing, drinking water and running and exercising way too much...My family got worried and took me to a doctor, I put weights around my ankles and that made me look like I weighed ten lbs more so they thought it was just a teenager thing...however it wasn't. I eventually did get to 100 even less. My brothers were so worried...I hated food, it was my worst enemy.

One day when I was running cross country I passed out and worried everyone. I was taken to the ER and they said I had anorexia I fought and argued that I didn't but

An earlier version of this chapter has been published as Simona Giordano, 'Eating or Treating? Ethical and Legal Issues Relating to Anorexia Nervosa', *Tip Etigi, Turkish Journal of Medical Ethics*, 712 (1999), 53–9.

they put me on a feeding tube because I just would not eat . . . when they weighed me and I gained 7 lbs. I ripped the tubes out and left . . . to this day I am still anorexic I am overcoming it day by day. I am currently 5'7 103 lbs.

Just a little advice—if you think someone is overweight, keep it to yourself. Nobody cares what you think. It may not affect some people but to others they can't get over it, so just mind your own business.

One day food will not be my enemy anymore and I will overcome anorexia.[1]

Nearly every day, cases of anorexia are reported in magazines and newspapers. Bookstores are replete with biographies of anorexics and bulimics. If you search on the web, you will find a vast number of sites publishing stories of people struggling with eating disorders, or who have been rescued by means of force-feeding.

Often the sufferer does not have the positive attitude shown by our anonymous writer ('one day food will not be my enemy anymore and I will overcome anorexia'). Many of these stories narrate episodes of hospitalization and tube feeding. People tell of how they were forced to stay in hospital, and of how they did their best to resist any medical intervention. Exercising in the shower, drinking loads of water and not going to the toilet before being weighed, or 'eating their way out'—getting fat enough to be discharged and then, once released, starting again with anorexia. The circle seems endless.

In none of the stories that I have read, however, does the sufferer seem to have starved *in order to die*. Eating disorders are not meant to be a suicidal choice. On the contrary, typically, anorexia is thought to be 'the route to happiness'—a false route, of course, as it soon becomes evident to the person herself. It is certainly not a feature of eating disorders that the person starves herself in order to die.[2]

---

[1] A43 anonymous. html.

[2] It has been pointed out to me that there was a case in which a 19-year-old woman had cystic fibrosis and had also had anorexia nervosa for about three years. Although cystic fibrosis was not directly life threatening, the patient claimed that her current refusal of food was based on her desire to die of anorexia rather than cystic fibrosis. This is an interesting case in which the refusal of food plays a part in the patient's articulation of medical choices. However, it seems to me that this case does not disprove the fact that generally anorexia is not a suicidal choice. When life is at risk, the person may well decide that death is better than living 'with fat'. Indeed, cases are reported of people who have been forcibly fed and who have committed suicide because they would not tolerate living with that sort of body. We have also seen early in the book that the mortality associated with eating disorders is extremely high, and death mainly results from suicide. This probably means that the life of people with anorexia is often miserable and intolerable, and that the person sees no way out. However, the choice to diet and to be thin is not *in itself suicidal*. On the contrary, it is widely accepted that the person develops anorexia to look better, to be better, to be happier, to be better satisfied with herself. She makes 'the wrong choice': anorexia will not improve her quality of life. Quite the contrary, after an initial period of satisfaction, the person normally spirals down into a condition of loneliness and unhappiness, and begins to suffer the hideous physical effects of abnormal eating. Death becomes preferable. However, the fact that people with anorexia sometimes want to die—and sometimes would

Although the person does not openly want to die or to harm herself, eating disorders involve high risks for the sufferer's health and life. On the one hand, one may then ask: should we respect abnormal eating (which sometimes amounts to non-eating), given that it clearly harms the person and threatens her life, and given that the sufferer typically *does not want to die*? On the other hand, one may also ask: given that eating-disorder patients are normally very intelligent, is it right to force them to eat and to live, when they consistently refuse food? Is it right to enforce treatment on intelligent people who constantly refuse it?

Typically the person with eating disorders refuses treatment and declares that she is fine, sometimes in the face of advanced emaciation. The sufferer is reluctant to question, let alone modify, her behaviour. Even when she recognizes the problem and claims that she wants to recover, she is often unwilling to take any significant measure to modify her eating habits. This ambivalence typically generates acute conflicts between the sufferers, on the one hand, and the family and medical staff, on the other.

'It is common—some family therapists report—for the individual with the eating disorder and her family to be at odds about the need for treatment. The most common situation is that where the patient is less critically ill and not interested in treatment. Very often the family and the patient end up in a polarized position with each hoping that the family therapist will side with them. The most dramatic of these situations involves involuntary treatment. While this is an issue in a number of psychiatric illnesses, the eating-disordered patient is often highly articulate and convincing about her opinions about the advisability of such treatment. Except for the most emaciated patient who looks very ill, most eating-disordered patients do not have the obvious changes in mental functioning that may accompany such illnesses as schizophrenia. Very often the family therapist can quickly find himself or herself caught right in the middle—with both the family and the patient attempting to recruit an ally'.[3]

In part, the conflict may be exacerbated by the dangers of eating disorders. Even when the person is not frighteningly emaciated, her health and even her life are at serious risk. Chapter 1 has discussed the side effects of low or abnormal nutrition. Eating disorders affect the entire life of the sufferer, her daily habits, her exercise regime, her work and social life. For both carers and health-care professionals, it is easy to see the extent to which the disorder affects and subverts the person's life, and how self-destructive and dangerous

rather die from starvation than be fed—is not incompatible with the finding that anorexia itself is not a directly suicidal choice.

[3] Jan B. Lackstrom and D. Blake Woodside, 'Families, Therapists and Family Therapy in Eating Disorders', in Walter Vandereycken and Pierre J. V. Beumont (eds.), *Treating Eating Disorders: Ethical, Legal and Personal Issues* (New York: New York University Press, 1998), ch. 5, pp. 106–26, at p. 115.

eating-disordered behaviour is. Consistently, studies show very high mortality rates.[4] It is understandable that carers become extremely anxious over the person refusing to deal with her disorder.

The question of whether one should respect the sufferer's manifest wishes or rather do what is thought to promote her welfare is one that may arise in all areas of health care and in the management of any disease. Beumont and Vandereycken have pointed out that health-care professionals normally have two responsibilities: on the one hand, they are responsible for treating the disease effectively, and, on the other, they are responsible for respecting the patient's autonomy, her preferences and values.[5] Inherent in medical practice, therefore, there is a potential conflict between respect for patient autonomy and promotion of his or her welfare. While these two responsibilities may come into conflict in the treatment of any disease, in the case of eating disorders the conflict is nearly 'endemic' and virtually omnipresent in the relationship between the eating-disorders sufferer, the family, and health-care professionals.

How doctors and carers decide to behave towards a person with eating disorders depends mainly on three things. One is their clinical judgement (including the judgement as to how important it is to respect the sufferer's autonomy in order to promote her long-term recovery—this issue will be discussed later in this chapter). The second is their 'moral judgement' (including, for example, the capacity to empathize with the patient and carers, for example, or ideas about the value of autonomy as compared with the imperative to treat the disease effectively). The third important determinant is the law.

The question of whether eating-disordered people should be respected or treated without their consent involves legal as well as ethical issues. The management of the disorder is also determined by legal provisions, not only by value choices. There is an important legal dimension that guides medical choices. In this chapter I will focus on the duties and responsibilities of health-care professionals in the treatment of the eating-disordered patient. The legislation on anorexia is an interesting and complex one. This chapter will explain it in broad and plain terms. It will focus on the law of England and Wales.

---

[4] Rosalyn Griffiths and Janice Russell, 'Compulsory Treatment of Anorexia Nervosa Patients', in Vandereycken and Beumont (eds.), *Treating Eating Disorders*, 127. Stephen Zipfel, Bernd Lowe, and Wolfang Herzog, 'Medical Complications', in Janet Treasure, Ulrich Schmidt, and Eric van Furth (eds.), *Handbook of Eating Disorders* (2nd edn., Chichester: Wiley, 2003), ch. 10, pp. 169–90, at p.195.

[5] Pierre J. V. Beumont and Walter Vandereycken, 'Challenges and Risks for Health Care Professionals', in Vandereycken and Beumont (eds.), *Treating Eating Disorders*, ch. 1, p. 8.

It has to be noted that refusal of food does not characterize only eating disorders. In some mental disorders—such as in some personality disorders and some psychotic disorders—patients may refuse food. Refusal of food is also sometimes utilized as a weapon for political protest (hunger strike). Bridget Dolan has analysed the legal provisions applying to different forms of food refusal (starving prisoners, the suffragettes, the IRA hunger-strikers) and has explored the provisions relating to compulsory force-feeding both in anorexia and in the absence of an eating disorder.[6] I will focus here on legal provisions relating to eating disorders. I shall discuss both the Statute and the case law. I will also offer a critical analysis of these provisions. The sections containing a critical analysis will be found in subheadings as 'ethical considerations'.

2. Hospitalization and Treatment of People with Mental Disorders: Coercive Assessment and Treatment

Specific provisions regulate the management of eating disorders in the UK. These are to be understood within the law on assessment and treatment for mental disorders in general. This section will present a brief account of the legal provisions on assessment and treatment of mental disorders in force in England and Wales. This will help us to understand the legal provisions relating specifically to eating disorders.

In England and Wales the Mental Health Act 1983 (MHA) regulates assessment and treatment of people with mental disorders. Scotland has a partly different statute (Mental Health Act Scotland 1984). We need to note that other European countries do not have any statute for the regulation of involuntary assessment and treatment of people with mental illness.

People suffering from mental illness, mental impairment, severe mental impairment, and psychopathic disorder[7] can be 'sectioned' under the MHA. This means that they can be compulsorily hospitalized for assessment (s. 2) and treatment (s. 3).

The conditions for admission are reported in Box 11.1. Admission for treatment can be for up to six months, and may be renewed for a further six months. Afterwards, renewals last one year. According to the Mental Health Act Review Expert Group, established in 1999 by the government for reforming the statute, where the order exceeds three months, the patient should be entitled to appeal to the Tribunal. The Tribunal may order

---

[6] Bridget Dolan, 'Food Refusal, Forced Feeding and the Law of England and Wales', in Vandereycken and Beumont (eds.), *Treating Eating Disorders*, 151–78.

[7] Definitions of these conditions may be found in the Mental Health Act 1983, s. 1(2); see also B. Hale, *Mental Health Law* (4th edn., London: Sweet & Maxwell, 1996), 30–5.

BOX 11.1. Admission for Treatment Under the MHA 1983

1. The patient must suffer from mental illness, severe mental impairment, psychopathic disorder, or mental impairment, and the mental disorder must be of a nature or degree that makes it appropriate for the patient to receive medical treatment in hospital; and
2. in the case of psychopathic disorder or mental impairment such treatment is likely to alleviate or prevent a deterioration of the patient's conditions; and
3. it must be necessary for the health or safety of the patient or for the protection of others that he should receive this treatment and it cannot be provided unless he is detained under section 3.

---

renewals on the recommendation of the clinical supervisor. The clinical supervisor may discharge a patient subject to an order, but only with the approval of the Tribunal.[8]

With regard to the sectioned patients' right to decide about treatment, s. 63 states that the patients' consent shall not be required for any medical treatment given to them for the mental disorder they are suffering from. Consent is required only for treatment given within ss. 57 (psychosurgery) or 58 (electro-convulsive therapy and long-term medical treatment) of the Act. However, it should be noticed that treatments mentioned in s. 58 may be enforced in some circumstances.[9] Therefore, in fact, the only strict limit on coerced treatment for patients compulsorily hospitalized is psychosurgery.

2.1. Ethical considerations

S. 63 represents a radical departure from a general legal principle that applies to all adults. English common law presumes that all adults are competent, and no medical intervention may be operated on them without their informed consent. Under common law, a doctor is liable for trespass, assault or battery if he or she administers any treatment without the patient's consent. A competent adult may select medical options that are offered to him or her, and reject medical treatment for reasons that may be rational, irrational, unknown, or even non-existent (*Re T* [1992]), even when the

---

[8] Mental Health Act Review Expert Group, *Draft Proposals for the New Mental Health Act* (April 1999), http://www.hyperguide.co.uk/mha/rev-prop.htm.

[9] Treatments that are regulated by s. 58 require either consent or a second opinion. According to the Mental Health Act Review Expert Group, this section has received most powerful criticism. See *Draft Proposals*, para. 138.

outcome of his or her decision will be serious harm or death. Whereas this principle stands for any competent adult, the capacity of sectioned psychiatric patients to make decisions about their mental condition is not assessed. Once sectioned under the act, these patients will be treated without consent, irrespective of whether they are competent to participate in therapeutic decisions. It may be argued that people with mental illnesses by definition cannot be competent to participate in the therapeutic process. However, as we shall now see, this is not the case, and the law recognizes that mental illness does not necessarily jeopardize the patient's capacity to make medical decisions.

3. *Can People with Mental Illness be Competent to Make Medical Decisions?*

As we have just seen, s. 63 reads that consent to treatment for the *mental disorder* shall not be required to patients sectioned under s. 2 and s. 3 of the MHA. However, the Mental Health Act Commission has declared that valid consent should always be sought for the *medical* treatment proposed, following the guidance given in chapter 15 of the Code of Practice.[10] This chapter stresses the importance of giving adequate information to make sure that the patient understands in broad terms the nature, the likely effects, and the risks of that treatment, and any alternatives to it (para. 2.3.1).[11]

The patient's consent is sought because it is understood that the presence of a mental disorder does not necessarily affect capacity to consent.[12] The law has recognized that incapacity in some areas of a person's life does not entail incapacity in all areas of her life, 'nor does it remove the *presumption of competence* to refuse [medical treatment]'.[13] The law assumes that people

---

[10] It should be noticed that in *Re F* it was stated that a doctor can impose treatment for a mentally disabled person in so far as the treatment is in the patient's best interest. *Re F* is one of the disputed cases concerning sterilization of people suffering from mental illness. The law met with difficulties in regulating cases of sterilization for mentally impaired patients. For the controversial character of *Re F*, see J. K. Mason and R. A. McCall Smith, *Law and Medical Ethics* (5th edn., London: Butterworths, 1999), 253, and ch. 4.

[11] It should be noticed that the Code of Practice does not have statutory force, but 'it is widely expected (including by the Mental Health Act Commission) that those involved with the management of the Mental Health Act will comply with the Code, and failure to comply might be cited in civil legal proceedings as indicating poor practice or negligence' (see Department of Health and Welsh Office, *Code of Practice: Mental Health Act 1983* (3rd edn., London: The Stationery Office, 1999), http://www.hyperguide.co.uk/shop/mh9901.htm).

[12] Code of Practice (15.9 to 15.11); see also *Re C (adult refusal of treatment)* [1994] 1 All ER 819; for comments, see J. McHale and M. Fox, *Health Care Law* (London: Maxwell, 1997), 275.

[13] Mason and McCall Smith, *Law and Medical Ethics*, 263–4, emphasis added.

(including people with mental disorders) are competent to refuse medical treatment, even if they lack capacity in some areas of their life.

According to Mason, McCall Smith, and Laurie, the case of *Re C* is particularly relevant to respect for people's choices. This was the case of a 68-year-old patient with chronic schizophrenia. He developed gangrene in his foot. The consultant diagnosed a 15 per cent chance of survival unless the foot was amputated from the knee downward. The patient refused the operation, saying that he preferred to die with two legs rather than live with one. Prima facie every adult has the right and capacity to accept and refuse treatment. The patient has to understand the nature, purposes, and effects of the proffered treatment, has to be able to comprehend and retain the relevant information, believe in it, and weigh it in the balance with other considerations. According to Mason, McCall Smith, and Laurie, this case is particularly important for three reasons: (1) the law reaffirms its commitment to the principle of respect for patient autonomy; (2) there is a prima facie presumption of autonomy for every adult, including those with mental disorders; (3) incapacity in one or several areas of one's life does not preclude autonomous behaviour in other areas, 'nor does it remove the presumption of competence to refuse' treatment.[14]

However, the authors also identify some problems with the notion of competence.

1. The important question to determine the patient's competence is: does he or she understand? One problem is that the medical staff may not be willing to ensure that the patient understands if they believe that the patient will make a decision that in their judgement is 'wrong'. Whether the patient understands depends, to an important extent, on whether the medical staff enables the patient to understand. It may be difficult to determine whether the patient's lack of understanding depends on inappropriate disclosure of information or on genuine incapacity.

2. What does the patient need to understand? The law requires that patients understand the nature, purpose, and effects of treatment. Moreover, as we have seen above, the patient has to be able to retain information, believe in it, and weigh it in the balance with other considerations. According to Mason, McCall Smith, and Laurie, this is a potentially very broad concept. Most lay persons would not be able fully to understand the nature of treatment, its purposes and effects, and only people with special medical knowledge may be really competent to make an informed choice. This cannot mean that most lay people without medical training are to be considered incompetent to

[14] J. K. Mason, R. A. McCall Smith, and G. T. Laurie, *Law and Medical Ethics* (6th edn., London: Butterworths, 2002), 332.

make medical choices, but what degree of understanding of the nature and purposes of treatment is necessary or sufficient in order to deem a patient competent to make a decision relating to medical treatment?

According to Mason, McCall Smith, and Laurie, these circumstances are likely to cause acute conflicts, especially when patients refuse life-saving treatment. In these cases, invariably the determination of competence gives rise to contests. Whereas the law commits itself to the principle of respect for people's autonomy, at least prima facie, the tests to determine competence give only a general idea of where the limits of the principle of respect for autonomy lie.[15] A number of other studies have also pointed out difficulties relating to the determination of competence, particularly in the case of anorexia nervosa.[16]

The case of *Re B* is one example of the problems that emerge in court, when it has to be decided whether the patient should be allowed to refuse life-saving treatment. This is the case of a 43-year-old woman paralysed from the neck downward, and sustained by means of a ventilator. The patient refused to continue with this treatment. A psychiatrist assessed her competence and deemed her incompetent to refuse treatment. Four months later, an independent clinician declared that she was competent. Nonetheless, her attending physician refused to interrupt treatment and also suggested that she attend a rehabilitation programme despite scarce chance of improvement. Ms B refused to participate in the rehabilitation programme. The President of the Family Division attended Ms B's bedside and discussed the matter with her. In court it was reiterated that the patient has an absolute right competently to refuse treatment, whatever the consequences of his or her decision. Health-care professionals have a corresponding duty to involve patients in the decision-making process as much as possible.[17]

According to Mason, McCall Smith, and Laurie this case shows the difficulties inherent in the determination of the patient's competence, especially when refusal of treatment is likely to result in the death of the patient. Although the law demands respect for people's autonomy and requires that competent decisions be respected, irrespective of their consequences, the determination of competence is still a matter of individual judgement, and therefore there is room for disagreement and conflict. The problematic nature of the notion of competence and of the determination of competence

---

[15] Ibid. 333–4.

[16] Kirsty Keywood, 'Rethinking the Anorexic Body: How English Law and Psychiatry "think" ', *International Journal of Law and Psychiatry*, 26/6 (2003), 599–616; Jacinta Tan, Tony Hope, and Anne Stewart, 'Competence to Refuse Treatment in Anorexia Nervosa', *International Journal of Law and Psychiatry*, 26/6 (2003), 697–707.

[17] Mason, McCall Smith, and Laurie, *Law and Medical Ethics*, 6th edn., 334.

becomes evident when life-saving decisions have to be made by both patients and health-care professionals.

Indeed, the notion of 'capacity to consent' or 'competence' has been a hard nut to crack for the English law.

4. *Competence in English Law*

The Mental Health Act Review Expert Group has recognized the difficulties inherent in the characterization of competence. According to the group, these difficulties are linked in part to the fact that there are different types of capacity required for different tasks. For example, writing a will requires a certain kind of capacity, while giving consent to hazardous treatment requires another kind. As the group points out, there is even a 'criminal' capacity. The group acknowledges that the Law Commission has made considerable efforts to find an appropriate definition of incapacity. Many consultation papers have been issued,[18] culminating in 1995 with the publication of the Law Commission Report on Mental Incapacity,[19] and in 1997 with a Green Paper.[20] Following this paper, in October 1999 the Government published a Policy Statement, *Making Decisions*.[21] On 27 June 2003 the Government published a draft Mental Incapacity Bill and accompanying notes.[22] The Joint Committee of both Houses published a report on the draft Bill in November 2003. In February 2004, the Government presented its response to the Joint Committee. The Bill has now been renamed Mental Capacity Bill.[23] This Bill is meant to clarify the legal uncertainties in the law relating to decisions made on other people's behalf. It covers both cases in which people lose mental capacity at some point in their lives, for example, as a result of dementia or brain injury, and cases in which people were born with an incapacitating condition. The Bill includes new rules to govern research involving people who lack capacity. Among other things, the Bill contains provisions defining 'Persons who lack capacity' (Part I). It states that people

[18] Mason, McCall Smith, and Laurie, *Law and Medical Ethics*, 6th edn., 276.

[19] Law Commission Report on Mental Incapacity, No. 231 (1995).

[20] 'Who Decides? Making Decisions on Behalf of Mentally Incapacitated Adults', A consultation paper issued by the Lord Chancellor's Department (December 1997).

[21] Department for Constitutional Affairs, *Making Decisions*, The Government's proposals for making decisions on behalf of mentally incapacitated adults. A Report issued in the light of responses to the consultation paper *Who Decides?* Presented to Parliament by the Lord High Chancellor by Command of Her Majesty (October 1999). Available at http://www.dca.gov.uk/family/mdecisions/indexfr.htm.

[22] Secretary of State for Constitutional Affairs, *Draft Mental Incapacity Bill*, presented to Parliament in June 2003. Available at http://www.dca.gov.uk/menincap/meninc.pdf.

[23] Department for Constitutional Affairs, *Mental Capacity Bill* (Dec. 2004). Available at www.parliament.the-stationery-office.co.uk/pa/cm200304/cmbills/120/04120.i-vi.html.

must be assumed to have capacity, unless the contrary is established. It reiterates the importance of respect for people's competent decisions; it reinforces the idea that competence is a decision-relative concept (people may be competent to make one decision but not another, or may be competent to make a decision at one time but not at another).[24]

A number of cases are relevant to the characterization of competence. These are summarized in Box 11.2. The approach to competence that is adopted in English law is known as the 'functional approach', as opposed to the 'outcome approach'. According to this approach, a person's competence is to be determined on the basis of her understanding of the matter, and not on the basis of the results of her choice. It should be noticed that this approach is coherent with a procedural conception of autonomy and with a weak form of paternalism. We have discussed these notions in Chapter 2. I have argued that, prima facie, weak paternalism combined with a procedural conception of autonomy constitutes the only ethically legitimate version of paternalism.

But there are other problems that complicate the determination of the patient's competence. Although the courts provided a characterization of competence, it was also argued that other factors—such as the presence of undue influences exerted on the patient,[25] misunderstanding of available alternatives, or the effect of a chronic mental illness—may jeopardize people's competence. These factors, so it was argued, may render the patient unable adequately to understand the nature, purpose, and effect of the proposed treatment.[26] Several tests for the assessment of competence have also been suggested.[27] In *Re C*, the court held that, in order to be deemed competent to make a medical decision, the patient should understand and retain information about treatment, believe in it, and weigh it in the balance to arrive at a choice.[28] In another case,[29] other factors jeopardizing the

---

[24] Ibid., in particular Part I, 1–3.

[25] *Re T* [1992] 4 All ER 649.

[26] *Re C* [1994] 1 All ER 819; see McHale and Fox, *Health Care Law*, 273.

[27] In this section I shall consider only suggestions presented to the courts. For further discussion, see T. Arie, 'Some Legal Aspects of Mental Capacity', *British Medical Journal*, 313 (July 1996), 156–8; B. Hale, 'Mentally Incapacitated Adults and Decision-Making: The English Perspective', *International Journal of Law and Psychiatry*, 20/1 (1997), 59–75; R. P. Smith et al., 'Competency and Practical Judgement', *Theoretical Medicine*, 17 (1996), 135–50; B. Freedman, 'Competence, Marginal and Otherwise', *International Journal of Law and Psychiatry*, 4 (1981), 53–72; B. F. Hoffman, 'Assessing the Competence of People to Consent to Medical Treatment: A Balance between Law and Medicine', *Medicine and Law*, 9 (1990), 1122–30; M. Katz et al., 'Psychiatric Consultation for Competency to Refuse Medical Treatment', *Psychosomatic*, 1 (1995), 33–41; P. Fulbrook, 'Assessing Mental Competence of Patients and Relatives', *Journal of Advanced Nursing*, 20 (1994), 457–61; L. Tancredi, 'Competency for Informed Consent', *International Journal of Law and Psychiatry*, 5 (1982), 51–63.

[28] *Re C* [1994] 1 FLR 31; see McHale and Fox, *Health Care Law*, 222.

[29] *Re MB* [1997] 8 Medical Law Report 217.

BOX 11.2. Cases Relevant to Characterization of Competence

Understanding is of vital importance, in order to assess the patient's capacity to give valid consent (*Gillick* v. *West Norfolk and Wisbech AHA* [1985] 3 All ER 402 at 409 e-h per Lord Fraser and at 422 g-j per Lord Scarman).

To be competent to give a legally effective consent, the patient must be *able to understand the nature and purpose of treatment, and to weigh its risks and benefit* (*F* v. *West Berkshire Health Authority* [1989] 2 All ER 545; see also *State of Tennessee* v. *Northern* [1978] 563 SW 2d 197).

Capacity to give valid consent is *not determined by the result of the choice and is not determined by the apparent rationality of it* (*St George's Healthcare NHS Trust* v. *SR* v. *Collins and others, ex part S* [1998] 3 All ER 673). For what is known as the 'outcome approach', see Jane McHale and Marie Fox, *Health Care Law* (London: Maxwell, 1997), 280.

The person has a right to refuse consent to medical treatment *for reasons that are irrational or unreasonable, or for no reason at all* (*Sidaway* v. *Board of Governors of the Bethlem Royal Hospital and the Maudsley Hospital* [1985] 1 All ER 643 at 509 b per Lord Templeman; see also *R* v. *Blame* [1975] 3 All ER 446).

The patient has the right to be unwise (*Lane* v. *Candura* [1978] 376 NE 2d 1232 Appeal Court of Massachusetts).

The patient has the right *to be wrong as long as she has the required understanding* (*Hopp* v. *Lepp* [1979] 98 DLR (3d) 464 at 470 per J. Prowse).

It has been deemed *unlawful to force compulsory feeding, as long as the person was found competent to refuse it* (*Secretary of State for the Home Department* v. *Robb* [1995] 1 All ER 677); in this case a prisoner with personality disorders refused food. The court decided that the prisoner's wishes should have been respected, as long as he retained the capacity to refuse hydration and nutrition. In *Airedale NHS Trust* v. *Bland* [1993] 1 All ER 281, it was stated that forced feeding of a competent patient who is not detained under the Mental Health Act is unlawful.

---

individual's competence to refuse medical treatment were outlined. They included inability to comprehend and retain the information that is material to the decision, especially relating to probable consequences of the decision, inability to use information and weigh it, temporary factors (such as confusion, shock, fatigue, pain, or drugs), panic, and, in some circumstances, compulsive disorders or phobias.[30]

The Law Commission has suggested that a person basically lacks capacity in two situations: (1) when she is unable to understand or retain the relevant information; and (2) when, although able to understand the relevant information, she is prevented from using this information in order to arrive at a choice by her mental disability.[31]

The case of anorexia nervosa has posed a further challenge on the courts. I will focus mainly on the legal and ethical issues relating to the adult sufferer, as this relates directly to the main theme of this book—that is, respect for people's autonomy versus concern for their welfare. The minor (under 16 years of age) is generally considered incapable of consenting to or refusing medical treatment. Parents are normally vested with the power to decide for their children. I will not discuss whether children under 16 can be autonomous to make medical decisions, as this would bring us towards a field of investigation that goes beyond the scope of this book.[32] I will focus only on the legal provisions relating to the treatment of the patient with anorexia nervosa. Some of the cases that influence UK law concern minors.

5. *The Case of Anorexia Nervosa*

It has been stressed that a patient with anorexia nervosa, though able to understand the nature, likely effects, and risks of treatment in broad terms, may nonetheless be unable to make an informed choice.[33]

In *Re W* Lord Donaldson MR argued that anorexia nervosa by its very nature is capable of destroying the sufferer's decision-making capacity with regard to treatment. This case concerned a 16-year-old girl with anorexia nervosa. She refused force-feeding, and the court was asked to decide 'whether it could authorise [...] treatment against her stated wishes in the exercise of its inherent jurisdiction'.[34] The crucial issue was whether W was competent to decide on this treatment. Whereas the trial judge (J. Thorpe) argued that 'W [was] a child of sufficient understanding to make an informed decision',[35] Lord Donaldson MR argued that anorexia nervosa 'creates a

---

[30] See also *Banks* v. *Goodfellow* [1870] LR 5 QB 549 at p. 569 per lord C. J. Cockburn.

[31] See the Mental Health Act Review Expert Group, *Draft Proposals*, para. 152.

[32] For a comprehensive account of the legal issues relating to treatment of the minor, see Margaret Brazier, *Medicine, Patients and the Law* (3rd edn., London: Penguin, 2003), 339–71.

[33] Law Commission, Consultation Paper No. 129, *Mentally Incapacitated Adults and Decision-Making: Medical Treatment and Research*, para. 2.18 from *Re W* [1992] 3 WLR 758 (London: HMSO, 1993).

[34] Ian Kennedy and Andrew Grubb, *Medical Law* (London: Butterworths, 2000), 639.

[35] As quoted in ibid. 639.

compulsion to refuse treatment or only to accept treatment which is likely to be ineffective. This attitude is part and parcel of the disease and the more advanced the disease, the more compelling it may become'.[36] A similar conclusion was reached in the case of *Re C*,[37] another case involving a 16-year-old girl. In this case the judge held that C was not competent to make a decision about the treatment for her mental disorder, because of the effect of her illness.

The Mental Health Act Commission (MHAC) also points out that some patients with anorexia nervosa may be unable to give and sustain valid consent. It assumes that capacity to consent may be affected by fears of obesity or denial of the consequences of their actions, notwithstanding retention of the intellectual capacity to understand the nature, purpose, and probable effects of treatment (para. 2.3.2).

5.1. *Ethical considerations*

These provisions are controversial for two reasons. First, there is a conceptual problem. The Law Commission suggests that mental illness *may render the patient* unable to use the relevant information to arrive at a choice. Lord Donaldson also argued that 'anorexia' *creates a compulsion* to refuse meaningful therapy. I discussed in Chapter 3 the logical fallacy involved in claims that mental illness *leads people* to behave in certain ways. I have argued that claims of these sorts are tautological. 'Schizophrenia', 'depression', 'anorexia', 'bulimia', 'agoraphobia', and most other psychiatric categories *refer to* patterns of experiences and behaviours. These categories summarize in one word a number of experiences and behaviours. They neither explain nor cause the phenomena or behaviours to which they refer. I shall not return to the issue here. However, it has to be pointed out that one cannot simplistically assume that 'mental illness' is something that 'may make' a person unable to use information, or that 'compels' the person to refuse treatment.

---

[36] *Re W (a minor) (medical treatment court's jurisdiction)* [1993] Fam 64 at 81, [1992] 4 All ER 627 at 637, quoted in Mason, McCall Smith, and Laurie, *Law and Medical Ethics*, 6th edn., 633. In their discussion of this case, Mason, McCall Smith, and Laurie point out that, in the course of the judgment, several issues had to be clarified. First, it was made clear that the powers of the court in wardship are irrespective of the provisions of the Family Law Reform Act 1969 and that the decision to force-feed W did not conflict with the Children Act 1989, which gives a mature minor the right to refuse psychiatric or medical treatment in some circumstances. They also point out that this judgment may in theory conflict with the Human Rights Act 1998. Articles 2, 3, 5 and 8 of the Act state that failure to respect a refusal by a mature minor would be a breach of human rights. I will not discuss any further the legal issues of consent by mature minors here. For a comprehensive account, see ibid., ch. 10.

[37] *Re C (a minor) (detention for medical treatment)* [1997] 2 FLR 180 (Fam Div). Discussed in Kennedy and Grubb, *Medical Law*, 639–41.

Logical flaws cannot be used consistently in defence of an ethical or legal stance.

Secondly, there is an 'empirical' problem. People with eating disorders are typically intelligent, and are not at all the stereotypical 'insane' person, detached from reality. People with eating disorders are generally skilled, intelligent, and able to run their life in many important ways, like everybody else. It is hard to believe that *all of them*, when they refuse treatment, are *incompetent*. Given that we are dealing with intelligent and generally competent people, it seems that one cannot assume a priori that every time a person with eating disorders refuses treatment, she is incompetent. It seems that their incompetence should be assessed, not presumed.

6. *Eating-Disordered Patients and Competence to Refuse Treatment*

The law recognizes that incapacity in one area of a person's life does not entail incapacity in all areas of that person's life, or incapacity to make medical decisions. The law has also committed itself to respect people's autonomy. Therefore it seems to follow that the capacity of eating-disordered people to refuse treatment should be assessed on an individual basis. In Chapter 3 I have accepted that saying that a person has a mental disorder puts her behaviour 'in a determined context'. It gives us a certain frame of mind in looking at that behaviour. If I am told that, for example, Anne has an eating disorder, I will expect her to show determined concerns about her shape. If Anne refuses my invitation for dinner, I shall not be surprised or offended—I will look at her choices under a certain perspective. This, however, is not to say that 'her behaviour lacks autonomy' or that she is incompetent. This, instead, may give us an extra reason to look at the person's competence. The fact that a person has received a diagnosis of mental illness does not give us reason to assume that she is incompetent. It may instead give us reason to investigate further her capacity to consent. This position is in line with the general principle of respect for autonomy that is accepted by UK law.

However, this position is hard to defend for a number of reasons. Saying that we should assess the capacity of eating-disordered people to refuse treatment gives rise to a number of difficult questions, and may give rise to an interminable debate on the nature of competence. What does it mean to be competent to refuse treatment? The law has provided an answer, but one that is open to discussion and that may sometimes raise more problems than it resolves (see above for the observations of Mason, McCall Smith, and Laurie). Is it true that 'the underlying mental disorder' may render a person incompetent? What is 'a mental disorder'? When is an action or a choice autonomous? Is eating-disordered behaviour 'autonomous' in any relevant sense?

It is, of course, unrealistic to expect health-care professionals dealing with an eating-disordered patient whose life is at risk to sit around a table discussing epistemological issues on the nature of mental illness, or philosophical issues on the nature of autonomy and on the freedom of the will, before deciding what they should do. Moreover, the issues involved are conceptually so complicated that nobody can guarantee finding a solution that may gain the consensus of those involved. The law has thus taken a different route. It has been decided that treatment for eating disorder is enforceable, irrespective of patients' competence.

7. *Treatment for Eating Disorders is Enforceable, Irrespective of Patients' Competence*

For English law, anorexia nervosa is a mental disorder.[38] This has a precise clinical and legal relevance, since, as we have seen above, in the UK special statutes regulate assessment and treatment of people with a diagnosis of mental disorder (MHA) (in England and Wales, the Mental Health Act 1983; in Scotland, the Mental Health Act Scotland 1984).

Because anorexia nervosa is regarded as a mental disorder, people who have been diagnosed as having anorexia nervosa may be forcibly detained and treated under s. 2 and s. 3 of the Act. In 1992 the Royal College of Psychiatrists published a report, stating that around 10 per cent of patients with anorexia admitted in England were admitted under the Act.[39]

S. 63 of the MHA states that consent for the treatment of the *mental* disorder shall not be required for patients who are detained under the Act. One of the problems with this statement is that it does not specify (and it is hard to see how it could without embarking in complex metaphysical issues on the dual nature of human beings) what kind of treatment may be considered treatment of the mental disorder, and may therefore be lawfully enforced under the Act.[40] In particular, is feeding treatment for emaciation

---

[38] Department of Health, *Mental Health Act: Memorandum on Parts I to VII, VIII and X* (London: The Stationery Office), (MHA 1998); see also Mental Health Act Commission (MHAC), *Guidance on the Treatment of Anorexia under the Mental Health Act 1983* (London: HMSO, August 1997), para. 2.2.2.

[39] Rosalyn Griffiths and Janice Russell, 'Compulsory Treatment of Anorexia Nervosa Patients', in Vandereycken and Beumont (eds.), *Treating Eating Disorders*, 139.

[40] In part, this difficulty is linked to the controversial character of the notion of treatment. The Mental Health Act Review Expert Group has recognized the unfortunate uncertainties to which the characterization of the notion of treatment has given rise. See Mental Health Act Review Expert Group, *Draft Proposals*, paras. 134–6.

or for anorexia? As we shall see later, this is a problem that, for its impossibility, could be paired to the famous chicken-and-egg issue: which comes first?

The Mental Health Act Commission (MHAC) has published *Guidance on the Treatment of Anorexia Nervosa under the Mental Health Act 1983*. In the *Guidance* the MHAC states that patients with anorexia nervosa may be detained under the Act, either for assessment or for treatment. It states:

'Where the diagnosis of anorexia nervosa is established, it is the MHAC's view that this condition does constitute a mental illness within the meaning of the Act and that such a patient could be detained under Section 3 of the Act on the grounds that it is necessary for the health of the patient, provided always that the other criteria involved are satisfied and a valid application is made.'[41]

The MHAC also states that where a patient with anorexia is detained under the Act, her consent should always be sought for any medical treatment proposed, according to the guidance given in chapter 15 of the Code of Practice. 'This Chapter particularly stresses the importance of giving sufficient information to ensure that the patient understand in broad terms the nature, likely effects and risks of that treatment, including the likelihood of its success and any alternatives to it.'[42]

Importantly, the MHAC recognizes that 'every adult is presumed to have the capacity to decide whether or not to accept medical treatment even if the reasons for refusing are irrational or non-existent. A person suffering from mental disorder is not necessarily incapable of giving consent.'[43] However, this stands only for *medical treatment*. As we have seen above, s. 63 of the MHA states that 'the consent of a patient shall not be required for any medical treatment given to him *for the mental disorder* from which he is suffering' (emphasis added). The MHAC includes among the treatments for the mental disorder behavioural programmes.[44] But is feeding treatment for the *mental* disorder?

Whether or not feeding is *treatment for the mental disorder* has been widely debated (para. 2.4). The Mental Health Act Review Expert Group has recognized concern that feeding contrary to the will of the patient has caused

[41]   MHAC, *Guidance*, para. 2.2.2.
[42]   Ibid., para. 2.3.1.
[43]   Ibid., para. 2.3.2.
[44]   For treatment legitimacy limits, see s. 127 of the Mental Health Act; see also anon., *British Medical Journal*, 311 (1995), 635–6. This, written in the form of an open letter, describes a patient's experiences of a strict behavioural regime. The patient deplores the lack of privacy— 'giving the effect of a museum exhibit case' and the fact that even visits to the bathroom were forbidden. The author also emphasizes the long-term effects of such humiliating treatment. Quoted in MHAC, Guidance Note 3, *Guidance*, issued August 1997 and updated March 1999 to accord with the 3rd edn. of the Code of Practice, note 5.

in recent years, and has acknowledged the need for clarification on this matter. Moreover, it has recommended that coercive feeding should be included among treatments requiring special safeguards.[45]

In November 1999, the Secretary of State for Health published the 'Proposals for Consultation relating to the MHA (1983)'. In these Proposals it is said that the Secretary of State accepts the Committee's recommendation on feeding contrary to the will of the patient.[46]

The MHAC concludes that force-feeding may be enforceable irrespective of the patient's competence. This treatment is enforceable under s. 63 of the MHA:

For a responsible medical officer to prescribe such treatment [force-feeding] he has to be satisfied that he is treating food refusal as part of the mental disorder. The MHAC recognizes that in these circumstances further diagnostic and monitoring procedures may need to be carried out, including venepuncture, as part of the medical treatment for the mental disorder of the patient. In addition, action which is taken in an emergency as the minimum necessary to prevent serious injury or loss of life may be justified under Common law.[47]

The MHAC concludes that in certain situations, patients with severe anorexia nervosa whose health is seriously threatened by food refusal may be subject to detention in hospital and further that there are occasions when it is necessary to treat the self-imposed starvation to ensure the proper care of the patient. This treatment might include compulsory feeding to treat the physical complications of anorexia nervosa insofar as this is a necessary precondition for the treatment of the underlying mental disorder. In these circumstances artificial means of providing nutrition could reasonably be regarded as medical treatment for the mental disorder. However, the MHAC advises that such treatment must be carefully and regularly reviewed and, on the principle of using the least restrictive alternative, discontinued when the patient's compliance can be secured for normal methods of feeding to which compulsion would not apply. Such a review should be multidisciplinary in nature and may need to include the patient's representative.[48]

8. *Force-Feeding can be Enforced under the MHA 1983: The Cases*

Despite the fact that anorexia is considered a mental illness, it has not been straightforward to understand whether naso-gastric therapy was enforceable under the MHA. As Mason, McCall Smith, and Laurie point out, 'the courts

[45] Mental Health Act Review Expert Group, *Draft Proposals*, paras. 19, 145–6.

[46] Secretary of State for Health, *Reform of the Mental Health Act 1983: Proposals for Consultation* (London: The Stationery Office, November 1999).

[47] MHAC, *Guidance*, para. 2.4.2.

[48] Ibid., para. 3.1.

have to decide whether or not force-feeding constitutes treatment for mental disorder which can be given without consent under the terms of the Mental Health Act 1983, s. 63, or, alternatively is justified within the broad envelope of s. 145'.[49] According to s. 145, treatment for mental disorders includes nursing, care, habilitation, and rehabilitation. Habilitation includes education, training in work, and social and independent living skills.[50]

To summarize, there were two options for the law on treatment of eating-disorder patients:

1. The first option is to assess patients' competence to decide on force-feeding. This would have the advantage of guaranteeing respect for people's real competence. The downside is that lawyers and health-care professionals may risk embarking on interminable discussions of the nature of competence, mental illness, and autonomy of behaviour.
2. The second option is to show that force-feeding is a treatment for the mental disorder. The advantage is a practical one. Ethical or not, the treatment for the mental disorder is enforceable by law. Thus the patient's life is saved and health-care professionals are protected. The downside here is the difficulty to show that *food* is a psychiatric therapy.

The problem of whether or not force-feeding may be imposed under the MHA was presented in the Family Division in *Re KB*.[51] This was the case of an 18-year-old woman with anorexia nervosa detained under s. 3 of the MHA. Following the court's decision in *Airedale NHS Trust* v. *Bland*,[52] it was stated that naso-gastric feeding was medical (and not psychiatric) treatment, but the problem was whether or not this treatment, namely force-feeding, was given for the *physical* symptoms (for example, to increase weight), or for the *mental* disorder. Ewbank J. argued that 'relieving symptoms was just as much a part of treatment as relieving the underlying cause'; therefore, naso-gastric feeding could be given under s. 63.[53]

The MHA allows symptomatic treatment,[54] and, on this basis, in *B.* v. *Croydon District Health Authority*[55] it was decided that naso-gastric feeding could be lawfully administered under the MHA. Naso-gastric treatment could be regarded as a 'symptomatic' treatment for a mental disorder.

---

[49] Mason, McCall Smith, and Laurie, *Law and Medical Ethics*, 6th edn., 633.

[50] Ibid.

[51] *Re KB (adult) (mental patient: medical treatment)* [1994] 19 BMLR 144.

[52] *Airedale NHS Trust* v. *Bland* [1993] 1 All ER 281 (1993) 12 BMLR 64.

[53] Mason and McCall Smith, *Law and Medical Ethics*, 5th edn., 517–18.

[54] See MHA 1983, *Memorandum*, sections 3, 63, and 145; see also M. Serafaty and S. McCluskey, 'Compulsory Treatment of Anorexia Nervosa and the Moribund Patient', *European Eating Disorders Review*, 6/1 (1998), 27–37.

[55] *B.* v. *Croydon District Health Authority* [1995] 1 All ER 683.

B. v. *Croydon District Health Authority* was not about anorexia. It was a case about a patient with a 'personality disorder', with self-harming and self-punishing behaviour. Hoffman L.J. argued that treatment designed to alleviate the consequences of a mental disorder is ancillary to treatment designed to alleviate or prevent the deterioration of the mental disorder. Treating the consequences or the effects of a disorder is part of treating the disorder.[56] Moreover, in *Re KB*[57] the judge declared that the refused treatment was linked to the mental illness and that, therefore, the person did not retain capacity to refuse or to consent to it.

Similar criteria were used in *Riverside Health NHS Trust* v. *Fox*.[58] In this case, the judge declared that feeding was treatment within s. 145 of the MHA. Section 145 states that treatment for mental disorders includes nursing, care, habilation, and rehabilitation under medical supervision. According to Sir Stephen Brown, feeding 'is an essential part of nursing and care', and 'feeding a person suffering from anorexia nervosa is an essential part of that treatment'.[59] In fact, in *Riverside*, the judge held that coercive feeding represents legitimate treatment, in the case of anorexia, because any other therapy would be ineffective if the person is severely underweight.

As we have seen in the previous section, this is now the position accepted and reformulated by the MHAC in its *Guidance on the Treatment of Anorexia Nervosa*.

8.1. *Ethical considerations*

As has been pointed out above, demonstrating that force-feeding is treatment for the mental disorder is an alternative to determination of competence. This alternative seems to allow health-care professionals to avoid the tricky conceptual problems involved in the determination of competence (given that treatment for the mental disorder is enforceable under the MHA). However, the route that is taken here is not at all 'easier' or less controversial than the other. How can one possibly demonstrate that administering food is treatment *for the mental condition* instead of treatment *for the physical condition*? How can one distinguish between the effects of food 'on the body' and 'on the mind'? How do we draw a line between the psychological

---

[56] Mason, McCall Smith, and Laurie, *Law and Medical*, 6th edn., 634.

[57] *Re KB (adult mental patient: medical treatment)* [1994] 19 BMLR 144 at 146.

[58] *Riverside Health NHS Trust* v. *Fox* [1994] 1 FLR 614.

[59] *Sir Stephen Brown*, P (1993) 20 BMLR 1 at BMLR 5, quoted in Mason and McCall Smith, *Law and Medical Ethics*, 5th edn., 518; see also *B.* v. *Croydon District Health Authority* [1995] 1 All ER 683; for a detailed account, see McHale and Fox, *Health Care Law*, 547; see also K. Keywood, '*B v Croydon Health Authority* 1994 CA: Force-Feeding the Hunger Striker under the Mental Health Act 1983', 3 Web JCLI (1995); see also *Re C (adult: refusal of medical treatment)* [1994] 1 All ER 819.

suffering of the anorexic and her physical state, her thinness? If the question of whether food is treatment for the mental disorder has to be taken seriously, then a number of metaphysical issues on the nature of the human being should be addressed and resolved. Should the human being be considered as composed of two entities, as, for example, Descartes believed? Descartes proposed a model of human being as composed of *two things* (literally): *res cogitans*, the thinking thing, and *res extensa*, the extended thing, its material part. Are we accepting the Cartesian model? Court decisions will allow doctors to intervene promptly to save people's lives, and some may think that this is what matters. However, to those who value individual autonomy, the arguments in support of the legal stance will appear poor and ultimately insufficient to force people to accept treatment or to live.

Once the principle of respect for people's competent decisions has been accepted, the logical consequence is that we should assess whether people are competent to refuse treatment for their condition—in this case, whether they are competent to refuse naso-gastric therapy. Whether or not eating-disordered patients are competent to refuse naso-gastric therapy is independent of the resolution of metaphysical issues about the dual nature of the human being and of the Cartesian body/mind split. The real issue is not whether we are composed of two ontologically distinguishable substances, body and mind, and whether a particular therapy affects one or the other, or one before the other, or one as a consequence of the other. The real issue is whether people are competent to make that decision. Whether that treatment cures their mind rather than their body is irrelevant. What matters is whether people are competent to accept or to refuse it. Once again, focus should be on people's competence to make the specific medical decision and to accept or refuse medical advice.

I would like now to turn to a partly different issue, still relating to the legitimacy of forceful treatment for eating disorders. The conclusions on the lawfulness of force-feeding are based partly on some assumptions and clinical judgements. In order to understand the ethical legitimacy of these provisions, it is important to clarify what these assumptions and clinical judgements are, and to evaluate their consistency and validity. The assumptions and clinical judgements are, first that food refusal in anorexia nervosa is part of the mental disorder, and, secondly, that weight gain is preliminary to any significant therapeutic programme—at least in severely emaciated patients.

Let us consider first whether food refusal in anorexia nervosa is part of the mental disorder.

English law assumes that 'food refusal [is] part of the mental disorder'.[60] The assumption here is that there is an *underlying mental disorder* of which

---

[60] MHAC, *Guidance.*

food refusal is a part. The idea here is that there is some disease that is hidden in some unidentified locus in the person's mind, or maybe brain, which produces a certain pattern of behaviour or which produces obsessions and fears to which the person responds by articulating a certain type of behaviour. Food refusal is, so the argument goes, the manifestation, 'the symptom' of something *behind* the mere behaviour—namely—a mental disorder that drives the person to act in a certain way. '[R]elieving symptoms—it was stated—was just as much a part of treatment as relieving the *underlying cause*.'[61] I discussed this assumption in Chapter 3. I have argued that control of food intake cannot be considered the effect of 'a mysterious disease' that lies somewhere within the person and that compels her to act in a certain way. Whereas there may be some scientific ground to claim that there may be genetic or other physiological factors that may contribute to the arousal and maintenance of the disorder, there are no scientific grounds for claiming that there is an *underlying mental disorder*.

My claim that eating-disordered behaviour is not 'symptomatic' of an 'underlying disorder' does not mean that eating-disordered behaviour is necessarily autonomous and that we have a moral obligation to let people starve to death, or that paternalism in this situation is always necessarily unethical. It is possible that some behaviours lack autonomy—and therefore there may be grounds for paternalistic interventions, in the case of eating disorders as well as in many other cases (psychiatric or non-psychiatric). Still, it is mistaken (conceptually mistaken) to say that disordered behaviour is due to (or a part of) the mental illness. Claims such as these either are tautological, or, if they identify 'mental illness' with a subject (for example, in statements such as 'mental illness causes/is responsible for this person's experiences and behaviours'), are comparable to those old explanations of mental illness that said that the person was 'possessed' by demons, or 'spirits' or 'evil forces' lying somewhere within the person, in an unspecified place, maybe the soul, and which compelled the person to behave in the odd way. Saying that eating-disordered behaviour is the result of an 'underlying *mental* illness' is not much better than those claims. Underlying what? And under, but where?

The second assumption is that weight gain is preliminary to any significant therapeutic programme. At the basis of the legal provisions there is also a clinical judgement. The law accepts that compulsory feeding may be 'a necessary precondition for the treatment of the underlying mental disorder'.[62] This follows the court decision in *Riverside Health NHS Trust* v. *Fox*.[63] The law accepts that it is sometimes necessary to enforce treatment for eating disorders in order for therapy to be effective in the long term. It is understood that

---

[61] Mason and McCall Smith, *Law and Medical Ethics*, 5th edn., 517–18, emphasis added.
[62] MHAC, *Guidance*.
[63] *Riverside Health NHS Trust* v. *Fox* [1994] 1 FLR 614.

meaningful therapy for anorexia is psychotherapy, and not force-feeding. However, psychotherapy is meaningless for severely underweight patients, given that severe malnutrition subverts people's cognitive capacities. Therefore, if the patient refuses to be fed, in the most severe cases of emaciation, it is appropriate to impose feeding in order to organize a meaningful programme of therapy. This is a *clinical judgement* on the course of action that it is appropriate to take with severely emaciated anorexics. It is important to notice that this clinical judgement is not universally accepted by experts.

Broadly speaking, there are three positions on the appropriateness of force-feeding for anorexia nervosa.

1. Some therapists believe that coercive treatment is the right option at least in the most severe cases, in which the person's life is directly at risk.
2. Other experts recognize that force-feeding may have negative effects on the patient's long-term recovery, but believe that sometimes coercive feeding is a necessary 'first step' towards recovery. They argue that, because of the negative psychological effects that it carries, coercive treatment should always be discouraged. However, there are cases in which it is necessary for the patient to regain some weight in order for the therapy to be meaningful. The conclusion is that, in some cases, enforcing treatment is clinically necessary.
3. A third group of experts deny that coercive treatment for anorexia could ever be clinically appropriate. This group believes that enforcing treatment for eating disorders is not really an option, and that coercive treatment is meaningless at best, counter-productive at worst.

We shall discuss these three positions in turn in the next three sections. First we should note that the position accepted by law seems to be a mixture of 1 and 2. The law allows doctors to section anorexic patients and treat them against their will, but restricts force-feeding to the most severe cases, where the patient's life is at risk, and to a limited period of time. The law allows coercive feeding *in order for other therapies to be meaningful.*

9. *Force-Feeding is Clinically Appropriate and Ethically Uncontroversial*

Some clinicians argue that enforcing treatment for severe anorexia is the right thing to do.[64] If doctors cannot gain the patient's consent, the appropriate thing to do is coercive therapy. This is the right thing to do not only from a

---

[64] Christopher J. Williams, Lorenzo Pieri, and Andrew Sims, 'We should Strive to Keep Patients Alive', *British Medical Journal*, 317 (July 1998), 195–7.

clinical point of view (effective treatment—in terms of weight gain) but also from an ethical point of view. For example, Rebecca Dresser argues that 'the refusing anorexia nervosa patient presents a case in which the discord between individual freedom and optimal health care is less extreme than in other instances of treatment refusal'.[65] Birley even argues that 'compulsory treatment is not an option but a right':[66] patients have a right to life and the doctors' duty is to provide the best therapy for their patients' disorders. Among the reasons brought in support of this stance, the most common is that force-feeding in some cases is necessary to preserve the health and safety of the patient.[67] The Eating Disorders Association reports that 50 per cent of those who have been force-fed declare, with the insight of the 'afterward', that this was a good thing for them.[68] Some clinicians have also argued that force-feeding is the right option because it is a demonstration of the clinician's devotion to the patient.[69]

10. *Force-Feeding may be Necessary to Render Other Therapies Meaningful*

One of the first and most important experts of eating disorders to advocate this position was Hilde Bruch. She argued that psychotherapeutic treatment is meaningless if the person is too emaciated, for two reasons. One is that severe emaciation may significantly affect the psychological responses of the person. The second reason is that, while treating a severely emaciated patient, the psychotherapist will probably be worried for the safety of the sufferer, and his or her anxiety and concern are likely to interfere with the efficacy of the therapy.[70] Starvation is believed to affect (1) the possibility of providing a

---

[65] Rebecca Dresser, 'Legal and Policy Considerations in Treatment of Anorexia Nervosa Patients', *International Journal of Eating Disorders*, 3 (1984), 43–51, at 44, quoted in Griffiths and Russell, 'Compulsory Treatment of Anorexia Nervosa Patients', 133.

[66] J. L. Birley, 'Psychiatrists as Citizens', *British Journal of Psychiatry*, 159 (1991), 1–6, quoted in Griffiths and Russell, 'Compulsory Treatment of Anorexia Nervosa Patients', 133.

[67] Janet Treasure, G. Todd, and G. I. Szmukler, 'The Impatient Treatment of Anorexia Nervosa', in G. I. Szmukler, Chris Dare, and Janet Treasure (eds.), *Handbook of Eating Disorders* (New York: Wiley, 1995), 275–92, quoted in Griffiths and Russell, 'Compulsory Treatment of Anorexia Nervosa Patients', 130.

[68] www.edauk.com.

[69] J. Yager, 'The Management of Patients with Intractable Eating Disorders', in K. D. Brownell and C. G. Fairburn (eds.), *Eating Disorders and Obesity: A comprehensive handbook* (New York: Guilford Press, 1995), 374–8, at 376, quoted in Griffiths and Russell, 'Compulsory Treatment of Anorexia Nervosa Patients', 130.

[70] H. Bruch, *The Golden Cage: The Enigma of Anorexia Nervosa* (London: Open Books, 1980), 90.

meaningful treatment, and (2) the patient's capacity to make medical decisions. Hence force-feeding should be considered as a means that will counteract the effects of starvation. The legal provisions presented in previous sections seem to be based on clinical judgements similar to those summarized in this section and in the previous section. The law accepts that force-feeding may be clinically appropriate, based on the idea that it is necessary for the severely emaciated patient to regain weight in order for any other therapy to be effective and in order to restore the patient's competence. However, a number of experts of eating disorders raise objections to the clinical efficacy of any coercive intervention towards eating-disordered patients.

11. *Coercive Treatment is Always a Clinical Mistake*

A third group of experts argues that coercive treatment for anorexia should never be considered an option. Mara Selvini Palazzoli and her team, for example, claim that forceful treatment will compromise both the efficacy of the therapy and the long-term recovery of the person. It will inevitably cause a sense of violation in the person. Given that eating disorders are the expression of an inner need for autonomy and control, coercive interventions will necessarily have counter-productive effects. Their position is one of the 'bravest' one can meet. Mara Selvini Palazzoli and her team stress that at the beginning of the therapy the sufferer often loses further weight. They suggest that therapists should not only ignore the fact, but even subtly praise and encourage it. Since the therapists give a response that is exactly opposite to the one that the patient expects, the sufferer's modality of behaviour gets destabilized. By disappointing the patient's expectation to create concern, irritation, frustration, and disapproval, the therapists render the anorexic's strategy unsuccessful. In their experience, this typically induces the sufferer to abandon the strategy of losing weight as a valid modality of behaviour.[71]

Many other experts on eating disorders strongly discourage any forceful intervention. For example, Pierre Beumont and Walter Vandereycken argue that 'to speak of enforced treatment of anorexia nervosa is misleading. True therapy necessarily involves the patient's co-operation'.[72] The clinical reasons for rejecting forceful treatment of anorexia are generally as follows.

---

[71] This is known as 'paradoxical method' or 'paradoxical therapy'. I am not evaluating the ethics of this clinical approach. I am here only pointing out the different attitudes towards force-feeding. M. Selvini Palazzoli, S. Cirillo, M. Selvini, and A. M. Sorrentino, *Ragazze anoressiche e bulimiche: La terapia familiare* (Milan: Cortina, 1998), 96.

[72] Pierre Beumont and Walter Vandereycken, 'Challenges and Risks for Health Care Professionals', in Vandereycken and Beumont (eds.), *Treating Eating Disorders*, 10.

- There is no evidence that force-feeding is beneficial to the patient.
- Short-term weight gain will be followed by higher long-term mortality.[73]
- The most likely outcome is that the patient will be fattened up in the hospital, and as soon as she is released she will starve herself again. Generally, once released, the patient is even more aggressive and determined in her behaviour, more frustrated, angry, and lonely than before.
- Compulsory therapy compromises the relationship with the therapist and other professionals and will thus have a negative outcome in the long term.
- Coercive weight gain encourages other compensatory behaviours, such as binging and purging.
- Force-feeding erodes further the already fragile autonomy of the patient. If eating disorders are a fight for autonomy and control, force-feeding will necessarily worsen the patient's psychological condition. It is not coincidental that patients who are treated against their will are more likely to commit suicide when discharged.[74]
- Data (such as those provided by the Eating Disorders Association,[75] for example) are regarded as merely anecdotal in scientific settings. No study has been published that has followed up patients with anorexia who have been compulsorily treated. Nor are there comparative studies of treatment outcome of compulsorily treated patient versus voluntarily treated patients.[76] The lack of empirical research on the outcome of coercive treatment may depend on different factors. Some researchers argue this is due to the fact that most anorexia patients who have been treated compulsorily do not wish to engage in follow-up studies.[77]

As said above, the law has endorsed a position that is supported by the clinical judgements summarized above (Sections 9 and 10). However, as we have just seen, the clinical judgement on which the law is based is widely debated in scientific settings. A 2003 study focused on how patients and families experience compulsory treatment. It seems that even those who considered compulsory treatment 'the right choice' still experienced it as a

---

[73] R. Ramsay, A. Ward, J. Treasure, and G. F. Russel, 'Compulsory Treatment in Anorexia Nervosa: Short-Term Benefits and Long-Term Mortality', *British Journal of Psychiatry*, 175 (1999), 147–53.

[74] Griffiths and Russell, 'Compulsory Treatment of Anorexia Nervosa Patients', in Beumont and Vandereycken, *Treating Eating Disorders*, 130–1.

[75] www.edauk.com.

[76] Günther Rathner, 'A Plea against Compulsory Treatment of Anorexia Nervosa Patients', in Vandereycken and Beumont (eds.), *Treating Eating Disorders*, 187.

[77] Griffiths and Russell, *Compulsory Treatment of Anorexia Nervosa Patients*, 143.

form of punishment and imprisonment. The experience was invariably reported as negative and traumatic.[78]

Moreover, a general objection may be made to the very existence of a Mental Statute.

12. *Why is a Mental Statute Necessary?*

Other objections may be raised to the provisions that regulate the management of the mental-disordered patient in the UK. These objections apply to the management of mental disorders in general, and therefore also to anorexia and bulimia nervosa.

In the UK the law accepts that people may be competent to make some decisions but not others, or to make a decision at one time but not another. The legal concept of competence is decision-relative, as we have explained above.

In other European countries the concept of 'competence' is generic and 'fictional'.[79] In other legislations, when a person is declared legally incompetent, there will be a list of actions and decisions that she is not entitled to make (for example, getting married, preparing a will, and disposing of her money). Whether or not the person is *de facto* unable to make competent decisions in those areas is irrelevant. Once the person is declared legally incompetent, she has no right in those areas, even if she is *de facto* capable of making decisions of that sort. The person is *legally* incapacitated, even if he or she is in reality capable of certain acts.

Competence, as it is understood in UK law, tries to reflect the *real capacity* of the person to make a specific decision, and is therefore based on the principle of genuine respect for people's autonomy. The law in the UK accepts that capacity for decision-making is not a general ability, and does not depend on the status[80] of the person. Competence is relative to the specific decision at stake and to the time it has to be made.[81]

As we have seen in previous sections, UK law recognizes that the fact that a person has a mental disorder does not necessarily mean that she is incompetent to make medical decisions. On the contrary, the law *presumes* that

---

[78] Jacinta O. A. Tan, Tony Hope, and Anne Stewart, 'Control and Compulsory Treatment in Anorexia Nervosa: The Views of Patients and Parents', *International Journal of Law and Psychiatry*, 26/6 (2003), 627–45.

[79] For example, in Italy; see 'Incapacità di intendere e di volere', in Codice Civile, artt. 414–19.

[80] For an account of the 'Status' approach, see McHale and Fox, *Health Care Law*, 280.

[81] *Gillick* v. *West Norfolk Wisbech AHA* [1985] 3 All ER 402 at 409 e-h per Lord Fraser and at 422 g-j per Lord Scarman; see also *Estate of Park* [1959] P 112; *Re C (adult: refusal of medical treatment)* [1994] 1 All ER 819, (1993) 15 BMLR 77.

people with mental disorders (including those who are compulsorily hospitalized under the Act) *are* competent to make *medical decisions*. They will be asked to consent to any medical procedure that is unrelated to the treatment of their mental disorder (s. 63). However, if they prove incompetent to make any such a decision, doctors may act independently of the person's consent. The legal instrument of 'competence' allows doctors to protect the health and life of people who are incompetent to make medical decisions at the time the decision needs to be made.

As we have also seen, patients who are admitted under the Act need not be required to consent to the treatment of their mental disorder (s. 63). However, it is unclear why the legal notion of competence, understood as a decision-relative concept, is not applied to the administration of therapy *for the mental disorder*. The determination of the patient's competence would enable doctors to treat patients who are at the time incompetent to make decisions about their mental health, in the same way in which it enables doctors to treat patients for their physical illnesses when they are incapable of participating in therapeutic decisions.

The assessment of the patients' competence is sufficient to guarantee protection of those sufferers who are unable—for whatever reason—to make decisions about their health. It is unclear why those who are incompetent because they have hallucinations or paranoia, for example, should be treated differently from those who are incompetent because of, let us say, drug abuse, and should be submitted to a different legislation. The principle that we should protect the health and life of those who are incompetent to make medical decisions is sufficient to allow health-care professionals to intervene paternalistically towards people with mental disorders who are unable to make medical decisions.

From this point of view, the very existence of a mental statute is objectionable and may be regarded as discriminatory. One may respond that, whereas everybody, including those who have mental disorders, may be competent to make medical decisions, those who have a mental disorder will necessarily be unable to make decisions *about their mental illness*. For example, a person with schizophrenia will necessarily be unable to make decisions about treatment for schizophrenia.

Indeed, many people seem to believe that there is something *inherent* in mental illness that disrupts the sufferer's autonomy, and that makes the person unable to make decisions relating to her mental illness. One of the myths surrounding mental illness is that the person with mental illness is unaware of her mental disorder and experiences her condition as normal. Therefore she will necessarily refuse treatment for her disorder— she does not think she has a disorder in the first instance, and therefore cannot recognize her need for therapy. Any similar belief is very far from reality. People with mental disorders are in the vast majority of cases well aware of their disorder, suffer a great deal, and do not at all live as if their situation is normal. Quite the contrary, they often realize that there is something terribly abnormal going on and realize they are very much in need of help.

Unfortunately, the history of management of mental disorders in Europe and elsewhere has been one of marginalization. The general public seems to know very little about mental illness and most people have never been in contact with a person with a severe psychiatric disorder. The information that the general public has of mental disorders is poor and often misguided. Most of us have been in a hospital and have dealt with people suffering from medical conditions, but very few of us have ever been in a psychiatric clinic or in close contact with a person with a psychiatric disorder. As always, ignorance is sister to fear and prejudice. The reality is that the vast majority of people with mental disorders are capable of engaging in a meaningful therapeutic relationship. They often seek help, are ready to participate in a therapeutic programme, and when they refuse medical advice they often do so for important reasons.[82]

As I have argued before, it is true that knowing that a person has a mental illness may give us a further reason to investigate the reasons why that person makes determined choices or behaves in a certain way, and may give us a further reason to investigate her capacity to consent to treatment. This, however, does not mean that we may assume that the person lacks autonomy or is incompetent to give consent.

It is simply mistaken to believe that there is 'a class of choices' that, by definition, the person with a mental disorder is unable to make. In psychiatry as anywhere else, each person is different, and from time to time her situation may raise particular ethical dilemmas. Those who suffer from mental illness (as is true of everybody else) are never (or almost never) entirely able or entirely unable to make autonomous decisions or to act autonomously. All persons (including those who suffer from mental illness) possess variable capacities to act and choose more or less autonomously in particular circumstances.

From the point of view of respect for people's autonomy, the very existence of a mental statute is therefore the signal of a discriminatory attitude towards those who receive a psychiatric diagnosis. This attitude is based on mistaken assumptions relating to the nature of mental illness. The patient's

---

[82] Allen E. Buchanan and Dan W. Brock, *Deciding for Others: The Ethics of Surrogate Decision Making* (Cambridge: Cambridge University Press, 1989), 18; M. D. Sullivan and S. J. Youngner, 'Depression, Competence, and the Right to Refuse Lifesaving Medical Treatment', *American Journal of Psychiatry*, 151/7 (July 1994), 971–7; Hoffman, 'Assessing the Competence'.

competence to consent to or to refuse treatment—whether or not related to her mental disorder—should always be assessed. It is unclear why overlooking a person's competent decision about her own mental health should be *lawful*, when the law forbids and punishes the overriding of competent decisions on other matters.

One may also argue that a mental statute is the most appropriate and efficient means of intervention for the management of mental illnesses, and this is why it is acceptable. Doctors need to be able to act promptly, and continuing assessments of patient's decision-making capacity would be time-consuming and costly. From this point of view, the mental statute would be 'a method of rationing', a method of making the health-care system more efficient. While it is easy to agree in principle with the idea that the health-care system should be efficient and that wastage should be avoided, it is debatable whether the best way of achieving these objectives is to violate the autonomy of a specific group of persons.

13. *Conclusions*

This chapter has explored the legal provisions regulating assessment and treatment of mental disorders in general and of eating disorders in particular. A critical analysis has also been offered. I have pointed out that the provisions that in England and Wales regulate the case of eating disorders are based on assumptions that are either controversial or mistaken.

I argued in Chapter 2 that, at least prima facie, the only reason that might justify paternalism is a detectable defect in autonomy (weak paternalism). The legal instrument of competence guarantees respect for people's autonomy and also protection of their welfare, when they prove incompetent to make decisions for themselves. People's capacity to make medical decisions is assessed, and, in principle, only if they are found incompetent may their decision be overruled.

If the arguments articulated so far are persuasive, it follows that the determination of people's competence should also be applied to the treatment of mental disorders. Prima facie, people should be entitled to make medical decisions, whether or not relating to their mental disorder, unless they are found incompetent to do so. Also people with eating disorders should, at least prima facie, be entitled to make competent decisions. They should be free from interference unless their behaviour lacks autonomy. In cases of medical decisions, they should be allowed to refuse medical treatment, unless they are found incompetent to do so. The conclusions on the ethics of paternalism towards the eating-disordered patients are summarized in Box 11.3.

BOX 11.3. Principle of Respect for the Autonomy of the Eating-Disordered Person

People with eating disorders, *at least prima facie*, should be entitled to consent to or to refuse any medical treatment, whether or not related to their mental disorder, unless they are found incompetent to do so.

BOX 11.4. Legal Competence: Cases and Documents

- *Banks* v. *Goodfellow* [1870] LR 5 QB 549 at p.569 per Lord C. J. Cockburn.
- *R* v. *Blame* [1975] 3 All ER 446.
- *Lane* v. *Candura* [1978] 376 NE 2d 1232 Appeal Court of Massachusetts
- *State of Tennessee* v. *Northern* [1978] 563 SW 2d 197.
- *Hopp* v. *Lepp* [1979] 98 DLR (3d) 464 at 470 per J. Prowse [1985] 3 All ER 402 at 409 e-h per Lord Fraser and at 422 g-j per Lord Scarman.
- *Sidaway* v. *Board of Governors of the Bethlem Royal Hospital and the Maudsley Hospital* [1985] 1 All ER 643 at 509 b per Lord Templeman.
- *Re T (adult refusal of treatment)* [1992] 4 All ER 649.
- *Airedale NHS Trust* v. *Bland* [1993] 1 All ER 281.
- *Re C (adult refusal of treatment)* [1994] 1 All ER 819.
- *Secretary of State for the Home Department* v. *Robb* [1995] 1 All ER 677.
- *Re MB* [1997] 8 Medical Law Report 217.
- *St George's Healthcare NHS Trust* v. *SR* v. *Collins and others, ex part S* [1998] 3 All ER 673.
- Department of Health, Mental Health Act 1983 Revised Code of Practice (15.9–15.24), issue date 1 March 1999, revised 1 March 2000.
- Law Commission Report on Mental Incapacity, No. 231 (1995).
- 'Who Decides? Making Decisions of Behalf of Mentally Incapacitated Adults', A consultation paper issued by the Lord Chancellor's Department (December 1997).
- Mental Health Act Review Expert Group, *Draft Proposals for the New Mental Health Act* (April 1999), http://www.hyperguide.co.uk/mha/rev-prop.htm, para. 15.
- Mental Health Act Commission, Guidance Note, Use of the Mental Health Act 1983 in General Hospitals without a Psychiatric Unit, Commission ref: GN 1/2001. Issued September 2001, Review date September 2003.

This is a principle that I propose as prima facie. In the next chapters I shall discuss the following issues:

1. Is eating-disordered behaviour autonomous?
2. Can a person with eating disorders competently refuse treatment for her disorder?
3. Should people with eating disorders who are found competent to refuse medical treatment be entitled to do so?

BOX 11.5. Competence and Anorexia Nervosa: Cases and Documents

- *Riverside Health NHS Trust* v. *Fox* [1994] 1 FLR 61, *Sir Stephen Brown*, P (1993) 20 BMLR 1 at BMLR 5.
- *Re KB (adult) (mental patient: medical treatment)* [1994] 19 BMLR 144.
- *B.* v. *Croydon District Health Authority* [1995] 1 All ER 683.
- Mental Health Act MHA 1983, s. 127.
- Department of Health, *Mental Health Act: Memorandum on parts I to VII, VIII and X* (London: Stationery Office, 1998), sections 3, 63, and 145.
- Mental Health Act Review Expert Group, *Draft Proposals for the New Mental Health Act* (April 1999), http://www.hyperguide.co.uk/mha/rev-prop.htm, paras. 134–6, para. 19 and paras 145–6.
- Mental Health Act Commission, Guidance Note 3, *Guidance on the Treatment of Anorexia Nervosa under the Mental Health Act 1983*, issued August 1997 and updated March 1999.
- Secretary of State for Health, *Reform of the Mental Health Act 1983: Proposals for Consultation* (London: The Stationery Office, November 1999).

12

Autonomy and Control in Eating Disorders

1. *Introduction*

Another anonymous story:

I'm not anorexic, I do eat.
   3 meals a day, almost every day.
   Breakfast, lunch, dinner.
   So I tell myself, my friends, my parents, my boyfriend, I'm OK.
   'How can you accuse me? You see me eat, I'm not starving myself.'
   It's amazing how much lettuce you can eat and keep below 100 calories, the soups
you can make at 50–100 calories per serving. The meals you can make and show
people you eat to calm them down.
   I'm a master at these meals.
   I'm not anorexic, I do eat.
   I'm 5′6″ and 99 pounds, I know I'm skinny.
   I look at myself in the mirror, find the fat, find the places where more pounds can be
shed, tell myself that I'm not unhealthy, I'm still safe, there is no reason to stop yet.
   I know I'm wrong.
   I know I'm reaching a point where it becomes dangerous, I remember the anemia,
the bad immune-system, the never-ending line of illnesses from the last time I was
here. I feel it closing in, I know the feeling in my bones.
   Soon.
   Not there yet, but soon.
   Some days I try to fight it, force myself to eat. I tell myself off, try to get some sense
into my stubborn head. Most times I lose, the food I promised myself becomes a tiny
cracker with tomato, tea, a piece of fruit, something like that.
   I'm not gonna go there again, I'm going to start eating, I'm not going to keep on
like this, I am gonna find another way of feeling the control.
   Tomorrow.[1]

A conflict is inherent in the management of eating disorders. The person with
eating disorders generally defends her eating habits and is unwilling to
engage in any meaningful programme of therapy. She often refuses to
admit that her behaviour is dangerous. Even when she does recognize that

---

[1] Anonymous 5 at http://www.eating.ucdavis.edu/speaking/told/anorexia/a37feeding.html.

her behaviour is dangerous, as in the anonymous story reported above, she does not modify it. It is inevitable that carers and health-care professionals will ask themselves whether they should respect the person's choices or whether they should force the person not to perform self-destructive and apparently unmotivated behaviour.

Cases of refusal of treatment for anorexia have appeared before the judges in the UK. Two main issues have been discussed in courts: (1) whether anorexic patients may competently refuse treatment for eating disorders; (2) whether force-feeding may be enforced under s. 63 of the MHA—and therefore irrespective of the patient's competence (see previous chapter). Following a number of court decisions, the law now provides that people with eating disorders may be compulsorily hospitalized and forcibly fed.

In the previous chapter, I discussed the legal provisions relating to management of mental disorder in general and of eating disorders in particular. I suggested that people with eating disorders (and generally people with mental disorders, like anybody else) prima facie should be entitled to participate in the therapeutic process, to assess alternatives, and to refuse treatment for the disorder they have, unless they are found incompetent to do so. Their incompetence should not be *presumed*, but *assessed*.

This conclusion is the practical application of the theory of weak paternalism that I articulated in Chapter 2. There I argued that, prima facie, the only form of ethically justifiable paternalism is weak paternalism combined with a procedural conception of autonomy. In plain words, it may be ethical to prevent self-harming actions and choices when these lack autonomy in some significant way. The autonomy of an action or of a choice is to be assessed on the basis of the process of reasoning and deliberation leading to that action or choice, not on the basis of their content or outcome.

This raises an obvious issue. Is eating-disordered behaviour autonomous? Is the process of reasoning and deliberation that leads to eating-disordered behaviour autonomous in any relevant sense? Among eating-disordered behaviours we should include all clinical features of anorexia and bulimia: for example, dieting, over-training, vomiting, and purging. Are these 'autonomous behaviours'? And, in the most extreme cases of refusal of life-saving treatment (normally naso-gastric feeding), may this be an autonomous choice? I will analyse the case of refusal of life-saving treatment in the next chapter.

In this chapter I analyse eating-disordered behaviour—including dieting, rituals around food, compensatory behaviour—in order to assess whether it is significantly autonomous or not. By 'eating-disordered behaviour' I mean behaviour that is described in clinical literature as well as in the *DSM-IV* and in the *ICD-10*, and that has been described in Chapter 1.

We should first ask what is meant by 'autonomy'. Characterizations of autonomy have been innumerable, and sometimes remarkably different from one another.[2] Autonomy has been considered from various theoretical perspectives. It raises metaphysical issues relating to freedom and causation, and therefore is central in the debate between 'compatibilists' and 'incompatibilists'[3]—that is, between those who believe that human beings have a free will, despite factors that may influence their decision, and those who believe that human beings do not have a free will, because these factors determine their decisions. It raises problems of moral agency and of intentionality, and therefore both political and moral philosophy, as well as philosophy of mind, deal with it. Given the complexity of the notion, it is important to characterize its essential traits. Some of the issues discussed in the following sections have already been addressed in Chapter 2. However, we shall now see them in relation to the notion of autonomy.

2. *Autonomy as Self-Control*

'Autonomy' is a word that has Greek origins, and that etymologically means 'self-rule' (*autos* = self + *nomos* = rule of law). This term was originally applied to city states of ancient Greece, where it indicated the independence of the *polis* of external political influences. Later on, its meaning was extended to the condition in which individuals' actions and choices are 'their own', and therefore are self-determined.[4]

Lawrence Haworth has pointed out that the ancient meaning is not comparable with what we currently mean by 'autonomy'. The Greek meaning was essentially negative (autonomy as independence), whereas autonomy has a positive meaning to us (autonomy as self-control).[5]

However, Alfred Mele has argued that autonomy cannot be considered simply in terms of self-control ('reductionist conception of autonomy' = autonomy as self-control). In other words, the notion of autonomy cannot be considered co-extensive with the notion of self-control. Mele argues that a worker, for example, may force herself to work very hard, and to do that she must exert self-control. Nonetheless, she can be acting non-autonomously,

---

[2] For a brief catalogue of the different uses of the term 'autonomy' in both political and moral philosophy, see G. Dworkin, *The Theory and Practice of Autonomy* (Cambridge: Cambridge University Press, 1988), 5.

[3] W. Bechtel, *Philosophy of Mind: An Overview for Cognitive Science*, Hillsdale, NJ: Lawrence Erlbaum, 1988).

[4] G. Dworkin, *The Theory and Practice*, 12–13.

[5] L. Haworth, *Autonomy: An Essay in Philosophical Psychology and Ethics* (London: Yale University Press, 1986), 11–12.

according to the *kind* of self-control that she exerts. If the person has been induced to such hard work by means of brainwashing, for example, that person, though acting with self-control, cannot be considered autonomous. Mele concludes that, if deliberation founding self-controlled conduct is based on *non-authentic*[6] values and beliefs, self-control is insufficient to make the action autonomous.

Theories evaluating the *kind* of self-control, such as Mele's, are called 'externalist'[7] because they pay attention to 'external' factors that may affect the process of acquisition of preferences, desires, and values founding individual behaviour.[8] Mele's argument seems to be particularly pertinent to the case of eating disorders, because of the problematic character of self-control in this condition. People with anorexia are 'masters' of self-control. However, claiming that they are autonomous, and, further, that they are autonomous because of their self-control, is highly counter-intuitive.

Eating disorders are always characterized by a strain towards control. People with eating disorders typically struggle between the urge to exert control and the drive to lose it. The person with eating disorders generally tries to maintain control over food intake, and, in many cases, periodically loses it. Generally she mainly experiences the *loss of control* as a problem. Generally she is happy and satisfied when she succeeds in her diet—and the more she can go without food, the better. Normally she feels that the worse thing that can happen to her is being unable *to control* eating. Bulimia is her nightmare: bulimia is shameful and disgusting. Although the person with eating disorders typically considers the loss of control as the major problem, probably the loss of control is *only a part* of the problem. The person with eating disorders has an eating disorder not only when she, for example, overeats and vomits, but also when she calculates calories, over-exercises, and *when she is satisfied* with herself because of *the control* that she has been able to exert on herself. This is the reason why not only bulimia and bulimic anorexia are regarded as disorders, but also restrictive anorexia. The fact that the anorexia exerts control does not make anorexia unproblematic.

Vandereycken, for example, argues that the *main problem* involved in eating disorders is 'self-control regarding weight/shape and the fear of losing

---

[6] A. Mele, *Autonomous Agents: From Self Control to Autonomy* (Oxford: Oxford University Press, 1995), ch. 10.

[7] Ibid., ch. 9; you can also find examples of externalist views in T. L. Beauchamp and J. Childress, *Principles of Biomedical Ethics* (4th edn., Oxford: Oxford University Press, 1994); H. T. Engelhardt, Jr., *The Foundation of Bioethics* (London: Oxford University Press, 1986); 2nd edn., Oxford: Oxford University Press, 1996); J. Harris, *The Value of Life* (London: Routledge, 1992).

[8] On the link between autonomy and authenticity of beliefs and values, see Mele, *Autonomous Agents*, ch. 10.

it'.[9] He considers bulimic episodes as a *breakthrough or violation of the restricted alimentary regime*. If Vandereycken is right, others may see things in a way that is directly opposite to the way the eating-disordered person sees them. While the eating-disordered person normally considers bulimia as the major threat, if we accept that self-control is the main problem, then we may even consider the 'bulimic' side as the 'healthy side', rather than as the 'problematic' one. Bulimia is the 'sane' self, the one that 'protests' against the 'tyranny' of the 'perfectionist' one. The 'loss of control' characterizing bulimia would therefore be not the expression of the incapacity to exercise autonomy, but, rather a 'rebellion' against the inflexible attempt to attain perfect control over oneself. In spite of the feeling of defeat that overeating normally generates in the person who binges, maybe this 'loss of control' is a sort of 'healthy protest', a way in which the person can claim, to herself, that she is not and cannot be 'perfect'. The 'anorexic' rises 'to the Empyrean', whereas the 'bulimic' grasps her by the feet and pulls her down to earth.

Conceptualizing autonomy in terms of self-control is potentially misleading, in that it reduces the problem of eating disorders to the *loss of control*, without ascribing due importance to the problematic (and meaningful) character of the strain towards control. As Mele's argument suggests, the fact that we are able to exert control does not necessarily mean that we are acting autonomously. Mele argues that desires, preferences, and values that move us to act in a particular way should be *authentic*. The main feature of *authenticity* is the presence of correct information.[10]

There is an evident link between autonomy and information. In order to be able to make an autonomous choice or action, we need to possess relevant information. John Stuart Mill produced a classic and still convincing argument that it is not infringing on one's autonomy to impose restraints on someone's self-harming actions, if these actions are based on ignorance of some relevant facts. In his *On Liberty*, he wrote: 'If either a public officer or any one else saw a person attempting to cross a bridge which had been ascertained to be unsafe, and there were no time to warn him of his danger, they might seize him and turn him back, without any real infringement of his liberty'.[11] Only if the person were sufficiently informed and warned, Mill would probably say, should we let him jump. The first thing we need to do, therefore, is to assess whether eating-disordered behaviour is based on correct information. A few preliminary remarks are necessary.

---

[9] W. Vandereycken and R. Van Deth, *From Fasting Saints to Anorexic Girls: The History of Self-Starvation* (London: Athlone Press, 1994), 98.

[10] For a similar externalist argument, see M. F. Hanser, 'Intention and Teleology', *Mind*, 104/426 (1998), 381–401.

[11] J. S. Mill, *On Liberty*, in *On Liberty and Other Essays* (Oxford: Oxford University Press, 1991), 106–7.

3. *Autonomy and Information in Psychiatry*

The issue of information is always central to the analysis of autonomy, at least in moral philosophy and medical ethics. Legislation also acknowledges the fundamental importance of information in decision-making.[12]

In psychiatry, it is often particularly difficult to assess whether people 'own' the relevant information. This problem becomes particularly evident when it has to be decided whether people are competent to consent to or to refuse medical treatment. In this case, what should be assessed is whether or not they possess relevant information relating to treatment, probable results, and available options. Moreover, assessment must be made as to whether they possess adequate information relating to themselves.[13] These tasks, obviously, are not confined to psychiatry. However, in psychiatry particular problems arise. Some psychiatric conditions, in fact, are typically characterized by the denial of the problem. For example, people with bi-polar disorders, when in their manic phases, typically deny that there is anything wrong with their extraordinary excitation. As we have seen in Chapter 1, eating disorders are also often characterized by the denial of the state of emaciation. Other psychiatric conditions are characterized by what has been called 'incomplete or floating information'.[14] In such cases individuals may be aware of some relevant facts but not others, or they may be aware of them at one time but not at another. For example, in some cases of schizophrenia, people may be aware of the fact that they suffer from delusions of reference, but at the very time they perceive something as referring to them, they may not recognize that the impression they have is false.

Moreover, there may be a defect in understanding and using relevant information. It may be argued that, in order for behaviour to be autonomous, people should be able to take relevant information into account in evaluating the conditions and options they have.

Obviously, it is sometimes extremely difficult, and sometimes even practically impossible, to assess whether the relevant information is actually understood and utilized in the decision-making process.[15] Despite both

---

[12] With regard to Italy, see A. Santosuosso, 'Il consenso informato: Questioni di principio e regole specifiche', in A. Santosuosso (ed.), *Il consenso informato* (Milan: Cortina, 1996), 26–7. With regard to England, see Department of Health's 1993 Code of Practice of the Mental Health Act 1983, para. 15.12, quoted in G. H. Jones, 'Informed Consent in Chronic Schizophrenia?', *British Journal of Psychiatry*, 167 (1995), 565–8.

[13] B. F. Hoffman, 'Assessing the Competence of People to Consent to Medical Treatment: A Balance between Law and Medicine', *Medicine and Law*, 9 (1990), 1122–30.

[14] R. P. Smith et al., 'Competency and Practical Judgement', *Theoretical Medicine*, 17 (1996), 135–50.

[15] J. Savulescu and R. W. Momeyer, 'Should Informed Consent be Based on Rational Beliefs?', *Journal of Medical Ethics*, 23 (1997), 282–8; see also P. S. Appelbaum and T. Grisso,

theoretical and practical difficulties involved, we should try to understand whether eating-disordered behaviour is based on correct information, since a lack of information would be the first signal of a defect in autonomy. There are at least two areas in which the use of information is problematic: (1) self-perception and (2) food.

4. *Information and Self-Perception*

People with eating disorders (1) typically claim that they are not 'thin enough', even when they risk dying from malnutrition,[16] and (2) seem unable to recognize impulses of hunger and (especially) satiety.[17]

First let us consider the claim that they are not 'thin enough', or not 'too thin', or that they are 'too fat', or similar. It is sometimes believed that they make these claims because they have a distorted perception of their body image. If people with eating disorders really had a distorted perception of their body image, then we could reasonably argue that their deliberation is significantly defective, as diet would be based (among other things) on *false information* about the way they look.

However, as has been shown in Chapter 1, the nature of the claim of looking fat, or the nature of the overestimation of the body size, is still unclear. People with eating disorders tend to err in the estimation of the whole body, whereas the estimation of single parts of the body is generally more realistic. This is puzzling, as usually perceptual disorders do not depend on whether the subject looks at a whole object or a part of it (a colour-blind person does not see colours whether he is looking at a whole object or at its parts).

Moreover, the perception of body image is a complex operation, being affected by cognitive, affective, and optative responses. This means that, in the way they *look at* their body and *perceive* their body, people express not only what they *see*, but also how they *think* they look, how they *feel* they look, and how they *want* to look.

Finally, as we have also seen in Chapter 1, the different tests that are currently utilized to assess the estimation of body dimensions give discordant results.

'Assessing Patients' Capacities to Consent to Treatment', *New England Journal of Medicine*, 319/25 (1988), 1635–8.

[16] P. J. McKenna, 'Disorders with Overvalued Ideas', *British Journal of Psychiatry*, 145 (1984), 579–85; I shall return to the importance of beliefs in later sections.

[17] They may also find it difficult to acknowledge tiredness. In my understanding, these problems relate to restrictive anorexia, bulimic anorexia, and bulimia.

All this considered, it seems that there is insufficient scientific ground to claim that people with eating disorders have a disordered perception of their body. Thus, we cannot claim that eating-disordered behaviour is not autonomous *because of perceptual disorders*.

Secondly, there is the difficulty of acknowledging hunger and satiety. With regard to the experience of body impulses, both Hilde Bruch and Mara Selvini Palazzoli have acknowledged a 'defect in information'. Selvini Palazzoli stresses that people with eating disorders are always totally uncertain about their appetite and satiety. It is particularly unclear to them whether they have eaten enough. People with eating disorders never 'know', by inner and unreflective awareness, if they should eat, how much they should eat, whether they have eaten enough, and when they should stop. The fear of having eaten too much, or having been unable to regulate themselves, always affects them.[18] The typical questions that the eating-disordered person asks herself are: Is it right to be hungry at this particular time? What is the degree of 'right hunger'? What should one feel to be sure that one has had enough?[19]

Hilde Bruch stressed that most anorexics and obese patients manifest a functional deficit (functional means that it is not an organic failure) in the perception of hunger and satiety. Studies on the movements of gastric juices in these patients show that they do not have a realistic perception of the real signals of appetite.[20] In her seminal work *Eating Disorders*, Hilde Bruch argued that the perception of hunger is not innate, but is the result of a complicated learning process. An essential part of this process is the way weeping is answered. Typically the hungry baby cries. The way the mother responds to this call is decisive to a functional development of the perception of hunger.[21] This process begins during the first stages of life and is consolidated through the relationship with the mother. Research on non-human animals in isolation has confirmed this.[22]

It is today accepted that a multifactorial pathway leads to the development of eating disorders. Family and school environment are thought to have a decisive influence on the development of eating disorders. Although the specific contribution of each influence may be discussed, there is little debate on the relevance of the early attachment patterns between an infant and his

---

[18] M. Selvini Palazzoli, *L'anoressia mentale: Dalla terapia individuale alla terapia familiare* (9th edn., Milan: Feltrinelli, 1998), 70.

[19] Ibid. 180.

[20] H. Bruch, *Eating Disorders: Obesity, Anorexia Nervosa and the Person within* (London: Routledge and Kegan Paul, 1974), ch. 4.

[21] D. O. Hebb, *The Organization of Behavior* (New York: Wiley, 1949).

[22] H. F. Harlow and M. Harlow, 'Learning to Love', *American Science*, 54 (1966), 244–72.

or her primary caregiver. Overall, research consistently reveals abnormal attachment patterns in eating-disordered populations.[23]

The perception of appetite and satiety, in people with eating disorders, is unrealistic and anomalous. It is not that they *do not feel* the signals of hunger and satiety; *they perceive* gastric contractions, but they interpret them in an abnormal way.[24] It is possible to give different interpretations to this phenomenon. Bruch, for example, interprets this in terms of 'conversion'; people have other types of emotional tensions and various types of problems and conflicts, but all these problems and conflicts converge on food. Food becomes their focus and the 'pseudo-solution' to these problems. The incapacity to perceive hunger and satiety is, according to Bruch, expressive of the incapacity to detect other types of emotional needs.[25]

Whether or not this interpretation is correct, what matters, from an *ethical point of view*, is that people with eating disorders appear to have an abnormal interpretation of hunger and satiety, whatever the deepest reasons for this. It may be argued that this compromises the process of deliberation leading to eating behaviour, and therefore is ethically relevant. The problematic perception of hunger and satiety 'diminishes' the autonomy of eating-disordered behaviour. Within the framework of 'weak paternalism', this may provide a prima facie ethical justification for non-consensual intervention.

However, it does not follow that carers and health-care professionals are entitled to seize the person with eating disorders and force her to eat or not to purge or not to exercise simply because of her 'defects in perception'. Why this is so will become clear in the following sections of this chapter.

5. *Information Relating to Food*

The *way* people with eating disorders utilize information relating to food provides an extraordinary representation of how the *way* in which information is utilized is relevant to autonomy.

People with eating disorders are usually very well informed about food. They normally know by heart both the nutrition and the caloric contents of principal foods. However, as Hilde Bruch noticed, they are *unable to apply* their knowledge.[26] The selection of right and wrong foods, or allowed and forbidden foods, is not characterized by a lack of information relating to

---

[23] Anne Ward and Simon Gowers, 'Attachment and Childhood Development', in Janet Treasure, Ulrich Schmidt, and Eric van Furth (eds.), *Handbook of Eating Disorders* (2nd edn., Chichester: Wiley, 2003), ch. 6, pp. 103–20, at p. 115.

[24] Bruch, *Eating Disorders*, ch. 4, sect. 4.

[25] Ibid., ch. 4, sect. 1.

[26] Ibid. 384.

nutrition needs or to food's nutrition contents. It is rather 'the way', inflexible and severe, people apply this information that seems somewhat
problematic.

Duker and Slade, for example, note: 'even after stating correctly that 1,400
calories is the daily minimum requirement for an unconscious head injury
patient, an anorexic nurse will firmly insist: "I'm different, 300 calories a day
is plenty for me." The attitude is: "Whatever you're saying, it doesn't apply
to me." ' Duker and Slade argue that these cognitive distortions are due to
brain function impairments at low weight.[27] They argue that being underweight alters brain chemistry and produces a number of cognitive changes.
They write:

Sometimes, when a person is extremely low weight, the psychological changes this
produces are so bizarre it is difficult to know what psychiatric condition she or he is
suffering from [...] This very extreme or bizarre behaviour tends to occur when the
less complex brain functions begin to disappear. These are the functions [...] that are
concerned with memory, with controlling the movements of the body, and with being
able to know where one is, or locating oneself in relation to the rest of the world.
Sufferers may experience themselves at this stage as being controlled by their sur-
roundings. They may, for example, hear physical objects demanding that they behave
in a particular way, or hear voices that are continually criticizing them [...] Generally
they will have no awareness of the way in which cognitively they become constrained
[...] Consistent food restriction does not produce uniformity solely in terms of
physical emaciation or 'slimness'. It produces psychological uniformity too. The
more constrained the anorexic or indeed any other starving person is the less variation
there is in that person's actions and responses. At low weight sufferers are all much the
same in the way they think, feel, relate to others and experience day-to-day events.
The lower their weight, the more 'standard' they become.[28]

People with eating disorders do not use information on food's nutrition
contents, caloric contents, food combinations, and so on to improve the
quality of their diet or their general well-being. Such information becomes
rather the frame of their cage. It provides a justification for their diet, to
themselves and to others. In other words, that information is utilized as an
'excuse' for both restrictive diet and food selection. People with eating
disorders do not eat in response to their physiological impulses or needs,
but rather 'commit' or 'delegate' their eating to self-imposed rules relating to
when and what to eat. They utilize detailed information about caloric content, association, digestion, and assimilation modes as 'instructions' for the
use. Their knowledge is what makes their restrictive regime both 'right' and
indisputable. In these cases, eating-related choices are not based on fully

---

[27] Marilyn Duker and Roger Slade, *Anorexia and Bulimia: How to Help* (2nd edn., Buckingham: Open University Press, 2003), 163.
[28] Ibid. 102–4.

correct information—not in the sense that relevant information is lacking, but in the sense that relevant information is not utilized *correctly*. Instead of being used for improving health and well-being, it is utilized *as a justification* for an unhealthy and clearly harmful lifestyle.

This is relevant to the ethics of treatment of eating disorders. It may be argued that inability to utilize information jeopardizes the autonomy of behaviour. Given the relationship between autonomy and information, inability to use information in a functional way strengthens the prima facie entitlement to paternalism. However, as was pointed out at the end of the previous section, the limits of justifiable paternalism need to be determined. Important considerations will be made below, in Sections 9.1, 9.2 and 9.3.

6. *Eating Disorders and Beliefs*

K. W. M. Fulford has suggested that psychopathologies should be understood in terms of disturbances of agency or failures of action. He points out that in psychiatry sometimes a failure in judgement and beliefs characterizes people's actions. For example, in the case of paranoia, delusions may take the form of value judgements and beliefs in informing actions.[29] As we shall see, it seems that something similar happens in the case of eating disorders, where beliefs inform behaviour in a peculiar way.

We should first clarify what the term 'belief' means. The following account of belief has been suggested. A belief may be defined in terms of (1) entertainment (I entertain p) and (2) disposition to act (I have a disposition to act as if p were true). While entertainment refers to the mental experience, disposition to act refers to physical behaviour—that is, while entertainment is subjective or phenomenological, disposition to act is objective or behavioural.[30] Charles S. Peirce also argued that beliefs guide our desires and shape our actions.[31] 'The essence of belief is the establishment of a habit; and different beliefs are distinguished by the different modes of action to which they give raise.'[32] Beliefs are, therefore, strictly linked to actions.

Moreover, when I believe something, it is possible that what I believe is not true. I may be 'very tenacious' in my belief, and indeed many people seem to 'fix' their beliefs with what Peirce called 'the method of tenacity'. As Peirce

---

[29] K. W. M. Fulford, 'Mental Illness, Concept of', in *Encyclopedia of Applied Ethics* (London: Academy Press, 1998), iii. 213–33, at 230; see also Hanser, 'Intention and Teleology'.

[30] R. B. Braithwaite, 'The Nature of Believing', in A. Phillips Griffiths (ed.), *Knowledge and Belief* (London: Oxford University Press, 1967), 28–40.

[31] Charles S. Peirce, 'The Fixation of Belief', *Popular Science Monthly*, 12 (Nov. 1877), 1–15, s. III.

[32] Charles S. Peirce, 'How to Make our Ideas Clear', *Popular Science Monthly*, 12 (Jan. 1878), 286–302, s. II.

pointed out, steady and immovable beliefs (a faith) yield a great peace of mind.[33] But, however tenaciously I may cling to my beliefs, there must be something else—apart from the fact that I hold them—that makes them true. By definition, thus, beliefs are *fallible*. Moreover, beliefs are characterized by 'indirectness'. This means that there must be some further fact, beyond the fact that I believe *p*, which makes *p* true. Instead, knowledge is by definition infallible. Of course it may not be exhaustive, but it cannot be 'true' or 'false'.[34]

In cases of eating disorders, there seems to be a superimposition of knowledge and belief. People with eating disorders articulate abnormal eating patterns on the basis of firm beliefs in the same way a rational agent would act on the basis of the knowledge of facts. Obviously, it is not necessary to suppose that a rational agent would *always only act based on knowledge*. She could give assent to her belief about *p*, when she has *reasons to believe p*. Having reasons to believe *p* means knowing some fact making *p* more likely than its alternatives. But, perhaps, what matters is that when we act on the basis of a belief, we should be aware that there are alternatives, and that the evidence on which our belief is based is, by definition, incomplete. Instead, people with eating disorders act on the basis of beliefs that do not have any 'indirect' confirmation, and elevate such beliefs at the level of evidence, accepting them as granted and being unable (or unwilling) to doubt them.

For example, they may refuse some food, typically *animal* fat food, on the basis of the belief that it will immediately take the form of *body* fat. They typically select food on the basis of, for example, the belief that 100kcal of cheese or eggs will 'fatten' more than 100kcal of vegetables and fruit, whereas how exactly human organism assimilates different kinds of food is still unclear.[35] It has been reported that *excess calories* are more easily stored as fats if they are ingested as fat.[36] But this does not mean that 'fats become body fat', or that if we ingest fats (animal or vegetable fats, in the form of, for example, cheese or oils or nuts) we will store more fat; or that the fat that we find on our thighs or abdomen comes from ingested fats. It is not *fat* (animal or vegetable fat) that becomes *body fat*, but *the excess of calories*. The evidence that *calories in excess* will be more easily stored as body fat if ingested in the form of fats has not much to do with the (rather simplistic) belief that ingested fats will transform themselves into body fat.

---

[33] Peirce, 'The Fixation of Belief', s. V.

[34] H. H. Price, 'Some Consideration about Belief', in Phillips Griffiths (ed.), *Knowledge and Belief*, 41–59.

[35] See E. Faccio, *Il disturbo alimentare: Modelli, ricerche e terapie* (Rome: Carocci, 1999), 97.

[36] Julia Dalgleish and Stuart Dollery, *The Health and Fitness Handbook* (Harlow: Longman, 2001), 135.

Clinical literature is full of examples of how people with eating disorders determine a rigid dietary regime on the basis of beliefs that have no solid scientific support (let us call these, for simplicity, *false beliefs*). This fact is relevant to the ethics of dealing with the person with eating disorders. It may be argued that autonomous behaviour is behaviour that is based on correct information—part of which is *knowledge of the relevant facts* and *belief in that knowledge*. If clinical literature is correct, then eating behaviour is based on beliefs that are *false* (on the basis of available scientific evidence and experience[37]). It follows that the person with eating disorders is not acting autonomously (at least in a relevant sense), in so far as her eating habits are based on these sorts of beliefs.

Obviously, we should not assume that only behaviour that is based on *knowledge* can be classified as autonomous. We all act on the *basis of beliefs*. We make 'simple' choices, like going to the cinema, *believing* that the film will be good, and our belief can be confirmed or not. We also make more important choices—for example, we get married on the basis of a number of beliefs (relating to our partner, to ourselves, to our job, and so on) that may be disproved. The fact that we often act and choose on the basis of *beliefs* (which, by definition, may be true or false, and are therefore fallible) does not, of course, entitle others, maybe better informed than we are, to force us to do otherwise. It may give them reason to talk to us and give us richer information that would allow us to make a more informed decision. It may give them reason to try to persuade us with words, but not to force us to behave in a different way.

In the case of eating disorders, however, some beliefs (sometimes evidently false beliefs) are utilized as an indisputable guide to practical conduct. People with eating disorders seem to attach the value of absolute and unquestionable truth to their beliefs. This contradicts the nature itself of beliefs. As happens with information, it is not the presence of a belief, but rather the *way* this belief is employed in practical conduct that 'rings the bell'.

The importance of the way information and beliefs inform behaviour in the case of eating disorders is acknowledged in clinical psychology. In particular, the cognitive approach to eating disorders focuses on the

---

[37] For example, the belief that 100kcal of animal fats fatten more than 100kcal of vegetable fats is based on no solid scientific ground. In this sense, it lacks scientific evidence. The belief that if you miss your training today you will be fatter tomorrow may be disproved by experience. There are 'known and observed facts', as Peirce wrote in 'The Fixation of Belief', s. V, that make these beliefs *false*. We should consider true those beliefs whose conceivable effects are in harmony with the practical effects. Peirce still talks at this level of beliefs (scientific beliefs), not of knowledge. What matters to our purposes is not whether this level of knowledge is still fallible and therefore should still be included in the category of beliefs, but, rather, that this level of knowledge is to be distinguished by the 'tenaciously held' belief that is not supported by either scientific or empirical basis of any sort.

way people with eating disorders process information. Cognitive studies suggest that the deliberation process of the eating-disordered person is dysfunctional.

7. *The Cognitive Approach to Eating Disorders*

Cognitivism is one of the branches of contemporary experimental psychology that is interested in the study of cognitive processes. Memory, thinking, language, and perception represent the central interests of cognitivism. Cognitivism stresses the importance of mental processes and, in particular, focuses on the crucial role of information. According to the *human information processing* model,[38] human behaviour depends on the way external information, coming from the senses, is elaborated at several stages and particularly in the decision-making centres. This information, in fact, elaborated and interpreted, affects decision-making processes and directs the answer (output).[39]

The cognitive approach has been utilized in the study of eating disorders since the 1980s. *Information* is considered one of the central aspects of eating disorders. All the phases through which information is obtained, elaborated, and utilized appear dysfunctional in subjects with eating disorders.

The cognitive process can be structured in four phases:

1. *perception* of the input of information;
2. *interpretation*;
3. *decision* relating to what action will be undertaken;
4. *output*.

It has been noticed that, in people with eating disorders, *perception* is distorted at two levels: (i) at the level of selection of the relevant information (typically, people with eating disorders ignore the most important information and focus on the less relevant[40]); (ii) at the level of acknowledgement of stimuli (typically, these people are unable to recall the information stored inside the memory and to utilize it to identify new information coming from the outside[41]). *Interpretation* also appears dysfunctional: 'You look good

---

[38] U. Neisser, *Cognitive Psychology* (New York: Appelton Century-Crofts, 1967).

[39] *Enciclopedia Garzanti di filosofia* (Milan: Garzanti, 1994), 183.

[40] Elena Faccio makes the following example: whereas many people might not pay attention to how they are fitting into their clothes because many other stimuli capture their attention, the person with anorexia might be focusing only on that factor, regardless of the many other things she could pay attention to. Another example could be: I still have some fat around my hips. The fact that I am underweight is irrelevant.

[41] Faccio, *Il disturbo alimentare*, 83.

today' is typically interpreted as 'You've put on weight'.[42] Finally, *decision-making process* and *output* seem dysfunctional in that eating-disordered behaviour is nothing but a pattern of ways of avoiding 'fat'.[43]

Among the typical cognitive dysfunctions of anorexic and bulimic people the following have been identified. The following schema is taken from Shafran and De Silva.[44]

- *Selective abstraction.* People select parts of a situation without considering any other evidence and come to conclusions only on the basis of the evidence they look at. Typical expression of selective abstraction is: 'Other people will like me more if I am thin.'
- *Dichotomous reasoning.* Thinking in terms of extremes and absolutes. 'If I'm not thin I'm fat.'
- *Overgeneralization.* 'I was unhappy when I was at normal weight... so I know that putting on weight is going to make me unhappy'.
- *Magnification* (exaggerating the significance of events). 'Gaining 2 pounds has made me unattractive.'
- *Superstitious thinking.* 'If I eat this, it will be converted into fat on my stomach immediately' (false belief; see above, Section 6).

There are other cognitive models of explanation of anorexia and bulimia.[45] Overall, there is a general agreement among cognitivists as to the kind of cognitive distortions that characterize anorexia and bulimia nervosa. It is generally accepted that the cognitive process underlying eating disorders is based on false or irrational beliefs that contribute to distort the interpretation of information.[46]

This, of course, is not intended to be a comprehensive account of the cognitive approach to eating disorders. The conclusions that have been briefly summarized here, however, seem coherent with the conclusions of this chapter and seem to confirm the validity of this type of analysis of eating disorders. The results of this analysis may have important ethical implications.

---

[42] A. Freeman and V. B. Greenwood (eds.), *Cognitive Therapy: Application in Psychiatry and Medical Settings* (New York: Human Science, 1987), quoted in Faccio, *Il disturbo alimentare*, 83.

[43] E. P. Garfinkel and D. M. Garner, *Handbook of Psychotherapy for Anorexia and Bulimia Nervosa* (New York: Guilford Press, 1985), quoted in Faccio, *Il disturbo alimentare*, 84.

[44] Roz Shafran and Padmal De Silva, 'Cognitive-Behavioural Models', in Treasure, Schmidt, and van Furth (eds.), *Handbook of Eating Disorders*, ch. 7, pp. 121–38, at p. 126.

[45] Ibid. 121–38, for a comprehensive account.

[46] Faccio, *Il disturbo alimentare*, 83.

8. *The Ethics of Paternalism towards People with Eating Disorders*

Chapter 2 argued that paternalism may be ethical in some circumstances—that is, when a person is performing self-harming behaviour that is based on factors (such as a lack of relevant information) that significantly undermine autonomy. As Feinberg suggests, paternalism may also be justifiable when a temporary intervention is necessary to assess whether self-harming conduct is significantly autonomous or not.[47] Defects in autonomy should not be inferred by the mere fact that the conduct is *harmful*, or that it may appear irrational to other people (doctors or carers) or that it differs from what the majority would do in similar circumstances. It should instead be determined on the basis of the analysis of the process of reasoning and deliberation that leads up to a particular action or choice.

In the above sections, I have looked at the process of deliberation underlying eating disorders. It seems that this process is dysfunctional in some important way. In the light of the compromising factors that have been highlighted in this chapter, we may conclude that there is a prima facie entitlement to paternalism in the care and treatment of people with eating disorders. Although eating-disordered people do not directly harm others with their eating-related choices, although they are normally skilled and capable of self-determination in most areas of their life, and although they typically do not complain about their situation and even defend it, acts of paternalism may still be an ethically legitimate option, given that self-harming behaviour is based on a dysfunctional deliberation process.

However, it is necessary to make some considerations that in a way 'mitigate' the (already weak) theory of paternalism articulated here, and that may raise further doubts as to the most appropriate way of approaching the eating-disordered person. If the theory articulated here is acceptable, and if the considerations that will be made in the next three sections are persuasive, cases in which paternalism may be acceptable towards people with eating disorders are very limited. There is room for paternalism towards eating-disordered people, but that space is very small, and is one in which paternalism is shorn of much of the normative strength that it may have in other circumstances.

---

[47]   J. Feinberg, 'Legal Paternalism', *Canadian Journal of Philosophy*, 1 (1977), 105–24.

9. *Factors that Limit the Strength of Paternalism towards the Eating-Disorders Sufferer*

9.1. *The first factor: When harmful is harmful enough*

According to the theory of paternalism articulated before, a person may be entitled to prevent the *harmful* conduct of another person only when this other person is acting non-autonomously. Conduct should be harmful, as paternalism has to be justified on the ground that the person is to be protected. But when is a conduct harmful? And when is it harmful enough to justify paternalism?

Some acts are intuitively harmful. Acts that will result in death or that seriously compromise bodily integrity or health are clearly harmful. An act of self-mutilation is clearly harmful. Severe malnutrition is clearly harmful, even when it is not directly lethal (see Chapter 1). Repeated compensatory behaviour, especially vomiting, is also clearly harmful, given the consequences it has, for example on people's electrolyte balance, heart rhythm, muscular strength, and fluids balance.

These types of behaviour are clearly harmful. However, eating-disordered behaviour is not always *clearly harmful*. Eating-disordered behaviour involves a wide pattern of acts and choices that affect and modify the entire life of the sufferer and are often not directly related to eating. In many of these acts (like checking weight several times in a day) there is nothing seriously harmful. Why should one stop a person from standing on the scale ten times a day, if this is what she likes to do? Food selection, to take another example, is not in itself dangerous (many vegans operate strict food selection and keep healthy). What types of behaviour related to eating disorders are sufficiently harmful to justify non-consensual intervention? How do we assess the amount of harm that may follow some acts or choices, when these actions or choices do not directly threaten the life, the integrity, or the health of the person?

An additional problem is that a modality of behaviour that may be harmless (or nearly so) in the short term may produce harmful consequences in the long term. The person with eating disorders may, for example, feel nervous at the prospect of going to the restaurant (on the basis of catastrophic thoughts such as: 'If I go to the restaurant today I'll end up stuffing for the rest of my life'). In individual cases, the strict discipline that characterizes eating disorders will produce no harm, but, if it becomes a modality of behaviour, it may prevent the person from enjoying and achieving many important things in life. The person with eating disorders may experience a wide range of 'normal' activities as threats to her own regime. She may find it reassuring to avoid all situations that may distract her from her strict self-discipline, and this 'beneficial' effect (reduction of anxiety) may induce her to avoid a wide range of pleasurable and important activities. As seems to happen to people with obsessions, a fixed behaviour or ritual (compulsion) may become the easiest modality to reduce anxiety (obsession). The positive effect of behaviour (reduction of anxiety) may trap the person in the cage of a ritual and may make it difficult for the person to do otherwise.[48]

If this happens, it may contribute to making the person more and more isolated, increasingly concentrated on herself, and, consequently, trapped in a miserable condition of overall loneliness and unhappiness.

Should behaviour be considered *harmful* only when it is directly harmful, or also when it is likely to produce harm in the future? Moreover, should it be considered harmful only when it is *physically harmful* or also when it involves non-physical harm?

The theory of weak paternalism does not provide us with an answer to these crucial questions. It allows us to intervene to prevent non-autonomous conduct that is harmful, but does not say when harmful is harmful enough. In some cases, eating-disordered behaviour is intuitively harmful enough to justify paternalism. But, in other cases, it may be difficult to determine whether eating-disordered behaviour is harmful, or harmful enough to justify paternalism. Since the theory of paternalism articulated here allows us to intervene only to prevent harm, in cases in which it is unclear whether behaviour associated with eating-disorders is harmful, or harmful enough to justify paternalism, we cannot be sure that paternalism is justifiable. I am not saying that paternalism *is unethical* whenever it is unclear whether eating-disordered behaviour is harmful enough. I am saying that *it is unclear* whether paternalism is ethical or not whenever it is unclear whether eating-disordered behaviour is harmful enough, and the theory does not help us make this assessment. This problem does not invalidate the theory, but makes it very weak in practice, as in many cases we seem unable to assess whether one of the conditions of justifiable paternalism is met.

9.2. *The second factor: The value of autonomy*

Clinical studies show that the sense of autonomy is extremely important to people with eating disorders. The search for control over the self and over the surrounding environment is considered the expression of people's profound need to perceive themselves as *autonomous beings*, capable of self-

---

[48] This should not be taken as an attempt to apply a behavioural model to eating disorders. I only wish to point out that behaviour that is not harmful in the short term may be harmful in the long term.

determination.[49] For this reason, it has been argued that, whereas physicians always confront these potentially conflicting responsibilities, in the case of eating disorders they have 'to face an additional *therapeutic* dilemma: encouraging greater autonomy and freedom in the patient, while at the same time taking control over the patient's food intake and body weight'.[50] The dilemma here is not simply *ethical*, but also *therapeutic*. Respect for autonomy is not only an ethical issue, but also a clinical issue. With a paternalistic action, we may risk worsening the eating-disordered person's condition. As we have seen in the previous chapter, there are not sufficient empirical studies on the long-term effects of 'coercive' intervention on anorexia sufferers to support one view or the other. However, a number of experts contend that paternalistic actions towards people with eating disorders are most likely to compromise both the efficacy of the therapy and the long-term recovery of the person. Paternalistic acts will inevitably cause a sense of violation in the person. Given that eating disorders are the expression of an inner need for autonomy and control, coercive interventions will necessarily have counter-productive effects. They will erode further the already fragile autonomy of the sufferer. They will also erode the trust necessary for clinical success. If eating disorders are a fight for autonomy and control, force-feeding will necessarily worsen the patient's psychological condition. Paternalistic interventions are likely to render the sufferer even more aggressive and determined in her behaviour, more frustrated, angry, and lonely than before. Acts of paternalism in the management of eating disorders are, therefore, a particularly delicate choice, probably more delicate than in the management of other diseases.

9.3. *The third factor: Are there true 'dysfunctions' or true 'defects' in deliberation?*

The final important consideration concerns the type of 'defects' that characterize the deliberation in eating disorders. This has to do with the way we think about eating disorders—or eating-disordered behaviour. As we have seen, there are 'defects' in the deliberation process leading to eating-disordered behaviour—defects relating to information and beliefs. However, we need to ask: how should we think of these defects?

These 'defects' consist mainly of *peculiar ways* of interpreting and using information and beliefs. This is very important, because there is not simply 'a piece of information missing', or 'a belief that is taken for granted', but a

---

[49] M. Selvini Palazzoli, S. Cirillo, M. Selvini, and A. M. Sorrentino, *Ragazze anoressiche e bulimiche: La terapia familiare* (Milan: Cortina, 1998), 96–7.

[50] Günter Rathner, 'A Plea against Compulsory Treatment of Anorexia Nervosa Patients', in Pierre J. V. Beumont and Walter Vandereycken, *Treating Eating Disorders: Ethical, Legal and Personal Issues* (New York: New York University Press, 1998), 198.

person who *interprets* and *uses* that information and those beliefs in that particular way. The fact that the person *gives that interpretation* means that the person is *active* in this process. The fact that the eating-disordered person believes that if she goes to the restaurant one day she will get fatter is not something that 'just happens to her' because she has some mistaken information, but is part of the modality of behaviour of the eating-disordered person. It is part of her system of thought, her fears, her emotional life, her feelings, and her objectives.[51] The defects in information and beliefs, if seen through this perspective, are not factors that jeopardize deliberation. They are not 'external' forces, so to speak. They are instead the expression of the complex emotional contents of the eating-disordered person. They are 'a part' of that person, part of what being that particular person means to the person herself.

From this point of view, eating-disordered behaviour is not 'characterized by dysfunctions'. There are not real 'dysfunctions' in eating disorders. All aspects of eating disorders that seem to be 'dysfunctional', or 'disordered', or 'defective', are indeed coherent and functional to the disorder. They are part of what it is to have an eating disorder.

In Chapter 2 we discussed Mill's example of the man crossing the unsafe bridge. That man was lacking relevant information. *Therefore* his action of crossing the bridge was non-autonomous. If the man knew the bridge was unsafe, he might not cross it. In this case we have a 'genuine' lack of information and therefore a 'genuine' defect in autonomy. The case of eating disorders is different in an important way.

In the case of eating disorders, the 'defects' in deliberation *are* the eating disorder and not what leads to eating disorders. These 'defects' are wanted and accepted to the same extent and in the same way as eating-disordered behaviour is wanted and accepted. Having those 'defects' in deliberation is not 'the reason why' people adopt abnormal eating: it is *the same as* adopting abnormal eating. Above I discussed the example of a person who decides not to go to the restaurant because she (mistakenly) believes that interrupting her diet for one meal will make her fatter. If this person did not have this type of belief, not only would she go to the restaurant tonight, but she would not have an eating disorder. In other words, a person would not articulate these types of beliefs if they were not important to her, and if they were not useful to support her 'project' of food and weight control.

This view is supported by a recent study published by Jacinta Tan, Tony Hope, and Anne Stewart. They report the replies of their eating-disorder patients, to the question: 'Do you think you would make it magically disappear if you could?' (referring to the eating disorder).

---

[51] Cf. Section 2 above.

c. 'If I knew that I could be happy—but it would be a completely different me, it would be a completely different way of thinking, because I don't think I could be the person I want to be, at the moment, without anorexia, because it's a part of me; so if I could change the kind of person I wanted to be, then yes, I would take that pill, but until then I probably wouldn't . . . I wouldn't know who I was. And I would be completely and utterly lost in what I was doing . . . '

I. 'Everything. My personality would be different. It's been, I know it's been such a big part of me, and—I don't think you can ever get rid of it, or the feelings, you always have a bit—in you.'[52]

As the authors also recognize, the 'disorder' is not an entity that the sufferers perceive as distinct from themselves, amenable in the same way as the lack of information of Mill's man is. You cannot simply provide the information or correct the patient's beliefs in order to modify the eating-disordered behaviour. 'Dysfunctional' information and beliefs are a part of the disorder itself, and a part of the *person* herself.

The fact that 'dysfunctions' in the deliberative process are a *part* of the person herself, a part of having eating disorders, has important consequences for the ethics of paternalism.

We have to distinguish two different points of view from which eating disorders may be seen. From one point of view, the deliberation underlying eating disorders *is* dysfunctional in that it is characterized by 'defects' in information and beliefs. Eating-disordered behaviour lacks autonomy in some important respects. There is thus a prima facie entitlement to paternalism. From another point of view, however, all apparent 'dysfunctions' in the deliberation process of the person with eating disorders are not dysfunctions but 'functions' of the system of thought/emotions and of the modality of behaviour of the person with eating disorders. From this point of view, it would be inappropriate and maybe too simplistic to claim that eating-disordered behaviour is non-autonomous *because there are such defects*. The peculiarities of the deliberation process should be seen as meaningful aspects of the whole condition, and not simply as the 'causes' of abnormal behaviour. These 'defects', in other words, do not qualify behaviour as non-autonomous. Only at one level do they qualify behaviour as non-autonomous. At another level, they do not, as they are a *part* of that behaviour. There seems to be no clear-cut distinction between deliberation, on the one hand, and actions and choices, on the other, as that particular type of deliberation is part of eating disorders and not simply what 'leads up to eating disorders'.

---

[52] Jacinta O. A. Tan, Tony Hope, and Anne Stewart, 'Anorexia Nervosa and Personal Identity: The Accounts of Patients and their Parents', *International Journal of Law and Psychiatry*, 26/5 (Sept.–Oct. 2003), 533–48.

These considerations make paternalism towards people a conceptually obscure area. The entire question of 'what it is ethical to do' when caring for eating-disordered people appears misleading, because, from a certain point of view, nothing is 'defective' and everything is important and meaningful, and worth attention and consideration.

So far as we do not lose interest in eating-disordered behaviour and curiosity about it, and so far as we investigate the reasons for people's behaviour, we find that moral categories lose their force and meaning; they do not help us either to understand the problem or to cope with it. Deliberation is not just defective, as defects cannot be there 'by chance'. There are reasons why the person articulates those 'defects'. It follows that the whole question of whether paternalism towards eating-disordered people may be ethical loses a significant part of its meaning. If we consider eating-disordered behaviour from the point of view of the meaning of behaviour, the question of whether or not behaviour is autonomous appears inappropriate.

10. *Conclusions*

In this chapter I have tried to determine whether behaviour that is typical of people with eating disorders is significantly autonomous. It has been shown that the way information is interpreted and utilized, together with beliefs, to direct practical conduct appears problematic. This seems to provide carers and health-care professionals with a prima facie entitlement to act paternalistically towards the eating-disordered person.

However, acts of paternalism towards this group of people are extremely controversial. The peculiarities of eating disorders make paternalism a very weak option. However, this theory of paternalism, weak as it may be, is still the best we can have. It is the most consistent with both ethical and clinical requirements, and is the only one that is theoretically clear and appropriate to the complex circumstances of the phenomenon. The main points of the theory may be summarized as follows.

1. We should reject all forms of paternalism according to which it is morally legitimate, right, or even mandatory to restrict individuals' *autonomy*, in order to prevent self-harm. Consequences on the good or on the well-being of the individual who wants to act so do not represent a criterion, either necessary or sufficient, for the moral legitimacy of restrictions on *autonomy*. The assessment of consequences is instead important, as it results from the definition of weak paternalism given above, in cases of relevant defects in autonomy.

2. We should reject all forms of apparently weak paternalism based on a substantive notion of autonomy, according to which individuals are autonomous only as far as their conduct satisfies determinate criteria of rationality. Whether or not an action or a choice is autonomous depends on the process of reasoning and deliberation informing them, not on the content or outcome of their decisions.
3. We should reject all forms of paternalism based on the fact that the person has been diagnosed as having a mental illness. The diagnosis of mental illness is ethically irrelevant: it does not produce any reason that may justify paternalism. If the criterion that may legitimate paternalism is a defect in autonomy, the fact that this defect is linked to a psychological or a psychiatric condition is surely clinically important, but has no moral relevance.

As I have pointed out above, it is still unclear whether and in what way carers and health-care professionals are entitled to force the eating-disordered person to modify her behaviour. In many cases, it would be difficult in practice to determine whether behaviour is harmful, especially considering it in perspective, and whether it is 'autonomous'. Whereas at one level eating-disordered behaviour is based on ill information and beliefs, at a deeper level these defects may be 'chosen' and 'wanted' to the same extent as eating-disordered behaviour itself is chosen and wanted. These 'defects' may not be real 'defects', but meaningful parts of behaviour itself.

From this point of view, the issue of the autonomy of eating-disordered behaviour becomes a complex one, a matter for psychologists rather than for ethicists. The whole issue of autonomy of behaviour becomes 'shaded' and loses part of its ethical significance. This is the 'frustrating' side of the story, for the ethicist. The ethicist who follows this book in its journey towards the heart of eating disorders, with the aim of finding out what it is ethical to do in these cases, is left in the same position as the cook who takes off all the leaves of the artichoke in the search for the artichoke. They are both left with nothing.

The real issue is why people want what they want, why they want it so much, why they are ready to sacrifice their health and even their life in order to get it, why they manage to frame a coherent set of beliefs in support of their self-destructive behaviour. From this point of view, ethics collapses into psychology. The ethicist who gets to this point has to accept that there may be no definite answer to the ethics of 'paternalism' towards people with eating disorders and that in an important sense asking whether behaviour is autonomous is somehow missing the point—because what matters is the meaning of people's behaviour, what they need, not whether they are autonomous. Maybe there is no such a thing as incompetence or lack of autonomy: there are needs.

However, the frustrated ethicist may object. Maybe you are right. Maybe the question of the autonomy of behaviour is partly misleading. Maybe we cannot have definite answers to the questions on the ethics of paternalism. Maybe it is true that 'ethics collapses into psychology', as you say. But still we *have to make choices* at some point. And these choices are *ethical choices*. When somebody is taken into hospital dehydrated and malnourished, we have to make a choice. Maybe the analysis of autonomy of behaviour does not provide us with valid grounds to make such a choice, but we still have to make a choice. Should we let the person decide? Should we let her die? Should we rescue her? Should we consider her relatives' wishes? Ethics may collapse into psychology, but what do we do? You may say: 'I don't have to do anything. Thank God I'm not a doctor, I'm a philosopher and my job is to think, not to act.' But this is still a *value choice*? Or maybe you might dwell on your philosophical impasse: 'Hold on! Don't do anything before we resolve philosophical and psychological dilemmas.' This would also be a *value choice*. The patient dies, the relatives cry out, and you think it *more important* to resolve your philosophical and psychological dilemmas before acting. The arguments of this book show that the ethicist needs to somewhat abandon his or her ethical categories in order to understand eating disorders. The ethicist needs to depart from the point of view of ethics and to embrace the point of view of psychology—understanding the values and needs of the person with eating disorders. However, ethics cannot be ruled out entirely, as eating disorders continue to impose on us choices that are ethical in nature.

The objection of the ethicist is a compelling one. We will always have to make some value choices. Even if we decided not to make any choice and 'let things happen' this would also be a value choice. Probably the most dramatic situation is when the patient refuses to eat, and the only means to save her life is by forcibly feeding her. The next chapter will discuss the case and try to answer the question as to whether the wishes of the dying anorexic should be respected.

13

Anorexia Nervosa and Refusal of Life-Saving Interventions

1. *Introduction*

A case history:

In 1994, in Sheffield, UK, a patient with anorexia was left to die. She was 24, and she had had anorexia since she was 16. After several admissions into hospital, she was deemed incurable. Hence she was administered only palliative care. She received symptomatic treatment for pain due to her osteoporosis. She died within a week of admission.[1]

Another case history:

A 22-year-old woman was admitted to hospital in Canada, in 1991. She was in a state of extreme emaciation and cardio-vascular collapse. She had had anorexia for eight years. Once admitted, as she had been before, she refused medical treatment and pulled out the infusion line. Previously, she had pulled out a naso-gastric tube. The case was discussed in the ethics committee with the parents and physicians. It was agreed that the patient should not be treated. She died the next day.[2]

Were these decisions ethically acceptable?[3] Some people have objected that we should always strive to keep anorexic patients alive, because it is possible

---

An earlier version of this chapter has been published as Simona Giordano, 'Anorexia Nervosa and Refusal of Naso-Gastric Treatment: A Response to Heather Draper', *Bioethics*, 17/3 (2003), 261–78.

[1] Walter Vandereycken, 'Viewpoint: Whose competence Should We Question?', *European Eating Disorders Review*, 6 (1999), 1–3.

[2] Ibid.

[3] It may be asked whether these patients would or should have been treated differently if they were minor. For a comprehensive account of the legal issues relating to treatment of the minor, see Margaret Brazier, *Medicine, Patients and the Law* (London: Penguin, 2003), 339–71. From the point of view of the arguments developed in this book, prima facie the child's wishes should be respected provided that they are autonomous (or competent, in legal language). The law assumes that there is an 'age' at which people may be presumed to be competent, that is 18 years. It is clear that each individual matures at a different pace and with different modalities, and therefore this age (18) is necessarily arbitrary and possibly does not capture the real capacity of the individual person. Therefore it cannot be determined a priori what physicians *should have done* if these two patients were minor.

even for people with long-standing severe anorexia to recover fully. The feelings of negativism and distress should not prevent us from offering therapy and we should always give people a chance.[4] Should patients with anorexia be allowed to make decisions about the treatment of their condition, even if they will die as a result? Is paternalism justifiable? If so, why? On what basis can we intervene?

In Chapter 2 I articulated a theory of paternalism. According to this theory of paternalism, prima facie we have an entitlement to protect a person from self-harm when she is acting or choosing non-autonomously. UK law accepts a similar principle: people cannot be forced to accept medical treatment unless they are found incompetent. The theory is summarized in Box 13.1.

For the purposes of this discussion I will use the terms 'competence' and 'autonomy' as equivalent. We have analysed the issue of autonomy of behaviour in Chapter 12. At the end of that chapter, it was unclear whether eating-disordered behaviour could be considered as non-autonomous. But now we need to shift to a specific choice—that is, the choice to refuse life-saving treatment. May that choice in some cases be a competent choice?

The question of whether the refusal of life-saving treatment may ever be a competent decision is in part related to the discussion of the autonomy of behaviour. Refusal of food in the hospital, when the patient is about to die, is in fact the result of a long chain of actions and choices—the eating-disordered behaviour. If we have problems in determining the autonomy of dieting and refusing food in general, we will also have problems in determining whether refusing food when death is imminent is a competent decision.

In part, however, the issue of whether the refusal of life-saving treatment may be a competent decision is unrelated to the autonomy of eating-disordered behaviour in previous phases of the patient's life. As we shall see in this chapter, a person may make a competent decision not to live with

---

BOX 13.1 Principle of Respect for the Autonomy of the Eating-Disordered Person

People with eating disorders, at least prima facie, should be entitled to consent to or to refuse any medical treatment, whether or not related to their mental disorder, unless they are found incompetent to do so.

---

[4] Christopher J. Williams, Lorenzo Pieri, and Andrew Sim, 'We Should Strive to Keep Patients Alive', *British Medical Journal*, 317 (1998), 195–7.

anorexia, whether or not anorexia is autonomous behaviour. If it is found on one particular occasion that this choice is a competent one, does this necessarily mean that we should respect the patient's decision to refuse life-saving treatment? If it is found on one particular occasion that this choice is not a competent one, does this necessarily mean that we should treat the patient against her expressed wishes?

In this chapter I will show that the refusal of life-saving treatment may in some cases be a competent choice; certainly, we cannot a priori assure it is not. However, this does not necessarily mean that we are ethically obliged to respect that choice. Some factors *weaken* the normative strength of the principle of respect for people's competent decisions in the case of anorexia nervosa,[5] and we shall see the reason why this is so. In the same way, if a patient is not competent, this does not necessarily mean that we should always strive to keep her alive.

I will argue that the fact that the anorexic patient is competent to refuse life-saving treatment is not a sufficient ground to justify omission or withdrawal of treatment. Whereas in general we assume that a patient's competence is sufficient to warrant her respect for medical decisions, in the case of anorexia this assumption is not self-evident. The reason why this is so is that the principle of respect for patient autonomy, in the case of anorexia nervosa, is weaker than it is in other cases. I shall explain why this is so by reference to the position of another philosopher, Heather Draper. She has argued, or so it seems, that omission or withdrawal of life-saving treatment for anorexia should rest on determination of the patient's competence. However, as soon as she expresses this position, a number of problems come to the fore. I will argue that the decision to omit or to withdraw life-saving treatment for anorexia will have to rest on our capacity to identify ourselves with the suffering of the patient, and on our willingness to end the pains of the sufferer. In one word, on our *compassion*. I will not advocate compassion as a moral virtue. In other words, I will not argue that carers and health-care professionals should develop empathy or similar forms of identifications with the patient.[6] My point is that it is somewhat misleading to think that the principle of respect for autonomy may, in the case of anorexia, be a sufficient ground for accepting the sufferer's decision to die. If and when we decide to accept the anorexic's refusal of life-saving treatment, given the particular circumstances of the case, we would not do this only for the sake of respect for patient autonomy. Of course the belief that the person's autonomous

---

[5] This may also be true with non-psychiatric conditions.

[6] Jodi Halpern has argued that doctors should develop empathy towards their patients. She has articulated carefully what type of empathy doctors should have in her book *From Detached Concern to Empathy: Humanizing Medical Practice* (Oxford: Oxford University Press, 2001).

choices should be respected will play a fundamental role in the way we relate to the patient who refuses life-saving treatment. However, in the case of anorexia, compassion will play a similarly fundamental role, and compassion for the sufferer will have a strong part to play in any decision that results in our acceptance of the subject's own autonomous choice.

2. Can People with Anorexia be Competent to Refuse Naso-Gastric Feeding?

Heather Draper points out that 'there may be circumstances under which a sufferer's refusal of consent to treatment should be respected. This argument will hinge upon whether someone in the grip of an eating disorder can actually make a *competent decision about the quality of life*.'[7]

In Chapter 12 I discussed the features of eating disorders that may jeopardize the sufferer's autonomy of behaviour. Since refusal of life-saving treatment is basically refusal of food, the same observations seem to apply here. Whereas people with anorexia may be competent to manage most areas of their life, the person may be unable to decide competently about food and the body, and, consequently, about the therapy that is inevitably related to these.

I will briefly summarize here how UK law defines competence (for a fuller account, see Chapter 11) and how the features of eating disorders may jeopardize the patient's capacity to consent to or to refuse life-saving treatment (that is, nutrition).

3. Competence

In UK law, 'competence' is a task-specific concept.[8] This means that a person may be able to make a competent decision at one time, but not at another, or he or she may, at the same time, be able to make one decision but not another.[9] Moreover, competence is independent of the result of the

---

[7] Heather Draper, 'Anorexia Nervosa and Respecting a Refusal of Life-Prolonging Therapy: A Limited Justification', *Bioethics*, 14/2 (2000), 120–33, at 120, emphasis added. This paper is a development of Draper's previous ideas, published in Heather Draper, 'Treating Anorexics without Consent: Some Reservations', *Journal of Medical Ethics*, 24 (1998), 5–7.

[8] I am referring to the English cases, to which Draper also refers. *Gillick* v. *West Norfolk Wisbech AHA* [1985] 3 All ER 402 at 409 e-h per Lord Fraser and at 422 g-j per Lord Scarman; see also *Estate of Park* [1959] P 112; *Re C (adult: refusal of medical treatment)* [1994] 1 All ER 819, (1993) 15 BMLR 77; John Harris, *The Value of Life* (London: Routledge, 1992), 200 ff.

[9] Brazier, *Medicine, Patients and the Law*, chs. 2, 4, 5.

choice.[10] People are acknowledged to have the right to be unwise[11] and wrong,[12] and to refuse treatment for reasons that are irrational or unreasonable, or for no reason at all.[13] People are considered competent to make a medical decision when they are able *to understand the nature and purpose of treatment, and to weigh its risks and benefits.*[14] Moreover, 'being classed as suffering from a mental illness is [not] necessarily an indication that one is an incompetent individual';[15] for example, in the case of a prisoner with a diagnosis of personality disorders who refused food, coercive feeding was deemed unlawful, because, despite the ongoing mental disorder, he was found competent to refuse that treatment.[16]

In all discussions about competence, fundamental importance is given to the understanding of correct information.[17] The Law Commission has stated that a person is lacking capacity (1) when he or she is unable to *understand or retain the relevant information*; (2) when, although able to understand the relevant information, he or she is prevented from *using* it by his or her mental disability.[18]

With regard to clinical studies of anorexia nervosa, cognitive psychology has focused especially on the *information process* leading to eating-disordered behaviour. We have seen in Chapter 12 that this process appears dysfunctional at various levels: *perception* of the input of information, *interpretation*, *decision-making process*, and *output*. For example, typically, people with anorexia are unable to recall information stored in their memory and to utilize it to identify new information coming from the outside; the interpretation of information is also distorted: 'You look good, today' is typically interpreted as 'You've put on weight'.[19]

It has also been shown that people with eating disorders do not have a realistic perception of actual signals of appetite and satiety. They never

[10] *St George's Healthcare NHS Trust* v. *SR* v. *Collins and others*, ex part S [1998] 3 All ER 673.

[11] *Lane* v. *Candura* [1978] 376 NE 2d 1232 Appeal Court of Massachusetts.

[12] *Hopp* v. *Lepp* [1979] 98 DLR (3d) 464 at 470 per J. Prowse.

[13] *Sidaway* v. *Board of Governors of the Bethlem Royal Hospital and the Maudsley Hospital* [1985] 1 All ER 643 at 509 b per Lord Templeman; see also *R* v. *Blame* [1975] 3 All ER 446.

[14] *F* v. *West Berkshire Health Authority* [1989] 2 All ER 545; see also *State of Tennessee* v. *Northern* [1978] 563 SW 2d 197; *Gillick* v. *West Norfolk Wisbech* AHA [1985] 3 All ER 402 at 409 e-h per Lord Fraser and at 422 g-j per Lord Scarman.

[15] Draper, 'Anorexia Nervosa', 129. See also the Law Commission Report on Mental Incapacity, No. 231 (1995); 'Who Decides? Making Decisions of Behalf of Mentally Incapacitated Adults', A consultation paper issued by the Lord Chancellor's Department, December 1997; Mental Health Act Review Expert Group, *Draft Proposals for the New Mental Health Act* (April 1999) http://www.hyperguide.co.uk/mha/rev-prop.htm.

[16] *Secretary of State for the Home Department* v. *Robb* [1995] 1 All ER 677.

[17] *Re C* [1994] 1 FLR 31; *Re MB* [1997] 8 Medical Law Report 217; *Banks* v. *Goodfellow* [1870] LR 5 QB 549 at p. 569 per Lord C. J. Cockburn.

[18] See the Mental Health Act Review Expert Group, para. 152.

[19] Elena Faccio, *Il disturbo alimentare: Modelli, ricerche e terapie* (Rome: Carocci, 1999), 83.

know, by inner and unreflective awareness, if they should eat, how much they should eat, whether they have eaten enough, and when they should stop.[20]

The use of information about food is also dysfunctional. Although people with eating disorders are typically very well informed about food, they seem *unable to apply* this information. Rather than using it to improve the quality of their diet or their general well-being, they use it as an 'excuse' for both restrictive diet and food selection.[21] It has also been stressed that the capacity to make medical decisions may be affected by fears of obesity or denial of the consequences of actions.[22]

This, as we have seen in Chapter 12, may be taken as evidence that the autonomy of the deliberative process leading to eating-disordered behaviour is somewhat defective. However, we should not conclude that all people with anorexia are necessarily incompetent *to refuse treatment*.

The question of whether the refusal of life-saving treatment is a competent decision is only partly related to discussion of the autonomy of behaviour. As pointed out earlier, the decision to refuse food, even when death will almost certainly result, is the result of behaviour that has been perpetrated for months and often years. If we cannot say whether dieting and refusing food in general is autonomous, we will also often be unable to determine whether refusing food when death is imminent is a competent decision.

In part, however, the issue of whether refusal of life-saving treatment is a competent decision is unrelated to the autonomy of eating-disordered behaviour in previous phases of the patient's life. A person may make a competent decision not to live with anorexia, whether or not anorexia is autonomous behaviour. Her decision to refuse treatment may be a decision

---

[20] Mara Selvini Palazzoni, *L'anoressia mentale: Dalla terapia individuale alla terapia familiare*, (9th edn., Milan: Feltrinelli, 1998), 70.

[21] H. Bruch, *Eating Disorders: Obesity, Anorexia Nervosa and the Person within* (London: Routledge and Kegan Paul, 1974), 384.

[22] Law Commission, Consultation Paper No. 129, *Mentally Incapacitated Adults and Decision-Making: Medical Treatment and Research*, para. 2.18 from *Re W* [1992] 3 WLR 758 (London: HMSO, 1993), in particular para. 2.3.2. The legitimacy of force-feeding is a highly controversial issue. Anorexia nervosa is considered a mental illness, and therefore patients can be compulsorily detained and treated under sections 2 and 3 of the Mental Health Act 1983. According to s. 63 of the Act, consent to treatment *for the mental disorder* will not be required for sectioned patients, and polemics arose as to whether naso-gastric feeding should be considered as a treatment for the mental disorder and could therefore be legally imposed under s. 63, or should instead be considered as a treatment for the physical conditions, for which consent must be obtained. Although in the cases of *Re KB* (adult) (mental patient: medical treatment) [1994] 19 BMLR 144, *Riverside Health NHS Trust* v. *Fox* [1994] 1 FLR 614, *B.* v. *Croydon District Health Authority* [1995] 1 All ER 683 the court decided that artificial feeding could be imposed, debate on the legitimacy of force-feeding is ongoing. In April 1999, the Mental Health Act Review Expert Group suggested that feeding contrary to the will of the patient should be included among treatments that deserved special safeguards. See Mental Health Act Review Expert Group, para. 19.

about the *quality of her life*. Being aware of what it is to live with anorexia, the patient may competently decide that the quality of her life is too low and that her life is for her not worth living. As Heather Draper puts it, we should 'be open to the possibility that sufferers are actually *as competent as anyone else* to make decisions about the quality of their lives, and to assess the relative value of their lives in the light of its quality'.[23] Draper asks:

What of the sufferer from anorexia who refuses therapy, not because she thinks that her condition is not life-threatening, nor because she refuses to accept that she has a problem at all, but because for her [. . .] the burden of therapy and the side-effects of successful therapy—in terms of the body with which she will be left—are such that she prefers to take her chances with death?[24]

According to Draper, a person with anorexia nervosa is competently refusing artificial feeding when she decides 'to withdraw from therapy not on the grounds that she didn't want to eat, nor that she was "fat" but because the quality of her life was so poor that the therapy was no longer of benefit to her, or that it was on balance more of a burden than benefit'.[25]

In other words, the sufferer may be unable to manage with food;[26] however, she may still be able to decide that she is no longer willing to live in such conditions. She may therefore be incompetent at the level of diet management, but competent at the level of medical decisions. At this level, in fact, she may *possess all necessary information* about herself and the quality of her life, and may be *able to use it* to arrive at a choice. It may be on the grounds of her considerations about herself and the quality of her life that she may refuse therapy.

The refusal of artificial feeding may thus be considered as a competent decision if the sufferer is able to judge the quality of her life, and when she founds her decision on such a judgement, rather than on the basis of her fears and cognitive dysfunctions. Probably, this concerns only a 'tiny minority'[27] of sufferers, but this minority still matters.

The problems that I shall discuss from now onwards relate not to this characterization of competence, which is perfectly acceptable, but to the arguments that follow this characterization.

---

[23] Draper, 'Anorexia Nervosa', 132–3, emphasis added.

[24] Ibid. 131.

[25] Ibid. 122.

[26] This apparent inability to control eating often leads to the idea of anorexia as a form of addiction. Besides generic similarities between the two conditions, however, they present crucial differences that make the comparison improper, even at a logical level. See S. Giordano, 'Addicted to Eating Disorders? Eating Disorders and Substance Use Disorders, Differences and Fallacies', *Italian Journal of Psychiatry*, 11/2–3 (2001), 73–7.

[27] Draper, 'Anorexia Nervosa', 133.

4. *Following the Arguments*

From the above arguments, we understand that, for Draper, if someone in the grip of anorexia is able to make a competent decision about the quality of her life, and, in the light of this judgement, decides not to be treated, her refusal of treatment should be respected.

Surprisingly, however, Draper does not argue this. Draper, instead, suggests that the refusal of force-feeding, *under some circumstances*,[28] should be respected (we shall see Draper's words in Section 9). According to Draper, the reason why *in these cases* the refusal of artificial feeding should be respected is because *in these cases* it is *not a request for euthanasia*.

As I anticipated in the Introduction, as soon as Draper makes the claim that people with anorexia who are competently refusing life-saving treatment should be respected—*because they are competent*—the issue becomes extremely complicated.

In the next section we shall ask why Draper, rather than following her arguments, tries to demonstrate that the refusal of artificial feeding is not a request for euthanasia and whether she succeeds in her attempt.

5. *A Paradoxical Distinction between Passive Euthanasia and Refusal of Treatment*

Draper tries to demonstrate that the refusal of artificial feeding, *in some cases*, is not a request for euthanasia. Why Draper makes such an attempt is quite obvious. While passive euthanasia 'may be viewed as murder or a similar crime [...] respecting a competent patient's decision to refuse life saving or life prolonging therapy [...] is part of respecting the right to consent'.[29] Indeed, many believe that 'euthanasia' (even in its passive and voluntary form) is unethical. Moreover, active euthanasia is unlawful in the UK, as it is in most European countries, and, consequently, practitioners have to be sure that withdrawal from artificial feeding will not be regarded as euthanasia, if they do not want to incur legal or ethical problems.

It is worth reporting a case that shows the controversial nature of letting an anorexic patient die.

In 1990, a doctor provided suicide drugs to a 25-year-old woman treated unsuccessfully for anorexia for sixteen years. A jury acquitted the doctor after viewing a video of the woman explaining her decision. In 1994, the Dutch Supreme Court

---

[28] Draper, 'Anorexia Nervosa', 122.   [29] Ibid. 123.

ruled that emotional suffering, not just physical suffering, was a basis for euthanasia.[30]

The 1990 case may be considered more controversial than other cases because it involved the 'active' provision of a lethal substance and the 'active' swallowing of the substance on the part of the patient (physician-assisted suicide). However, even in cases in which a lethal substance is not administered, accepting the request for omission or withdrawal of artificial feeding closely resembles passive euthanasia. The doctor is asked to withhold a procedure with the consequence that the patient will die.

Therefore, Draper tries to make a distinction between passive euthanasia and competent refusal of treatment:

In passive euthanasia therapy is withdrawn or omitted with the intention that the patient will die as a result. [...] The final judgement about whether or not to omit therapy rests with the clinician and not the patient even when the patient is party to the decision, or even when the patient goes to considerable lengths to persuade the clinician of her point of view. Considerable weight may be given to what the patient thinks. The clinician may even decide to be bound by what the patient thinks, but the final decision still rests with him [...] The moral difference between passive euthanasia and competent refusal of therapy lies in who makes the final decision.[31]

Although the person 'who makes the final decision' is a pivotal figure in Draper's distinction between passive euthanasia and refusal of treatment, it is unclear what Draper means by that. There are in fact only three cases in which it is possible to determine who makes the final decision, or, in other words, in which the decision rests only on *one* party.

1. In case of suicide, the decision seems to rest entirely on the person who commits suicide (apart from exceptional debatable cases); if the patient, for example, pulls out the drips and, before the doctor realizes it, dies, then surely the decision *rests entirely with the patient*. But perhaps we would not think of it as a genuine case of *refusal of treatment*.
2. If the patient is incompetent and has left no advance directives to which doctors may refer, the decision clearly rests with doctors (putting aside the issue of the role taken by relatives—for example, in interpreting the patient's wishes).
3. If the patient is *competent* and *asks for* life-saving treatment, or asks to carry on with it, and the doctor refuses to comply with this wish, then the decision clearly *rests entirely with the doctor*. However, this

---

[30] Joseph P. Shapiro, Euthanasia's Home, US News, 30 March 2001, available at www. globalaging.org/elderrights/us/euthanasia.htm.

[31] Draper, 'Anorexia Nervosa', 124.

case is precisely the opposite to the one we are discussing, in which the patient *refuses* life-saving treatment and the doctor wants to administer it.

In all other cases there seems to be nothing like *the person with whom the final decision lies*. There is at most what parties *believe* about this. I may believe that I have made the final decision. You may believe the same, or the other way round. Since there is no way to decide who is right, it is impossible to distinguish between passive euthanasia and refusal of treatment on the grounds of what the parties involved in it believe (however strong their belief may be), and it is impossible to determine *on whom the final decision rests*, unless we look at what each party believes.

Since Draper's distinction between passive euthanasia and refusal of treatment 'lies in who makes the final decision',[32] we must conclude that Draper fails to provide a persuasive distinction between the two, and, consequently, that she fails to demonstrate that refusal of artificial feeding is unequivocally 'refusal of treatment' and not a 'request for euthanasia'.[33]

Another argument brought to support the view that in some cases the refusal of artificial feeding should be respected is that *in some cases* 'the decision to refuse therapy is *on a par* with other decisions to refuse life-prolonging therapy made by sufferers of debilitating chronic, or acute onset of terminal illness'.[34]

In the next section we shall see that chronic anorexia nervosa cannot be considered 'on a par' with chronically debilitating and terminal illnesses, even in the cases specified by Draper.

---

[32] Draper, 'Anorexia Nervosa', 124.

[33] It should also be noticed that, in order to defend people's entitlement to make decisions relating to their life, we do not need to demonstrate that their decisions have nothing to do with 'euthanasia'. Draper assumes that 'euthanasia is unethical', and therefore tries to define 'euthanasia' in a way in which refusal of artificial feeding appears to be something different from a request for 'euthanasia'. However, a defence of people's entitlement to make decisions relating to their life would be more consistent and persuasive if we openly claim that sometimes ethics demands respect for a person's decision, even if that decision results in the person's death. Rather than saying that respect for refusal of artificial feeding may be legitimate because *it has nothing to do with 'Euthanasia'*, we should rather say that we should sometimes respect the request for omission or suspension of life-saving treatment, even if this involves some kind of 'euthanasia'. What should be demonstrated, in other words, is not that a decision does not fall under the category of 'euthanasia', but rather that some decisions, although they involve the death of the person who competently make those decisions, should be respected, and that it is unethical to violate the person's competent wishes about her own life, even if someone may call this 'euthanasia'.

[34] Draper, 'Anorexia Nervosa', 123, emphasis added.

6. *Refusal of Artificial Feeding is not 'on a Par' with Refusal of Treatment in Debilitating Chronic and Terminal Illnesses*

Chronic anorexia nervosa presents important similarities with debilitating chronic or terminal illnesses. The patient is severely emaciated and manifests a wide range of physical complications related to malnutrition; unless artificially hydrated and fed, she will die. In spite of efforts, this situation may sometimes persist for many years. In up to 20 per cent of cases, unfortunately, it concludes tragically with the death of the patient (notably, mortality is mainly due to suicide).[35]

Despite the similarities, there is a remarkable difference between chronic anorexia nervosa and debilitating chronic or terminal illnesses. The condition of those who suffer from debilitating chronic or terminal illnesses is *unavoidable*—that is, the situation is going to be at least as it is, despite the efforts of all parties involved. Both the condition and the death of people with anorexia are, instead, *avoidable*. We can avoid the patient's death simply by feeding her, and making sure that she does not commit suicide (it is another matter whether this is the right thing to do). Moreover, the physical complications (the so-called 'secondary symptomatology') resulting from starvation are completely reversible, more or less quickly depending on the case, as normal weight is gained.[36] Despite the difficulties surrounding the notion of 'recovery', surely death is (at least 'technically' speaking) *avoidable*, physical complications are *reversible*, and, more significantly, people with anorexia can actually get over their misery.[37]

---

[35] Janet L. Treasure, 'Anorexia and Bulimia Nervosa', in G. Stein and G. Wilkinson (eds.), *Seminars in General Adult Psychiatry* (London: Royal College of Psychiatrists, 1998), 858–902.

[36] Allan S. Kaplan and Paul E. Garfinkel, 'The Neuroendocrinology of Anorexia Nervosa', in R. Cullu, G. M. Brown, and Glen R. Van Loon (eds.), *Clinical Neuroendocrinology* (Oxford: Blackwell, 1998), 105–22.

[37] Draper points out that in some cases people with eating disorders are prepared to live only on the condition that they maintain an abnormally low weight. In these cases, physical complications are typical, and the concern about thinness fills the person's mind and grossly reduces the quality of her life. This shows the problematic nature of the notion of 'recovery'. We should also admit that some people never get better. A high number of those who have eating disorders die. The majority die because they commit suicide. No doubt, many people who have eating disorders feel unbearably unhappy. However, we should also consider that, according to the same estimates reported by Draper, the majority of those who develop eating disorders recover (according to Lang, *The Harvard Medical Letter*, recovery rate is between 50 and 70 per cent over ten years. E. D. Eckert et al. ('Ten Year Follow-up of Anorexia Nervosa: Clinical Course and Outcome', *Psychological Medicine*, 25 (1995), 143–56) report 24 per cent full recovery and just under 50 per cent benign outcome. Quoted in Draper, 'Anorexia Nervosa', n. 27. In this note Draper concludes that 'taken together these sources suggest a failure rate of between 25–50% over ten years'. Obviously, this means that the recovery rate, over ten years, is about 50–75 per cent). Moreover, there is empirical evidence of considerable improvement when the appropriate approach is adopted. See, e.g. results reported by M. Selvini Palazzoli, S. Cirillo, M. Selvini,

7. *The Brave Claim*

The fact that the decision to refuse artificial feeding is in no case equivalent to the decision to refuse therapy in cases of debilitating chronic or terminal illnesses has important ethical implications.

In cases of debilitating chronic and terminal illnesses, respect for the patient's decision is not only supported by the principle of respect for competent decisions. In these cases the fact that the condition is *irreversible* and (in terminal illnesses) the fact that premature death is *unavoidable* represent additional ethical reasons for respecting the patient's competent decision. Because of these additional ethical reasons, respect for the patient's request for the omission or withdrawal of life-saving therapy is (relatively) less controversial than respect for a similar request when the patient does not suffer from a similar condition.

In anorexia nervosa, as we have just seen, strictly speaking the condition is not *irreversible,* and death is not *unavoidable.* Therefore, these additional ethical reasons are lacking. Consequently, it seems that the competent refusal of life-saving or life-prolonging treatment can be respected only on the ground that people are entitled to make competent decisions about their life (and its termination) (the principle of autonomy).

This is what I call the *brave claim*: people with anorexia nervosa who competently decide not to be artificially fed should be respected *because* everybody is entitled to the exercise of their autonomy, not only 'in the middle' of their life, but also at the end of it, or when their own life is at stake. The principle of autonomy binds us to respect people's competent decisions about their life and its termination, precisely because autonomy extends also to the most difficult moments of our life, and, ultimately, 'stretches [. . .] far out into the distance',[38] to the end of it.

In the next sections, we shall see *why* Draper *should have made* the *brave claim*; that she *has not* made it; and *why* she *has not* made it; (and we shall ask whether we can sensibly defend the *brave claim* in the case of anorexia nervosa).

8. *Why Draper should have Made the Brave Claim*

Draper should have made the brave claim, not because the brave claim is indisputable (on the contrary, as we shall see in Section 11, the brave claim

---

and A. M. Sorrentino, *Ragazze anoressiche e bulimiche: La terapia familiare* (Milan: Cortina, 1998).

[38] Milan Kundera, *Immortality* (London: Faber & Faber, 1991), 73.

is disputable), but because it follows from her premises. In fact, Draper acknowledges that having an eating disorder does not entail incompetence,[39] distinguishes between irrationality and incompetence,[40] and acknowledges the ethical and legal right to make competent medical decisions.[41]

From these premises, it follows that people are entitled to refuse life-saving or life-prolonging treatment, if they are deciding competently. It seems to follow that people with anorexia are entitled competently to refuse artificial feeding, and that, if this is the case, they are entitled to have their decisions respected *because* they are deciding competently.[42]

Although this conclusion follows from Draper's premises, as we have seen, she does not draw it.

9. *Draper has not Made the Brave Claim, although She Should Have*

Instead of making such a claim, as we have seen, Draper has tried, on the one hand, to reassure us that a competent refusal to accept artificial feeding is not a request for passive euthanasia, and, on the other, to demonstrate that in some cases this decision is on a par with the decision to refuse treatment in cases of debilitating chronic or terminal illnesses. We should now focus on these cases.

Where those who are refusing have been afflicted beyond the natural cycle of the disorder (which is between one and eight years); have already been force-fed on previous occasions; are competent to make decisions concerning their quality of life; have insight into the influence which their anorexia has over some aspects of their lives, and are not at death's door (they may, for instance, have just been released from a section for compulsory treatment).[43]

Draper contends that *under these circumstances* force-feeding would represent a failure 'to respect their competent refusal of therapy'.[44]

This statement is clearly wrong. In fact, coercive treatment represents a failure to respect competent refusal of therapy not only *in these cases*, but *every time competent refusal of therapy is not respected*.

Force-feeding is a violation of competent refusal of therapy in all cases in which the patient competently refuses and doctors fail to comply with the refusal. It is another matter whether such a violation is *justifiable*. So, by

---

[39] Draper, 'Anorexia Nervosa', 122.

[40] Ibid. 125–6.

[41] Ibid. 126.

[42] I am here assuming that the entitlement to refuse medical treatment entails an obligation of health-care professionals to respect our decision.

[43] Draper, 'Anorexia Nervosa', 122–3.

[44] Ibid. 122.

saying that *in these cases* force-feeding represents a failure to respect competent refusal of therapy, perhaps Draper means that, *in these particular cases*, force-feeding represents a failure to respect competent refusal of therapy that is *ethically unjustifiable*. The implication is that *in other cases* doctors may legitimately fail to comply with competent refusal of artificial feeding.

Now, it should become clear why it is significant that Draper has not made *the brave claim*. In fact, we are led to ask: what is it, for Draper, that makes force-feeding ethically unjustifiable? Is it the fact that it is a failure to respect competent refusal of therapy? Or is it the fact that the person has 'been afflicted beyond the natural cycle of the disorder [...] [has] already been force-fed [...] [has] insight into the influence which their anorexia has over some aspects of their lives, and are not at death's door (they may, for instance, have just been released from a section for compulsory treatment)'?[45] Draper does not clarify this point. However, this would be important, because if one claims that force-feeding is ethically unjustifiable when the person is making a competent refusal, and that it is ethically wrong to lack respect for people's competent choices, then why should one specify that, to claim respect, the patient must have been afflicted beyond the natural cycle of the disorder, or that she must have been force-fed before?

10. *Why Draper has not Made the Brave Claim*

One of the reasons for specifying that only force-feeding of patients belonging to this group is ethically unjustifiable may be 'playing safe'. The cases selected by Draper present some similarities with debilitating chronic and terminal illnesses, and therefore, it seems that, *in these cases*, we have *additional ethical reasons* for respecting the refusal of artificial feeding. As we have seen in Section 7, in fact, respect for the patient's refusal of life-saving or life-prolonging therapy may be supported not only by the principle of respect for autonomy. In debilitating chronic illnesses the condition is unfortunately *irreversible* and, in terminal illnesses, premature death is *unavoidable*. These circumstances may provide additional ethical reasons for respecting the patient's decision, and seem to make the respect for such a decision (relatively) less controversial than in cases where the death is somewhat avoidable and the condition is totally reversible, such as in anorexia. In anorexia, even in the cases selected by Draper, these additional ethical reasons are lacking, and this is why respect for the patient's decision will always be more controversial than in cases of debilitating chronic or terminal illnesses.

---

[45] Draper, 'Anorexia Nervosa', 122–3.

These considerations raise another question, which relates to the plausibility of the brave claim in the case of anorexia nervosa.

11. *Can we Defend the Brave Claim in the Case of Anorexia Nervosa?*

One might wonder whether the principle of autonomy preserves all its normative strength in the particular circumstances characterizing anorexia nervosa, and it might be argued that, taken alone, the principle of autonomy may not be strong enough to justify respect for refusal of artificial feeding.

In the first part of this book, I have articulated a theory of paternalism, which proposes that prima facie strong paternalism is unjustifiable. Strong paternalism entails restriction of autonomy for the sake of the person's welfare. From that theory, it follows that, if a person with anorexia autonomously (or competently) refuses treatment, we should respect her wish, even if this means that the person will die as a result of her choice. This is because, prima facie, autonomy generally has a compelling normative strength.

However, in the case of anorexia, there are, as we have seen, other important considerations to make that arguably 'weaken' the normative strength of the principle of respect for autonomy.

The premature death of a loved one is often intolerable to us, and may be a profoundly devastating experience. It is not euphemistic that sometimes it is said that people become 'crazy' after the premature death or suicide of a loved person. The tragic event of bereavement is intolerable even when it is *unavoidable*, and this is understandable. If it is understandable that people sometimes find the *unavoidable* death of a loved person intolerable, perhaps even more understandable is the fact that people may find the death of a close friend or relative intolerable when her death is *avoidable*. And this, perhaps, is not only *understandable*, but also *ethically relevant*.

When artificial feeding is to be administered to a person with anorexia, it is because dehydration and malnutrition threaten her life. The person, normally young, generally declares that she is not fasting to death, and that she does not want to die, but, if dying is the price she has to pay to be thin, then she will pay it.[46] Families literally fall apart. The person herself seems not to know how to cope; neither do her relatives. However, as we have repeatedly seen, death is *avoidable*, and the condition is *reversible*. Clinical studies show

---

[46] A novel based on a real story expresses well the paradox of accepting misery and death, while longing for happiness and life. D. Hautzig, *Second Star to the Right* (London: Fontana Lions, 1982).

that people in desperate conditions have recovered, and such empirical evidence supports not a nebulous faith in miracles, but the concrete hope that everything could 'come back to normal', that the nightmare could finish.[47]

In these circumstances, does the principle of autonomy preserve intact all its normative strength? In other words, does the fact that both the condition and death are *reversible* and *avoidable* weaken its normative strength? Do they weaken the duty, which we all share, to respect other people's autonomy?

Whereas in principle the theory of paternalism articulated prima facie in Chapter 2 is the most ethically appropriate, whereas in principle we should aim at respect for people's autonomous decisions, the case of anorexia is so peculiar that it raises further issues relating to both to the real autonomy of the person's behaviour and to the impact of the choice on carers. This does not mean that coercion should be justified every time that carers, relatives, or health-care professionals are not psychologically prepared to accept the patient's decisions. This means that the particular circumstances that may take place in extreme situations, such as those characterizing severe anorexia, should also be taken into consideration, and that they may mitigate the normative force of the principle of respect for autonomy.

12. Conclusions

Draper makes an important point. She stresses that 'when a competent patient refuses therapy—whether or not she has a terminal illness or a poor quality of life or will die as a result—professional carers are ethically and legally bound to accept this refusal'.[48] She also points out that some people with anorexia nervosa, even if this is only a tiny minority, may be competently refusing naso-gastric feeding. As Draper also suggests, people with anorexia may be considered competent to refuse therapy if they make their decision on the basis of a reasoned judgement upon the quality of their life, rather than on the basis of dysfunctional cognitive processes, or of irrational beliefs of other sorts. From these arguments, one would expect Draper to conclude that, when people with anorexia competently refuse naso-gastric therapy, professionals are ethically bound (and should also be legally bound) to respect their choice. However, as we have seen, Draper avoids this conclusion, and claims that *competent* refusal of naso-gastric therapy should be respected *in some cases* (thus, not in all cases in which it is competent).

---

[47] See Selvini Palazzoli et al., *Ragazze anoressiche e bulimiche*, 115–18.
[48] Draper, 'Anorexia Nervosa', 124.

The reason why Draper appears reluctant to draw the conclusions that follow from her initial arguments probably lies in the peculiarities of anorexia nervosa. Anorexia nervosa, strictly speaking, is not a lethal illness, in the sense that there are courses of action that may prevent death, and the effects of abnormal eating, severe as they may be, are completely reversible. The refusal of artificial feeding and hydration may therefore be profoundly devastating for carers, possibly more devastating than the refusal of therapy in cases of untreatable degenerative or mortal illnesses. Perhaps, this is not only humanly understandable, but also ethically relevant, and seems to weaken the normative strength of the principle of respect for people's competent decisions. For this reason, whereas it is widely accepted that people generally have both the ethical and the legal right to make competent medical decisions, and competently to refuse life-saving treatment, the claim that people with anorexia should have the same right appears as an extremely *brave claim*, which may not always be defensible in cases of anorexia nervosa. This does not mean that the anorexic patient's refusal of therapy should always be disregarded, or that it should be disregarded every time that the carers or family members find it too hard to accept, but rather that the fact that the sufferer is making a competent decision may not be sufficient to bind carers to respect refusal of life-saving therapy. In other words, competence does not seem to produce, in the case of anorexia, the same ethical obligation that it produces in other cases.[49]

Although a substantial part of Draper's paper is about competence, about demonstrating that people have both the ethical and the legal right to make competent decisions, whatever the results may be, and about demonstrating that people with anorexia may retain capacity to refuse therapy, Draper is probably allowing for the fact that the circumstances characterizing anorexia nervosa may weaken the normative strength of the principle of respect for people's competent choices. For this reason, she takes a number of 'safety measures' and argues that respect for the *competent* refusal of naso-gastric treatment should be accorded only *in some cases*. She does not err, however, on the side of safety. Her mistake is a methodological one. The problem with her argument is not that the number of cases in which she would accord respect is too small, but that she moves from particular premisses and reaches conclusions that are not implied from those premisses. She assumes that competent decisions should be respected and demonstrates that some people with anorexia nervosa may competently refuse artificial feeding. Then, instead of concluding that, on this basis, we should respect these decisions (and

---

[49] See e.g. the case of Ms B., a woman paralysed from the neck downward. The High Court acknowledged her right to have her life-support machine turned off. See BBC news, Friday, 22 March 2002, at the website www.bbc.co.uk.

perhaps take extra precautionary measures, due to the peculiarity of the case), she tries to demonstrate that the competent refusal of artificial feeding is not a request for passive euthanasia and that, in some cases, it is on a par with refusal of treatment in debilitating chronic and terminal illnesses. This shift was not only methodologically incorrect, but also unsuccessful, for Draper has failed to demonstrate these two points.

We should now return to the fundamental issue raised by Draper. The author argues that there are cases in which refusal of artificial feeding should be respected. We should ask two questions. Is she right, and if she is, what are these cases?

There may be cases in which the person's wishes should be respected, despite the normative 'weakness' of the principle of autonomy in cases of anorexia. It would be inappropriate, and, perhaps more importantly, not respectful of the tragic peculiarities of each individual case, to provide general guidelines or to draw a list of circumstances in which the patient's wishes should be respected. Although the theory of paternalism articulated in Chapter 2 is still prima facie the framework that we should keep in mind when relating to other people and to patients in the health-care context, there are circumstances that should be evaluated through a careful analysis of each individual case. As we have seen, we should consider both the person's competence or incompetence and the feelings of those who are closely involved. There is also another aspect of the problem that we should not neglect. In some cases, the life of people with anorexia is intolerable to them. With their skeleton-like bodies, they survive their emaciation, while suffering, sometimes for years, the severe side effects of malnutrition. Whereas the majority of sufferers, sooner or later, recover, or at least get much better, a minority of sufferers never seem to get better, and there might be a point at which further therapeutic attempts seem to condemn them to agony. From this point of view, I think it makes sense to consider how many years the person has been ill, and how many attempts she has made to recover. After many years and many therapeutic attempts, and after many reiterated competent requests for suspension of therapy, I believe we should probably consider the patient's request, not necessarily because the person is now *more competent* than before, but, more probably, *out of pity*.

As I have said above, it would be inappropriate to provide general guidelines that tell people how they should behave in these circumstances. However, I believe that carers should be encouraged to consider all aspects of the problem. Among those aspects, we should also include the condition and the suffering of the person who refuses therapy. Understanding the condition and the suffering of the person with anorexia involves not only a critical attitude toward the situation, but also *compassion* (in its etymological meaning: *com-* = with + *patī* = to bear, suffer). Identification with the patient and participation to her suffering may clearly be burdensome for carers. More-over, it is 'a double edged sword'. Empathy and compassion may improve understanding of the patient and her condition, but probably carers can never, nor should they ever, think they are able to grasp completely what the patient experiences. To think that we ourselves may be able to identify completely with the patient and her suffering may actually be disrespectful.[50] However, compassion enables us to give the patient a genuine understanding and to cultivate a refined sensitivity, more attentive to the peculiar aspects of each individual case, and therefore it is essential when considering the sufferer's request not to be artificially fed and hydrated.

---

[50] Halpern, *From Detached Concern to Empathy*, in particular 77–84.

14

Conclusions: The Need for Change

How should we behave when dealing with a person with eating disorders? Should we prevent the sufferer from dieting, over-exercising, vomiting, and spiralling down into the grip of the eating disorders? And when malnutrition threatens the person's life, should he or she be fed against his or her will?

In this book I have tried to answer these ethical questions. In order to do this, I have done two things: one has been to analyse eating disorders, and the other has been to provide an ethical theory that may be applied in the case of eating disorders. I have argued that eating disorders are not illnesses like cancer or heart diseases, but rather behaviours that reflect dominant Western values. They are caused in an important way by our ordinary morality, not by some pathogen or insult.

I have proposed a way of thinking about eating disorders (anorexia and bulimia nervosa). Chapter 1 describes the clinical features of eating disorders. It explores the clinical perspective on aetiology, incidence, and prevalence of anorexia and bulimia, and reports the risks for health that are caused by abnormal nutrition. The central feature of anorexia is *deliberate weight loss*, which is tenaciously pursued and/or sustained by the reduction of food intake and the strict selection of permitted food. Low weight is upheld by compensatory behaviour, practised in order to reduce the assimilation of calories. Compensatory behaviour includes vomiting (which is generally self-induced), the abuse of laxatives, excessive exercise, the use of appetite suppressants and/or diuretics.

Bulimia or 'bulimic' phases generally refer to binging, which is experienced as being 'out of one's own control', and which is followed by compensatory behaviour. The person feels compelled to overeat. This is normally done in secrecy. The person is overwhelmed by the thought of eating and tries to set up a situation in which she may perform her food orgy. She normally feels ashamed about this urge and will find it difficult to talk about it. She will feel disgust over her orgy and will normally compensate binging with either self-induced vomiting and/or other cathartic practices (restrictive diet over the next days, until the next breakthrough, exercise, diuretics, laxatives). These practices are experienced as a purification from the pollution of food.

A dread of fatness and a morbid fear of weight gain are commonly reported features of eating disorders. In cases of open emaciation or rapid weight loss, denial of the state of emaciation is typical. Sometimes, even though severely emaciated, people with eating disorders claim that they 'look fat' (or that they are still too fat, or make similar claims). Sometimes it is believed that these claims may depend on a disordered perception of body shape, but it has not been proved that people with eating disorders suffer from a disorder in perception.

Many experts consider anorexia and bulimia as related phenomena, as the two sides of the same relentless concern towards weight and body shape.

Eating disorders are highly destructive behaviour: the side effects of low and abnormal nutrition are severe and may include endocrine and metabolic changes, heart disorders, electrolyte disorders, gastrointestinal complications, bone mineral density loss, and kidney complications. Mortality is among the highest in psychiatry. In the light of the possible scenario resulting from eating disorders, it is understandable that carers ask themselves whether they should force the person who refuses to change to adopt less destructive eating patterns.

Chapter 2 highlights the ethical issues created by eating disorders. The major ethical issues are related to whether carers and health-care professionals should be or are allowed to intervene paternalistically to protect the welfare of the person with eating disorders. I have proposed a theory of weak paternalism that says that there is a prima facie entitlement to protect a person from self-harm when the action/choice that the person is making lacks autonomy in some important way. Autonomous behaviour, however harmful, should be respected. The issue will then be to understand whether eating-disordered behaviour (dieting, vomiting, over-exercising, food selection, and so on) can be autonomous. If these behaviours were autonomous, there would be a prima facie obligation to respect them.

Against this argument, an objection may be raised. Eating-disordered behaviour cannot be autonomous and therefore cannot be respected. The objection may take two forms: one is to say that eating-disordered behaviour is the result of a mental illness. Mental illness jeopardizes people's autonomy, and this entitles others paternalistically to intervene in the person's best interests. The other form that the objection may take is that eating-disordered behaviour cannot be autonomous because it results from a genetic mutation or from an organic dysfunction (hypothalamic disorder, for example, or endocrine disorder).

Chapter 3 deals with the first form of the objection. I show that the argument that mental illness jeopardizes people's autonomy rests on a tautology. Saying that people 'starve and vomit' because they are anorexic is saying no more that they starve and vomit because 'they starve and vomit'.

Anorexia is, in fact, the name given to a pattern of experiences and behaviours, and is not the explanatory cause for those experiences and behaviours. So, when people (and clinicians) say, for example, that anorexics diet because they are anorexic, or that anorexia causes the anorexic to diet, they are not really providing an explanation for the anorexic's behaviour. They are just describing succinctly that behaviour, or naming it. Eating disorders are patterns of behaviour, and not 'an entity' that causes people to have those patterns of behaviour.

Another form the objection may take is that eating-disordered behaviour is not autonomous because it is the result of an organic illness that is yet to be identified. In Chapter 4 I analyse the genetics/neuro-physiology of eating disorders. A number of organic imbalances are related to abnormal eating. However, they are often the result of abnormal eating, and not their primary cause. Gene variations do seem to be associated with the disorder. However, these alone cannot explain why eating disorders occur. In conclusion, despite the importance of genetic/neuro-physiological factors, it cannot be claimed that they are purely 'determined' behaviour.

In the light of these arguments, I offer a critical discussion of legal provisions on the assessment and treatment of people with mental illness and with eating disorders in particular. In Chapter 11 I analyse both the Mental Health Act 1983 and the case law on eating disorders, and I provide a critical analysis of the legal provisions.

Given that eating disorders are not purely determined behaviour, in Chapters 5 and 6 I focus on the purposes and meanings of eating-disordered behaviour. At the heart of anorexia and bulimia there is 'deliberate weight loss' (*ICD-10*). This means that anorexia and bulimia are a deliberate pursuit of 'lightness'. I tried to understand why lightness is important by looking at various contexts in which lightness is valued. For a long time, lightness has been presented as a positive value and a worthwhile goal in literature, poetry, and music. Lightness/thinness are often associated not only with beauty, but also with feelings of liberation and purity, and with elation. Historically, the search for purity and moral integrity has often led people to mortify the flesh, and fasting has always been praised as an ascetic technique. Many people seem to believe that anorexia and bulimia have to do with youngsters' desire to emulate extra-thin top models pictured in magazines. However, anorexia is not merely a modern phenomenon of girls emulating supermodels; it is a pattern of behaviour with a long history. Lightness/thinness are not merely 'aesthetic' ideals. Lightness often symbolizes the transcendence of the body. The person who pursues lightness/thinness pursues control over the passions of the 'flesh'. This ideal has to do with values such as spirituality as opposed to carnality, intellect as opposed to the body. The ideal of physical beauty is here rooted in ideals of 'moral' beauty. The light/thin body incarnates ideals of spirituality and purity, which are an important part of Western morality. The pursuit of lightness/thinness is rooted in ancient moral values, which have become an essential part of the ordinary morality in Western societies. Eating disorders signify the person's belonging and adherence to a determined moral context. The disorder is the *consistent* expression of values that have ancient roots in Western culture and that have been incorporated into ordinary morality.

This has important implications in terms of how eating disorders are understood. Eating anomalies are not the *symptom of an underlying mental disorder*, as is often argued. They are the symptoms of ordinary morality, which is just being *taken seriously*—or more seriously than usual. The logic of anorexia and bulimia nervosa is not a *dysfunctional logic*: it is a *moral logic*.

How deeply and imperceptibly morality shapes eating disorders becomes even more striking when we look at the family and society of the eating-disordered person. Chapters 7–10 report results of studies of the family and the societies in which eating disorders are most often found. According to clinical and sociological studies, eating disorders are a response to family and social dynamics and are better understood if they are considered as a relational problem, and not simply as a problem of the individual. The person who develops eating disorders is typically submitted to a number of high and contradictory expectations—typically she is supposed to be successful in her school/professional life, competitive, and able to take on roles that were traditionally assigned to males, but at the same time she has to be feminine, maternal, and obedient, and she is supposed stick to traditional female roles within the family. Moreover, she has to be fit and thin and the ideal of beauty, which becomes more and more androgynous, which is in open contradiction to the physiology of the woman. Clinical and sociological studies argue that the whole set of very high or openly contradictory expectations of the future anorexic/bulimic induce her to develop the disorder. The person develops eating disorders as an opposition to other people's contradictory expectations of her, as a defence against other people's demands, and as a way to regain some sort of control over her life.

The studies on the family and society of the eating-disordered person provide information that is essential to the understanding of the condition. However, there is a gap in these explanations of eating disorders. Why should one be made to 'suffer' by these pressures? And why should one develop a 'disorder' in order to regain control over others?

There are two assumptions in these arguments: one is that other people's expectations of us may 'make us suffer'. It is very common for people to suffer or get angry because other people have inappropriate expectations of them, but the fact that this is a common reaction does not mean that it is obvious. Why should we not be indifferent to other people's expectations of us?

The other assumption is that a 'disorder', or the exhibition of suffering, may give us some power over others. This is also not obvious. Why do people 'suffer' in order to obtain power over others? Why do not they laugh or sing? Why do they think that suffering, rather than laughing or happiness, may give them power over others?

I argue that both assumptions may be explained with reference to a particular moral context.

The reason we are made to suffer by others' expectations is that we 'expect' them not to have those expectations of us. If we thought that others' expectations were 'a problem of those who have them', it would be impossible for us to 'suffer'. We suffer because we think we have a moral right for others not to exert inappropriate pressure on us. In other words, we suffer from a 'moral wrong': what makes us suffer is not the expectation in itself, but the sense of being morally wronged (which is independent of whether others mean to wrong us). Thus, the 'pain' that the future anorexic/bulimic has is a 'moral pain', in the sense of receiving a moral wrong. The 'persecutors' expect the future anorexic to conform to their ideals (perfection, beauty, obedience, and so on). The 'victim', the future anorexic, expects the persecutors to conform to her ideals (to change the inappropriate and constraining expectations). At the basis of the pain of the eating-disordered person, thus, there is a circular moral logic that traps all those involved. It is far from obvious that people are made to suffer from others' expectations of them. The reason why they suffer is that they share with the significant others a moral logic in which other people's behaviour is understood in moral terms and in which expectations and disappointments are perceived as morally right or morally wrong.

The strategy implemented by the eating-disordered person to regain power has also to do with moral beliefs. According to clinical studies (see Chapter 7) eating disorders are a strategy to achieve control and power over others. But why does the person adopt a self-destructive behaviour, in order to regain power? The answer is to be found in the belief that causing suffering is morally wrong. The person is saying 'do you see how much you are making me suffer?'—and expects others to change accordingly. It is in fact a rather common belief that people should feel sorry for other people's suffering and do something about it. Therefore, it is common for people to try to achieve a change in others by displaying their misery to them and maybe blaming them for it (an illustrative case is that of hunger-strikers). According to one of the most macabre tales narrated in the Scriptures, God used a similar strategy to save humanity. In order to save humanity from eternal death, He killed His only Son after torture. It is unclear why He did not choose to make the sky blue and the fields full of flowers to save the humankind. There must be a reason why, among the many possible things God could have done to save humankind, He decided to do the most atrocious of all and condemned His Son Jesus to torture and slow death. The idea here is that the best and most efficient way of changing the course of history, or changing other people's behaviour, is by exhibition of pain and suffering. Display of suffering is supposed to elicit a sense of guilt, which is a powerful mental constraint. These sorts of strategies may of course work only in contexts in which people believe that causing suffering is morally wrong. Again, the anorexic strategy rests upon moral values and beliefs.

These conclusions deeply affect the ethics of the treatment of the eating-disordered person. After having analysed eating disorders, I have gone back to the initial questions—should we intervene paternalistically towards eating-disordered people? Should we force the dieting anorexic to eat? Should we empty the fridge and cupboards for the bulimic not to have food to binge with? And, in the most dramatic cases, should we force-feed the anorexic who starves to death?

The theory of paternalism articulated in Chapter 2 says that, prima facie, autonomous decisions should be respected, whatever the consequences of these decisions on the person's welfare. Conversely, the theory also says that it may be ethical to intervene independently of or against people's wishes to protect their welfare when their harmful actions and choices are undermined by significant defects in autonomy (weak paternalism).

In the case of eating disorders, this means that eating-disordered behaviour should be respected provided that it is autonomous. Chapter 12 has thus explored eating-disordered behaviour, such as dieting, vomiting, over-exercising, to assess whether it may be considered autonomous and should therefore be respected. This investigation provided inconclusive results. Eating-disordered behaviour seems to be associated with important defects in autonomy—defects in information and beliefs. For example, people with eating disorders are normally very well informed about food and nutrition, but will also have a number of beliefs relating to food that do not have any scientific basis (for example, the idea that animal food fattens 'more' than vegetable food—so that 100kcal of cheese fatten more than 100kcal of bread). Moreover, people with eating disorders have unrealistic perceptions of hunger and satiety. Their beliefs are also often false or based on few if any scientific grounds. For example, the belief that, if they eat at a restaurant one night, the next day they will be fatter, or that, if they do not exercise one day, they will spend the rest of their life binging on the sofa (catastrophic thinking). Cognitive psychology has shown how the process of thinking of the eating-disordered person is dysfunctional at different levels. The process of deliberation that leads up to eating-disordered behaviour thus appears, from this point of view, defective. This seems to give us a prima facie ethical entitlement to intervene paternalistically to protect the sufferer's welfare.

However, these 'defects' in information and beliefs are also a part of the deeper meaning of anorexia and bulimia. So, not only are they 'defects' underpinning the process of deliberation leading up to eating-disordered behaviour; they are also a part of the complex psychological world of the person with eating disorders and constitutive of that person's behaviour. The way these 'defects' determine the person's behaviour is different from the way in which genuine defects make people's behaviour non-autonomous. For example, I may not eat dairy food because a doctor made a wrong diagnosis and told me that I am intolerant to lactose, when in fact I am not. In this case, we may say that a genuine defect in information affects my choice not to eat dairy products. Once I receive the correct information, the likely outcome is that I will start eating dairy food again. My choice to avoid cheese is based on wrong information and on a false belief about myself. The case of anorexia and bulimia is different. There is no real evidence to support some beliefs—such as that animal food will fatten more than other types of food, or that, if one does not exercise one day, one will put on weight. In fact, some of these beliefs are clearly false. However, the person will be reluctant to accept that they are false. It seems that the person at some level 'wants to believe' what she believes in order to support her modality of behaviour. In this sense I have argued that those defects in information and beliefs are a part of anorexia and bulimia. If the person did not have these defects, she would not have eating disorders at all. Having those 'dysfunctions' is equal to having eating disorders, and is not what leads up to disordered eating.

These defects, thus, tell us something about eating-disordered behaviour, but do not tell us whether that behaviour is autonomous. They do, at one level—because it remains true that the person has false information and false beliefs and that the process of deliberation is dysfunctional. But, at another level those dysfunctions *are* eating disorders, and not what leads up to eating disorders. At this level, these dysfunctions make us understand better the problems that the person with eating disorders has, her way of thinking, her fears, but do not tell us whether the behaviour is autonomous or not.

Since we cannot claim that eating-disordered behaviour is autonomous or non-autonomous, any action—or inaction—towards the person with eating disorder is morally *uncertain*. Any decision to intervene paternalistically or not to intervene will be associated with significant *moral doubt*.

The question of whether carers are entitled to intervene paternalistically towards the person with eating disorders extends to the most dramatic cases in which the only way to rescue a person from death is by administering force-feeding. Chapter 13 has discussed the ethics of force-feeding. These cases are also extremely problematic, from an ethical point of view, and the decision to respect the patient's wishes will always have a degree of moral doubt. I have argued that in some cases the decision to refuse force-feeding may be a competent one. Based on the theory of paternalism proposed in Chapter 2, it seems that we should respect the refusal of artificial feeding, if or to the extent that it is an autonomous (competent) decision.

However, again it is unclear whether we should respect the competent refusal of food by the dying anorexic. And it is unclear on which basis we should decide whether we should respect the competent refusal or not. The case of anorexia is in fact different from other cases of refusal of life-saving treatment. Although the severely emaciated anorexic looks similar to people with terminal diseases, anorexia is not lethal or chronically debilitating in the same way as terminal or chronically debilitating diseases are. The person is normally young and healthy, and the symptomatology she is suffering is the result of the hideous effects of extreme diet—not some untreatable disease. She could recover completely, and all the symptoms of starvation could disappear with normal eating patterns. The person's life could be saved by simply feeding her. Thus, it is not true that anorexia is a lethal or chronically debilitating disease in the same way as other diseases are. The decision to let the person die is therefore an extremely hard one to make, for carers and health-care professionals.[1] Even if one is committed to the principle of respect for autonomy, and thus believes that autonomous decisions should be respected even if they cause harm, this may not be enough for someone to accept the patient's refusal of life-saving treatment. When people decide to accept a patient's decision to die, they are probably thinking not only of whether the person is being autonomous, but also—and maybe mainly—of how much the person is suffering, how many attempts they have all made to help her, and how many years the person has lived in those conditions; ultimately they will have compassion for the sufferer. Whether or not one accepts the sufferer's competent decision to refuse life-saving treatment will depend not only on how much weight one gives to respect for autonomy, but also, to an important extent, on one's sense of empathy and compassion for the person's suffering.

When we face the dying anorexic, thus, we cannot have a definite answer as to whether we should force-feed her or not. I have suggested that carers and health-care professionals should make a judgment about the autonomy/ competence of the person's decision, but should also be empathetic and compassionate towards the sufferer.

---

[1] It has been pointed out to me that a similar situation may arise when a young person has a curable disease but refuses life-saving treatment—for example, for religious reasons. It seems to me that the situation in this case is very similar, and poses similar ethical dilemmas to carers and health-care professionals, and similar psychological strains.

The questions with which we started—Should we force the dieting anor-exic to eat? Should we lock up the toilet to prevent her from making herself sick? Should we stop her exercising? Should we forcibly feed her?—have remained to an important extent unanswered. I would now like to attempt to explain this.

Many studies have investigated the causes of eating disorders. Many explanations have been provided, and all of them probably contain an element of truth. However, the crucial aspect of eating disorders, which is often underestimated, is *morality*. Eating-disordered behaviour is the con-sistent implementation of moral values that the person (the sufferer) *takes seriously*. Eating disorders are in an important way an expression of ordinary (or prevalent) morality. Without shared basic concepts of good/bad and right/wrong (the most fundamental of which is probably the idea that causing suffering is *morally wrong*), eating disorders could not be articulated. I have argued that people with eating disorders are just people who have taken some moral values *seriously*—maybe more seriously than others. Although other variables are also likely to play a role in the articulation of such a complex syndrome, the fight for control that is at the heart of anorexia and bulimia appears unintelligible unless one takes into account the fundamental part played by moral beliefs and ideals. Eating anomalies should be seen as the coherent implementation of moral imperatives that are just being taken seriously. These moral imperatives are part of ordinary morality; stripped of their original religious significance, they express moral codes that are routinely applied to all areas of daily life. Eating disorders thus challenge our ordinary morality, and to force us to accept that 'morality' 'rightness', and 'goodness'—if taken seriously—may cause great psychological harm, and may threaten people's life.

The analysis of eating disorders and of the ethics of the treatment of eating-disordered people touches our very moral values and beliefs. We face eating disorders armed with a set of moral values—we want to do what is right or good for the person. But eating disorders challenge these moral values, as the disorder is an expression of them. The fact that eating disorders have to do with the concept of *right and wrong*, and therefore are a *moral issue*, makes the ethics of care and treatment an extremely complex and fragile field of investigation.

If eating disorders stem from ordinary moral concepts (right and wrong, good and bad), we will find that asking what it is right to do with the person with eating disorders is in some way asking the wrong question. The real issue is *why* people want what they want, why they want it so much, why they are ready to sacrifice their health and even their life in order to get it. This book has shown how searching for an answer to these questions represents a challenge to common moral beliefs. The question 'What is it ethical to do with the eating-disordered person?' is therefore somehow bound to remain, to some extent, unanswered. Often ethical arguments are deductions from ethical values or principles. For example, given that we believe we should promote people's welfare, it follows that... Or given that we believe we should respect people's autonomy, it follows that... However, our very moral principles, beliefs, and attitude towards other people get challenged in the analysis of eating disorders. So the person who tries to understand eating disorders will have the impression that in an important sense searching for 'what is the right or good thing to do' is just missing the point and even gets trapped in the same logic that gives rise to eating disorders.

The analysis of eating disorders will have, as a likely outcome, a *moral doubt*. The search for an ethical answer will lead us to ask a number of other questions. Why do we believe these things? Why do we believe that causing suffering is a moral wrong? Why do we think that parents have 'moral' obligations to their children? Why do people get upset if others disappoint them? Why do people perceive disappointment as a moral wrong? Why do people perceive other people's behaviour as morally right or wrong to them? Eating disorders induce us to question and unmask a *moral logic*, a way of understanding human behaviour and human relationships in moral terms.

Wittgenstein said that anyone who understands his book the *Tractatus Logicus Philosophicus* must *throw it away*. 'He must, so to speak, throw away the ladder after he has climbed up it.'[2] In some way, something similar will happen to this book, once it has been read and understood. The perspective from which eating disorders are normally observed needs to be surpassed. Eating disorders are normally understood in terms of eating, fasting, binging, autonomy, or competence. This book has shown that eating disorders should be understood in terms of moral values. We need to discuss not eating disorders but eating disorders in the context of the moral values that are prevalent in the societies where the disorder arises. Shared moral notions, such as moral perfection and moral integrity, and other familiar moral categories are an essential key to the understanding not only of the way in which eating disorders work but also of the way in which they make sense.

If we really want to understand eating disorders, and to understand *what it is right to do* with eating-disordered people, we do not need to focus on how people eat, but rather to look at *what they believe*, and more generally at *what we all believe*—at our morality.

The clinical and social implications of this may be important in terms of how eating disorders are understood and approached. When approaching eating disorders, what one should discuss is not primarily *eating*, but

---

[2] Ludwig Wittgenstein, *Tractatus Logico-Philosophicus*, trans. D. F. Pears and B. F. McGuinness (London: Routledge & Kegan Paul, 1961), 6.54.

morality. The focus should shift from the person with eating disorders, from her eating habits, and from what happens 'in her mind' to *our* shared moral assumptions about what is 'good' and 'right' and their repercussions. Eating (normal or abnormal) is not important *per se*. Eating is important as an expression of people's moral beliefs, and it is these beliefs that need to be unmasked and discussed. Anorexia and bulimia express values such as the superiority of the spirit/mind/soul over the body, the control over the body, the idea that the moral person is 'strong-willed', capable of mastering his or her emotions and physical impulses. These values, though sometimes mitigated and implemented in many different ways, are part of ordinary morality in Western societies. The eating-disordered person is just someone who has taken these values seriously, and eating disorders can be understood as a consistent implementation of them. Eating disorders, thus, are not so much about eating as about what people believe and value and how they apply their beliefs and values.

It is true, however, that carers and health-care professionals still have to make decisions as to how to deal with an eating-disordered person. We may all agree that anorexia is not about dieting—it is about shared morality. And we may agree that the issue is not 'shall we force her to eat?' but 'how do we address our shared beliefs and how do we get rid of these harmful moral concepts?' However, the person still is starving herself—she is still vomiting. We still have the choice of locking up the toilet and forcing her to eat. We are still in the situation of having to make a value judgement and a value choice, and whatever we do or do not do is a value choice.

I have not provided a clear and definite answer to the issue of paternalism towards eating-disordered people—maybe others studies will. However, hopefully I have offered a deeper insight into eating disorders and a new way of thinking about 'what one should do'. Most people think that what they should do is to try to change the self-destructive modality of the behaviour of the person with eating disorders—either change the dieting, vomiting, or over-exercising, or change the psychology of the eating-disordered person, change her deepest needs. If the arguments of this book are accepted, nobody's behaviour needs to be changed. There is in fact nothing 'wrong' with the eating-disordered person—and there is nothing 'wrong' with the family and the society of the anorexic person. There are no 'wrong' behaviours; there are, instead, *meaningful* behaviours, expressive of people's values and needs. The most effective way to resolve eating disorders, therefore, is not to find a way of changing the person's eating patterns, or changing others' expectations of them. It is, rather, to change, or at least rearticulate, the way we—*all of us*—think about concepts such as right and wrong, good and bad, and the way in which we seem to be bound to judge human behaviour and people's interactions in moral terms.

Bibliography

1. Clinical Studies

Abraham, Suzanne, *Eating Disorders: The Facts* (Oxford: Oxford University Press, 1997).

American Psychiatric Association, *Diagnostic and Statistical Manual of Mental Disorders, DSM-IV-TR (Text Revision)* 4th edn., Washington: APA, 2000.

Andersen, Arnold, E., 'Atypical Anorexia Nervosa', in R. A. Vigersky (ed.), *Anorexia Nervosa* (London: Raven Press, 1977).

—— *Practical Comprehensive Treatment of Anorexia Nervosa and Bulimia* (London: Edward Arnold, 1985).

—— *Eating Disorders and Obesity* (2nd edn., London: Guilford Presss, 2002), ch. 33, pp. 188–92.

Aravich, P. F., Rieg, T. S., Lauterio, T. J., and Doerries, L. E., 'Beta-Endorphin and Dynorphin Abnormalities in Rats Subjected to Exercise and Restricted Feeding: Relationship to Anorexia Nervosa', *Brain Research*, 622/1–2 (1993), 1–8.

Baily, Andrew, 'Neurosis: A Conceptual Examination', *International Journal of Applied Philosophy*, 11/2 (1997), 51–61.

Bell, R. M., *Holy anorexia* (Chicago: University of Chicago Press, 1985). Italian version, *La santa anoressia: Digiuno e misticismo dal medioevo a oggi* (Rome: Laterza, 1987).

Bemporad, Jules, R., 'Cultural and Historical Aspects of Eating Disorders', *Theoretical Medicine*, 18/4 (1997), 401–20.

Beumont, Pierre J. V., and Vandereycken, Walter, 'Challenges and Risks for Health Care Professionals', in Walter Vandereycken and Pierre J. V. Beumont (eds.), *Treating Eating Disorders: Ethical, Legal and Personal Issues* (New York: New York University Press, 1998), ch. 1, pp. 1–29.

Birley, J. L., 'Psychiatrists as Citizens', *British Journal of Psychiatry*, 159 (1991), 1–6.

Blinder, B. J., Blinder, M. C., and Sanathara, V. A., 'Eating Disorders and Addiction', *Psychiatric Times*, 15/12 (1998), http://www.mhsource.com/edu/psytimes/p981230.html.

Bordo, Susan, 'Anorexia Nervosa: Psychopathology as the Cristallization of Culture', *Philosophical Forum*, 17 (1985–6), 73–104.

—— *Unbearable Weight, Feminism, Western Culture and the Body* (Berkeley and Los Angeles: University of California Press, 1993).

Boskind-Lodahl, M., 'Cindarella's Stepsister: A Feminist Perspective on Anorexia Nervosa and Bulimia', *Signs*, 2/2 (1976), 342–56.

Bowden, P. K., et al., 'Distorting Patient or Distorting Instrument? Body Shape Disturbance in Patients with Anorexia Nervosa and Bulimia', *British Journal of Psychiatry*, 155 (1989), 196–201.

Brambilla, F., et al., 'Plasma Concentration of Interleukin-1 Beta, Iterleukin-6 and Tumor Necrosis Factor-Alpha in Anorexia and Bulimia Nervosa', *Psychoneuroendocrinology*, 23/5 (1998), 439–47.

Bruch, Hilde, 'The Insignificant Difference: Discordant Incidence on Anorexia Nervosa in Monozygotic Twins', *American Journal of Psychiatry*, 126 (1969), 123–8.

—— *Eating Disorders: Obesity, Anorexia Nervosa and the Person within* (London: Routledge and Kegan Paul, 1974). Italian version, *Patologia del comportamento alimentare* (Milan: Feltrinelli, 1977).

—— *The Golden Cage: The Enigma of Anorexia Nervosa* (London: Open Books, 1980). Italian version, *La gabbia d'oro, l'enigma dell'anoressia mentale* (Milan: Feltrinelli, 1983).

—— 'Four Decades of Eating Disorders', in D. M. Gardner and P. E. Garfinkle (eds.), *Handbook for the Psychotherapy of Anorexia Nervosa and Bulimia* (New York: Guilford Press, 1985), ch. 1.

—— 'Perils of Behavioural Modification in Treatment of Anorexia Nervosa', *American Association of Medicine*, 230 (1994), 1419–21.

Bulik, C. M., and Sullivan, P. F., 'Comorbidity of Bulimia and Substance-Abuse Perceptions of Family of Origin', *International Journal of Eating Disorders*, 13/1 (1993), 49–59.

—— —— McKee, M., Weltzin, T. E., and Kaye, W. H., 'Characteristics of Bulimic Women with and without Alcohol Abuse', *American Journal of Drug and Alcohol Abuse*, 20/2 (1994), 273–83.

—— et al., 'Heritability of Binge-Eating and Broadly Defined Bulimia Nervosa', *Biological Psychiatry*, 44/12 (1998), 1210–18.

Caillot Augusseau, A., Lafage Proust, M. H., Margaillan, P., Vergely, N., Faure, S., Paillet, S., Lang, F., Alexandre, C., and Estour, B., 'Weight Gain Reverses Bone Turnover and Restores Circadian Variation of Bone Resorption in Anorexic Patients', *Clinical Endocrinology*, 52/1 (2000), 113–21.

Campbell, D. A., Sundaramurthy, D., Markham, A. F., and Pieri, L. F., 'Fine Mapping of Human 5-HTR2 a Gene to Chromosome 3914 and Identification of Two Highly Polymorphic Linked Markers Suitable for Association Studies in Psychiatric Disorders', *Genetic Testing*, 1/4 (1997), 297–9.

Carter, F. A., and Bulik, C. M., 'Exposure Treatments for Bulimia Nervosa, Procedure, Efficacy and Mechanisms', *Advances in Behaviour Research and Therapy*, 16/2 (1994), 77–129.

Cash, T. F., and Deagle, E. A., 'The Nature and Extent of Body-Image Disturbances in Anorexia Nervosa and Bulimia Nervosa: A Meta-Analysis', *International Journal of Eating Disorders*, 22/2 (1997), 107–25.

Casper, Regina C., 'Depression and Eating Disorders', *Depression and Anxiety*, 8, suppl. 1 (1998), 96–104.

—— 'Recognising Eating Disorders in Women', *Psychopharmacological Bulletin*, 34/3 (1998), 267–9.

—— and Davis, M. John, 'On the Course of Anorexia Nervosa', *American Journal of Psychiatry*, 134/9 (1977), 974–6.

Cochran, C., Malcom, R., and Brewerton, T., 'The Role of Weight Control as a Motivation for Cocaine Abuse', *Addictive Behaviors*, 23/2 (1998), 201–7.

Collo, Robert, Brown, Gregory M., and Van Loon, Glen R., *Clinical Neuroendocrinology* (Oxford: Blackwell, 1998).

Corcos, M., 'Sexuality and Eating Disorders: True–False Sexual Toxin and Endogenous Pleasure', *Evolution Psychiatrique*, 64/3 (1999), 543–65.

Crisp, H. Arthur, *Anorexia Nervosa: Let Me Be* (London: Baillière Tindall, 1990).

Crow, S., Praus, B., and Thuras, P., 'Mortality from Eating Disorders: A 5-to-10 Year Record Linkage Study', *International Journal of Eating Disorders*, 26/1 (1999), 97–102.

Cuntz, U., Frank, G., Lehnert, P., and Fichter, M., 'Interrelationships between the Size of the Pancreas and the Weight of Patients with Eating Disorders', *International Journal of Eating Disorders*, 27/3 (2000), 297–303.

Dalgleish, Julia, and Dollery, Stuart, *The Health and Fitness Handbook* (Harlow: Longman, 2001).

Dally, Peter, and Gomez, Joan, *Obesity and Anorexia Nervosa* (London: Faber & Faber, 1980).

—— —— and Isaacs, A. J., *Anorexia Nervosa* (London: Heinemann, 1979).

Dansky, B. S., Brewerton, T. D., and Kilpatrick, D. G., 'Comorbidity of Bulimia Nervosa and Alcohol Use Disorders: Results from the National Women's Studies', *International Journal of Eating Disorders*, 27/2 (2000), 180–90.

Darley, J. M., Glucksberg, S., Kamin, L. J., and Kinchla, R. A., *Psychology* (Englewood Cliffs, NJ: Prentice Hall, 1984).

Davis, C., and Claridge, G., 'The Eating Disorders as Addiction: A Psychological Perspective', *Addictive Behaviors*, 23/4 (1988), 463–75.

Davis, M. John, 'On the Course of Anorexia Nervosa', *American Journal of Psychiatry*, 134/9 (1977), 974–6.

De Silva, Padmal, and Eysenk, Sybil, 'Personality and Addictiveness in Anorexic and Bulimic Patients', *Personality and Individual Differences*, 8/5 (1987), 749–51.

De Zwaan, Martina, 'Basic Neuroscience and Scanning', in Janet Treasure, Ulrich Schmidt, and Eric van Furth (eds.), *Handbook of Eating Disorders* (2nd edn., Chichester: Wiley, 2003), ch. 5, pp. 89–101.

Dolam, Bridget, 'Food Refusal, Forced Feeding and the Law of England and Wales', in Walter Vandereycken and Pierre J. V. Beumont (eds.), *Treating Eating Disorders: Ethical, Legal and Personal Issues* (New York: New York University Press, 1998), ch. 7, pp. 151–78.

Draper, Heather, 'Treating Anorexics without Consent: Some Reservations', *Journal of Medical Ethics*, 24 (1998), 5–7.

—— 'Anorexia Nervosa and Respecting a Refusal of Life-Prolonging Therapy: A Limited Justification', *Bioethics*, 14/2 (2000), 120–33.

Dresser, Rebecca, 'Feeding the Hungry Artists: Legal Issues in Treating Anorexia Nervosa', *Wisconsin Law Review,* 2 (1984), 297–374.

—— 'Legal and Policy Considerations in Treatment of Anorexia Nervosa Patients', *International Journal of Eating Disorders*, 3 (1984), 43–51.

Duker, Marilyn, and Slade, Roger, *Anorexia and Bulimia: How to Help* (2nd edn., Buckingham: Open University Press, 2003).

Dunne, E. G., Feeney, S., and Schipperheijn, J., 'Eating Disorders and Alcohol Misuse: Features of an Addiction', *Postgraduate Medical Journal*, 67/784 (1991), 112–13.

Eckert, E. D., et al., 'Ten Year Follow-up of Anorexia Nervosa: Clinical Course and Outcome', *Psychological Medicine*, 25 (1995), 143–56.

Ehrenreich, B., *For her Own Good: 150 Years of the Experts' Advice to Women* (London: Pluto Press, 1979).

Eisler, Ivan, Le Grange, Daniel, and Asen, Eia, 'Family Interventions', in Janet Treasure, Ulrich Schmidt, and Eric van Furth (eds.), *Handbook of Eating Disorders* (2nd edn., Chichester: Wiley, 2003), ch. 18, pp. 291–310.

Estok, P. J., and Rudi, E. B., 'The Relationship between Eating Disorders and Running in Women', *Research in Nursing and Health*, 19/5 (1996), 377–87.

Faccio, Elena, *Il disturbo alimentare: Modelli, ricerche e terapie* (Rome: Carocci, 1999).

Fairburn, G. Christopher, and Brownell, Kelly D. (eds.), *Eating Disorders and Obesity* (2nd edn., London: Guilford Press, 2002).

—— and Wilson, G. Terence, *Binge Eating* (New York: Guilford Press, 1993).

—— Shafran, R. and Cooper, Z., 'A Cognitive-Behavioural Therapy of Anorexia Nervosa', *Behavioural Research Theory*, 37/1 (1999), 1–13.

Fallon, P., *Feminist Perspective on Eating Disorders* (New York: Guilford Press, 1994).

Fedoroff, I. C., Stoner, S. A., Andersen, A. E., Doty, R. L., and Rolls, B. J., 'Olfactory Dysfunction in Anorexia Nervosa', *International Journal of Eating Disorders*, 18 (1995), 71–7.

Fichter, Manfred, and Krenn, Heidelinde, 'Eating Disorders in Males', in Janet Treasure, Ulrich Schmidt, and Eric van Furth (eds.), *Handbook of Eating Disorders* (2nd edn., Chichester: Wiley, 2003), ch. 23, pp. 369–83.

Freeman, A., and Greenwood, V. B. (eds.), *Cognitive Therapy: Application in Psychiatry and Medical Setting* (New York: Human Science, 1987).

Fullerton, Donald T., Swift, W. J., Getto, C. J., and Carlson, I. H., 'Plasma Immunoreactive Beta-Endorphin in Bulimics', *Psychological Medicine*, 16 (1986), 59–63.

Gardner, D. M., and Garfinkle, P. E. (eds.), *Handbook for the Psychotherapy of Anorexia Nervosa and Bulimia* (New York: Guilford Press, 1985).

Gardner, R. M., and Bokenkamp, E. D., 'The Role of Sensory and Non-Sensory Factors in Body Size Estimations of Eating Disorders Subjects', *Journal of Clinical Psychology*, 52/1 (1996), 3–15.

Garfinkel, Paul E., *Anorexia Nervosa: A Multidimensional Perspective* (New York: Brunner/Mazel, 1982).

Garfinkel, Paul E., 'Classification and Diagnosis of Eating Disorders', in Christopher G. Fairburn and Kelly D. Brownell (eds.), *Eating Disorders and Obesity* (2nd edn., London: Guilford Presss, 2002), ch. 28, pp. 155–61.

Gendall, K. A., Bulik, C. M., and Joyce, P. R., 'Visceral Protein and Hematological Status of Women with Bulimia Nervosa', *Physiology and Behavior*, 66/1 (1999), 159–63.

Giannini, A. J., Newman, M., and Gold, M., 'Anorexia and Bulimia', *American Family Physician*, 41/4 (1991), 1169–76.

Goldbloom, D. S., Garfinkel, P. E., Katz, R., and Brown, G. M., 'The Hormonal Response to Intravenous 5-Hydroxytryptophan in Bulimia Nervosa', *Journal of Psychosomatic Research*, 40/3 (1996), 289–97.

Goodwood, P., Bouvard, M., Mouren-Simeoni, M. C., Kipman, A., and Ades, J., 'Genetics and Anorexia Nervosa: A Review of Candidate Genes', *Psychiatric Genetics*, 8/1 (1998), 1–12.

Gordon, Richard, *Anorexia and Bulimia: Anatomy of a Social Epidemic* (Oxford: Blackwell, 1990). Italian version, *Anoressia e bulimia: Anatomia di un'epidemia sociale* (Milan: Raffaello Cortina, 1991).

Grice, D. E., Halmi, K. A., Fichter, M. M., Strober, M., Woodside, D. B., Treasure, J. T., Kaplan, A. S., Magistretti, P. J., Goldman, D., Bulik, C. M., Kaye, W. H., and Berrettini, W. H., 'Evidence for a Susceptibility Gene for Anorexia Nervosa on Chromosome 1', *American Journal of Human Genetics*, 70 (2002), 787–92.

Griffiths, Rosalyn, and Russell, Janice, 'Compulsory treatment of Anorexia Nervosa Patients', in Walter Vandereycken and Pierre J. V. Beumont (eds.), *Treating Eating Disorders: Ethical, Legal and Personal Issues* (New York: New York University Press, 1998), ch. 6.

Grossman, Sebastian P., 'Contemporary Problems concerning our Understanding of Brain Mechanism that Regulate Food Intake and Body Weight', in A. J. Stunkard and Eliot Stellar (eds.), *Eating Disorders* (New York: Raven Press, 1984), 5–15.

Haley, J., 'The Family of the Schizophrenic: A Model System', *Journal of Neurologic and Mental Disorders*, 129 (1959), 357–74.

Halmi, K. A., 'Current Concepts and Definitions', in G. I. Szmukler, C. Dare, and Janet Treasure (eds.), *Handbook of Eating Disorders* (Chichester: John Wiley & Sons, 1995), 29–44.

—— 'Physiology of Anorexia Nervosa and Bulimia Nervosa', in Christopher G. Fairburn and Kelly D. Brownell (eds.), *Eating Disorders and Obesity* (2nd edn., London: Guilford Presss, 2002), ch. 48, pp. 267–71.

Han, L., et al., 'No Coding Variant of the Tryptophanhydroxylase Gene Detected in Seasonal Affective Disorder, Obsessive-Compulsive Disorder, Anorexia Nervosa and Alcoholism', *Biological Psychiatry*, 45/5 (1999), 615–19.

Hardin, K. Pamela, 'Shape-Shifting Discourses of Anorexia Nervosa: Reconstituting Psychopathology', *Nursing Inquiry*, 10/4 (2003), 209–17.

Harlow, H. F., and Harlow, M., 'Learning to Love', *American Science*, 54 (1966), 244–72.

Hautzig, Deborah, *Second Star to the Right* (London: Fontana Lions, 1982).

Hayes, Nicky, *Foundations of Psychology* (London: Thomason Learning, 2000).

Herzog, D. B., Nussbaum, K. M., and Marmor, A. K., 'Co-Morbidity and Outcome in Eating Disorders', *Psychiatric Clinics of North America*, 19/4 (1996), 843–61.

Herzog, D. B., Greenwood, D. N., Doer, D. J., Flores, A. T., Ekeblad, E. R., Richards, A., Blais, M. A., and Keller, M. B., 'Mortality in Eating Disorders: A Descriptive Study', *International Journal of Eating Disorders*, 28/1 (2000), 20–6.

Hill, K. K., Hill, D. B., Humphries, L. L., Maloney, M. J., and McClain, C. J., 'A Role for Helicobacter Pylori in the Gastrointestinal Complaints of Eating Disorder Patients?', *International Journal of Eating Disorders*, 25/1 (1999), 109–12.

Hill, O. W., 'Epidemiological Aspects of Anorexia Nervosa', *Advances in Psycholomatic medicine*, 9 (1977), 48–62.

Hinney, A., et al., 'No Evidence for Involvement of Leptin Gene in Anorexia Nervosa, Bulimia Nervosa, Underweight or Early Onset of Extreme Obesity', *Molecular Psychiatry*, 28/4 (1998), 539–43.

—— et al., 'Systematic Mutation Screening of the Pro-Opiomelanocortin Gene: Identification of Several Genetic Variants Including Three Different Insertions, One Nonsense and Two Missense Point Mutations in Probands of Different Weight Extremes', *Journal of Clinical Endocrinology and Metabolism*, 83/10 (1998), 3737–41.

Hoek, Hans Wijbrand, 'Distribution of Eating Disorders', in Christopher G. Fairburn and Kelly D. Brownell (eds.), *Eating Disorders and Obesity* (2nd edn., London: Guilford Press, 2002), ch. 41, pp. 233–7.

Holderness, C. C, Brooks-Gunn, J., Warren, M. P., 'Comorbidity of Eating Disorders and Substance Abuse: Review of Literature', *International Journal of Eating Disorders*, 16/1 (1994), 1–34.

Holland, A. J., Hall, A., Murray, R., Russel, G. F., and Crisp, A. H., 'Anorexia Nervosa: A Study of 34 Pairs of Twins and One Set of Triplets', *British Journal of Psychiatry*, 145 (1984), 414–19.

Horne, R. L., Vanvactor, J. C., and Emerson, J., 'Disturbed Body Image in Patients with Eating Disorders', *American Journal of Psychiatry*, 148/2 (1991), 211–15.

Hudson, J. I., Weiss, R. D., Pope, H. G., McElroy, S. K., and Mirin, S. M., 'Eating Disorders in Hospitalised Substance Abuser', *Journal of Drug and Alcohol Abuse*, 18/1 (1992), 75–85.

Hugo, P. J., and Lacey, J. H., 'Disordered Eating: A Defense Against Psychosis?', *International Journal of Eating Disorders*, 24/3 (1998), 329–33.

Huline, Dickens S., 'Anorexia Nervosa: Some Connections with the Religious Attitude', *British Journal of Medical Psychology*, 73/1 (2000), 67–76.

Jack, L., and Katz, M. D., 'Eating Disorders', in M. M. Shangold and G. Mirkin (eds.), *Women and Exercise: Physiology and Sports Medicine* (Philadelphia: Davis Company, 1994), 292–312.

Jarman, Maria, Smith, A. Jonathan, and Walsh, Sue, 'The Psychological Battle for Control: A Qualitative Study of Health Care Professionals. Understanding the Treatment of Anorexia Nervosa', *Journal of Community and Applied Social Psychology*, 7 (1997), 137–52.

Jimerson, D. C., Lesem, M. D., Kaye, W. H., and Brewton, T. D., 'Low Serotonin and Dopamine Metabolite Concentrations in Cerebrospinal Fluid from Bulimic Patients with Frequent Binge Episodes', *Archives of General Psychiatry*, 49/2 (1992), 132–8.

Johnson, R. D., 'Opioid Involvment in Feeding-Behavior and the Pathogenesis of Certain Eating Disorders', *Medical Hypotheses*, 45/5 (1995), 491–7.

Kaplan, Allan S., and Garfinkel, Paul E., 'The Neuroendocrinology of Anorexia Nervosa', in R. Collu, G. M. Brown, and Glen R. Van Loon (eds.), *Clinical Neuroendocrinology* (Oxford: Blackwell, 1988), 105–22.

Kaye, H. Walter, 'Central Nervous System Neurotransmitter Activity in Anorexia Nervosa and Bulimia Nervosa', in Christopher G. Fairburn and Kelly D. Brownell (eds.), *Eating Disorders and Obesity* (2nd edn., London: Guilford Press, 2002), ch. 49, pp. 272–7.

Kaye, W., Gendall, K., and Strober, M., 'Serotonin Neuronal Function and Selective Serotonin Reuptake Inhibitor Treatment in Anorexia and Bulimia Nervosa', *Biological Psychiatry*, 44/9 (1998), 825–38.

Kayloe, J. C., 'Food Addiction', *Psychotherapy*, 30/2 (1993), 269–75.

Kennedy, A. H., and Garfinkel, E. Paul, 'Advances in Diagnosis and Treatment of Anorexia Nervosa and Bulimia Nervosa', *Canadian Journal of Psychiatry*, 37/5 (1992), 309–15.

Kipman, A., Bruins-Slot, L., Boni, C., Hanoun, N., Adès, J., Blot, P., Hamon, M., Mouren-Siméoni, M. C., and Gorwood, P., '5-HT2A Gene Promoter Polymorphism as a Modifying rather than a Vulnerability Factor in Anorexia Nervosa', *European Psychiatry*, 17 (2002), 227–9.

Klump, Kelly L., Wonderlich, Stephen, Lehoux, Pascale, Lilenfeld, Lisa R., and Bulik, Cynthia M., 'Does Environment Matter? A Review of Nonshared Environment and Eating Disorders', *International Journal of Eating Disorders*, 31 (2002), 118–35.

Krahn, D. D., Dequardo, J., and Gobnell, B. A., 'Opiate Addiction and Anorexia Nervosa: A Case Report', *International Journal of Eating Disorders*, 9/4 (1990), 453–6.

—— Piper, D., King, M., Olson, L., Kurth, C., and Morberg, D. P., 'Dieting in Sixth Grade Predicts Alcohol Use in Ninth Grade', *Journal of Substance Abuse*, 8/3 (1996), 293–301.

Krugovoy Silver, Anna, *Victorian Literature and the Anorexic Body* (Cambridge: Cambridge University Press).

Lackstrom, Jan B., and Woodside, D. Blake, 'Families, Therapists and Family Therapy in Eating Disorders', in Walter Vandereycken and Pierre J. V. Beumont (eds.), *Treating Eating Disorders: Ethical, Legal and Personal Issues* (New York: New York University Press, 1998), 106–26.

Landau, C., 'Substance Abuse', in *Encyclopedia of Psychology* (New York: Wiley 1994), 382–3.

Lawrence, Marlin, 'Anorexia Nervosa: The Control Paradox', *Women's Studies International Quarterly*, 2 (1979), 93–101.

—— (ed.), *Fed Up and Hungry: Women, Oppression and Food* (London: Women's Press, 1987).

—— *The Anorexic Experience* (3rd edn., London: Women's Press, 1995).

Le Grange, D., Telch, C. F., and Tibbs, J., 'Eating Attitudes and Behaviors in 1435 South African Caucasian and Non-Caucasian College Students', *American Journal of Psychiatry*, 155/2 (1998), 250–4.

Lemberg, R., and Cohn, L. (eds.), *Eating Disorders: A Reference Sourcebook* (Phoenix: Oryx Press, 1999).

Lester, R. J., 'The (Dis)embodied Self in Anorexia Nervosa, Social Science and Medicine', *Social Science and Medicine*, 44/4 (1997), 479–89.

Lilenfeld, L. R., and Kaye, W. H., 'The Link between Alcoholism and Eating Disorders', *Alcohol, Health and Research World*, 20/2 (1996), 94–9.

—— et al., 'Psychiatric Disorders in Women with Bulimia Nervosa and their First-Degree Relatives: Effects of Comorbid Substance Dependence', *International Journal of Eating Disorders*, 22/3 (1997), 253–64.

—— Kaye, W. H., Greeno, C. G., Merikangas, K. R., Plotnikcov, K., Pollice, C., Rao, R., Strober, M., Bulik, C. M., and Nagy, L., 'A Controlled Family Study of Anorexia Nervosa and Bulimia Nervosa: Psychiatric Disorders in First-Degree Relatives and Effect of Proband Co-Morbidity', *Archives of General Psychiatry*, 55/7 (1998), 603–10.

Loumidis, K. S., and Wells, A., 'Assessment of Beliefs in Exercise Dependence: The Development and Preliminary Validation of the Exercise Beliefs Questionnaire', *Personality and Individual Differences*, 25/3 (1998), 553–67.

Lyn, Patrick, 'Eating Disorders: A Review of the Literature with Emphasis on Medical Complications and Clinical Nutrition', *Alternative Medicine Review* (June 2002), 184–207.

Lyons, M. A., 'The Phenomenon of Compulsive Overeating in a Selected Group of Professional Women', *Journal of Advanced Nursing*, 27/6 (1998), 1158–64.

McCann, U. D., Rossiter, E. M., King, R. J., and Agras, W. S., 'Non-Purging Bulimia: A Distinct Subtype of Bulimia Nervosa', *International Journal of Eating Disorders*, 10/6 (1999), 679–87.

McKenna, P. J., 'Disorders with Overvalued Ideas', *British Journal of Psychiatry*, 145 (1984), 579–85.

MacSween, Morag, *Anorexic Bodies: A Feminist and Social Perspective* (London: Routledge, 1995). Italian version, *Corpi anoressici* (Milan: Feltrinelli, 1999).

Mahowald, Mary Briody, 'To Be or Not To Be a Woman: Anorexia Nervosa, Normative Gender Roles, and Feminism', *Journal of Medicine and Philosophy*, 17/2 (1992), 233–51.

—— *Women and Children in Health Care: An Unequal Majority* (New York: Oxford University Press, 1993).

Malson, H., *The Thin Woman: Feminism, Post-Structuralism and the Social Psychology of Anorexia* (New York: Routledge, 1998).

Marazzi, M. A., Lubi, E. D., Kinzie, J., Munjal, I. D., and Spector, S., 'Endogenous Codeine and Morphine in Anorexia and Bulimia Nervosa', *Life Sciences*, 60/20 (1997), 1741–7.

—— McQuarters, A., Barnes, C., Lawhorn, J., and D'Amico-Rasmussen, Q., 'Male/Female Comparison of Morphine Effect on Food Intake: Relation to Anorexia Nervosa', *Pharmacology, Biochemistry and Behavior*, 53/2 (1998), 433–5.

Marcos, A., 'Eating Disorders: A Situation of Malnutrition with Peculiar Changes in Immune System', *European Journal of Clinical Nutrition*, 54, supp. 1 (2000), 61–4.

Mayer, L. E., and Walsh, B. T., 'The Use of Selective Serotonin Reuptake Inhibitors in Eating Disorders', *Journal of Clinical Psychiatry*, 59, suppl. 15 (1998), 28–34.

Meijboom, A., Jansen, A., Kampman, M., and Schouten, E., 'An Experimental Test of the Relationship between Self-Esteem and Concern about Body Shape and Weight in Restrained Eaters', *International Journal of Eating Disorders*, 25/2 (1999), 327–34.

Mental Health Act Commission, *Guidance on the Treatment of Anorexia under the Mental Health Act 1983* (London: HMSO, 1997; updated 1999).

Mickley, D. W., 'Medical Dangers of Anorexia Nervosa and Bulimia Nervosa', in R. Lemberg and L. Cohn (eds.), *Eating Disorders: A Reference Sourcebook* (Phoenix: Oryx Press, 1999).

Mills, I. H., and Medlicott, L., 'Anorexia Nervosa as a Compulsive Behavior Disease', *Quarterly Journal of Medicine*, 83/303 (1992), 507–22.

Minuchin, Salvador, *Families and Family Theory* (London: Routledge, 1991).

Mond, M. Jonathan, Philoppa, J. Hay, Rodgers, Bryan, and Beumont, J. V. Pierre, 'Beliefs of Women concerning Causes and Risk Factors for Bulimia Nervosa', *Australian and New Zealand Journal of Psychiatry*, 38/6 (2004), 463.

Monteleone, P., Di Lieto, A., Tortorella, A., Longobardi, N., and Maj, M., 'Circulating Leptin in Patients with Anorexia Nervosa, Bulimia Nervosa or Binge-Eating Disorder: Relationship to Body Weight, Eating Patterns, Psychopathology and Endocrine Changes', *Psychiatric Research*, 94/2 (2000), 121–9.

Morley, J. E., Levine, A. S., and Krahn, D. D, 'Neurotransmitter Regulation of Appetite and Eating', in B. J. Blinder, B. F. Chaitin, and R. S. Goldstein (eds.), *Eating Disorders: Medical and Psychological Bases of Diagnosis and Treatment* (New York: PMA, 1988), 11–19.

Murray, R. M., Jones, P., O'Callaghan, E., Takei, N., and Sham, P., 'Genes, Viruses and Neurodevelopmental Schizophrenia', *Journal of Psychiatric Research*, 26/4 (1992), 225–35.

Nagel, K. L., and Jones, K. H., 'Sociological Factors in the Development of Eating Disorders', *Adolescence*, 27/105 (1992), 107–13.

Nasser, Mervat, and Katzman, Melanie, 'Sociocultural Theories of Eating Disorders: An Evaluation in Thought', in Janet Treasure, Ulrich Schmidt, and Eric van Furth (eds.), *Handbook of Eating Disorders* (2nd edn., Chichester: Wiley, 2003), ch. 8, pp. 139–50.

Neisser, Ulric, *Cognitive Psychology* (New York: Appelton Century-Crofts, 1967).

Neyer, Lynn, and Lemberg, Raymond, 'Fat is not a Feeling! The Using of Reframing in the Treatment of Anorexia Nervosa and Bulimia', *British Review of Bulimia and Anorexia Nervosa*, 3/1 (1988), 7–12.

Nielsen, Søren, and Carril, Núria Bará, 'Family Burden of Care and Social Consequences', in Janet Treasure, Ulrich Schmidt, and Eric van Furth (eds.), *Handbook of Eating Disorders* (2nd edn., Chichester: Wiley, 2003), ch. 11, pp. 191–206.

Nillsson, E. W., Gillberg, C., and Rastam, M., 'Family Factors in Anorexia Nervosa: A Community Based Study', *Comprehensive Psychiatry*, 39/6 (1998), 392–9.

Nishizono, Maher, A., 'Eating Disorders in Japan: Finding the Right Context', *Psychiatry and Clinical Neurosciences*, 5/55 (1998), 320–3.

Noordenbos, Greta, 'Differences between Treated and Untreated Patients with Anorexia Nervosa', *British Review of Bulimia and Anorexia Nervosa*, 3/2 (1989), 55–60.

Orbach, Susie, *Fat is a Feminist Issue* (New York: Hamlyn, 1978).

—— *Hunger Strike: The Anorectic's Struggle as a Metaphor for our Age* (London: Faber & Faber, 1986).

Palmer, R. L., *Anorexia Nervosa: A Guide for Sufferers and their Family* (2nd edn., London: Penguin, 1989).

Pawlikawski, M., and Zarzycki, J., 'Does the Impairment of the Hypothalamic–Pituitary–Gonadal Axis in Anorexia Nervosa Depend on Increased Sensitivity to Endogenous Melatonin?', *Medical Hypotheses*, 52/2 (1999), 111–13.

Peterson, T. Robin, 'Bulimia and Anorexia in an Advertising Context', *Journal of Business Ethics*, 6 (1987), 495–504.

Pierce, E. F., Daleng, M. L., and McGowan, R. W., 'Scores on Exercise Dependence among Dancers', *Perceptual and Motor Skills*, 76/2 (1997), 531–5.

Polivy, Janet, and Herman, C. Peter, 'Causes of Eating Disorders', *Annual Review of Psychology*, 53 (2002), 187–213.

Pomeroy, Claire, and Mitchell, James E., 'Medical Complications of Anorexia Nervosa and Bulimia Nervosa', in Christopher G. Fairburn and Kelly D. Brownell (eds.), *Eating Disorders and Obesity* (2nd edn., London: Guilford Presss, 2002), ch. 50, pp. 278–83.

Pope, H. G., Jr., Hudson, J. I., Yurgelun-Todd, D., and Hudson, M. S., 'Prevalence of Anorexia Nervosa and Bulimia in Three Student Populations', *International Journal of Eating Disorder*, 3 (1984), 33–51.

Probst, Michel, Vandereycken, W., Vanderhaden, Johan, and Van Coppenolle, Herman, 'The Significance of Body Size Estimation in Eating Disorders: Its Relationship with Clinical and Psychological Variables', *International Journal of Eating Disorders*, 24/2 (1998), 167–74.

Ramsay, R., Ward, A., Treasure, J., and Russel, G. F., 'Compulsory Treatment in Anorexia Nervosa: Short-Term Benefits and Long-Term Mortality', *British Journal of Psychiatry*, 175 (1999), 147–53.

Rathner, Günter, 'A Plea against Compulsory Treatment of Anorexia Nervosa Patients', in Walter Vandereycken and Pierre J. V. Beumont (eds.), *Treating Eating Disorders: Ethical, Legal and Personal Issues* (New York: New York University Press, 1998), ch. 8, pp. 179–215.

Razzoli, Guido, *La bulimia nervosa: Definizione, sintomatologia e trattamento* (Milan: Sonzogno, 1995).

Reneric, J. P., and Bouvard, M. P., 'Opioid Receptor in Antagonists in Psychiatry: Beyond Drug Addiction', *Drugs*, 10/5 (1998), 365–82.

Rosen, J. C., and Ramirez, E., 'A Comparison of Eating Disorders and Body Dysmorphic Disorder on Body Image and Psychological Adjustment', *Journal of Psychosomatic Research*, 44/3–4 (1998), 441–9.

Rosenkranz, K., et al., 'Systematic Mutation Screening of the Estrogen Receptor Beta Gene in Probands of Different Weight Extremes: Identification of Several Genetic Variants', *Journal of Clinical Endocrinology and Metabolism*, 83/12 (1998), 4524–7.

Ross, H. E., and Ivis, F., 'Binge-Eating and Substance Use among Male and Female Adolescents', *International Journal of Eating Disorders*, 26/3 (1999), 245–60.

Russel, F. M. Gerald, Szmukler, G. I., Dare, C., and Eister, I., 'An Evaluation of Family Therapy in Anorexia Nervosa and Bulimia Nervosa', *Archives of General Psychiatry*, 44 (1987), 1047–56.

Russon, Lynne, and Dawn, Alison, 'Palliative Care does not Mean Giving up', *British Medical Journal*, 317 (1998), 21–4.

Sansone, R. A., Fine, M. A., and Nonn, J. L., 'A Comparison of Borderline Personality Symptomatology and Self-Destructive Behavior in Women with Eating Disorders, Substance Abuse and Both Eating Disorders and Substance Abuse Disorders', *Journal of Personality Disorders*, 8/3 (1994), 219–28.

Sarramon, C., Baheux, C., Charitat, H., Dorso, M. E., Cadilhac, P., Sztulman, H., and Schmitt, L., 'Psychodynamic Profile of Personality among Anorexia Nervosa and Opioid Addiction Patients', *Annales Medico-Psychologiques*, 157/6 (1999), 422–7.

Schmidt, U., Tiller, J., Andrews, B., and Treasure, L. Janet, 'Is there a Specific Trauma Precipitating Anorexia Nervosa?', *Psychological Medicine*, 27 (1997), 523–30.

Scott, W. Derek, 'Alcohol and Food Abuse: Some Comparisons', *British Journal of Addiction*, 78 (1973), 339–49.

Selvini Palazzoli, Mara, *L'anoressia mentale: Dalla terapia individuale alla terapia familiare* (9th edn., Milan: Feltrinelli, 1998).

—— Cirillo, S., Selvini, M., Sorrentino, A. M., *Ragazze anoressiche e bulimiche: La terapia familiare* (Milan: Cortina, 1998).

Shafran, Roz, and De Silva, Padmal, 'Cognitive-Behavioural Models', in Janet Treasure, Ulrich Schmidt, and Eric van Furth (eds.), *Handbook of Eating Disorders* (2nd edn., Chichester: Wiley, 2003), ch. 7, pp. 121–38.

Shan, P. J., 'Clinical and Psychometric Correlates of Dopamine D2 Binding in Depression', *Psychological Medicine*, 27/6 (1997), 1247–55.

Shelley, Rosemary, *Anorexics on Anorexia* (London: Jessica Kingsley, 1992).

Silverstein, B. and Perdue, L., 'The Relationship between Role Concerns, Preferences for Slimness, and Symptoms of Eating Problems among College Women', *Sex Roles*, 18 (1988), 101–6.

—— Peterson, B., and Perdue, L., 'Some Correlates of the Thin Standard of Bodily Attractiveness for Women', *International Journal of Eating Disorders*, 5 (1986), 895–905.

—— Perdue, L., Peterson, B., Vogel, L., and Fantini, D. A., 'Possible Causes of the Thin Standard of Bodily Attractiveness for Women', *International Journal of Eating Disorders*, 5 (1986), 905–16.

—— et al., 'Binging, Purging, and Estimates of Parental Attitudes regarding Female Achievement', *Sex Roles*, 19 (1988), 723–33.

Slade, Roger, *The Anorexia Nervosa Reference Book: Direct and Clear Answers to Everyone's Questions* (New York: Harper & Rowe, 1984).

Smith, D. K., Hale, B. D., and Collins, D., 'Measurement of Exercise Dependence in Body Builders', *Journal of Sports, Medicine and Physical Fitness*, 38/1 (1998), 66–74.

Shisslak, C. M., and Crago, M., 'Eating Disorders among Athletes', in R. Lemberg and L. Cohn (eds.), *Eating Disorders: A Reference Sourcebook* (Phoenix: Oryx Press, 1999), 79–83.

Sobel, S. V., 'What's New in the Treatment of Anorexia Nervosa and Bulimia?', *Medscape Womens Health eJournal*, 1/9 (1996), available at www.medscape.com.

Stephenson, G. M., Maggi, P., Lefever, R. M. H., and Morojele, N. K., 'Excessive Behaviours: An Archival Study of Behavioural Tendencies Reported by 471 Patients Admitted to an Addiction Treatment Centre', *Addiction Research*, 3 (1995), 245–65.

Steel, Z. P., Farag, P. A., and Blaszczynsky, A. P., 'Interrupting the Binge-Purge Cycle in Bulimia: The Use of Planned Binges', *International Journal of Eating Disorders*, 18/3 (1995), 199–208.

Striegel Moore, R. H., et al., 'Eating Disorders in a National Sample of Hospitalised Female and Male Veterans: Detection Rates and Psychiatric Comorbidity', *International Journal of Eating Disorders*, 25/4 (1999), 405–14.

Strober, Michael, and Bulik, M. Cynthia, 'Genetic Epidemiology of Eating Disorders', in Christopher G. Fairburn and Kelly D. Brownell (eds.), *Eating Disorders and Obesity* (2nd edn., London: Guilford Press, 2002), ch. 42, pp. 238–43.

—— Freeman, R., Bower, S. and Rigali, J., 'Binge Eating in Anorexia Nervosa Predicts Later Onset of Substance Use Disorder: A Ten-Year Prospective, Longitudinal Follow-up of 95 Adolescents', *Journal of Youth and Adolescence*, 25/4 (1996), 519–32.

—— Freeman, R., Lampert, C., Diamond, J., Kaye, W., 'Controlled Family Study of Anorexia and Bulimia Nervosa: Evidence of Shared Liability and Transmission of Partial Syndromes', *American Journal of Psychiatry*, 157 (2000), 393–401.

Stunkard, J. Albert, and Stellar, Eliot (eds.), *Eating and its Disorders* (New York: Raven Press, 1984).

Sullivan, D. Mark, and Youngner, J. Stuart, 'Depression, Competence and the Right to Refuse Lifesaving Medical Treatment', *American Journal of Psychiatry*, 151/7 (July 1994), 971–7.

Sullivan, P. F., Bulik, C. M., Fear, J. L., and Pickering, A., 'Outcome of Anorexia Nervosa', *American Journal of Psychiatry*, 155/7 (1998), 939–46.

Suzuki, K., Higuchi, S., Yamada, K., Komiya, H., and Takagi, S., 'Bulimia Nervosa with and without Alcoholism', *International Journal of Eating Disorders*, 16/2 (1994), 137–46.

Szmukler, G. I., and Tantam, D., 'Anorexia Nervosa: Starvation Dependence', *British Journal of Medical Psychology*, 57/4 (1984), 303–10.

—— Dare, Chris, and Treasure, Janet (eds.), *Handbook of Eating Disorders: Theory, Treatment and Research* (Chichester: Wiley, 1995).

Taber, M. T., Zernig, G., and Fibiger, H. C., 'Opioid Receptor Modulation of Feeding-Evoked Dopamine Release in the Rat Nucleus Accumbens', *Brain Research*, 785/1 (1998), 24–30.

Tan, Jacinta O. A., Hope, Tony, and Stewart, Anne, 'Anorexia Nervosa and Personal Identity: The Accounts of Patients and their Parents', *International Journal of Law and Psychiatry*, 26/5 (September–October 2003), 533–48.

Taylor, Ann. E., Hubbard, Jane, and Anderson, Ellen J., 'Impact of Binge Eating on Metabolic and Leptin Dynamics in Normal Young Women', *Journal of Clinical Endocrinology and Metabolism*, 84/2 (1999), 428–34.

Touyz, Stephen W., 'Ethical Considerations in the Implementation of Behaviour Modification Programmes in Patients with Anorexia Nervosa: A Historical Perspective', in Walter Vandereycken and Pierre J. V. Beumont (eds.), *Treating Eating Disorders: Ethical, Legal and Personal Issues* (New York: New York University Press, 1998), ch. 9, pp. 216–29.

Treasure, Janet L., 'Anorexia and Bulimia Nervosa', in G. Stein and G. Wilkinson (eds.), *Seminars in General Adult Psychiatry* (London: Royal College of Psychiatrists, 1998).

—— Todd, G., and Szmukler, G. I., 'The Impatient Treatment of Anorexia Nervosa', in G. I. Szmukler, Chris Dare, and Janet Treasure (eds.), *Handbook of Eating Disorders* (New York: Wiley, 1995), 275–92.

—— Schmidt, Ulrich, and van Furth, Eric (eds.), *Handbook of Eating Disorders* (2nd edn., Chichester: Wiley, 2003).

—— and Holland, A., 'Genetic Factors in Eating Disorders', in G. I. Szmukler, Chris Dare, and Janet Treasure (eds.), *Handbook of Eating Disorders: Theory, Treatment and Research* (Chichester: Wiley, 1995), 49–65.

Troop, A. Nicholas, and Treasure, L. Janet, 'Setting the Scene for Eating Disorders', *Psychological Medicine*, 27 (1997), 531–8.

Tuomisto, T., Hethenngton, M. M., Morins, M. F., Tuomisto, M. T., Turjanmaa, V., and Lappalainen, R., 'Psychological and Physiological Characteristics of Sweet Food Addiction', *International Journal of Eating Disorders*, 25/2 (1999), 169–75.

Turner, Brian S., *The Body and Society: Explorations in Social Theory* (Oxford: Blackwell, 1984).

Ugazio, Valeria, 'La semantica de potere: Anoressia, bulimia e altri affanni alimentari', in Valeria Ugazio, *Storie permesse storie proibite: Polarità semantiche familiari e psicopatologiche* (Tuni: Bollati Boringhieri, 1988).

Van Deth, Ron, and Vandereycken, Walter, 'Food Refusal and Insanity: Sitophobia and Anorexia Nervosa in Victorian Asylums', *International Journal of Eating Disorders*, 27/4 (2000), 390–404.

Vandereycken, Walter, *The Family Approach to Eating Disorders: Assessment and Treatment of Anorexia and Bulimia* (New York: PMA, 1989).

—— 'Family Interaction in Eating Disorder Patients and Normal Controls', *International Journal of Eating Disorders*, 8/1 (1989), 11–23.

—— 'The Addiction Model in Eating Disorders: Some Critical Remarks and a Selected Bibliography', *International Journal of Eating Disorders*, 9/1 (1990), 95–101.

—— 'History of Anorexia Nervosa and Bulimia Nervosa', in Christopher G. Fairburn and Kelly D. Brownell (eds.), *Eating Disorders and Obesity* (2nd edn., London: Guilford Press, 2002), ch. 27, pp. 151–4.

—— 'Viewpoint: Whose Competence should we Question?', *European Eating Disorders Review*, 6 (1999), 1–3.

Vandereycken, Walter, and Beumont, Pierre J. V. (eds.), *Treating Eating Disorders: Ethical, Legal and Personal Issues* (New York: New York University Press, 1998).

—— and Van Deth, Ron, *From Fasting Saints to Anorexic Girls: The History of Self-Starvation* (London: Athlone Press, 1994). Italian version, *Dalle sante ascetiche alle ragazze anoressiche: Il rifiuto del cibo nella storia* (Milan: Cortina, 1995).

Vigersky, R. A. (ed.), *Anorexia Nervosa* (London: Raven Press, 1977).

Wade, T., Martin, N. G., and Tiggeman, M., 'Genetic and Environmental Risk Factors for the Weight and Shape Concerns Characteristic of Bulimia Nervosa', *Psychological Medicine*, 28/4 (1998), 761–77.

Ward, Anne, and Gowers, Simon, 'Attachment and Childhood Development', in Janet Treasure, Ulrich Schmidt, and Eric van Furth (eds.), *Handbook of Eating Disorders* (2nd edn., Chichester: Wiley, 2003), ch. 6, pp. 103–20.

Wardle, Jane, Bindra, Renu, Fairclough, Beverly, and Westcombe, Alex, 'Culture and Body Image: Body Perception and Weight Concern in Young Asian and Caucasian British Women', *Journal of Community and Applied Social Psychology*, 3 (1993), 173–81.

Waskett, Carole, *Counselling People in Eating Distress* (Rugby: British Association for Counselling, 1993).

Waugh, E., and Bulik, C. M., 'Offspring of Women with Eating Disorders', *International Journal of Eating Disorders*, 25/2 (1999), 123–33.

Weiner, S., 'The Addiction of Overeating: Self-Help Groups as Treatment Models', *Journal of Clinical Psychology*, 54/2 (1998), 163–7.

Welch, S. L., Doll, H. A., and Fairburn, C. G., 'Life Events and the Onset of Bulimia Nervosa: A Controlled Study', *Psychological Medicine*, 27 (1997), 512–22.

Westermeyer, J., and Specker, S., 'Social Resources and Social Function in Comorbid Eating and Substance Disorder: A Matched-Pairs Study', *American Journal on Addiction*, 8/4 (1999), 332–6.

Williams, Christopher J., Pieri, Lorenzo, and Sims, Andrew, 'We Should Strive to Keep Patients Alive', *British Medical Journal*, 317 (1998), 195–7.

Williamson, D. A., et al., 'Equivalence of Body Image Disturbances in Anorexia and Bulimia', *Journal of Abnormal Psychology*, 102/1 (1993), 171–80.

Wilson, G. Terence, 'The Addiction Model of Eating Disorders: A Critical Analysis', *Advances in Behaviour Research and Therapy*, 13/1 (1991), 27–72.

—— 'Eating Disorders and Addictive Disorders', in Christopher G. Fairburn and Kelly D. Brownell (eds.), *Eating Disorders and Obesity* (2nd edn., London: Guilford Press, 2002), ch. 35, pp. 199–203.

Winchester, Elizabeth, and Collier, David, 'Genetic Aetiology of Eating Disorders and Obesity', in Janet Treasure, Ulrich Schmidt, and Eric van Furth (eds.), *Handbook of Eating Disorders* (2nd edn., Chichester: Wiley, 2003), ch. 3, pp. 36–64.

Woodruff, P. W. R., 'Structural Brain Abnormalities in Male Schizophrenics Reflect Fronto-Temporal Dissociation', *Psychological Medicine*, 27/6 (1997), 1257–65.

Woodside, D. B., Field, L. L., Garfinkel, E. Paul, and Heinmaa, M., 'Specificity of Eating Disorders Diagnoses in Families of Probands with Anorexia and Bulimia Nervosa', *Comprehensive Psychiatry*, 39/5 (1998), 261–4.

World Health Organization, *Manual for the Statistical Classification of Diseases, Injuries, and Causes of Death* (9th edn., Geneva: WHO, 1967).

World Health Organization, *International Classification of Diseases* (10th edn., Geneva: WHO, 1992).

Yager, J., 'The Management of Patients with Intractable Eating Disorders', in K. D. Brownell and C. G. Fairburn (eds.), *Eating Disorders and Obesity: A Comprehensive Handbook* (New York: Guilford Press, 1995), 374–8.

Zerbe, K. J., 'Anorexia Nervosa and Bulimia Nervosa: When the Pursuit of Bodily Perfection Becomes a Killer', *Postgraduate Medicine*, 99/1 (1996), 167–9.

Zipfel, Stephen, Lowe, Bernd, and Herzog, Wolfang, 'Medical Complications', in Janet Treasure, Ulrich Schmidt, and Eric van Furth (eds.), *Handbook of Eating Disorders* (2nd edn., Chichester: Wiley, 2003, ch. 10, pp. 169–90.

2. *Philosophical and Literary Studies*

Ackerman, A. Bruce, *Social Justice in the Liberal State* (London: Yale University Press, 1980).

Anderson, R. Charles, *Emily Dickinson's Poetry: Stairway of Surprise* (New York: Holt Rinehart and Winstone, 1960).

Apel, K. O., 'Causal Explanation, Motivational Explanation and Hermeneutical Understanding. (Remarks on the Recent Stage of the Explanation–Understanding Controversy)', in G. Ryle (ed.), *Contemporary Aspects of Philosophy* (London: Oriel Press, 1976), 161–76.

Aristotle, *De Anima* (*On the Soul*) (Harmondsworth: Penguin, 1986).

—— *Metaphysics* (London: Penguin, 1998).

Ayer, A. J., *Language, Truth and Logic* (London: Penguin, 1990).

Beauchamp, Tom, 'Paternalism', in W. T. Reich (ed.), *Encyclopedia of Bioethics* (rev. edn., New York: Simon and Schuster, Macmillan, 1995), iv. 1914–20.

—— 'The Failure of Theories of Personhood', *Kennedy Institute of Ethics*, 9/4 (1999), 309–24.

—— and Childress, James, *Principles of Biomedical Ethics* (4th edn., Oxford: Oxford University Press, 1994). Italian version, *Principi di etica biomedica* (Florence: Le Lettere, 1999).

Bechtel, William, *Philosophy of Mind: An Overview for Cognitive Science*, Hillsdale, NJ: Lawrence Erlbaum, 1988). Italian version, *Filosofia della mente* (Bologna: Il Mulino, 1992).

Berlin, Isaiah, *Four Essays on Liberty* (Oxford: Oxford University Press, 1969).

Braithwaite, R. B., 'The Nature of Believing', in A. Phillips Griffiths (ed.), *Knowledge and belief* (London: Oxford University Press, 1967), 28–40.

Bridge, C., 'Adolescent and Mental Disorder: Who Consent to Treatment?', *Medical Law International*, 3 (1997), 51–74.

Buchanan, Allen R., 'Medical Paternalism', *Philosophy and Public Affairs*, 7 (Summer 1978), 372.

Byrne, Peter, 'Divergence on Consent: A Philosophical Assay', in G. R. Dunston and Mary J. Seller (eds.), *Consent in Medicine* (London: King Edward's Hospital Fund for London, 1983), 45–56.

Caney, S., 'Sandel and the Self', *International Journal of Moral and Social Studies* (Summer 1991), 161–71.

Capron, A., 'The Authority of Others to Decide about Biomedical Interventions with Incompetents', in W. Gaylin and R. Macklin (eds.), *Who Speaks for the Child?* (New York: Hastings on Hudson, 1982), 115–52.

The Catholic Encyclopedia, vol. i, (copyright © 1907 by Robert Appleton Company; online edition copyright © 2003 by Kevin Knight, available at http://www. newadvent.org/cathen/01767c.htm).

Cheung, P., et al., 'Studies of Aggressive Behaviour in Schizophrenia: Is there a Response Bias?', *Medicine, Science and the Law*, 37/4 (1997), 345–8.

Childress, James, 'The Place of Autonomy in Bioethics', *Hastings Center Report*, 20 (Jan.–Feb. 1990), 12–16.

De André, F., *Via della Croce* (Milan: Edizioni Musicali BGM Ricordi, 1971).

DeGrazia, David, 'Autonomous Action and Autonomy-Subverting Psychiatric Conditions', *Journal of Medicine and Philosophy*, 19/3 (1994), 279–97.

Dennett, Daniel, *The Intentional Stance* (Cambridge, Mass.: MIT Press, 1987). Italian version, *L'atteggiamento intenzionale* (Bologna: Il Mulino, 1993).

—— *Kinds of Minds* (London: Weidenfeld & Nicolson, 1996). Italian version, *La mente e le menti* (Milan: Sansoni, 1997).

Diderot, D., *Pensées philosophiques* (Paris: Garnier-Flammarion, 1746).

Dombrowisky, Daniel, 'Process Thought and the Liberalism, Communitarianism Debate: A Comparison with Rawls', *Process Studies*, 26/1–2 (1996), 15–32.

Downie, R. S., and Telfer, E., 'Autonomy', *Philosophy*, 46/178 (1971), 293–301.

Dresser, Rebecca, 'Dworkin on Dementia, Elegant Theory, Questionable Policy', *Hastings Center Report*, 25 (Nov.–Dec. 1995), 32–8.

Dworkin, Gerald (ed.), *Determinism, Free Will and Moral Responsibility* (Englewood Cliffs, NJ: Prentice-Hall, 1970).

—— 'Paternalism', *Monist*, 56 (1972), 64–84.

—— *The Theory and Practice of Autonomy* (Cambridge: Cambridge University Press, 1988).

Dworkin, Ronald, 'Liberalism', in S. Hampshire (ed.), *Public and Private Morality* (Cambridge: Cambridge University Press, 1978), 113–43.

—— *Life's Dominion* (London: Harper Collins, 1993).

Elster, John, *The Multiple Self* (Cambridge: Cambridge University Press, 1986).

Enciclopedia Garzanti di filosofia (Milan: Garzanti, 1994).

Engelhardt, Tristram H., Jr., *The Foundation of Bioethics* (London: Oxford University Press, 1986; 2nd edn., Oxford: Oxford University Press, 1996). Italian version, *Manuale di bioetica* (Milan: Il Saggiatore, 1991; 2nd edn., 1999).

Feinberg, Joel, 'Legal Paternalism', *Canadian Journal of Philosophy*, 1 (1977), 105–24.

Frankfurt, G. Harry, 'Freedom of the Will and the Concept of a Person', *Journal of Philosophy*, 68/1 (1971), 5–21.

Fray, R. G., 'Act-Utilitarianism, Consequentialism and Moral Rights', in R. G. Fray (ed.), *Utility and Rights* (London: Blackwell, 1985), 61–85.

Friedman, M., 'Autonomy and the Split-Level Self', *Southern Journal of Philosophy*, 24/1 (1986), 19–36.

Frohock, M. Fred, 'Conceptions of Persons', *Social Theory and Practice*, 23/1 (1997), 129–58.

Gilligan, Carol, *In a Different Voice: Psychological Theory and Women's Development* (London: Harvard University Press, 1982). Italian version, *Con voce di donna* (Milan: Feltrinelli, 1987).

Gilbert, Margaret, 'Agreement, Coercion and Obligation', *Ethics*, 103/4 (1992–3), 679–706.

Glover, Jonathan, *Responsibility* (London: Routledge and Kegan Paul, 1970).

—— (ed.), *The Philosophy of Mind* (Oxford: Oxford University Press, 1976).

—— *Causing Death and Saving Lives* (9th edn., London: Penguin, 1988).

—— *I: The Philosophy and Psychology of Personal Identity* (London: Penguin, 1991).

Guidacci, M. (ed.), *Poesie e lettere* (Florence: Sansoni, 2000).

Hallgarth, W. Matthew, 'Consequentialism and Deontology', in *Encyclopedia of Applied Ethics* (London: London Academy Press, 1998), 609–29.

Hahn, E. Frank, 'On Some Difficulties of the Utilitarian Economist', in A. Sen and B. Williams (eds.), *Utilitarianism and Beyond* (3rd edn., Cambridge: Cambridge University Press, 1984), 187–98. Italian version, *Utilitarismo e oltre* (Milan: Il Saggiatore, 1990).

Halpern, Jodi, *From Detached Concern to Empathy: Humanizing Medical Practice* (Oxford: Oxford University Press, 2001).

Hanser, F. Mattehew, 'Intention and Teleology', *Mind*, 107/426 (1998), 381–401.

Hare, R. M., 'Backsliding', in G. Mortimore (ed.), *Weakness of Will* (London: Macmillan, 1971).

—— 'Brandt on Fairness to Happiness', *Social Theory and Practice*, 15 (Spring 1989), 59–65.

—— *Essays on Bioethics* (Oxford: Clarendon Press, 1993).

Harris, John, *Wonderwoman and Superman* (Oxford: Oxford University Press, 1992). Italian version, *Wonderwoman and Superman* (Milan: Baldini e Castoldi, 1992).

—— *The Value of life* (London: Routledge, 1992).

Harsany, J. C., *Essays on Ethics, Social Behaviour and Scientific Explanation* (Dordrecht: Reidel, 1976).

Haworth, Lawrence, *Autonomy: An Essay in Philosophical Psychology and Ethics* (London: Yale University Press, 1986).

Held, Virginia, *Feminist Morality: Transforming Culture, Society and Politics* (Chicago: University of Chicago Press, 1993). Italian version, *Etica femminista* (Milan: Feltrinelli, 1997).

Hirsch, R. Steven, and Harris, John (eds.), *Consent and the Incompetent Patient: Ethics, Law and Medicine* (Oxford: Gaskell, 1988).

Hodgson, D. H., *Consequences of Utilitarianism, a Study in Normative Ethics and Legal Theory* (Oxford: Clarendon Press, 1967).

Hohl, Reinhold, *Alberto Giacometti: Sculpture, Painting, Drawing* (London: Thames & Hudson, 1972).

Hope, Tony, Savulescu, Julian, and Hendrick, Judith, *Medical Ethics and Law: The Core Curriculum* (London: Churchill Livingstone, 2003).

Hume, David, *Treatise of Human Nature* (Oxford: Oxford University Press, 1967). Italian version, *Trattato sulla natura umana* (Rome: Biblioteca Universale Laterza, 1987).

Istituto della Enciclopedia Italiana, *Vocabolario della lingua italiana* (Rome: Treccani, 1986).

Jeffrey, P. (ed.), *Reading Nozick: Essays on Anarchy, State and Utopia* (3rd edn., London: Blackwell, 1981).

Johnson, T. H. (ed.), *The Letters of Emily Dickinson* (Cambridge, Mass.: Harvard University Press, 1958).

Kant, Immanuel, *Critical Examination of Practical Reason,* in *Critique of Practical Reason and Other Works on the Theory of Ethics,* trans. and ed. T. K. Abbott (London: Longmans, Green and Co., 1948), 87–200. Italian version, *Critica della ragione pratica* (Milan: Signorelli, 1959).

—— *Groundwork of the Metaphysic of Morals* (London: Hutchinson House, 1955). Italian version, *Fondazione della metafisica dei costumi* (Milan: Mondadori, 1995).

Keith, M. D. (ed.), *Preferences, Institutions and Rational Choice* (Oxford: Clarendon Press, 1995).

Kuflik, Arthur, 'The Inalienability of Autonomy', *Philosophy and Public Affairs,* 13 (1984), 271–98.

Kundera, Milan, *The Art of the Novel* (London: Faber, 1988). Italian version, *L'arte del romanzo* (Milan: Adelphi, 1988).

Kundera, Milan, *Immortality* (London: Faber & Faber, 1991).

Kymlicka, Will, *Contemporary Political Philosophy: An Introduction* (Oxford: Clarendon Press, 1990).

Lecaldano, Eugenio, *Etica* (Tunà: UTET, 1995).

—— *Bioetica: Le scelte morali* (Rome: Laterza, 1999).

Levi, Carlo, *Le mille patrie* (Rome: Donzelli, 2000).

Lindley, Robert, *Autonomy* (London: Macmillan, 1996).

Locke, John, *An Essay on Human Understanding* (London: Oxford University Press, 1975). Italian version, *Saggio sull'intelletto umano* (Tunà: UTET, 1971).

Lorenz, Konrad, *On Aggression* (London: Methuen, 1967).

Lyons, David, *Forms and Limits of Utilitarianism* (Oxford: Clarendon Press, 1965).

McGuinness, B. (ed.), *Wittgenstein and his Times* (London: Blackwell, 1982).

McMahan, Christopher, 'Autonomy and Authority', *Philosophy and Public Affairs,* 16 (1987), 303–28.

Martin, Wendy (ed.), *The Cambridge Companion to Emily Dickinson* (Cambridge: Cambridge University Press, 2002).

Mele, A., *Autonomous Agents: From Self Control to Autonomy* (Oxford: Oxford University Press, 1995).

Michalowski, S., 'Protection of Medical Confidentiality without a Medical Privilege? A Discussion of the English and the German Approach', *Medical Law International*, 2 (1997), 277–89.

Mill, John Stuart, *Three Essays, On Liberty, Representative Government, The Subjection of Women* (London: Oxford University Press, 1975).

—— *On Liberty* (New York: Cambridge University Press, 1989). Italian version, *Saggio sulla libertà* (Milan: Il Saggiatore, 1993).

Moodie, P., and Wright, M., 'Medical Research and Alzheimer's Disease: A Study of the Hazard of Conducting Research on the Incompetent Patient', *Medical Law International*, 2 (1997), 291–313.

Moon, Donald, 'Communitarism', in *Encyclopedia of Applied Ethics* (London: London Academy Press, 1998).

Mortimore, G. (ed.), *Weakness of will* (London: Macmillan, 1971).

Nagel, Thomas, 'Autonomy and Deontology', in S. Scheffler (ed.), *Consequentialism and its Critics* (Oxford: Oxford University Press, 1988), 142–72.

Nozick, Robert, *Anarchy, State and Utopia* (Oxford: Blackwell, 1974).

Oslon, E., *The Human Animal: Personal Identity without Psychology* (Oxford: Oxford University Press, 1997).

Parfit, Derek, 'Personal Identity', in J. Glover (ed.), *The Philosophy of Mind* (Oxford: Oxford University Press, 1976), 143–63.

Peirce, Charles S., 'The Fixation of Belief', *Popular Science Monthly*, 12 (Nov. 1877), 1–15.

—— 'How to Make our Ideas Clear', *Popular Science Monthly*, 12 (Jan. 1878), 286–302.

Pettit, P., and Smith, M., 'Freedom in Belief and Desire', *Journal of Philosophy*, 9 (Sept. 1996), 429–49.

Phillips Griffiths, A., 'How can One Person Represent Another', *Proceedings of the Aristotelian Society*, 34, suppl. (1960), 187–208.

Pink, Thomas, *The Psychology of Freedom* (Cambridge: Cambridge University Press, 1996).

Pitkin, H., *Representation* (New York: Atherton, 1969).

Plato, *Phaedo*, trans. G. M. A. Grube, *Five Dialogues* (Indianapolis: Hackett Publishing, 1981).

Price, H. H., 'Some Consideration about Belief', in A. Phillips Griffiths (ed.), *Knowledge and Belief* (London: Oxford University Press, 1967), 41–59.

Rawls, John, 'Construction and Objectivity', *Journal of Philosophy*, 78 (Sept. 1980), 554.

—— *A Theory of Justice* (Oxford: Oxford University Press, 1972). Italian version, *Una teoria della giustizia* (Milan: Feltrinelli, 1984).

Raz, Joseph, 'Authority and Justification', *Philosophy and Public Affairs*, 14 (1985), 3–29.

Reale, Giovanni, *La metafisica di Aristotele* (Naples: Luigi Loffredo Editore, 1968).

—— and Antiseri, Dario, *Il pensiero occidentale dale origini a oggi* (3rd edn., Rome: La Scuola, 1984).

Ridge, Michael, 'Humean Intentions', *American Philosophical Quarterly*, 35/2 (1998), 157–78.

Riley, J., *Liberal Utilitarianism* (Cambridge: Cambridge University Press, 1988).

Robins, H. Michael, 'Is it Rational to Carry out Strategic Intentions?', *Philosophia*, 25/1–4 (1997), 191–221.

Ryle, Gilbert, *The Concept of Mind* (London: Penguin, 1978).

Sandel, Michael, *Liberalism and the Limits of Justice*, 2nd edn. (Cambridge: Cambridge University Press, 1998). Italian version, *Il liberalismo e i limiti della giustizia* (Milan: Feltrinelli, 1994).

Savulescu Julian, 'Desire-Based and Value-Based Normative Reasons', *Bioethics*, 13/5 (1999), 405–13.

—— and Momeyer, R. W., 'Should Informed Consent Be Based on Rational Beliefs?', *Journal of Medical Ethics*, 23 (1997), 282–8.

Scanlon, T., 'A Theory of Freedom of Expression', *Philosophy and Public Affairs*, 1 (Winter 1972), 215.

—— 'Nozick on Rights, Liberty and Property', in P. Jeffrey, *Reading Nozick, Essays on Anarchy, State and Utopia* (3rd edn., London: Blackwell, 1981), 107–29.

Scarre, Geoffrey, 'Utilitarianism', in *Encyclopedia of Applied Ethics* (London: London Academy Press, 1998), 439–50.

Schiavone, Michele, *Bioetica e psichiatria* (Bologna: Patron, 1990).

Scoccia, Danny, 'Paternalism and Respect for Autonomy', *Ethics*, 100/2 (1989–90), 318–34.

Sen, Amartya, *Inequality Reexamined* (Cambridge, Mass.: Harvard University Press, 1992).

Sewall, R. B. (ed.), *The Lyman Letters: New Light on Emily Dickinson and her Family* (Amherst, Mass.: University of Massachusetts Press, 1965).

—— *The Life of Emily Dickinson* (New York: Ferrar, Straus and Giroux, 1974).

Singer, Peter, *Rethinking Life and Death* (Oxford: Oxford University Press, 1995).

Smart, J. J. C., 'Extreme and Restricted Utilitarianism', in M. D. Bayles, *Contemporary Utilitarianism* (Gloucester: Anchor Books, 1978), 99–116. Italian version, 'Utilitarismo estremo e ristretto', in E. Lecaldano and P. Donatelli (eds.), *Etica analitica* (Rome: CEA, 1996), 287–302.

—— and Williams, Bernard, *Utilitarianism for and against* (London: Cambridge University Press, 1996). Italian version, *Utilitarismo: un confronto* (Naples: Bibliopolis, 1985).

Smith, A. D., and Humphreys, M., 'Physical Restraint of Patients in a Psychiatric Hospital', *Medicine, Science and the Law*, 37/2 (1997), 145–9.

Sparti, Davide, *Soggetti al tempo* (Milan: Feltrinelli, 1996).

Thalberg, I., 'Hierarchical Analyses of Unfree Action', *Canadian Journal of Philosophy*, 8 (June 1978), 211–25.

Thomson, J. J., 'People and their Bodies', in J. Dancy (ed.), *Reading Parfit* (Oxford: Blackwell, 1997), 202–29.

Thorp, J., *Free Will* (London: Routledge, 1980).

Tolstoy, Leo N., *Anna Karenina* (London: Penguin, 1977). Italian version, *Anna Karenina* (Milan: Frassinelli, 1997).

Tooley, Michael, *Time, Tense and Causation* (Oxford: Clarendon Press, 1997).

Van Inwagen, P. (ed.), *Time and Cause: Essays Presented to Richard Taylor* (Dordrecht: Reidel, 1980).

Veatch, M. Robert, 'Autonomy's Temporary Triumph', *Hastings Center Report*, 14 (Oct. 1994), 38–40.

Veatch, M. Robert, 'Abandoning Informed Consent', *Hastings Center Report*, 25 (Mar–Apr. 1995), 5–12.

Velleman, J. D., 'The Possibility of Practical Reason', *Ethics*, 106/1 (1995–6), 694–726.

Vick, S., *What Makes a Perfect Agent? A Pilot Study of Patients' Preferences* (Aberdeen: Health Economics Research Unit, 1995).

Weber, Max, *The Protestant Ethic and the Spirit of Capitalism* (London: George Allen & Unwin, 1976). Italian version, *L'etica protestante e lo spirito del capitalismo* (Florence: Sansoni, 1984).

Wettstein, R. M., 'Competence', in W. T. Reich (ed.), *Encyclopedia of Bioethics*, rev. edn., New York: Simon and Schuster, Macmillan, 1995), 445–51.

Wittgenstein, Ludwig, *Tractatus Logico-Philosophicus*, trans. D. F. Pears and B. F. McGuinness (London: Routledge & Kegan Paul, 1961).

—— *Lectures and Conversations on Aesthetics, Psychology and Religious Belief*, ed. C. Barrett (Oxford: Blackwell, 1966). Italian version, *Lezioni e conversazioni sull'etica, l'estetica, la psicologia e la credenza religiosa*, ed. M. Ranchetti (Milan: Adelphi, 1967).

Wolff, Jonathan, *Robert Nozick: Property, Justice and the Minimal State* (Cambridge: Polity Press, 1991).

Wolff, Robert Paul, *In Defense of Anarchism* (New York: Harper & Row, 1970).

Woloski, Shira, 'Emily Dickinson: Being in the Body', in Wendy Martin (ed.), *The Cambridge Companion to Emily Dickinson* (Cambridge: Cambridge University Press, 2002), 129–41.

3. Legal Studies and Cases

Adler, M. W., 'HIV, Confidentiality and "a Delicate Balance": A Reply to Leone Ridsdale', *Journal of Medical Ethics*, 17 (1991), 196–8.

Airedale NHS Trust v. *Bland* [1993] 1 All ER 281.

Alexander, M. P., 'Clinical Determination of Mental Competence', *Archives of Neurology*, 45 (1988), 23–6.

Anon., *British Medical Journal*, 311 (1995), 635–6.

Appelbaum, P. S., and Grisso, T., 'Assessing Patients' Capacities to Consent to Treatment', *New England Journal of Medicine*, 319/25 (1988), 1635–8.

Arie, Tom, 'Some Legal Aspects of Mental Capacity', *British Medical Journal*, 313, (July 1996), 156–8.

B v. *Croydon District Health Authority* [1995] 1 All ER 683.

Banks v. *Goodfellow* [1870] LR 5 QB 549.

Black, D., 'Guide-Lines or Gumption? The Role of Medical Responsibility: A View from the Profession', in R. S. Hirsch and J. Harris (eds.), *Consent and the Incompetent Patient: Ethics, Law and Medicine* (Oxford: Gaskell, 1988).

Bolam v. *Friern Hospital Management Committee* [1957] 1 WLR 582.

Borsellino, Patrizia, 'Consenso informato', *Bioetica, rivista interdisciplinare*, 3 (1995), 433–45.

Boyd, K. M., 'HIV infection and Aids: The Ethics of Medical Confidentiality', *Journal of Medical Ethics*, 18 (1992), 173–9.

Brazier, Margaret, *Medicine, Patients and the Law* (3rd edn., London: Penguin, 2003).

Brody, B., Engelhardt, H. Tristram, Jr., *Mental Illness: Law and Public Policy*, (Boston: Reidel, 1980).

Brooke, H., 'Consent to Treatment or Research: The Incapable Patient', in R. S. Hirsch and J. Harris (eds.), *Consent and the Incompetent Patient: Ethics, Law and Medicine* (Oxford: Gastell, 1988).

Church of Scientology v. *Kaufman* [1973] RPC 635.

De Leo, G. and Patrizi, P., *La spiegazione del crimine* (Bologna: Il Mulino, 1998).

Department for Constitutional Affairs, *Making Decisions*, The Government's proposals for making decisions on behalf of mentally incapacitated adults. A Report issued in the light of responses to the consultation paper *Who Decides?* Presented to Parliament by the Lord High Chancellor by Command of Her Majesty (October 1999). Available at http://www.dca.gov.uk/family/mdecisions/indexfr.htm.

Department for Constitutional Affairs, *Mental Capacity Bill* (December 2004); available at www.parliament.the-stationery-office.co.uk/pa/cm200304/cmbills/120/04120.i-vi.html.

Department of Health, Mental Health Act 1983, Revised Code of Practice (15.8–15.24), issue date 1 March 1999, revised 1 March 2000.

—— *Mental Health Act: Memorandum on Parts I to VII, VIII and X* (London: Stationery Office, 1998).

Department of Health and Welsh Office, *Code of Practice: Mental Health Act 1983* (3rd edn., London: The Stationery Office, 1999), http://www.hyperguide.co.uk/shop/mh9901.htm.

Doyal, L., 'Advance Directives', *British Medical Journal* (Mar. 1995), 612–13.

Estate of Park [1959] P 112.

F v. *West Berkshire Health Authority* [1989] 2 All ER 545.

Fornari, Ugo, *Trattato di psichiatria forense* (Tunñ: UTET, 1997).

—— 'Accertamenti e trattamenti sanitari volontari e obbligatori sotto il profilo del rapporto medico-paziente: Il problema della scelta', in S. Jourdan and U. Fornari (eds.), *La responsabilità del medico in psichiatria* (Tunñ: Centro Scientifico Editore, 1997).

Freedman, B., 'Competence, Marginal and Otherwise', *International Journal of Law and Psychiatry*, 4 (1981), 53–72.

Fulbrook, P., 'Assessing Mental Competence of Patients and Relatives', *Journal of Advanced Nursing*, 20 (1994), 457–61.

Gillick v. *West Norfolk and Wisbech AHA* [1985] 3 All ER 402.

Giordano, Simona, 'Eating or Treating? Ethical and Legal Issues Relating to Anorexia Nervosa', *Tip Etigi, Turkish Journal of Medical Ethics*, 7/2 (1999), 53–9.

—— 'Anorexia Nervosa and Refusal of Naso-Gastric Treatment: A Response to Heather Draper', *Bioethics*, 17/3 (2003), 261–78.

Groves, T., 'Prison Policies on HIV under Revision', *British Medical Journal*, 303 (1991), 1354.

Hale, Brenda, *Mental Health Law*, 4th edn. (London: Sweet & Maxwell, 1996).

—— 'Mentally Incapacitated Adults and Decision-Making: The English Perspective', *International Journal of Law and Psychiatry*, 20/1 (1997), 59–75.

Hoffman, B. F., 'Assessing the Competence of People to Consent to Medical Treatment: A Balance between Law and Medicine', *Medicine and Law*, 9 (1990), 1122–30.

Hope, Tony, 'Advance Directives', *Journal of Medical Ethics*, 22 (1996), 67–8.

Hopp v. *Lepp* [1979] 98 DLR (3d) 464.

Hubbard v. *Vosper* [1972] 2 QB 14.

Jones, G. H., 'Informed Consent in Chronic Schizophrenia?', *British Journal of Psychiatry*, 167 (1995), 565–8.

Katz, M., et al., 'Psychiatric Consultation for Competency to Refuse Medical Treatment', *Psychosomatics*, 1 (1995), 33–41.

Kennedy, Ian, and Grubb, Andrew, *Medical Law* (London: Butterworths, 2000).

Keywood, Kirsty, '*B* v. *Croydon Health Authority* 1994 CA: Force-Feeding the Hunger Striker under the Mental Health Act 1983', 3 Web JCLI (1995).

—— 'Rethinking the Anorexic Body: How English Law and Psychiatry "think" ', *International Journal of Law and Psychiatry*, 26/6 (2003), 599–616.

Kirby, J. Michael, 'Consent and the Doctor–Patient Relationship', in R. Gillon (ed.), *Principles of Health Care Ethics* (New York: Wiley, 1994), 445–54.

Lane v. *Candura* [1978] 376 NE 2d 1232.

Law Commission, *Mentally Incapacitated Adults and Decision-Making: Medical Treatment and Research* (Consultation Paper No. 129; London: HMSO, 1993).

Law Commission Report on Mental Incapacity, No. 231 (1995).

Lee, A. M., and Tolle, W. S., 'Advance Directives', *British Medical Journal*, 310 (Mar. 1995), 612–14.

Legal Correspondent, 'Medical Confidence and the Law', *British Medical Journal*, 283 (1991), 1062.

McHale, Jane and Fox, Marie, *Health Care Law* (London: Maxwell, 1997).

Malette v. *Shulman* [1990] 67 DLR (4th) 321.

Marella, G. L., and Rossi, P., 'Accertamenti e trattamenti sanitari obbligatori per malati di mente nelle legislazioni nazionali', *Difesa sociale*, 2 (1996), 96–107.

Mason, J. K., and McCall Smith, R. A., *Law and Medical Ethics* (5th edn., London: Butterworths, 1999).

—— —— and Laurie, G. T., *Law and Medical Ethics* (6th edn., London: Butterworths, 2002).

Mental Health Act Commission, *Guidance on the Treatment of Anorexia under the Mental Health Act 1983* (London: HMSO, August 1997).

Mental Health Act Commission, Guidance Note, Use of the Mental Health Act 1983 in General Hospitals without a Psychiatric Unit, Commission ref.: GN 1/2001. Issued September 2001, Review date September 2003.

Mental Health Act Review Expert Group, *Draft Proposals for the New Mental Health Act* (April 1999), http://www.hyperguide.co.uk/mha/rev-prop.htm.

Mulloy v. *Hop Sang* [1935] 1 WWR 714.

Pomerantz, A. S., and Nesnera, A., 'Informed Consent, Competency and the Illusion of Rationality', *General Hospital Psychiatry*, 13 (1991), 138–42.

Re B [1981] 1 WLR 1421.

Re C [1994] 1 FLR 31.

Re C (adult: refusal of medical treatment) [1994] 1 All ER 819, (1993) 15 BMLR 77.

Re F [1989] 2 WLR 1063.

Re KB [1994] 19 BMLR 144.

Re MB [1997] 8 Medical Law Report 217.

Re R [1991] 4 All ER 177.

Re T (adult: refusal of medical treatment) [1992] 4 All ER 649, (1992) 9 BMLR 46, CA.

Re T [1993] Fam. 95 102.

Re W [1992] 3 WLR 758 (HMSO, 1993).

Riverside Health NHS Trust v. *Fox* [1994] 1 FLR 614.

R v. *Blane* [1975] 3 All ER 446.

Roth, L. H., Meisel, C., and Lidz, W., 'Test of Competency to Consent to Treatment', *American Journal of Psychiatry*, 134 (1977), pp. 279–84.

Samuel, A., 'The Duty of the Doctor to Respect the Confidence of the Patient', *Medicine, Science and the Law*, 20/1 (1980), 58–66.

Santosuosso, Amedeo, 'Il consenso informato: Questioni di principio e regole specifiche', in A. Santosuosso (ed.), *Il consenso informato* (Milan: Cortina, 1996), 26–7.

—— 'Il consenso informato e i medici: Tra aperture formali e conflitti radicali', *Bioetica, rivista interdisciplinare*, 2 (1997), 209–26.

Schloendorff v. *Society of New York Hospital* [1941] 105 NE 92.

Secretary of State for Constitutional Affairs, *Draft Mental Incapacity Bill*, Presented to Parliament in June 2003. Available at http://www.dca.gov.uk/menincap/meninc.pdf.

Secretary of State for Health, *Reform of the Mental Health Act 1983: Proposals for Consultation* (London: The Stationery Office, November 1999).

Secretary of State for the Home Department v. *Robb* [1995] 1 All ER 677.

Serafaty, Marc, and McCluskey, Sara, 'Compulsory Treatment of Anorexia Nervosa and the Moribund Patient', *European Eating Disorders Review*, 6/1 (1998), 27–37.

Sidaway v. *Board of Governors of the Bethlem Royal Hospital and the Maudsley Hospital* [1985] 1 All ER 643.

Silberfeld, M., 'Capacity Assessments for Request to Restore Legal Competence', *International Journal of Geriatric Psychiatry*, 10 (1995), 191–7.

Smith, R. P., et al., 'Competency and Practical Judgement', *Theoretical Medicine*, 17 (1996), 135–50.

St George's Healthcare NHS Trust v. *SR* v. *Collins and others* [1998] 3 All ER 673.

State of Tennessee v. *Northern* [1978] 563 SW 2d 197.

Sullivan, M. D., and Youngner, S. J., 'Depression, Competence and the Right to Refuse Lifesaving Medical Treatment', *American Journal of Psychiatry*, 151/7 (1994), 971–7.

Tan, Jacinta O. A., Hope, Tony, and Stewart, Anne, 'Competence to Refuse Treatment in Anorexia Nervosa', *International Journal of Law and Psychiatry*, 26/6 (2003), 697–707.

—— —— ——, 'Control and Compulsory Treatment in Anorexia Nervosa: The Views of Patients and Parents', *International Journal of Law and Psychiatry*, 26/6 (2003), 627–45.

Tancredi, L., 'Competency for Informed Consent', *International Journal of Law and Psychiatry*, 5 (1982), 51–63.

Tarasoff v. *Regents of the University of California* [1974] 529 P 2d 55.

W v. *Egdell* [1990] 1 All ER 835.

Whitehead, T., *Mental Illness and the Law* (Oxford: Blackwell, 1982).

'Who Decides? Making Decisions of Behalf of Mentally Incapacitated Adults', A consultation paper issued by the Lord Chancellor's Department (December 1997).

Wong, J. G., Clare, I. C. H., Gunn, M. J., and Holland, A. J., 'Capacity to Make Health Care Decisions: Its Importance in Clinical Practice', *Psychological Medicine*, 29 (1999), 437–46.

X v. *Y* [1988] 2 All ER 648.

4. *Psychiatry: Critical Studies*

Ardal, P. S., 'Depression and Reason', *Ethics*, 103/3 (1992–3), 540.

Baily, Andrew, 'Neurosis: A Conceptual Examination', *International Journal of Applied Philosophy*, 11/2 (1997), 51–61.

Baker, Robert, 'Conception of Mental Illness', in W. T. Reich (ed.), *Encyclopedia of Bioethics* (rev. edn., New York: Simon and Schuster, Macmillan, 1995), 1731–41.

Bleuler, Eugene, *Dementia Praecox* (New York: International University Press, 1966).

Bloch, Sidney, 'Psychiatry, Abuses of', in W. T. Reich (ed.), *Encyclopedia of Bioethics* (rev. edn., Simon and Schuster, Macmillan, 1995), 2126–33.

—— and Chodoff, Paul (eds.), *Psychiatric Ethics* (Oxford: Oxford University Press, 1981).

Bolton, D., and Hill, J., *Mind, Meaning and Mental Disorder: The Nature of Causal Explanation in Psychology and Psychiatry* (Oxford: Oxford University Press, 1996).

Boyers, R., *Laing and Antipsychiatry* (Harmondsworth: Penguin, 1972).

Buchanan, Allen, E., and Brock, Dan W., *Deciding for Others: The Ethics of Surrogate Decision Making* (Cambridge: Cambridge University Press, 1989).

Cooper, David, *Psychiatry and Antipsychiatry* (London: Paladin, 1970).

De Leo, G., *Psicologia della responsabilità* (Rome: Laterza, 1996).

Dunn, Caroline, *Ethical Issues in Mental Illness* (Ashgate: Aldershot, 1998).

Esterson, A., *The Leaves of Spring: A Study in the Dialectics of Madness* (Harmondsworth: Penguin, 1972).

Frances, Allen, 'DSM-IV Meets Philosophy', *Journal of Medicine and Philosophy*, 3 (1994), 207–18.

Fulford, K. W. M., *Moral Theory and Medical Practice* (Cambridge: Cambridge University Press, 1989).
—— *Medicine and Moral Reasoning* (Cambridge: Cambridge University Press, 1994).
—— 'Mental Illness, Concept of', in *Encyclopedia of Applied Ethics* (London: Academy Press, 1998), iii. 213–33.
Giordano, Simona, 'Il principio di autonomia nel trattamento e nella cura dei malati di mente: Una prospettiva deontologica', *Bioetica, rivista interdisciplinare*, 3 (1999), 482–91.
—— 'For the Protection of Others', *Health Care Analysis*, 8/3 (2000).
—— 'Addicted to Eating Disorders? Eating Disorders and Substance Use Disorders, Differences and Fallacies', *The Italian Journal of Psychiatry*, 11/2–3 (2001), 73–7.
—— ' Qu'un souffle de vent . . .', *Medical Humanities*, 28/1 (2002), 3–8.
—— 'Anorexia Nervosa and Refusal of Naso-Gastric Treatment: A Response to Heather Draper', *Bioethics*, 17/3 (2003), 261–78.
—— 'Persecutors or Victims? The Moral Logic at the Heart of Eating Disorders', *Health Care Analysis*, 11/3 (2003), 219–28.
Goffman, Erving, *Asylums: Essays on the Social Situation of Mental Patients and Other Inmates* (New York: Anchor Books, 1961).
Hebb, D. O., *The Organization of Behavior* (New York: Wiley, 1949).
Hundert, E. M., *Philosophy, Psychiatry and Neuroscience* (Oxford: Oxford University Press, 1989).
Jervis, Giovanni (ed.), *Psicoanalisi e metodo scientifico* (Turin: Einaudi, 1967).
—— *Manuale critico di psichiatria* (5th edn., Milan: Feltrinelli, 1997).
—— *La conquista dell'identità* (Milan: Feltrinelli, 1997).
Laing, Ronald David, *The Divided Self* (Harmondsworth: Penguin, 1990). Italian version, *L'io diviso* (Tunn: Einaudi, 1969).
—— *Sanity, Madness and the Family: Families of Schizophrenics* (Harmondsworth: Penguin, 1990).
Leifer, R., 'The Psychiatric Repression of Dr Thomas Szasz', *Review of Existential Psychology and Psychiatry*, 23/1–3 (1997), 85–106.
Minuchin, Salvadores, *Families and Family Theory* (London: Routledge, 1981).
Moore, M., 'Legal Conceptions of Mental Illness', in B. Brody and T. H. Engelhardt (eds.), *Mental Illness: Law and Public Policy* (Boston: Reidel, 1980).
Murphy, E., 'Psychiatric Implications', in S. R. Hirsch and J. Harris (eds.), *Consent and the Incompetent Patient: Ethics, Law and Medicine* (Oxford: Gaskell, 1988).
Orsi, Luciano, 'Il consenso informato, il prezzo della libertà', *Bioetica, rivista interdisciplinare*, 1 (1995), 55–61.
Passerieux, C., 'Heterogeneity in Cognitive Functioning of Schizophrenic Patients Evaluated by a Lexical Decision Task', *Psychological Medicine*, 27/6 (1997), 1295–1302.
Pepper-Smith, R., Harvey, W. R., and Silberfeld, M., 'Competency and Practical Judgement', *Theoretical Medicine*, 17 (1996), 135–50.
Reznek, L., *The Philosophical Defence of Psychiatry* (London: Routledge, 1991).
Robert, P. H., 'Use a Sequencing Task Designed to Stress the Supervisory System in Schizophrenic Subjects', *Psychological Medicine*, 27/6 (1997), 1287–94.

Ryan, C. J., 'Betting your Life: An Argument Against Certain Advance Directives', *Journal of Medical Ethics*, 22 (1996), 95–9.

Sacks, Olivier, *An Anthropologist on Mars: Seven Paradoxical Tales* (London: Picador, 1995). Italian version, *Un antropologo su Marte* (Milan: Adelphi, 1995).

Sass, A. Louis, *Madness and Modernism* (London: Harvard University Press, 1992).

Sidnan, M., 'Coercion in Educational Settings', *Behavioural Change*, 16/2 (1999), 79–88.

Szasz, Thomas, *The Myth of Mental Illness* (London: Paladin, 1984).

—— *A Lexicon of Lunacy: Metaphoric Malady, Moral Responsibility and Psychiatry* (London: Transaction Publisher, 1993).

Wilkes, Kathleen V., *Real People: Personal Identity without Thought Experiments* (Oxford: Clarendon Press, 1988).

Wing, J. K., *Reasoning about Madness* (Oxford: Oxford University Press, 1978).

Index